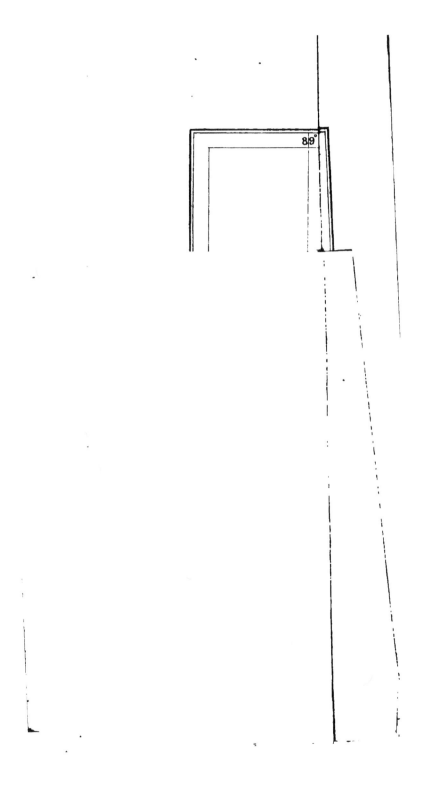

A

REPORT

ON THE

DISTRICT OF JESSORE:

ITS ANTIQUITIES,

ITS HISTORY, AND ITS COMMERCE.

BY

J. WESTLAND, Esq., C.S.
Late Magistrate and Collector of Jessore.

Calcutta:

PRINTED AT THE BENGAL SECRETARIAT OFFICE.

1871.

From J. WESTLAND, Esq.,

To RIVERS THOMPSON, Esq.,

Officiating Secretary to the Government of Bengal.

Dated Simla, the 25th October 1870.

Sir,

I have the honor to forward to you, and to request you to lay before the Lieutenant-Governor, a report upon the district of Jessore.

2. During the year or two for which the Lieutenant-Governor did me the honor to place me in charge of that district, I busied myself in collecting, from the sources thus placed at my command, such information as I could regarding subjects of local interest. This information, the result of inquiries and observations made in every part of the district, I have embodied in the present report, trusting it may prove to be of some use and of some interest to Government and to officers who have to do with the district, inasmuch as it is a collection from original sources of information otherwise unprocurable. In fact, with the exception of two matters which are included among the subjects dealt with in my chapters III and IV, nothing of what I have written has, so far as I know, been previously placed on record.

3. I shall indicate briefly the subjects I have treated in my report.

The first part contains some geographical notes, and the chief portion of it is the account given in the second chapter of a great change which during the last hundred years has taken place in the formation of the Gangetic delta.

4. The second part I have named "The antiquities of the district," and I have in it described the ancient ruins which are to be found in some parts of Jessore, narrating the legends and stories which the people in their vicinity connect with them, and seeking to cull from these tales what

of history may be in them. An account—in one case a partly legendary one—is also given of one or two of the ancient families of the district.

5. The third part is for the most part a compilation from early official records; it is a history of the first thirty years, the most interesting period, of British rule in the district. From the old regulations, and especially from their preambles, it is possible to gain an idea of the general outlines of the Company's administration in those days; but avoiding what might be a mere recapitulation of the general or legal history of Bengal, I have concerned myself rather to give a view of the state of affairs with which the district officers in those days had to deal, to give a history of the various attempts that were made to put matters on a better footing, to shew the difficulties that had to be encountered, and the successes or failures which attended the various measures adopted. I imagine that few who have not examined the early records of the Bengal districts have any conception of the ordeal through which these districts passed during the period whose history I have attempted to narrate, the period of transition from the old *régime* to the new. Viewing the quiet and settled state of the districts now, one is apt to forget that eighty or a hundred years ago their condition in all that regarded internal administration was but a few degrees removed from barbarism; and one's present experience affords little aid in measuring the bearing and effects of even the most prominent public measures of that time.

6. The fourth part describes the distribution of landed property in the district; and I have given in it a historical account of some of the zemindaris, and of the rise, and in a few instances the fall, of some of the families who hold or have held land in the district. Of what I have narrated in this section, I obtained a small part from some papers which my predecessor in the district, Mr. Monro, had procured from some of the leading families of the district, and which he handed to me. The rest is mostly part of the floating unwritten history of the district.

7. The fifth part has to do with commerce and agriculture, and contains what I have gathered in visiting and inquiring among the various trading places in Jessore. A description of the cultivation and manufacture of sugar, and an account of the reclamation and cultivation of the Sundarbans, form the chief subjects of this part of the report, as they are the leading features in the commerce and agriculture of the district.

8. In the sixth part, the "Gazetteer," I have gathered together all I consider worthy of note, which found no place under any of the other headings.

9. I have added two or three statistical tables regarding population, agriculture, revenue and expenditure, which I compiled from official sources during my tenure of office in Jessore.

10. I have tried, of course, to be as nearly correct as possible in all that I have written; but since much is taken from such uncertain sources as oral tradition and verbal narration, there must be much in my report that would bear further inquiry; and even where I base my statements on personal observation, I feel a regret that I am unlikely to have any opportunity of comparing anew the things written with the things observed. There is much, too, which I would wish to re-write in better form; but to do so would require more leisure than I have at my command, and I am obliged to present my report in the somewhat rough form in which it was cast when I first melted down into a consecutive record the mass of scattered notes which I had collected.

11. I am afraid the Lieutenant-Governor will not esteem everything I have written to be worthy of being recorded; but such as it is, I place the report entirely at His Honor's disposal.

I have the honor to be,

Sir,

Your most obedient servant,

J. WESTLAND.

TABLE OF CONTENTS.

———♦———

[NOTE.—In several places in the body of the work appear references. G. is intended for Government; B. or Bd. for Board of Revenue; J. for Judge; C. for Collector; M. for Magistrate; C. B. for Commissioner of Bhusna; N. A. for Nizamut Adalut. These letters indicate in each case the writer of the letter quoted, and the figures that follow indicate the date.]

A REPORT

DISTRICT OF JESSORE.

———◆———

PART I.—GEOGRAPHICAL.

I.—The district of Jessore, its situation and physical character.

If that tract of land which forms the double delta of the Ganges and the Brahmapootra rivers be imagined to be divided by lines running north and south into three equally broad portions, then the western portion would represent the districts of Nuddea on the north and 24-Pergunnahs on the south, the eastern portion would comprise the districts of Furreedpore on the north and Backergunge on the south, and the central portion would be the district of Jessore. Except that the line of its length points a little to the west of north and the east of south, Jessore might be described as the rectangle included between

North latitude, 21° 45′ and 23° 45′;

East longitude, 89° 15′ and 89° 55′.

This would give a length of about 140 miles and a breadth of about 40, or an area of 5,600 square miles. The actual area is 3,805 square miles, besides 1,716 square miles of unsurveyed Sundarbans; total, 5,521 square miles.

2. The imaginary lines which we have made to do duty for the western and eastern boundaries are respectively (roughly speaking) the lines of the rivers Kabadak (Kapatáksha, "dove's eye") and Madhumati ("honey-flowing"). The boundaries generally, though not accurately, adhere to the lines of these rivers, and at the upper or north-western

end of the district the boundary is an arbitrary and irregular line drawn from Kotchandpur on the Kabadak to a point on the Gorai or Madhumati river.

3. In its general features the district is a plain intersected by *General features—First* rivers, which intercommunicate by cross rivers. *division.* But the district may be divided into three parts, each of which has a different physical character. Suppose a straight line to be drawn through the district in a direction south-west and north-east, passing through Keshabpur and Muhammadpur, and another straight line to be drawn through it from east to west, about the parallel of Baghahat. The land which lies north and west of the first line,—the northern division as we may call it,—is generally high land. The soil tends in some places to slight sandiness, and the country may be considered free from inundation. The rivers are beyond the reach of tides, and, except during the height of the rains, their waters are kept within bounds by banks which rise more or less high above the surface of the water.

4. The central tract of the district, namely that lying between *Second division.* our two supposititious lines, is low-lying land filled with marshes. The rivers flow backwards and forwards according to the tides, and though of course the rainy season filling the channels raises the level of the rivers, yet the change is not nearly so marked as it is farther north. The marshes which cover this part of the district communicate almost always with the rivers; they render the country in a great measure impassable to pedestrians during the dry weather, and for some months in the year the whole region may be said to be under water. The tract is not only liable to inundation, but the inundation is calculated upon, and the crops do not prosper without it. The configuration of the country is everywhere that characteristic of deltaic lands; the margins of the rivers are the highest land, and the land slopes away from the rivers, so that the surface seems to be a series of basins, into which the waters flow through the khals, which, leading from the rivers, penetrate the high marginal land.

5. The southern of our three divisions forms the Sundarbans, a *Third division.* vast plain intersected everywhere by rivers and khals, which, except with the tides, hardly vary in height. The level of the whole country is from 12 to 30 inches above high tide level. It is probably not actually higher in level than the marshy lands which lie to the north, because of course the rivers in the

north reach an absolutely higher level than they do farther south, and the lands which are marshy, because they lie beneath their northern level, may yet be considerably above their southern level. Of this southern division of the district, about a quarter or a third of the breadth on the northern side represents the lands where Sundarban reclamation has been and is going on, the rest of it, forming a third or a quarter of the whole area of the district, is the unpenetrated forest of the Sundarbans.

6. In the northern of the three divisions of the district the drainage is all in one direction—southward and south-eastward, the direction in which the rivers flow.

Drainage.

Although these rivers were once deltaic streams which performed their part in carrying the upland waters to the sea, they have, as will be shewn more at length in the next chapter, put off that character, and now serve only to drain off the water that falls within the limits of the district itself. The Kumar and the Nabaganga carry along their own courses the water which drains into them; but that which falls south of their limits finds its way, for the most part, by many channels into the Bhairab, which in the very centre of the district, at the point where it receives the Afra khal, presents a large channel, and seems to tap all the country lying north-west of it. The extreme southern part of this division drains into the Bhadra and the bheel country adjacent to it.

7. In the other two of our divisions the drainage is in no particular direction. Intersected in all directions by rivers, and full in some parts of morasses, the water, when it does drain away, finds its way out in whatever direction local circumstances may determine.

8. The Kabadak does not receive much of the drainage of the district, as the land slopes away from it to the eastward, causing the water to flow towards the Bhairab, or towards the net-work of rivers in the south. The Bhairab in fact, except for the south of the district, is the main channel by which the water of the district finds outlet. Not only does it receive, as just mentioned, the drainage of the region that lies between Jhenida and Jessore, but the Nabaganga also, after percolating through and collecting the drainage of Magurah and Naral, sends its waters by many streams to meet the Bhairab river on its eastern side. South of Baghahat and Khulna it is hardly possible to note any one stream as claiming more of the drainage than another. The rivers there form a perfect maze of large streams, which finally, towards the south, determine towards three large centres,—the

The Kabadak and Bhairab rivers.

Southern rivers.

Kabadak, the Passar, and the Haringhatta, each large enough to be called an arm of the sea.

9. In physical aspect each of the three divisions into which we have marked out the district is different. The higher division is well wooded, and especially groves, almost forests of date trees, cover it in many parts. We find scattered here and there a few low plains where *amun* rice may be cultivated, but for the most part *ous* is the rice which can best be cultivated, and in the cold season the usual cold weather crops grow in luxuriance. The villages and towns in this tract are comparatively large, and there is a prosperous and comfortable air about the people and their homes.

Physical aspect—First division.

10. In the central, the marshy division, it is different. On the banks of some of the rivers, such as the Bhairab, the Chitra, and the Nabaganga, there are large villages; and the margins of the Bhairab especially are rich in trees. The river banks are high land, and partake in the prosperous appearance of more favored tracts; but in the interior, where the lands are lower, the villages are poor and scant. Rice grows in abundance, but in some places, where the bheels do not dry up at any time during the twelve months, there are large tracts of land which shew no cultivation. There are many places where one can stand on the margin of a large uncultivated plain or marsh, and wonder that signs of human habitation can be so sparse when not very far off the country is rich in inhabitants and busy with the toil of human life.

Second division.

11. Farther south still, in our southern division, we reach the Sundarban clearings. There are few or no villages, properly speaking, here; that which is marked in the map as a village is perhaps only an expanse of rich rice land, with a few houses, those of the cultivators, scattered here and there. Every thing here is subordinated to rice and rice cultivation; in the forest clearings hardly a tree is left, and people live, not in villages, but far apart, among their rice fields. The khals and rivers of the Sundarbans wind about among the rice clearings, and their course can be traced by the fringes of brushwood that line their banks. Nearer the sea, in fact over the greater part of the area of this southern division, we find the primeval forest, impenetrable jungle, trees and brushwood intertwined, and dangerous-looking creeks running into their darkness in all directions.

Third division.

II.—*The river system and its changes—Progress of deltaic formation.*

IT is not my purpose under this head to describe the mere names and courses of the rivers that flow through the district. These matters a map will delineate more clearly than any description. But I propose to take up the river system as a whole—no unimportant feature in a deltaic district—to shew what its history is, and some remarkable changes that have taken place in it.

Change of river system.

2. For the deltaic rivers which pass through Jessore are utterly changed from what they were a hundred or a hundred and fifty years ago, and the change is no casual one, for in every instance it has been of the same character. Previously the water which came to be discharged through the Jessore rivers came from the north-west and passed to south-east. Now it entirely comes from the north-east and passes to the south. The rivers which once flowed south-eastward through the district are now dried-up streams, and carry nothing but local surface-drainage; the arteries of the district are supplied by the water that comes down the Gorai, and enters the district at its north-east corner.

3. Taking one by one the rivers which used to flow south-eastward, intersecting the district at intervals of about ten or fifteen miles, the first on the north is the Kumar river. It is an exception to the general rule, for it has still preserved its communication at its head with the great river. The connection, however, does not exist during the dry months, when a bar of sand shuts up the head of the Matabhanga or Haulia river, and the Kumar itself is rapidly silting up, especially near Alamdanga in Nuddea. — Where it passes through the Jessore district, the Kumar is a beautiful stream of brilliantly clear water, and it can carry large vessels all the year round.

The Kumar.

4. The next stream is the Nabaganga (or "new river"). In Rennel's map,* now a hundred years old, it flows out of what is now the Matabhanga, at a point just north of Damarhuda, in Nuddea, and following its present course past Jhenida, Magurah, Nohatta, Naldi, and Lakshmipassa, meets there the stream which is now the Madhumati. The Nabaganga is now, and has long been, completely shut up at its head; it cannot be traced

The Nabaganga.

---

* Published with Colonel Gastrell's (survey) report on Jessore, Fureedpore, and Backergunge. Calcutta: Government Press, 1868.

beyond a baor, or lake, which marks its bed at a point some six miles from its old head at Damarhuda. The river, too, is drying up year by year. Boats of forty or fifty maunds can pass up to Jhenida in December, but a little later it is completely impassable.

5. The Chitra ("variegated") river is shewn in the same map
The Chitra. flowing out of the Nabaganga, two or three miles from the point where the latter leaves the Matabhanga, and after that it flows in its present course—past Kaliganj, Khajura, Gorakhali, Naral, Gobra, and then loses itself in the low marsh country, so that no particular exit can be identified with it. According to Rennel's map it divides into two channels between Kaliganj and Gorakhali; one flowing, as described, in the course which is now called the Chitra, the other flowing farther north, in the course now called the Katki river. The head of the Chitra river is now completely shut up, not only by the shutting up of the Nabaganga, from which it flowed, but by a disconnection from the Nabaganga. I am told that this last disconnection was brought about immediately by an indigo planter's throwing an embankment across the head of the Chitra, about forty years ago. About December the Chitra can carry boats of two hundred maunds up to Kaliganj, but about February it is almost closed.

6. The Katki river, the northern bend of the Chitra, is now disconnected from the upper Chitra, and derives its water from the Benga river, a cross-stream from the Nabaganga, which passes Naldanga. Once this Benga river must have been a large river, else its bank would never have been chosen as the seat of the Naldanga family. Now, however, it is in the cold season almost a dry river bed.

7. The next river, the Bhairab, and those which follow it in our
The Kabadak. list, used to flow from the Kabadak: but we must first say a word about the Kabadak itself. North of Matiari, in the Nuddea district, the river Matabhanga once made a great bend to the eastward. The site of this bend is now a long semi-circular lake, which one sees on the east side of the Eastern Bengal Railway. From the easternmost point of this bend the Kabadak used to flow first eastward to Kotchandpur, and then southward to the sea. That it was once a very large river there is not a doubt. There are some ancient buildings on its shores, which will be described; there are many large churs, and many forsaken river beds near its banks; and all these things sufficiently attest its previous greatness.

8. About forty years ago, or more (so I have heard the story told), Mr. Shakespeare was magistrate of Nuddea, and he, for the benefit of the navigation, cut a channel across the neck of this bend in the Matabhanga. The river occupied this more direct channel, the bend began to silt up,—for it is now disconnected from the river,—and the Kabadak lost its connection with the Matabhanga. It was compelled to put on the character of all the other rivers,—streams filled with the local surface drainage in the rains, but during the latter part of the cold season unable to carry even small vessels. Below Trimohini the river becomes a large tidal stream, but between that and Chandkhali it winds about so much that its navigation is tedious. Still it has given birth to several large trading towns. Maheshpur, in Nuddea, and Kotchandpur, no doubt owe to it their existence, and in its still navigable parts it passes Chaugachha, Jingagatchha, Trimohini, Talla, Kopilmuni, Katipara, and Chandkhali.

Its closure.

9. Its name, Kabadak, is a corruption of the fuller form Kapatáksha ("dove's eye"), so called from the beautiful blue of its waters at some seasons.

10. The Bhairab used to flow out of the Kabadak just north of Chaugachha, and then take a south-easterly course through the district. It was once the great central stream of the district, and its name signifies "dreadful." Its head silted up somewhere about the end of last century, and now although that part of it which is tidal, namely all below Basantia, is still a large river capable of bearing vessels of any size, the rest of it, the part which lies between the Kabadak and Basantia, is in the dry weather little more than a marsh, and in the rains even no bigger than a khal.

The Bhairab.

11. In a letter of 18th July 1794, the then collector wrote that the Bhairab was shut up by a chur forming at its head (that is, that the head of the channel was silting up), and that the stream was in the dry season almost dry. To keep it open was important, as the civil station of Jessore was situated upon it, and the collector proposed to cut through the chur. Many years afterwards an attempt was made, by embanking the Kabadak below the exit of the Bhairab, to drive the water down the Bhairab channel. A formidable embankment was erected, which may still be seen near Tahirpur, but the river refused to be controlled. It entered the Bhairab channel certainly, but then immediately broke across country into its old bed, at a point below the embankment.

Its closure.

12. The towns on its bank are these: Jessore, Rajahat, Rupdia, Basantia, Noapara, Phultalla, Senhati, Khulna and Sen's Bazar, Alaipur, Faqirhat, Baghahat, Kochua—a long array of towns prominent in the commerce of the district.

13. The next river is the Harihar. It used to emerge from the Kabadak, just above Jingagachha, at the point where the Jingagachha factory subsequently stood. It flowed from thence south-eastward, past Manirampur and Keshabpur into the Bhadra. The head of the river has long been shut up, and in a list of bridges to be made upon the Calcutta and Jessore road (in the collector's letter of 2nd October 1810) the Harihar is not mentioned, which it certainly would have been if at the point where the road crossed the river bed there was then any current of water. At that point the bed is now cultivated. Farther down, near Manirampur, the river bed is a marsh, containing a little water. For two or three miles beside Keshabpur the river is navigable for small vessels when the high tide comes up to fill the otherwise nearly dry channel; but the merchants in Keshabpur are obliged to dig holes or tanks in the bed, in which the ships may lie while waiting cargo.

The Harihar.

14. There is still another river, the Bhadra, just mentioned, which used to emerge from the Kabadak at Trimohini, and after receiving the Harihar a mile or two beneath Keshabpur continue its south-eastward course to the Sundarban rivers. Upon the bank of this river, in the Mahomedan times, the house of the faujdar, or military governor of Jessore, used to stand; but now all between Trimohini and Keshabpur the bed is cultivated, and below that point it widens out into a tidal stream.

The Bhadra.

15. Thus every one of the rivers we have mentioned used to flow from the north-west, bringing down towards the sea the waters of the great river; but in every case their connection with the great river has within the last hundred years ceased to exist. Their heads have all silted up; that of the Kumar, it is true, only partly, but those of all the rest—the Nabaganga, the Chitra, the Kabadak, the Bhairab, the Harihar, and the Bhadra—completely.

16. But it is not only in the closing of the heads of these rivers that one has evidence of the nature of the change that has long been going on, and has now been nearly completed. We find from the old records of the collectorate that the northern and western parts of the district were far more liable

Ancient liability to inundation.

to inundation eighty years ago than they are now. The country between the Kumar and the Nabaganga at that time was under water regularly for some months of the year (C. 1-11-91; 18-7-94), whereas it is now reached only by an unusual inundation. The Nabaganga was then a dreaded river, and much money was spent in keeping up embankments along the south bank of it, the remains of which may be seen in the present day; its floods frequently caused very great damage, and sometimes poured silt and sand over the country. Even Saydpur and Isafpur were pergunnahs where creeks had to be embanked and inundations expected. The details of all these floods, and the history of the embankments, will be given in a subsequent place; but at present I mention them to shew that floods were once not uncommon where now the land is quite free from them, and that a river which is now a mere channel for local surface drainage was eighty years ago a source of constant dread.

17. If we look beyond the boundaries of the district we see the once great streams, the Matabhanga and the Jalinghi, both of them now having their heads closed, except during the rains; even the Bhagirati itself is rapidly silting up, and the cold weather traffic upon it is necessarily becoming less and less.

18. The conclusion from all this is, that this part of the country, all that lies north and west of my imaginary line from Keshabpur to Muhammadpur, is ceasing to be delta land; the work of formation there is nearly finished, and the building-up operations of the river are carried on now to the eastward and southward of the line which I give as the boundary between the high and already formed land, and the low land now in course of formation.

General conclusion.

19. I have stated the facts bearing on my first point, the general cessation of deltaic action in the high part of the district, and I now proceed to state those bearing on the second point, the commencement or marked increase of action in the low tract. And I notice, to begin with, that the changes in both these respects were contemporaneous, and occurred almost entirely during the last half of last century. They were not two independent matters, but both were effects of one cause.

Transfer of deltaic action.

20. A hundred years ago, as we may see from Rennel's map, the Kumar was a large stream which flowed across the north of what are now the districts of Nuddea, Jessore, and Furreedpore, rejoining the main stream on the other side

The opening of the Madhumati river.

B

of Furreedpore. At the point where, as we would now put it, the Gorai
receives the Kumar, the Kumar then received the Gorai, a cross-stream
from the Ganges, and a little farther down it discharged a stream, the
Barasi, which flowed southward, while the Kumar flowed eastward.

21. But when its western exits became closed to it, the waters of the
Ganges began to pour down the Gorai, which then began to swallow up
the Kumar and continue its course down in the direction of the Barasi,
leaving the eastern part of the Kumar channel comparatively deserted.
The Barasi was too small a stream to contain all this body of water, and
the current therefore opened up another channel on the west of the
Barasi, which channel was that of a mere khal, named the Alangkhali.
Barasi is a contraction of Bara-masi, "twelve months' stream"—a vari-
ation even now occasionally used; and I think we may infer from the
distinctiveness of this name that the western channel, the Alangkhali,
was not a twelve months' stream. Indeed, Rennel's map does not mark
it as a continuous channel.

22. The two channels united in the great marsh which anciently
occupied the site of Mokimpur pergunnah, where it was easier for them
to widen out a bed for themselves, so as to make one great river.

23. The recent formation of this great river is not a mere matter
of argument or probability. It is a fact perfectly well known in the
vicinity, being almost within the recollection of persons now living. It
occurred at the very beginning of the present century, and it is remarkable that at that time we find records of unusual inundations over the
country about Muhammadpur, which have clearly to do with the change
then going on. The water pouring down accumulated in that region, as
it had not yet formed a wide enough channel by which to proceed on its
course. A few years of inundation and the work of erosion was
performed; the stream flowed on regularly, and inundation ceased
to be perpetually recurrent.

24. The new channel obtained the name Madhumati ("honey-
flowing"), that being the name the lower part of it, that below the point
where it received the Nabaganga in the marsh just alluded to, used
to have. Farther south, where the stream became of a tidal character,
it was and is called the Baleshwar ("lord of strength"), and its estuary
is called Haringhatta ("deer-shore").

25. Even if the formation of this river were not so recent as to be
within men's memory, there is another argument by which we might
prove it. The division of the districts into pergunnahs is a very ancient

division, and it was in existence at the time when we first hear of the country in history. Now, where we find a river marking the boundary between adjacent pergunnahs, we may be sure that it was a land-mark in very ancient times, or at least at the period when the pergunnahs were constituted. The Kumar, the Bhairab, the Bhadra, the Kabadak, divide pergunnahs for almost their whole length, so that in that fact we have proof that they were once large streams. The Gorai and Madhumati, on the other hand, for almost their whole course, pass through the hearts of successive pergunnahs,—Nasratshahi, Sator, Mokimpur, Sultanpur, Selimabad. This could never have been the case if these rivers had been at the time of the pergunnah distribution anything approaching in size to what they are now.

26. It is necessary now to note the changes which the opening of this great river has caused in all the other rivers, namely, how the waters of the Gorai, breaking across country, fill at a lower point the channels of all those older rivers whose heads have been closed.

27. There is the Kumar river, which is filled by the Kaliganga and some other cross-streams from the Gorai. The Kumar.
In the rainy season so much water is thus received by the Kumar, that at Ramnagar, near Magurah, it discharges part of its water back again into the Gorai channel, following, in fact, the ancient channel of the Kumar; but in the cold season, when hardly any water comes down the Kumar, the water of this cross-stream at Ramnagar flows in the other direction, and brings down the water of the Gorai towards Magurah. Thus, both when the rivers are full and when they are low, it is the water of the Gorai, rather than that of the Kumar, which comes to the confluence at Ramnagar, and pours down by what was once only a cross-stream, but now is a principal river channel, into the Nabaganga at Magurah. The mere names are sufficient to shew that this was once only a cross-stream, for we see a channel, called the Muchikhali, joining two parallel streams, the Kumar and Nabaganga; and there could never have been this arrangement of names if the waters had always flowed as they do now, in one continuous river down the Kumar, across by the Muchikhali, and then down the Nabaganga.

28. The Nabaganga, then below Magurah, now derives all its water from the Gorai, through the above channels. The Nabaganga.
Above the point where this water pours into it, the Nabaganga itself is a small silting up stream; beneath this point it is worthy of the name of a river.

29. Like the Kumar then, the channel of the old Nabaganga carries the waters that have come from the Gorai as far as Naldi, and there similarly it divides into two parts. One part flows south-eastward by its old course past Lakshmipassa, the other breaks across country by a channel, also called the Muchikhali, into the Chitra, which it joins at Gorakhali.

30. Of the original formation of this Muchikhalli, the following
Formation of the Muchi-
·khali. story is told. At one of the villages upon this khal there lived last century a very wealthy mercantile family, who had some hundreds of boats trading upon all the rivers. At that time there was no khal here at all, but these merchants were desirous that their many boats should be able to come to their house. Fearing opposition to the cutting of a channel from the river to their house, they collected a lot of men, and in the course of a single night they had united the Nabaganga and Chitra rivers by a khal. The house in which they dwelt, and in which their descendants now live, stands out still very prominently on the bank of the khal.

31. This khal, small enough once, has now the size and aspect of a river. It is year by year widening out, because the other exit from the Nabaganga is becoming closed. The channel under Lohagara, which used to convey the Nabaganga waters into the Madhumati, has, during the last ten years, become completely closed, except during floods, so that all the water which comes down the south-eastern channel must find its way down the Bankana, toward Khalia. But this south-eastern channel itself is tending to silt up, so that the greater part of the waters of the Nabaganga discharge themselves through the Muchikhali into the Chitra.

· 32. The Chitra then carries on these waters, which have, as we
The Chitra. have stated originally, come from the Gorai, and spreads them over the bheel country of Naral and Khulna, whence they find their way by many channels into the Athara-banka or the Bhairab.

33. The Atharabanka ("eighteen bends") is also itself a stream which brings the waters of the Madhumati into the Bhairab. So abundant is the supply that it brings, that it not only fills all that part of the Bhairab which lies south-east of Alaipur, but turns back the Bhairab from Alaipur to Khulna, and drives all its water away from its own channel down the Rupsa.

34. Thus, then, the whole river system has been changed; the
many rivers that used to flow from north-west to
south-east have now their heads closed, and the
Madhumati sends its waters across their paths, changing the cross-streams
into principal streams, and determining a general south-westward flow
of the river currents.

General result.

35. The work that is at present being accomplished by the Madhumati it is easy to trace. When the rainy season
fills the rivers, the water of the Madhumati pours
in over its banks, inundating all the country which lies between the
Nabaganga and the Madhumati. This tract ought, according to its
original formation, to drain out south-eastward; but as the water
comes from the north-east, and operates first upon the east of it,
the channels there silt up, and the water is more and more pent
up within the bheels. Cultivation is decreasing there at present,
because the bheels are more and more overflowed each year. When
the Madhumati formed, it carried forward at one bound the formative
energy from the west of the district to the east of it, and there
necessarily exists a low tract of country in that place to which the
formation from the west or north-west had not reached when it was
discontinued, and to which the formation from the east or north-east
has not yet reached.

Deltaic formation—pre-
sent stage.

36. Lower down, as I have said, the Bankana and the Chitra
rivers carry the waters of the Madhumati over the lower bheel country.
It will be many generations before the effect of the rivers is seen in
the elevation of the land, but it is an effect which will follow with
certainty some time or other.

37. There is one part of the low tract lying between the old
formation on the west and the now progressing
formation on the east that requires special notice;
it is the country south of Magurah, included between the Nabaganga
and the Chitra. It ought to be flooded by the overflowing of the
Nabaganga, filled by the waters of the Gorai, and so it is in part. But
unfortunately we have adopted effective measures to prevent this.
Within the last ten years it was found that the waters pouring down
towards Magurah from the Gorai and the Kumar were flowing not
only *down* the Nabaganga, but were flowing up the Nabaganga as far
as Kasinathpur, and there breaking into the country to the south. A
river had almost already been formed, when, in order to prevent one of

Artificial interference.

the indirect effects of this determination of the current, namely, the destruction of the Magurah house, an embankment was thrown across at Kasinathpur. It has saved the house perhaps, but it has delayed for many many years the natural process of the elevation of the land. Had the embankment not been put up, we would have seen a new river coming down from Kasinathpur to the Katki channel, a new centre from which the silting up process in the delta might proceed. This piece of country now gets very little silt-laden water from higher rivers. The only channel that brings down to it any considerable quantity of water is one which, coming from the Kumar across the Nabaganga, near Jhenida, pours southward by a channel known as the Dhopaghatta channel.

PART II.—ANTIQUITIES.

III.—*Traditions of Khan Jahan Ali—The ruins at Baghahat, Masjidkur, &c.—A.D. 1450.*

SOME of the earliest traditions, and some of the oldest ruins in the district of Jessore, connect themselves with the name of Khanja Ali, who lived four centuries since; so long ago, that it is a matter of difficulty to find out exactly who and what he was. So much is certain, both from the traditions and from the marks that he has left behind him, that he came to the district with a large body of men, and that he and his men resided for a long time in the district. This is a matter, however, that can best be discussed when we have first described the traces which he has left of his presence.

Khanja Ali.

2. Ruins which there is reason to attribute to Khanja Ali are to be found in various parts of the district; but they occur in the greatest abundance near Baghahat, on the outskirts of the Sundarbans, the place which is declared by tradition to have been his residence.

3. From the bank of the Bhairab river at Baghahat there runs, in almost a straight line, a brick-laid road which was made by Khanja Ali. The bricks, which are smaller than those now used, being about five or six inches square, and less than two inches thick, are laid on edge to form the road; there are five equidistant

Road at Baghahat.

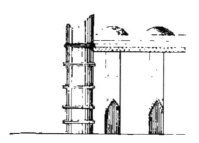

PLAN

longitudinal lines, each of two bricks' thickness, and between these the
bricks are laid transversely, forming in all a brick road of about ten feet
across, raised on a slightly elevated embankment. The surface is, as is
natural after 400 years' attrition, very irregular, and in most places the
embankment has been partly washed away, carrying with it some part
of the breadth of the brick road. But even now the road is continually
used as such, though there appears to have been no sort of repair effected
for the last 400 years.

4. Following this road for about three miles in a westerly direction
from Baghahat, we reach the largest of Khanja
Ali's buildings, the Satgumbaz, or "sixty domes."
This building presents to the east a face of massive
brick-work, terminated at both sides by circular towers. In the centre
is a large doorway, and at each side of this doorway, arranged at equal
distances, are five smaller ones; in all eleven doorways, all being of the
pointed-arch form. Above the doorways the face of the wall is a little
deeper than it is in the intervals, and the wall is dotted with circles,
by way of ornament. Entering by the doorways we find ourselves in
a large hall, whose dimensions are given by Baboo Gour Dass Bysack
(who visited and described the place) as 144 by 96 feet. The pillars
which support the roof, of which there are ten rows of six each, divide
the space into eleven aisles lengthwise and seven aisles crosswise.
The eleven doorways are of course opposite the aisles, and, in fact, as all
four sides of the building are penetrated with doorways, there is one at
each end of each of the aisles. The central aisle, that which is entered
by the large doorway mentioned above, is however closed at the western
end by an erection of stone. This was the place of prayer, the worshippers of course worshipping towards the west. On the north side of the
central aisle are the remains of two small platforms of brick; one near
the stone altar just described, which was for the worshippers, and one
near the doorway, the place where it is said Khanja Ali sat to
transact his business; for this large hall was both a place of business and
a place of worship, and even the altar served worldly purposes, for
two holes are shewn in it where Khanja Ali kept his boxes of money.

5. The roof is composed of seventy-seven cupolas or domes,
(eleven rows of seven), supported by arches on the pillars beneath.
It is all very massive, but the pillars are nevertheless very thin, not
more than 1¼ or 1½ feet square. The pillars were apparently originally
built of grey stone, encased in brick; but in all, except one or two,

the brick-casing has fallen away, and hence the apparently light structure of the pillars. Each pillar shews two or three of these grey stones placed one above the other, and cut quite smooth ; and about eight feet from the ground, where the arch springs which supports the cupola above, there is a sort of capital.

6.   At the four corners of the building four small towers rise a little above the roof. The two which are on the front are ascendible by winding staircases from the inside of the building, one of these being called the andhar kotha ("dark building"), and one the roshan kotha ("light building").

7.   Except that the tops of the towers are dilapidated, the rest of the masonry is in good order, and with mere surface repair would make what would even now be called a grand public building ; the roof, however, is covered with a forest of jungle, which completely obscures its form.

8.   The inside is kept clear by an old man, who gets a few pice from the pilgrims who travel to the place. During the méla or fair held every year in honor of Khanja Ali, it is used as a dwelling place by many hundreds of the visitors, who can find within its ample dimensions abundant accommodation. The natives regard the structure as Government property, and it is considered that Government, when it established the sub-division of Baghahat, should have used for its purposes the building whence the country was ruled 400 years ago.

9.   There are traces of a large wall which once surrounded the whole building, and the entrance to the enclosure
Archway.
within which it stands is even now by the ancient archway which formed part of this wall.

10.   Immediately at the back of the building there is a very large tank, which dates back to the same time. Khanja
Tank.
Ali always dug a tank where he erected a building.

11.   At a distance along Khanja Ali's high road of about a mile and a half from Baghahat, a side road strikes off
The mosque of the tomb.
to the south, and takes us to others of Khanja Ali's buildings. The road takes us up an artificial mound, and through a gateway in the wall which surrounds the whole of the buildings. Within this enclosure there is another smaller one, also surrounded by a wall, and within this is the mosque which contains the tomb of Khanja Ali. This structure appears square in the outside, but octagonal in the inside, and the roof of it is one large hemispherical dome, with an ornamental pinnacle standing out at the top. The

dimensions of the building are, according to Baboo Gour Dass Bysack, 45 feet square (this being therefore the diameter of the dome), and it is 47 feet to the top of the dome.

12. Khanja Ali's tomb occupies the centre of the mosque, and it is marked by a tombstone—a stone five or six feet long, and of rounded top, laid upon three steps. The stone is covered with Arabic inscriptions in relief, and the horizontal face of the two highest steps (which are also of stone) bear similar inscriptions. The lowest step, and the floor of the hall, are laid with hexagonal encaustic tiles, but the floor is very much broken up.

The tombs.

13. The stone used in the construction of the tomb is the same grey stone which is used in the pillars of the Satgumbaz. There is no such stone to be found in all the Gangetic delta, and the tradition is that Khanja Ali had it brought from Chittagong. But whence came the masons who fashioned and engraved it?

14. Immediately to the west side of this building, and outside it, there is another tomb, lying like Khanja Ali's, north and south, fashioned exactly similarly, but bearing no inscriptions. It is a cenotaph, and can be entered by a door leading beneath the tombstone. I did not go down, and could not verify what I was told, that there were inscriptions inside. This tomb is that of Muhammad Taher, the dewan of Khanja Ali. He is known in Bengal by the name of Pir Ali, and was a brahmin who had adopted the Mussulman religion. His zeal for religion is celebrated to the present day, and he gives his name to a certain sect of Hindoos, though how he does so I do not exactly know.

Pir Ali's tomb.

15. The mosque and these two tombs are all that is within the inner quadrangle; but just west of it, and within the outer enclosure, is another building similar in structure to the mosque but smaller in dimensions. It is said to have been used by Khanja Ali, when he dwelt here, as his cook-house.

Cook-house

16. All these buildings are in good repair, except so far as the surface goes. They are all in charge of two faqirs, who keep up the worship at the mosques and who use the cook-house as such. They claim descent from Khanja Ali, but acknowledge they cannot trace it; but they have rights in the place, for they hold some 368 beegahs of lakhiraj land, appropriated to the service of the place, and coming down from a very long time.

Faqirs.

There were larger lands once, and there were also lands attached to the Satgumbaz; but these were resumed by Government while the 368 beegahs were released. The tomb is also a great place of pilgrimage for devout Mahomedans, and people come from a long distance to make their vows at Khanja Ali's shrine.

17. Immediately to the south of the buildings I have described, and in front of the mosque, which faces south,

Tank.

is a very large and very fine tank. Baboo Gour Dass Bysack measured its water at the height of the dry season 1,560 feet square. Its depth the faqirs could not tell me, for they say no boat ever goes on its surface. Near the edges it is certainly very shallow, but the water is always good.

18. There are in the tank eight tame alligators, of which one only is large. They come at the faqir's call to

Tame alligators.

the ghât that leads from the water to the door of the mosque (a fine broad ghât, now somewhat dilapidated, but still the largest and widest by far in the whole district), and take food from the faqir; not from his hand however, for they might have some difficulty in regulating the fierce snap they make at their food, so as to make it avoid taking also the feeder's arm. It is chiefly by the offerings of pilgrims, or the thanksgivings of those who have made a successful vow at the mosque, that these alligators are supported. They have a grand feed once a year at the fair time, but at other times are not so well off. They do not eat each other, but apparently do not live on very friendly terms, and it seems to be one rule of their society that not more than one should grow big at one time. The present large one remained small for years, until the last king alligator was gathered to his fathers.

19. The alligators of course are sacred, for they are the descendants of Khanja Ali's, and it is through his sacred influence that they obey the faqir's calls. He had two alligators, who were called Kalapar and Dholapar ("black-side" and "white-side"), and when he called them by their names they would come to him from the remotest corner of the tank. So their descendants, the alligators of the present day, hear and obey the same call.

20. The story of these buildings is this: Khanja Ali lived first at the Satgumbaz, but when he was old and near

Legend of the tank.

the end of his days he asked God where he should go to die and be buried. God pointed out to him this place, and so he came here, erected the mosque and tomb for himself, and dug a tank, as he always did beside his buildings. It is said that in excavating this tank he had dug very deep indeed, and yet failed to find any water. The diggers at last dug out a Hindoo temple, into which Khanja Ali entered and found a devotee sitting inside. Him he asked for water, and the devotee at once caused the fountains of the deep to gush forth in such abundance, that it was with difficulty that Khanja Ali and the diggers escaped in time to the bank. The devotee's temple is fabled still to exist at the bottom of the tank, but it has been seen only by one man. This was a man who one day, mounted on a tree on the edge of the tank, was cutting its branches. All of a sudden he cried out, "Hallo! there is the devotee waking!" and the moment he said so, the branch on which he stood snapped, and he fell down and died. His body was buried close by, within the precincts of the mosque.

21. The legend of the tank is a curious one in one respect ; it is a Mahomedan fable, though its subject is Hindoo divinity.

22. The buildings described, though the most complete, are by no
Numerous ruins
means the only remains of Khanja Ali to be found in this place; for a two or three miles round about the country is full of ruins that date back to his time. In passing along the road I have described one sees several ruined mosques, some of them similar in structure to the mosque of the tomb, some simpler. The people who reside near them say that there are in all 360 mosques and 360 tanks, and that they were called by the names of Khanja Ali's leading men—Bakhtar Khan, Ikhtyar Khan, Alam Khan, Saadat Khan, Ahmad Khan, Deria Khan, and so forth.

23. The road which I have described is the one which shews most
and roads.
of its original structure, but I saw two or three others leading off from it at right angles, and I am informed that Khanja Ali's roads crop out all over the region round about. One of those I saw ran right through the village of Basabari, close to Baghahat, being in fact its principal road. This road, it is said, led right on to Chittagong; and I was told, though I cannot say with what truth, that fragments of it were traceable even at places far distant from Baghahat. Khanja Ali made this road in order to go to visit a great faqir at Chittagong, whose name was Bazid Bostan. They say that he bridged the rivers and khals in the way, but probably they

mean only the smaller ones (for the Megna was, I should imagine,
beyond even his engineering skill), and that long after the Nawab
Jangir Khan, who used part of the road in a journey from Dacca to
Calcutta, broke down all the bridges.

    *   *   *   *   *   *   *   *

    24. Leaving the Baghahat ruins for a while, let us describe
Ruins at Masjidkur.
(Plate II.) some which exist at the other side of the district.

    25. When, in the extension of cultivation into the Sundarban forest,
some people were clearing the jungle along the banks of the Kabadak
river, at a point about six miles south of Chandkhali, they came upon an
ancient mosque, close by the river bank, and they called the village by
the name of Masjidkur, "the digging out a mosque."

    26. The building thus found proclaims at the first glance that it
owes its origin to the same hand which built the
Mosque. Satgumbaz. The principle of structure is the
same, only instead of a breadth of eleven domes and a depth of seven,
we have here a breadth and depth of three domes only, or nine in all.
These are the same massive walls, for they are about six feet thick ; a
large central doorway is beneath the middle dome on each side, and
two smaller doorways on each face, one on each side of the central one.
But the building itself appears to the eye of so massive structure, that
the doorways seem dwarfed out of all proportion to the size of the face.
As in the Satgumbaz, so here also there are four towers at the four
corners of the buildings, but none of them appear to be ascendible ;
and the walls shew in several places the same little circlets traced on
the face of the brick which are used to ornament the larger structure
near Baghahat.

    27. Inside we find of course only four pillars supporting the roof,
one at each of the four interior depending cusps of the arches which
support the nine domes. The west, or rather the north-west side, I
should have mentioned, has no doorways like the other three sides ; but
looking from the inside, we find, at the places where the doorways should
be, three "bimbars" or niches,—the places towards which prayer was
made. The building is clean in the inside, and is all in very good
state. The tops of the corner towers are fallen away, but the rest of
the masonry looks as if it could stand for ages yet. The roof, too, is
kept clean, no jungle being allowed to grow, except a little grass only ;
and thus we see not only the forms of the nine domes, but the tracery

work along the upper edge of the four faces. As in most of these ancient buildings, the middle part of each face stands higher than the sides.

28. The pillars are made of stone—and here I come to a some-
Mystery about the stone pillars.what inexplicable part of the matter. Like the Satgumbaz pillars, they are formed by placing two or three long stones perpendicularly in line, but they shew none of the same regularity. Instead of rising out of the ground upon symmetrical bases, they rest upon one or two similar long stones laid horizontally upon the ground, without regularity, and not even at the same height: it is done as one would set up such stones roughly, and for a temporary purpose. Most of the stones are of the same grey stone we saw at the Satgumbaz, but there are one or two of a redder color, and one or two speckled stones among them. They are all cut in some sort of pattern, either square, or with a band, or with a groove upon one side. Two stones shew the same device, four tassels as it were dependent upon the four edges; but these two stones are in two different pillars, and are reverse ways; that is, the tassels hang up in one and hang down in the other.

29. So far therefore is clear: these stones were not brought there, and were not fashioned, for the purpose they at present fulfil. They belonged to some other structure, and they were taken from it, or from its ruins, to form pillars in this mosque.

30. Now, in the adjacent village of Amadi, where I shall presently describe some other remains of Khanja Ali's, there lies, and has lain during all the memory of the present generation, a cylindrical piece of grey stone about two feet long. Its ends are squared, and its circumference cut into twelve facets. Round the middle of it is a high band, and at either the bottom or the top (I can not say which) there is a device, alternate triangle and square, carried round the twelve facets. This stone, whatever it was meant for, came from a long distance away, for no such stone can be found for 150 miles round, and there is no other building near for which it could have been intended, except only the mosque I have described.

31. Two theories alone seem admissible to explain what I have stated. Either the builder of this mosque, finding some ancient structure in the place, and having no stone of his own to work with, built the mosque with temporary pillars taken from this more ancient structure, intending afterwards to procure and fashion and substitute other stones, of which we find one now lying in Amadi; or the building being properly finished, some Vandals of later times took away its

pillars for their own purposes or for some other temple, leaving behind
them only the one we now find in Amadi; and either they or the
worshippers at the mosque put up the pillars we now find, using for the
purpose the stones of the gateway, or of some similar erection close by.
The latter theory is the one I incline to. It seems to me impossible
that a man building what must then have been so fine a mosque, and
a man capable of building the Satgumbaz, would begin by laying down
pillars that are mere patch-work compared with the rest of his building.
It is also extremely improbable that, ancient as the mosque itself is,
the builders of it should have found in such a place as the Sundarbans
a still more ancient structure, and should have used its elements in their
own work.

32.   In favor of the explanation I give, it may be mentioned that
there are clear traces of a wall which once enclosed the mosque, and in
which there must have been a gateway. The removal of the old
pillars, and the substitution of new ones, is not so impossible a task as
may at first sight appear, for the whole structure is so massive that it
could easily support itself without the pillars. The present pillars
indeed are so small, and so weak in construction (one being actually
bent in the middle like an elbow), that they can bear but a small part
of the weight of the roof. Still I am not content with the explanation,
though the facts certainly demand explanation of some sort.

33.   Some of the faces, and some of the corners of the pillar stones,
shew marks of considerable attrition; and as in their present position
they are little liable to attrition, or at all events whatever attrition they
now suffer would be distributed regularly, and not so capriciously as we
find it the case, this is another evidence of their having once formed part
of another structure. A fable has been invented to account for the
wearing away of the corner of one pillar at a point almost out of reach
as it at present stands.—There is a fairy who comes at night and rubs
herself upon the pillar, and it is she who has polished away the corner.
I cannot find that she has ever revealed herself in any other way.

34.   The mosque is still used as a place of worship by the residents
in the vicinity. On the day of my visit there
was a grand service there, for it was the I'd-ul-fitr,
the breaking of the Ramazan fast. The mulla, who stood in front, read
the service—apparently first prayers and then lesson—to the crowd,
who remained in silence, occasionally changing position and intoning
at the same time some response. · There were viands presented at the

Worship.

altar, and I was told that they were presented in the name of Khanja
Ali, to whom they attributed the erection of the mosque.

35. Less than a mile down the stream, and on the same side of it,
is the village of Amadi, where there are other

Tomb at Amadi.

relics of Khanja Ali. Close on the river bank
are two tombs, placed lengthways, north and south; they are said to be
the tombs of Bura Khan and Fatah Khan, father and son, followers of
Khanja Ali. The tombs are no doubt ancient; but at first sight I
would not have dated them back 400 years. The northern one is now
falling into the river.

36. A little farther south is a raised piece of land with a brick
foundation in it. Two or three small tanks and a

Cutcherry and tanks.

long artificial trench surround this elevation, and
the place is stated to mark the cutcherry of Bura and Fatah Khan.
Farther south still is a very large tank, called the Kalki-diggi; it is
now a mass of marshy jungle, but the surface included within its high
embankments measured, I was told, 100 beegahs (a square of 1,200
feet a side). The tank has no masonry ghât, but in the centre of each
of the four sides rises a cluster of tamarind trees. Coming back to
the river bank at a point a little farther up than the tombs, we
pass another large tank whose name is Hathi-banda ("elephant-
binding"); like the former, it is far on its way to ruin, but it still
contains sweet water. The stone I have mentioned above lies not far
from this tank.

37. It is strange that these two large tanks have their length
north and south. This would be an argument for their Hindoo origin
were not the tombs and the mosque, which are no doubt connected with
them, so distinctly Mahomedan.

38. Close to the mosque there are two or three small tanks, but
they deserve no description.

   *   *   *   *   *   *   *

39. I have described the above as the principal traces of Khanja
Ali, but there are a few other marks of him

Other ruins.

scattered over the district. Of the connection
between Khanja Ali and the ruins at Baghahat and at Masjidkur, of
course no doubt can exist; but in the other cases I have been tempted to
think that it arises only from a desire to explain every thing ancient by
attaching it to the most ancient name known to the traditions of the
district. It must be remembered, however, that there are few things

that strike an inquirer more than the localization of traditions such as those I am narrating. Names and traditions seem to be hardly known beyond the circle where they sprung up; and when we find Khanja Ali's name known so far north as the town of Jessore, we may deem it pretty certain that the local tradition attached to his name arises from some connection which he had with the place, and not from the arbitrary appropriation of a hero who belongs to another part of the country.

40. It is also very much in favor of the reality of Khanja Ali's connection with the places I am about to note, that all the places fall in one line, apparently the line of march from the north-west of the district down to Baghahat.

41. There is first of all Bara Bazar, ten miles north of Jessore. There are some ruins here, but they make no great shew, and I have not had an opportunity to examine them in detail. There are also some tanks, one at least a very large one, and it is said that in and around Bara Bazar the whole number of tanks is six score and six. These are all put down to Khanja Ali, and this place was one stage of his journey to Baghahat. This, however, is very doubtful. (See note to chapter **XXXIX**.)

42. Next, in Jessore itself, we find the shrines of two old peers, or Mussulman sages,—Gharib Shah and Bahram Shah. The shrine of the first is just beside the collectorate, a place where Mussulmans make a salaam as they pass along the road; the other's shrine is a little distance off, in the direction of the cemetery. Gharib and Bahram Shah were companions of Khanja Ali, and it is said that when he was coming this way he sent them ahead to prepare food for him at Jessore. When he came up it was not ready, and he therefore left them behind when he went on. They remaining erected shrines; and as they were, like Khanja Ali, men of great piety and divine power, people resorted to them, and even now resort to their shrines, to pay their vows and make known their wishes.

43. There is a large tank at Ramnagar, four miles south-east of Jessore, which I have also heard connected with his name. But the people who live near it know nothing of it, and the tank itself, being a north and south one, is too pronouncedly Hindoo. I do not think it has anything to do with Khanja Ali.

44. In several places along the bank of the Bhairab there are
traces of an old road, raised upon a pretty high
embankment, but not metalled or brick-laid like
those near Baghahat. Portions of this road I have seen in and near
Nimai Ray's bazar (Senhati) and Sen's bazar (Khulna); in fact, both
these bazars are partly built on the road in question; and between
Sen's bazar and Sholepur, except where in some parts it is destroyed,
it forms the current road. Three or four years ago, one Madan Bawali
repaired that part of it above Nimai Ray's bazar which connected
that bazar with Digalia (his house) and Barakpur. At Sen's bazar it
apparently crossed the river, and then proceeded down towards Baghahat,
and traces of it are found four miles down the river, opposite Alaipur.
This road is known as Khanja Ali's road, and it is said to be the road
by which Khanja Ali and his men came through the district on their
way to Baghahat, making the road as they went along.

Road along the Bhairab.

45. I have not myself seen any other traces of Khanja Ali,
but I am informed that there exist such in Abhaynagar on the bank
of the Bhairab, and in Subalhara in Naral. The first of these two
places is on the line of march, the second is far from it.

    *   *   *   *   *   *

46. Who was Khanja Ali, or, to use his full name, Khan Jahan
Ali, the centre of all these traditions? The
inscriptions on his tomb tell us only these facts
about him, that he was a stranger in the land, and that he died in
the Mahomedan year 863, i.e., A.D. 1458. The works he has left
behind sufficiently shew that he must have been a ruler of many men.
With these facts all the traditions agree; for he is represented as
entering the district and marching through it with a large body of
men, making his road as he went along, and building mosques and tanks
here and there. The Senhati people say he brought along with him
sixty thousand diggers.

Who was he?

47. The tradition both at Baghahat and at Masjidkur is that he
came to reclaim and cultivate the lands in the
Sundarbans, which were at that time waste and
covered with forest. He obtained from the emperor, or from the
king of Gaur, a jaghir of these lands, and in accordance with it
established himself in them. The tradition of his cutcherry site in both
places corresponds with this view of his position, and the fact of his
undertaking such large works—works which involve the necessity of

A colonist of the Sundarbans.

D

supporting quite an army of laborers—also points to his position as receiver of the rents, or chief of the cultivators of the soil. His works in their nature correspond exactly with those that a century or two later were undertaken by other great zemindars.

48. The pergunnah near Baghahat, where all these works are found, is named Khalífat-abad ; and this name is a very ancient one, for it is given as one of the assessment divisions in Todarmal's assessment of Bengal in 1582. The meaning of the name is "reclaimed on the part of the emperor," or "by the emperor's command." It seems to me that this name is no small corroboration of our view of Khanja Ali's position. In 1578 Khalífat-abad, with other thirty-four pergunnahs included within its circle of assessment, was assessed at Rs. 1,35,053. But it seems to have extended north at least as far as Naldi pergunnah, and perhaps also still farther west and north-west. It does not argue that land worth Rs. 1,35,053 a year had been reclaimed from what we now regard as the Sundarbans.

49. Another testimony regarding Khanja Ali's position I find in the history I am about to narrate of Raja Pratapaditya. He came to the country a century later, and it is stated that the land had, before him, been occupied by a Mussulman ruler of the Khan race.

50. Such places as Masjidkur were likely out-stations of Khanja Ali's, where his lieutenants carried on the same work, and occupied the same position that he himself did in Khalífat-abad. Bura Khan and Fatah Khan were, as before said, the names of his lieutenants at Masjidkur.

51. Khanja Ali was a very holy man,—what the natives call a "buzurgi ;" that is, one who has, through his holiness, supernatural power. Mosques and tanks without number are the testimony he has left behind him of his existence ; and the Satgumbaz, where apparently he dwelt during the period of his greatness, was both a place of worship and a place of business. After he had lived a long time as a great zemindar, he withdrew himself from wordly affairs and dwelt as a faqir in the place which, as before narrated, had been pointed out to him as the place where he should die.

A holy man.

52. As there seems to have been no one before Khanja Ali, so there seems to have been no one after him. I find no tradition even of his leaving an heir to his greatness. I have mentioned that the faqirs at the mosque of the tomb

No successors.

claim to be his descendants; but they have no history of their tenure of office, and it is impossible to find out whether it has been continuous or not.

53. It would seem, in fact, that when Khanja Ali died, the work
The obliteration of tradi- he had come to accomplish died also. The land
tion. he had reclaimed fell back into jungle, to be
again reclaimed at some later date. It is to this that I attribute the fragmentary nature of the traditions regarding him. Had the occupation of the lands he ruled over been continuous from his time, no doubt we would find many more traditions of him. But when the jungle spread over the country, it buried most of his history; and the new inhabitants, when they came, picked up and preserved only those fragments which were thrust in their way. Masjidkur, for example, has been reclaimed, and has relapsed twice or thrice within this last century, and its present occupation dates only from 1253 (1846). Nothing tends to obliterate tradition so much as changes like these; and even where there is a continuous line of tradition, the absence among the natives of any spirit of inquiry tends of itself to bury in forgetfulness the unwritten history of the past. It is perfectly wonderful how a whole village can live under the shadow of some ancient building such as I have described, and never once trouble themselves to think or to ask how it came there, or who it was that built it.

54. An annual méla, or fair, is held on the grounds near the
Méla. mosque of the tomb upon the supposed anniversary of the death of Khanja Ali, the full moon
of Cheit (March-April). This fair is the largest, or one of the largest,
Pilgrims. held in the Sundarbans. The mosque is also
continually visited by Mussulman pilgrims, some
of them from long distances; many of these are pilgrims making a round of such visits, who pass on from this to the shrine in Chittagong, the place where Khanja Ali also is stated to have visited (para. 23).

[NOTE.—In 1867, Baboo Gour Dass Bysack read to the Asiatic Society an account of the buildings near Baghahat, which I have described above. There are one or two points of difference between my account and his, which I notice here:

(1) What the Baboo describes as Khanja Ali's pleasure ground, a place in Baghahat itself, belongs, as I believe, to a much later time than Khanja Ali's. I shall describe the thing subsequently in its proper place (chapter LI).

(2) The Baboo narrates somewhat differently the fable of the large tank; but every such fable has two or three forms.

(3) There is no white marble about the tomb, nor are there any golden letters; it is all grey stone, and the inscriptions are merely in relief. The Baboo has made some mistake in description here.

(4) I did not observe anything particularly artistic in the encaustic tiles, or in the chunam work; this, however, may be a matter of opinion.

I have borrowed from the Baboo's account two or three of his measurements, which I have acknowledged in the text. I borrow from it also the inscriptions which he caused to be copied from the tomb, adding to them a translation.

A.

انتقلَ العبْدُ الضعيفُ المُحْتاجُ الى رحمةِ ربِّ العالمينَ اَحَبُّ لا وَلاِدِمَبِدِ ۰
المرسلين المخلص للعلماء الراشدين المبغض للكفار و المشركين ۰ المعين
للاسلام و السلمين الخ خان جهان عليه الرحمة و الغفران من دارالدنيا الى
دارالبقا ليلة الاربعاني منة و عشرين من ذى الحجة و دفن يوم الخميس ني مبع
و عشرين منه سنة ثلث و ستين و ثمانماية ۰

B.

مَن ماتَ غَرِيباً فَقَدْ ماتَ شَهِدًا ۰

C.

الدنيا اولها بكاُء واوسطها عناُء واخرها فناُء

D.

هذه روضة مباركة من رياض الجنة لخان الاعظم خان جهان عليه الرحمة
والرضوان نصر يُبرا نى مت و عشرين من ذى الحجة سنة ثلث و ستين و
ثمانمائة ۰

E.

ياد آور يد اى دوستان الموت حق الموت حق
خار است اندر بوستان الموت حق الموت حق
مرگست خصمى محكمى بِه جمله جانان زو يقين
ـنِه همچو ديگر دشمنان الموت حق الموت حق ۰

A.—*Arabic* :—Here died a poor slave of God, who prays for his mercy. He was a friend of the descendants of the chief of all the prophets, a sincere well-wisher to the learned, and a hater of the infidels. His name was Alagh Khan Jahan Ali. (Peace to his memory.) He was a defender of Islamism. He left this world for a better one on the night of Wednesday, 26th Ze'l Hijjah, and was buried on Thursday, 27th, 863 Hijra.

B.—*Arabic* :—A man who dies in a strange place is entitled to be considered a martyr.

C.—*Arabic* :—The world is a place where a human being begins by crying, then he undergoes several hardships and trials, and at last he dies.

D.—*Arabic* :—This is the garden of heaven (*i.e.,* tomb) for the great khan, Khan Jahan Ali. The peace of God be on him. Dated 26th Ze'l Hijjah 863.

E.—*Persian* :—Remember, O friends, there comes death in the end : death in the end.

It is a thorn within the garden : death in the end : death in the end.

Death is a great enemy to all living things.

Not merely like other enemies : death in the end : death in the end.]

IV.—*History of Raja Pratapaditya—Origin of the name Jessore.—*
A.D. 1580.

AN account of Jessore would not be complete without reference to
King Pratapaditya. Though the ruins of his buildings are now within
the 24-Pergunnahs, I have not been able to visit them or to collect
the traditions which hang about them. I note therefore only that
which seems to be historical about Pratapaditya, and my information
has been obtained in part by the aid of Baboo Pratap Chandra Ghose,
who wrote a paper about this raja in the Asiatic Society's proceedings
of December 1868.

2. Rajah Vikramaditya was one of the chief ministers at the court
of Gaur during the time of King Daud, the last
sovereign of Bengal, and also during one or two
of the previous reigns. When Daud made rebellion against the emperor
of Delhi, about 1573-74, Raja Vikramaditya, a prudent counsellor, was
utterly opposed to the step, and knowing that ruin would shortly follow,
determined to provide himself a city to which he might retire. He
therefore obtained a raj in the Sundarbans, a place sufficiently remote
and difficult of access, and he there established a city, to which he
subsequently retired with his family and his dependants. He had
probably a very large following, for shortly after we find his family
the masters of a large tract of country, and holding it by considerable
military force.

(margin: Raja Vikramaditya founds a city called Jessore.)

3. To this new city Vikramaditya gave the name "Yasohara,"
which, the *y* being pronounced like a *j*, is the
vernacular spelling of Jessore. The name means
"glory-depriving," and I find it accounted for in the following way
in a small book, a popular history of Pratapaditya, which however
is not, in its details at least, of any reliability. When things
were going against King Daud, and Vikramaditya was just about to
proceed to the city which he had prepared for his retirement, Daud
thought it well to remove to a place of safety his wealth and his jewels,
and asked Vikramaditya to take them with him to the new city.
Vikram took with him so much of the wealth and adornments of Gaur
that the splendour of the royal city was transferred to Jessore, whose

(margin: Origin of the name.)

name accordingly was called "the depriver of glory." To me this derivation seems somewhat strained, especially as the city must have had some name before it was finished; and I am inclined to suggest another derivation, which, however, I have nowhere seen ascribed to the name. In the only ancient Hindu inscription which, so far as I know, now exists in the district, that on the temples at Kanhaynagar, which will be described in the next chapter, the Raja Sitaram Ray applies to his city the epithet *ruchira,ruchi,hara*, " depriving of beauty that which is beautiful," meaning simply that beautiful things compared with it no longer had any beauty. I think it possible, if not likely, that Yasohara has a similar meaning and application, and is intended merely to express the idea " supremely glorious."

4. The city thus founded is not the Jessore of the present day, but will be found on the map not far from Kaliganj police station, in the 24-Pergunnahs district.

5. Vikramaditya had a son whose name was Pratapaditya, and who was endowed with all the virtues under the sun, and this Pratapaditya succeeded him in the possession of the principality of Jessore. It is doubtful if Pratapaditya waited for his father's death, for he appears to have set up a rival city at Dhûmghat, close to the old Jessore, and to have taken possession a little time before his father's death. His dominions, either those which he acquired by inheritance, or those which he obtained by extending his inheritance, extended over all the deltaic land bordering on the Sundar-bans, embracing that part of the 24-Pergunnahs district which lies east of the Ichamati river, and all but the northern and north-eastern part of the Jessore district. The raja of Krishnanagar (Nuddea) was apparently the owner of the lands which lay on the north-west of Pratapaditya's.

Pratapaditya.

6. It is stated that at that time Bengal, or more likely only the lower part of it, was distributed among twelve such lords of principalities, who of course all paid rent and owed allegiance to the emperor of Delhi and the governor under him of Bengal. Among these twelve lords Pratapaditya apparently gained the pre-eminence, and in time considered himself strong enough to disclaim allegiance and refuse to pay his revenues to the court of Delhi. During the whole of that time.Bengal was in a very disturbed state, full of quarrelling and of rebellion, so that the opportunity afforded to Pratapaditya was no doubt a good one.

His revolt against the emperor.

7. The emperor several times sent armies to subdue this refractory vassal, but the Sundarbans gave Pratapaditya a strong position, and for a long time he bade defiance to the emperor. The little history referred to above makes him carry war into the open country, and fight the armies of Delhi in a place distant far from his own fortress. But this is not at all likely; the war waged against him had nothing of the character of a general warfare, and the silence of the Mahomedan historians regarding it makes it likely that the efforts made to capture Pratapaditya were little more than small expeditions sent to crush a local rebellion.

8. From the family records of the rajas of Chanchra, it appears that Khan Azim, who was one of Akbar's great generals, deprived Pratapaditya of some of his pergunnahs, for four of them were bestowed upon the raja's ancestor. It is possible, therefore, that Pratapaditya, though he was victorious over the imperial armies, and though they failed to fulfil their duty of capturing him, lost in the struggles part of his power and substance some time before he was finally reduced.

9. Unsuccessful as yet, the emperor now sent Raja Man Singh, his great general, with a large force, to capture the rebellious Pratapaditya. With great difficulty he succeeded in storming his fortress and taking him prisoner, and he conveyed him in an iron cage towards Delhi. The prisoner, however, died on the way, at Benares.

Raja Man Singh captures Pratapaditya.

10. The date of all these events may be gathered from the fact that Azim Khan was in power in 1582-84, and Man Singh was leader of the Delhi armies in Bengal from 1589 till 1606.

11. The name Jessore continued to attach itself to the estates which Pratapaditya had possessed. The faujdar, or military governor, who had charge of them, and who, as we shall see, was located at Mirzanagar, on the Kabadak, was called the faujdar of Jessore; and when the head-quarters of the district, which still differed not much in its boundaries from what it had been in Pratapaditya's time, were brought to Murali, and thence to Kusba (where they now are), the name Jessore was applied to the town where the courts and cutcherries thus were located. The district is now, of course, far from conterminous with Raja Pratapaditya's territories; but that is only because since 1786, the date of its establishment, it has been made to suffer changes of boundary so violent, that only half of what then was Jessore is within the limits of the district as it now stands.

Transfer of the name Jessore.

V.—*History of Raja Sitaram Ray—Ruins at Muhammadpur.—*
A.D. 1700.

AT the period to which belong the events about to be narrated,

Three zemindaris in Jessore. Jessore was at least to some extent a settled country. The present area of the district was divided chiefly among three zemindaris. The raja of Jessore held all the south, the raja of Naldanga held the zemindari of Muhammad-shahi, and the third zemindari, the subject of this chapter, including all Naldi and the greater part of Furreedpore, was called the zemindari of Bhusna. These three zemindars collected the revenues of the tracts within their jurisdiction, and paid them over to the nawab of Bengal, whose capital was then at Dacca. The boundaries of the zemindaris probably had not much of definition, the country being less extensively cultivated, and having far less facility of communication than now; and it is likely that, so far as the borders of their zemindaris went, the various rajas acted on the principle "that he should take who has the power, and he should keep who can."

2. The zemindari of Bhusna came, whether by hereditary descent

Raja Sitaram Ray. or by some other means, into the hands of Raja Sitaram Ray. The zemindari he held for fourteen years, during which time he built Muhammadpur for his capital, and adorned it with many fine buildings and tanks, the remains of which I am about to describe. Before his time Muhammadpur was not in existence, and its site was a mere rice plain, the capital being then probably at Bhusna, on the other side of what is now the Madhumati, but what was then only a small khal, the Alang Khalli. At the beginning of this century, Muhammadpur was one of the chief towns in the district; it is in fact only of late years, that is since 1836, that it has fallen from its high estate.

3. Of the origin of Sitaram Ray more than one story is current. The first story I shall narrate runs thus:—

4. On the other side the present Madhumati river there is a

Stories of his origin. village, Hariharnagar. In this village Sitaram had a talook. He held also a jumma in another village, Shyamnagar, close to the present Muhammadpur. One day he was riding across from his village, Hariharnagar, to see this jumma, when his horse's foot so stuck in the mud that it could not be got out. So he made some men dig up the ground so as to extricate the horse's foot, and in so doing they came upon a trishul, or Hindoo trident. Digging still further, they found it was the pinnacle of a temple, which they accordingly proceeded to dig up. Inside the temple they found the idol Lakshmi Narayn, which, be it observed, is not a carved stone in human image, but is merely a round stone of a certain shape.

5. Lakshmi Narayn is the god of good fortune; and when Sitaram was, in the manner just described, proclaimed the favorite of the gods, he was not long in finding adherents. He was himself an uttar-rári kayath (an up-country kayath by caste), and ever so many up-countrymen flocked to him. He either received thus, or he previously had in his service a certain giant, a mighty man of valor, named Menahathi, from his elephantine strength ; and this Menahathi was, or became the leader of a troop of fighting men.

6. Sitaram, strengthened by this accession, now planted himself at the place where Lakshmi Narayn had appeared. He founded a service which lasts to this day in the temple of Lakshmi Narayn, and he also built a house for himself close by. With the aid of his little army he commenced a war of aggression upon the possessors of the Bhusna zemindari, and having obtained the zemindari, fortified himself in it, refused to pay rents to the nawab, and lived in magnificence on the produce of his lands.

7. The story I have narrated I esteem to be a perversion of the true story (or the more authentic legend at least). The alleged origin from Hariharnagar arises from the fact that some of his descendants being there, it is supposed that that was his home. The finding of the buried temple is absurd, for the temple (which is alleged to be the original one) is far too high, and it has a flat top without any trishul, or trident, and it bears, or bore, an inscription to the effect that Sitaram erected it. For these and other reasons I consider the above story a mere dilution of the original legend, which I am now about to relate, and which is probably nothing more than an embellishment of the truth.

8. In this part of the country there were twelve provinces, and the rajas of these twelve provinces were (as was *More correct story.* much the custom in those days) rather remiss in sending to the emperor, or his nawab at Dacca, the revenues assessed

E

upon them. Sitaram was accordingly deputed by the emperor of Delhi to "investigate" the matter by force of arms, and this duty he performed with such effect that he not only turned the twelve rajas out of possession, but installed himself as lord of their domains. The nawab now demanded from Sitaram the revenues due upon his lands, but Sitaram refused to acknowledge his authority. He held his lands from the emperor alone, and to the emperor alone would he pay his rents. My informants, who were anxious that Sitaram's justice should appear in all his transactions, declared he never absolutely refused to pay his revenues; he claimed merely to pay them to the emperor. It was admitted, however, that he collected a revenue of a few lakhs of rupees, and as a matter of fact never paid one pice of it to any one.

9. Of Sitaram's history after his acquisition of the zemindary, the legend has only one form. The nawab being refused his revenues, levied war against Sitaram; but the latter, who had fortified himself in Muhammadpur, and gathered around him many soldiers and servants, chief of whom were Menahathi (mentioned before), Bakhtar Khan, Muchra Singh, and Ghâbar Dalan, was able to hold his own against the nawab's men.

His revolt.

10. Then the nawab sent against him his son-in-law, Abu-t-tarâb, and he had a battle with Sitaram's men; but again the redoubtable Menahathi was victorious, having slain Abu-t-tarâb with his own hand.

Expeditions against him.

11. So the nawab now sent a more formidable force under his great general Singharâm Shah; and he came to Bhusna and established his camp there. Profiting by the experience of his predecessors, he resolved to get Menahathi into his power first before making an attack. Watching for his opportunity he at last captured him as he was passing the dhol mandir in the morning on his way to do what natives mostly do in the fields in the morning. Another account says that, receiving information from a spy, he secretly crossed the river at night, and captured Menahathi sleeping at the "lion gate," which was, as will be presently described, the entrance to Sitaram's citadel, and close to the dhol mandir.

12. Menahathi thus caught unarmed was bound by his capturers, who kept him for seven days, belabouring him with sticks and hacking him with swords. But Menahathi kept continually about him a wondrous drug, which was buried under the skin in front of his right shoulder; and its virtue was such, that though it could not prevent him from feeling the pain

Menahathi's death.

of the blows, it rendered his body impenetrable by either stick or sword. Wearied, however, with the continual assaults of his revengeful enemies, and willing rather to suffer death than a life of such pain, he at last confessed the secret of the drug. The influence of it could be got rid of only by taking him to the bank of the Ram Sagar (a huge tank about to be described), plucking it out from his arm, and throwing it into the water of the tank. So they did, and so Menahathi died.

13. It is narrated that his head was sent to the nawab at Moorshedabad, and that the nawab, seeing the huge head, said—"A man like that you should have brought alive and not killed." He directed the head to be taken back to Muhammadpur, and it was there buried, and a great tomb raised over it. The spot marked by the brick foundation of the tomb is still shewn, close to the north-east corner of the present bazar.

His tombs.

14. When Sitaram heard of the capture and death of his faithful general, he knew that his time too was come. He accordingly went and surrendered himself, or, more likely, was carried captive, to the nawab at Dacca, who locked him up in prison. He lingered there for a little time, but at last, when an officer of the nawab's came to him and told him there was no hope, and he was sure to be hanged, he sucked poison from a ring which, Hannibal-like, he kept against such emergencies, and so he died. The nawab sent for Sitaram to his durbar, but found that he had placed himself beyond his power.

Capture and death of Sitaram.

15. There is some confusion here between the nawab at Dacca and the nawab at Moorshedabad. It is however excusable, seeing that these events occurred, at the very latest, about 1712 or 1714 (A.D.), less than ten years after the transfer of the nawab's capital from Dacca to Moorshedabad.

16. The outlines of Sitaram's story are given above: the details which are handed down respecting him attach themselves to various parts of the ruins that are found in Muhammadpur, and will be most conveniently related in connection with them. (See plate III.)

17. There is first the large quadrangle which encloses most of his buildings within which he kept his soldiers, and within which was his own house. It measures more than half a mile in each direction, and is surrounded on each side with an excavated ditch, the earth of which, thrown inwards, is used to raise the level of the quadrangle, and especially of the edges of it, leaving

Quadrangular fort.

as it were a ramp round it. The ditch on the eastern and northern sides has gradually filled in, principally through the influence of the river; but that on the western side is still full of water. On the southern side the ditch is of much more ample dimensions than on any other side; both it is much broader, and it extends westward far beyond the western side of the quadrangle. It forms a fine sheet of water, a mile long, looking almost like a river. By the earth obtained from these excavations, and by that obtained from tanks within its area, the level of almost the whole quadrangle has been considerably raised—a work which in itself represents an enormous amount of labor.

18. It is to this quadrangle that the name Muhammadpur is more The name "Muhammad-pur." properly applied, for Muhammadpur is not the name of any village or mouzah. Bagjanee is the name of the mouzah within which the chief buildings are, and the city which sprung up when Sitaram made this his capital spread over many others, as Naraynpur on the east, and Kanhaynagar and Shyamnagar on the west. The name Muhammadpur therefore extends over all these lands.

19. The origin of the name is this. At the place where Sitaram desired to build his house, he found that an old Mahomedan faqir, named Muhammad Khan, had established himself. Him Sitaram desired to leave the place, but he declared that he would not,—he would sooner be killed. However, on being pressed, he consented to go, provided his name were left as the name of the place; and therefore Sitaram gave his new city the name of Muhammadpur.

20. The chief entrance to within the quadrangle is, and probably was, at the south-east corner. Stationing ourselves here, we see, looking northward, the high and broad ramp upon which stood the bazar, and at the southern end of which, close to where we stand, is the more meagre bazar of the present day. Looking westward, we look along the river-like sheet of water which I have described as forming the southern side of the quadrangle; and looking southward, we see, just outside the boundary of the quadrangle, The Ram Sagar. Sitaram's great tank, the Ram Sagar. Though now 170 years old, it is still the noblest reservoir of water in the district. Its area I would estimate by sight at 450 or 500 yards from north to south, and 150 to 200 yards from east to west; and it contains rarely less than 18 to 20 feet of water. It is the greatest single work that Sitaram has left behind him,—the only one to which he himself attached his own name "Ram."

21. A tank like this has, of course, its place in the legends current in the locality, and one episode connected with it, the death of Menahathi, we have already related. Another story accounts for the making of the tank thus.

Legend of its origin.

There was a woman—a widow—who lived close to where the tank now is, and she had a boy whose name was Sita. One day she was calling for her boy by his name, "Sita, Sita," when Sitaram, who happened to be passing by, stepped up, and pretending to take the call for himself, asked the woman what she wanted with him; she of course explained that she was only calling for her son.

22. Now, Sitaram had one remarkable characteristic,—wherever hidden treasure was, there his good fortune perpetually led him to find it. Pointing therefore to a lau tree which overhung the widow's house, and under which his good spirit whispered to him that treasure was buried, he asked the widow for how much she would sell it to him. She said, "You are the raja of the place, you may take it at once." After a little resistance upon both sides, he at length said he would take the tree and would do for her in return anything she would like to have done. She replied she was badly off for water—would he dig a well for her?

23. So he took the tree, and digging at the foot of it found the treasure that was there buried. He handed it to Menahathi, who was standing by, and said to him,—"Take this treasure, and with it dig a tank as long as the flight of an arrow." The giant Menahathi placed himself where the north end of the tank now is, and drew his bow to shoot his arrow southward. The arrow sped away and lighted a thousand yards off, in the village of Naihati.

24. For such a display of strength Sitaram himself was not prepared; and as to cut the tank so long the village of Naihati would itself have been dug away, and with it some brahmins' lands which it included, he did not dig it so far, but restricted it to its present length.

25. The story, perhaps, is one which has gathered round an account of the widow's lands which Sitaram cut away, and the brahmins' lands which he did not.

26. A quarter of a mile to the west of this, and just outside the quadrangle, is another tank of Sitaram's. It is not one of unusual dimensions. In the middle of it is an island on which was once a house; and this was a sort of summer retreat of Sitaram's—a place where, in the hot weather, he used

The Sukh Sagar.

to come to seek the breezes blowing over the wide plain from the south. From this circumstance he named the tank the Sukh Sagar, "the lake of pleasure."

27. Going northward from the Ram Sagar, along the eastern ramp of the quadrangle, we are passing along what was Sitaram's bazar, the ramp being made high and wide expressly for its accommodation. By "bazar" I refer to the purely trading part of the town; for, with the exception of it, Sitaram apparently did not permit any but his own dependants to live within the quadrangle. The artificers, for example, all dwelt outside, on the east. The harlots were an exception; their quarter was inside, near the middle of the eastern ramp, from which point a road leads off into the middle of the quadrangle, where Sitaram's buildings are almost all aggregated.

Bazar.

28. At the corner of this road we find the ruins of a brick-built house, which is said to have been the old Kanungo cutcherry attached to the zemindari.

Kanungo cutcherry.

29. Proceeding along the road westward, towards the centre of the quadrangle, we pass between two tanks, now both decayed and become jungly marshes. The southern one is called the Padma or "lotus tank," and the northern one, the Chuna or "lime tank," because Sitaram prepared there the lime which he used in erecting his buildings.

30. After passing these we enter the central space which contains the ruins of Sitaram's greatness. The first building we come across is, however, not one of Sitaram's. It is the temple of the idol Ramchandra, which was erected about the year 1800 by the Nattore raja, whose family had obtained the zemindari after it passed out of Sitaram's hands. It is a two-storied building, the upper story being smaller in extent than the lower, and each story having an arched verandah in front. The building, which is still in good order, contains nothing remarkable. It was endowed with certain rent-free lands, which included the jalkar of the Ram Sagar, but its endowments were resumed by Government. The service is still carried on from the profits of these lands, and is managed by the same person who looks after the services in Sitaram's old temples.

Temple of Ramchandra.

31. The building just described is on the south of the road, and on the north side, in front of it, is an open space, in which is the "dhol mandir," that is, the place

Dhol mandir.

where drums are beat at the poojah of the full moon of Falgoon (the *dhol jattra*). This is a building of Sitaram's time, and it is still in good order, the plaster work being occasionally repaired. The form of the building is that of a magnified sentry-box,—a pointed arched roof, supported upon four columns placed square, these again elevated upon a pedestal of three tiers.

32. Next we pass between two buildings, the "punyaghar" on the north, and the cutcherry of pergunnah Naldi on the south. These do not date from Sitaram's time, being buildings (now ruined) which belonged to the zemindari of pergunnah Naldi, when its collections were made here, as they were up till thirty years since.

Zemindari buildings.

33. The next building is one which extends some little distance to the north of the road we are passing along. The part of it nearest the road was the cutcherry where Sitaram made his collections and kept his zemindari accounts. The long extension northward was his jail—the place where he used to confine, "during pleasure," those ryots who did not or could not pay up the demands on them. Of the cutcherry, the "Chakla," as it is called (signifying a cutcherry for a circle of pergunnahs), the walls are still standing; but of the jail it is possible only to trace the lines.

Sitaram's cutcherry and jail.

34. Along the western side of this cutcherry and jail-khana extends a tank, at the further side of which are the ruins of Sitaram's own house. The tank runs up close to the house, and a wall, the foundations of which are still easily traceable, ran round the tank on the east and north sides, enclosing it so as to be within Sitaram's private enclosure. This tank was used as a treasure-room. The wealth that Sitaram accumulated was thrown in here until it was wanted. It is said that great wealth even now remains buried at the bottom of the tank, beneath the grassy jungle which now fills it: and in modern days evidence of this wealth has been found. In 1248 (1841) one Ram Krishna Chakravarti, cook of the naib of Naldi, was lucky enough to find a box containing 500 goldmohurs, which he sold at Rs. 20 a-piece; and about 1861, quite recently, a boy of the teli caste found in the tank a goti (brass goblet) full of rupees.

The treasure-tank.

35. The Naral baboos, who for some time had possession of the temple lands (debuttar) at Muhammadpur, made diligent search in the tank to find any stray treasure which might be in it. They tried

to pump out the water, but there dwells a genius in the tank who frustrated their impious efforts. Every night the water rose as much as it had gone down by the pumping during the day, and they had to give up. Another tank, which is close to these central buildings, and which has also the reputation of containing much treasure, was similarly unsuccessfully searched by the same zemindars. It is not improbable that wealth still remains buried in these tanks, though, no doubt, by far the greater part of their contents was carried off when Sitaram was captured.

36. Sitaram's own house is unapproachable for the density of the jungle, which has been allowed to spread over almost the whole quadrangle. I cannot therefore say what sort of structure it was, except that it was of brick and that it had a tower.

Sitaram's house.

37. The road, immediately after passing in front of the Chakla cutcherry, passes under the "lion gate" (singh darwaza), which admitted to Sitaram's private buildings. This gate was once a large structure, but now only the arch of it remains. The top of the arch is in the shape of one-half of a dome, the hollow side facing outwards.

The "lion gate."

38. Adjoining this gate on the north, and therefore close to the cutcherry house, is the "punyaghar," that is, the place where the first collections of the year were made—a half-religious ceremony performed about Assar (June-July) in each year at the principal collecting place of the zemindari. This punyaghar is now nothing but a mass of jungle and bricks.

Punyaghar.

39. When we enter the "lion gate," we find ourselves in a little courtyard, with three buildings, one on each side, not much larger than ordinary natives' huts, but built of brick. That facing us is the malkhana, or treasure room of Sitaram, and that on our left side is the guard-house. These two buildings were used for these purposes by the rajas of Nattore, when, after Sitaram's time, they obtained the zemindari. When, however, their zemindari of Naldi was sold up (about 1800), the purchasers forcibly expelled the Nattore people from these houses, and they, obliged to erect a treasure-room for themselves, built the little one on the right hand side. All three are now in ruins.

Treasure-room.

40. Just south of the treasure-house there is a small gateway coming down from Sitaram's time, through which we pass into a small

courtyard at the back of the treasure-house. The building which here
faces us on the west is a common Shib mandir
(place of worship of Shiba), erected by the
Nattore rajas. It is much in the shape of a native hut, with its bent
roof and verandah in front, opening outward by three arches. The
plaster over the brick-work is sculptured, but much of it has fallen off.

Shib mandir.

41. Facing us, on the north, and built on the bank of the tank of
the treasure, which lies close to us in this direction,
is the smallest and the oldest of Sitaram's three
temples. In shape it resembles the newer structure just described—a
masonry erection in the shape and size of a native hut, with a verandah
in front. The arches opening out of the verandah have, however, fallen
down, and an attempt has been made to repair it by masonry of such
barbarian style that it would disgrace a cow-house. The deity worshipped here is a small idol, and is called Dasabhujá, "the ten-armed,"
an epithet of the goddess Kali. The temple once bore an inscription,
which has either been stolen, or, more likely, lies among the *débris* of
the broken arches. The inscription, which was in Sanscrit, ran thus :—

Temple of Kali.

Mahí,bhuja,rasa,kshauní,shake   Dasabhuj,álayam
Akári   Shrí   Sitáráma,ráyena   mandiram.

" In the year of the era called Shak, earth-arms-tastes-earth, this
temple, the abode of Dasabhujá, was built by Sitaram Ray."

42. The date here requires some explanation. The Shak era is a
sort of formal or sacred era, and the year 1 Shak
began 78 A.D. The date is given in a sort of
enigmatical manner, by the words " earth-arms-tastes-earth," and the
plan of the enigma will be seen from the explanation :—

Explanation of date.

" Earth" stands for *one*, for there is only *one* earth.

" Arms" means *two*, for every one has *two* arms.

" Tastes."—Hindoos enumerate *six* tastes: they are pungent, sour,
saline, bitter, acid, and sweet.

" Earth," as above, represents *one*.

The date is therefore 1 and 2 and 6 and 1; or, as we write it
with the largest denomination first, 1621.

This year began in April 1699.

43. Passing on in the same direction westward, past the Shib
mandir just described, and another smaller one,
also of the Nattore rajas, close to it, we find our-
selves in another courtyard. On the west and south sides it is closed by

Toshakhana.

F

the "toshakhana," a long shed, fronted with arches, in which in Sitaram's time all the vessels were kept which had anything to do with the temple service, and probably profane vessels also. This erection is in ruins.

44. This court is separated from the treasure-tank, on whose south side we still are (for all these smaller buildings are close together), by the temple of Lakshmi Narayn. It is an octagonal structure with two stories, having a flat roof, and has no pretensions to architectural form or beauty. In the upper story the god reposes at night, and for the day he is brought down to the lower story, where he remains upon a couch. In front of him, and upon the same couch, are two little idols of three or four inches high, Gobind and Lakshmi, who are probably his attendants. When I saw the temple, I saw placed in front of the couch some gaily-decked vessels containing food and other offerings; for the service at these temples is still kept up.

Temple of Lakshmi Narayn.

45. It is agreed by everybody that Lakshmi Narayn (which, as I have said, appears to the profane eye very like an ordinary round-shaped stone) was found by Sitaram under ground. One legend of the finding of the stone, temple, and all, I have already narrated. Another relates that Sitaram, when one morning he went out to perform among the bushes matutinal functions, saw and picked up the stone. He brought it to the pundits, and they told him that it had all the marks of Lakshmi Narayn, and he therefore erected to it the temple we now see. Another story says that Lakshmi Narayn himself revealed to Sitaram in a vision where the " Narayn" was to be found, and that, going to the place indicated, he extracted from the earth the buried god.

Legend of his finding.

46. There was a dedicatory stone upon this temple, which has been either stolen or lost. The inscription on it (which was furnished to me, like that of the Dasabhujá, by the superintendent of the temples,) ran thus :—

Lakshmi,naráyana,sthityai   tark,ákshi,rasa,bhú,shake,

Nirmitam   pitri,puny,ártham   Sitárámcna   mandiram.

" For the abode of Lakshmi Narayn, in the year of Shak Logic-eye-taste-earth, this temple was built by Sitaram for the sake of the beatitude of his father."

The date is thus read :—

" Logic."—There are *six* systems of logic.

" Eye."—Eyes always go by *twos*.

" Taste."—As explained before, there are *six* tastes.

" Earth."—As shewn above, stands for *one*.

Reading this with the last figure, the thousands first, as we do in English, we have the date 1626 of the Shak era, which commenced in April 1704.

47. It was of course solely through the influence of Lakshmi Narayn that Sitaram enjoyed all his prosperity, and that Muhammadpur rose to be a great city. Muhammadpur has been since 1836 a scene of desolation, and unbelievers might attribute it to Lakshmi Narayn's waning influence over human affairs. But this is not the case, and the faithful can account for the whole thing. The Lakshmi Narayn who is now worshipped at Muhammadpur is not, they say, the Simon Pure. When the Naral family had possession of the service lands, several years ago, they stole away the original image, and, substituting a false one, set up the real one at Naral. The natural consequence followed at once. A plague broke out that desolated Muhammadpur, and prosperity followed the Naral family, whose lands, extending and extending, now form one of the largest estates in Bengal.

Influence of Lakshmi Narayn.

48. Passing the Lakshmi Narayn temple, we find ourselves close to Sitaram's house, which, as we said before, is inaccessible through jungle.

49. I have now described all the buildings within the quadrangle, the remains of which, more or less complete, are still to be seen. The rest of the quadrangle is for the most part waste and jungly; but the many bricks scattered all over it, and the mounds which one sees in every direction, shew that it was once covered with buildings, probably those of Sitaram's retainers.

Other remains.

50. Besides the poojah in Falgoon which I have mentioned in connection with the dhol mandir, there was another great poojah which was established in this place by Sitaram, namely, the rath jâtra. Passing along the embankment on the inner side of the river-like trench, which, as I have said, forms the southern boundary of the quadrangle and extends far beyond it, there was a road which is still in very fair order. The "rath" was kept on it, near the bazar end, and on the rath jâtra day Lakshmi Narayn was brought from Sitaram's house, and Krishna and Balaram from their temples in Kanhaynagar (which I am just about to describe), and laid upon the "rath," which was wheeled away to the western end of the road, staid the customary nine days, and was then brought back. A recent lawsuit about the temple lands has caused the "rath" to fall into disrepair, and for some eight years this annual poojah

The rath jâtra.

has not taken place. But the suit is decided, and the "rath" will no doubt be shortly rebuilt, and the gods will have their annual outings as before.

51. When we pass along this southern trench, beyond the limits of the quadrangle, we find the village Kanhay-nagar, which lies west of the quadrangle. Buried amid its trees and houses is a square of temples built by Sitaram, one of them being the finest building of the sort in the district.

Temple of Krishna.
(Plate III.)

52. This building—a temple to Krishna—is that on the west side of the square, and therefore fronting east. It is a square building, with a tower surmounted by a pointed dome rising out of the middle of it. This tower is as high again as the building, and is composed merely of the cupola and the pointed arches which support it. The front of the temple shews a face gradually rising from the sides to the middle, and flanked by two towers which rise rather higher than the roof. The towers to the front present a face shewing three arches of the pointed form, one above the other, supporting a pointed dome.

53. The top of the front face is, as I have said, in the form of the arc of a circle—higher in the middle than at the sides. Beneath the top line, and parallel with it, two bands of ornamental tracery are carried across the face, and between them a series of little sculptured squares, perhaps about twenty in all. The top line is also itself ornamented, and, with the two bands noticed, occupies about a quarter of the height of the front. Beneath these the face is divided into five equally broad portions. The two outer parts contain each three perpendicular bands of ornamental tracery, with two lines of little sculptured squares between them. The other three parts contain doorways, of which the centre one is higher than the other two. In outline they are of the pointed arch form; but, instead of having their sides simple lines, they are waved so as to be a succession of semi-circles. Above each of the doorways is a large square, of equal breadth with the doorway, containing a device which at first sight looks remarkably like "the lion and the unicorn fighting for the crown." It is, however, intended to represent two lions supporting a chalice. The spaces between the sides of the arches and the squares above the doorways are also ornamented.

Its ornamentation.

54. The whole face of the building therefore, and partly also of the towers, is one mass of tracery and figured ornament. The

sculptured squares, as I have called them, of which there must be about fifty on this front face, represent each an episode in Krishna's life. The figures in them, as well as all the rest of the ornament, are done in relief on the brick-work of the building, the bricks being sculptured either before or after burning. The figures are very well done, and the tracery is all perfectly regular, having none of the slip-shod style which too often characterizes native art in these districts.

55. The sides of the building present much the same appearance as the front; but, instead of three doorways and two spaces, they have five doorways. Within the doorways, both in front and at the sides, is a verandah, and the entrance to the temple is from this verandah, the image of Krishna being inside. The whole temple is raised on a pedestal, whose floor is some three feet above the soil; and temple, pedestal, and all, are still in very good order, though signs of decay are shewing themselves.

56. On the top of the lowest arch of the tower, on your left side as you face the building, a small round
Inscription. stone, twelve or eighteen inches in diameter, is let into the face of the brick-work. It bears the dedicatory inscription written in the Sanskrit language, with Bengali letters, which, though fairly formed, are somewhat huddled together, and are not very easily read. The inscription, which is written in four lines of Prakriti metre, is as follows. It is more elaborate than the other inscriptions of Sitaram, and while I arrange it in the same lines in which it appears in the original, I mark the metric lines by a linear stop :

> Bána,dwandw,ánga,chandre
> pariganita,shake Krishna,tosh,á-
> bhiláshí—srímad,biswása,bháah,o-
> dbhaba,kula,kamale bhásako bhánu,-
> tulyah—ajasram sauda,yukte ruchira,ru-
> chi,hare Krishna,geham vichitram—sri,sitá,
> ráma,ráyo Yadupatinagare
> bhaktimán,utsasarjja.

"In the year of Shak, counted by arrow-pair-limb-moon, desirous of gratifying Krishna, Sitaram Ray, who is like a resplendent sun on the lotus of the family, to which attaches the great name of Biswas (that is, who casts a lustre on the great Biswas family, to which Sitaram belonged, as the sun casts a lustre on the lotus), erected in his devotion this splendid house of Krishna, within Yadupatinagar, a city filled with innumerable mansions, and [so beautiful that it] deprives of beauty that which is beautiful."

Yadupati and Kanhaya are both synonyms for Krishna ; Yadupatinagar is accordingly made, for metrical reasons, to do service for Kanhaynagar, the name of the village within which this temple is situated. Sitaram apparently considered that the many buildings which he had erected within his quadrangle were within the limits of the village Kanhaynagar, and therefore refers to the village as " filled with innumerable mansions."

The date remains to be explained :—

" Arrow" refers to the *five* arrows of Cupid.

" Pair" of course stands for *two*.

" Limb."—The Hindoos enumerate *six* limbs.

" Moon" of course there is only *one* moon.

The year therefore is 1625 Shak, which began in April 1703.

57. The building which looks into the same square, facing southward, is a temple of Balaram. It has no architectural pretensions, being in the shape of two native huts placed alongside each other ; the front one being a verandah opening in front with three arches, and the one farther back being the abode of Balaram.

Temple of Balaram.

58. The building on the east side of the square, and facing west, is a much finer one than the last, though not nearly so good as the temple of Krishna. Its frontage shews three doors, the centre one being higher than the other two, and all being of the pointed arch shape. They are each surmounted by a square containing, in relief, the same device which we saw in the finer structure, namely, two lions and a cup. The top of this building is in three domes, all of the pointed form, and finished off with pinnacles, and the central dome is higher than the two side ones ; it is both higher in position (as the frontage of the building rises towards the centre) and it is larger in form. Between the doors, and across the top of the face, there is a good deal of tracery-work executed in relief in the brick-work.

Third temple.

59. An octagonal building closes the square on the south. It was the place for keeping the vessels which belonged to the service of the idols. It is said they were very fine vessels once upon a time ; but some one of the zemindars who had control over them considered he could make them more useful in his own service and stole them away.

60. Of these buildings, which are all Sitaram's, the three-domed temple is almost torn asunder by the luxuriant peepul trees that have found root in it; but the rest, though they suffer a little from this cause, are still in fair order. Their fall, however, is a mere matter of two or three decades; disintegration is going on however slowly, and I had a curious example of it.

61. For while I was within the square, and was striving to make out the inscription, I suddenly felt giddy and saw some of the lime begin to stream down one of the cracks in the face of the temple. The trees began to wave a little backwards and forwards, until the group of natives who were with me began muttering to each other that it was an earthquake. This led to our talking about earthquakes, and as I expressed my ignorance of their cause, a little brahmin boy, who seemed very intelligent, and was certainly looked up to by his companions, began with great earnestness to explain their true theory.

An earthquake.

62. It appears that the world is supported on the head of a serpent, who, in his turn, rests upon a tortoise. Now, this serpent has many heads—a thousand at least—and after a little time he naturally begins to have a headache in that head which is supporting the world. He relieves himself by transferring the weight from the sore head to the next one, and it is the motion of transference that causes the earthquake. Now, it is not the material weight of the earth that wearies the serpent, but it is the weight of the sin on it. In the good days of old it took a long time—twelve years and more—to run up the amount of sin necessary to produce a headache. But in these degenerate days a year or two suffices, and earthquakes are hence of more frequent occurrence than they were of old.

Hindoo theory.

63. I asked, if the serpent rested on the tortoise, on what did the tortoise rest, and was told that it rested on nothing. So I said that the agency of the tortoise and the serpent seemed to me somewhat superfluous, since if the tortoise could rest upon nothing, the earth might equally rest upon nothing. But the little brahmin boy's philosophy was deeper than that it should fail before so obvious an argument, and I was told that the earth, being material, could not rest on nothing, but the tortoise is an avatar, and stood therefore in need of no support. My unbelieving objections were silenced, and I accepted the revelation.

64. Apparently a curious error has arisen among some of the
dwellers in the place, for they talk of the temple
Error of name.   of Krishna as the temple of Harkrishna. By that
name I heard it almost always called, but the inscription plainly shews
it is a temple to Krishna. I think it possible the mistake may be
derived from an ignorant reading of one part of the inscription—

ruchira,ru-
chi,hare Krishna

Some have read "ruchira,ruchi" as a sort of reduplication of the same
word, and left the "hare" to be tacked on to "Krishna." Certainly the
man who read it to me made that mistake.

An adjacent village is called Harkrishnapur: no doubt from this
mistake.

65. A little to the west of the village of Kanhaynagar is another
of Sitaram's large tanks, the Krishna Sagar (or
Krishna Sagar.   lake), so named from the god of the temple.
This tank is a fine large one, about half the size each way of the Ram
Sagar, and it is still in good condition. This probably results from a
peculiarity of construction, which might be with advantage copied in
making tanks in the present day. The excavated earth is carried ten
or twenty yards back from the edge of the excavation, so that there is
a large wide berme between.

66. Of Sitaram's there remains nothing else to describe at Muhammadpur; but in the vicinity there are some other
Remains in other places.   remains attributed to him, viz. at Hariharnagar
on the other side of the river, at Surjyakunda near Muhammadpur, and
at Shyamganj, a village a little distance off, on the road to Magurah.
In each of these places he built a summer-house and dug a tank, and
it is the remains of these that are to be seen. At Dighalia also, which
is some distance off, near Lakshmipassa, some erections of his are pointed
out; but I have not visited that place, and cannot describe them. The
people there say that Sitaram retired there one time when the pursuit
of the nawab became too hot.

67. When Sitaram was captured, his estates were all taken from
him, and they were made over to the Rajshahye
Story of Sitaram's son.   family and formed part of the great Rajshahye
estate. He had, however, a son named Prem Narayn Ray, who lived
in the Surjyakunda house, but was very poor. So he made a wish to
God that he might get something, and God appeared to him in a

dream and told him he would find something in the tank, and whatever he first touched that he should get. When he went to the edge of the tank, there rose to the surface two things,—a golden basin and a large jar full of rupees. His fate was that he touch the basin first, and so he got it, while the richer treasure sank out of sight.

68. Sitaram's posterity fell into obscurity, but they were recognized by, and received a pension from the Naldi zemindars, who, like them, were up-country Kayaths. Two persons now living, Adu Ghose of Muhammadpur and Gurudial Ghose of Hariharnagar, have some connection with the family.

[NOTE.—In Stewart's History of Bengal an account is given from the Mussulman point of view of this Sitaram Ray. It is to this effect: Sitaram was a refractory semindar, who kept in his pay a band of robbers and used to plunder the country around. Abu Tarab, the faujdar of Bhusna, desiring to extirpate this robber band, and being unable to get any assistance from the nawab, engaged an Afghan officer, Pir Khan, and sent him with a force of 200 men to attack Sitaram. On this Sitaram withdrew into another part of the country, where his followers happened to come across the faujdar and killed him.

This Abu Tarab was of illustrious family, and the nawab, afraid of having incurred the displeasure of the emperor by permitting his death, sent a large force, which effected the capture of Sitaram, his women and children, and his band of robbers. They were sent in irons to Mooshedabad, where Sitaram and the robbers were impaled alive, and the women and children sold as slaves.

This account, I presume, is taken partly from the version the nawab himself wrote in order to represent his own conduct favorably to the emperor. It is probably quite as far from the truth in its depreciation of Sitaram as the legends of Muhammadpur are in his glorification. The tanks and temples and ruins at Muhammadpur mark the existence of something more than a mere robber chief, and consist far better with the local legends than with the Mahomedan account. As for the impaling, admitting even its truth, still it was little more than the punishment which that particular nawab ordinarily inflicted on semindars who had fallen in arrear with their rents.]

Mahomedan account of Sitaram.

VI.—Ruins at Mirzanagar (Trimohini)—The Faujdar of Jessore.— A.D. 1700.

HALF a mile from Trimohini, along the road which now connects that place with Keshabpur, we pass the remains, still in sufficiently good state of preservation, of an old brick building which in the vicinity goes by the name of the Nawab-bari, or "nawab's house."

The Nawab-bari.

2. The building is composed of two square courtyards separated by a high wall, and on the north of the northern one, and on the south of the southern one, there are similar high walls. On the eastern side of both the squares is a double row of little arched dwellings, which seem rather to be built in the inside of a massive wall than to be

G

constructed with reference to convenience of dwelling. These were apparently the retainers' houses, and the only entrance to the court-yards is through them.

3. On the western side of the northern square is a three-domed structure, which was the residence proper. The masonry is dilapidated, but the domed roof still remains. In front of this, and within the courtyard, is a large masonry reservoir, which is said to have been a bath. The water was brought in by being pumped over the top of what I have termed the retainers' houses, and could be discharged by a subterranean channel. The source of the water was the river Bhadra, which, though now closed, was at the time when these buildings were occupied a flowing river, and flowed close beside.

4. The southern courtyard shews only a few Mussulman tombs, and there are some tombs outside the building also.

5. About a mile due south of this is what is called the Kilaabari, or "fort." It is a large area raised some eight

The fort.

or ten feet by earth excavated, in all probability, from a long and wide trench called the Motí Jhil, which bounds it on the south. This raised area was at one time, it is said, surrounded by a wall, but of that no traces now remain. Its length is east and west, and the principal entrance to it was upon the east.

6. The entrance appears to have been fortified, for there used to be three cannon lying here. Two of them were

Cannon.

taken away by Mr. Beaufort, when he was magistrate (1854); and according to the inhabitants, one of these was converted into fetters for prisoners and the other used as a roller on the roads. A native gentleman at Jessore, however, told me that he had purchased one of them for Rs. 3, and could, if I liked, let me have it. The third gun is still lying in a field close by. There is, according to the natives, some magic power in it which makes it refuse to be moved. Three hundred convicts and one elephant were at one time tried, but failed to raise it from its place. However, I should think that a strong arm and a stout bamboo would overcome the magic of its inertia. It is an iron gun, about five feet long, and composed of three or four concentric layers of metal.

7. Close outside the entrance is a low range of brick-built dark chambers, said to have been the prison-house. Two

Prison and wells.

of the chambers have small wells in them, and on the outside of the building there is a large and deep well. Into these, it is said, malefactors were cast, and the inside was smoothly plastered over, so that there might be no chance of the victims climbing up.

8. Close to the Trimohini bazar is what is probably another part of the same set of buildings—the imámbára, or "praying place." It is doubtful if it was ever a roofed structure. The simplest form of imámbára is a wall—usually of a certain ornamental structure—before which Mussulmans stand facing westward to make their prayers. This imámbára was probably a wall of that sort, and had likely a platform upon which the worshippers might stand. There is not any trace of anything more than this, and the wall itself is in a tumble-down condition. The whole is raised on the top of an artificial mound.

Praying place.

9. It is plain that this place was the residence of some man who had a military force; and the local tradition is that it was some nawab of Moorshedabad who occasionally stayed here. That was all I could find out, and I could not find any trace of a name, except of one Kishor Khan; and of him the people know nothing, except that he was a dreadful oppressor, and that they connect him in some way with the ruined buildings.

Local tradition.

10. So much I would have written had I derived my information only from the local tradition; but I have been fortunate enough to come across some further information, which will shew distinctly what the ruins I have described are the remains of.

True story.

11. The place where these remains are found is the village of Mirzanagar, Trimohini being the name of a modern suburb which has outgrown the old village; for Mirzanagar is a small enough village now, though a collector, writing in 1815 (C. 28-4-15), names it as one of the three largest towns in the district.

12. I find that in 1798 two persons, named Hidayat-ullah and Rahmat-ullah, made a petition to the collector to this effect:—

"Nur-ullah Khan, our great grandfather, was foster-brother of Aurangjíb (emperor of India), and was by him appointed nawab nazim of Bengal. He took up his residence in Mirzanagar, the seat of some former nazims. His successor was Mir Khalil, who also had the chief command as nazim. He had two sons, Daim-ullah and Kaim-ullah, but as they were minors they were excluded from the nawabship, whereupon they quarrelled and killed each other. Then Suja Khan was appointed nawab, and he set up his throne at

Moorshedabad, whither, by express order of the emperor, we were sent for. Nothing, however, was done for us, and being left destitute we returned to Mirzanagar and sold all we had. We are now eighty years old, and up till now have been supported by the raja who got his zemindari from our great-grandfather. But he is now ruined, and we can look only to you. Like Joseph, people are now in a well and now on a throne."

13. At the collector's recommendation the Government, on the faith of the collector's statements as to the reliability of the petition, granted Hidayat and Rahmat a pension of Rs. 100 each. But before the grant was made, " Providence," to use the pious words of the collector, "had been pleased to dispose of one of them," and the other died four years after. (O. 12-6-98. G. 11-7-98. O. 24-7-98 ; 8-9-02.)

14. Whether the two old men honestly believed what they wrote, I can't say ; but their statement of their lineage was far from correct. It is true that Aurangjíb once made his foster-brother nawab of Bengal; but that man's name was not Nur-ullah, but Fidai Khan, and his date was 1677-78. We find, however, that in 1696, while Aurangjíb was still emperor, a Hindoo zemindar, Subha Singh, and an Afghan chief, Rahim Khan, organized a petty rebellion and plundered the districts of Burdwan, Hooghly, and Moorshedabad; and that the nawab, who was then resident at Dacca, ordered Nur-ullah, the faujdar (or military commandant) of Jessore, to subdue the rebellion. Nur-ullah, taking a part of his force, which amounted to 3,000 horse, marched to Hooghly, and he shut himself up there when the rebels came to meet him. They attacked Hooghly, and Nur-ullah escaped at night by a boat and made his way back to Jessore.

15. This is no doubt the Nur-ullah mentioned in the petition, and Mirzanagar was therefore the residence of the faujdar of Jessore. In the Nawab-bari he likely resided, and his military force dwelt in the Kilaa-bari.

The faujdar of Jessore.

16. Suja Khan, referred to in the petition, was nawab from 1725 to 1739, and the petitioner is right in stating that he had his capital at Moorshedabad ; and the office which the petitioner's family desired and could not get was that of faujdar of Jessore, and not of nawab of Bengal.

17. It is hardly a century since these military faujdars disappeared, and it is strange that in so short a time all remembrance of them should vanish from a place like Mirzanagar, where the traces of them were continually before the eyes of the people. It would appear that

even by 1798 the traditions of the place made Mirzanagar a seat of the nazim instead of the residence of the faujdar.

18. The Kishor Khan of whom the villagers talk was apparently a petty zemindar, who, like many before and after him, was sold up by the civil courts; at least so I gather from a petition that refers to him and is among the judge's correspondence of April 1791.

19. In a work written in Sanskrit, called "Khitisa Charita," being a history of the rajas of Krishnanagar, I find Mirzanagar is mentioned as the residence of the faujdar of Jessore.

VII.—*Ancient Ruins at Kopilmuni, on the Kabadak.*

AT Kopilmuni, on the banks of the Kabadak, a little below Talla, there are some ancient ruins which deserve description.

2. There is first of all the abode of the sage (muni) Kopil. He established his abode here long long ago, when this place was likely still Sundarban forest. Beyond the fact that he was a devotee, and that he set up the idol Kopileshwari, who is still worshipped here, nothing is known of him. He of course had nothing to do with the great Kopil, who, in Hindoo mythology, destroyed the sons of King Sagar.

Kopil, the sage.

3. A large banyan tree, growing on the bank of the river, grasps by its roots what was once the house of the devotee; but one can only see the walls of the house by sailing in the river under the tree. The tree is one which began growing in the brick-work of the house and ended by tearing asunder the whole structure and binding together its broken parts.

4. The old temple of Kopileshwari has long fallen down, and a newer temple, a modern structure with a flat roof supported on beams, was built twenty-five years ago by the farmer of the place—Mr. Mackenzie of Jhingagachha. The cyclone of 1867, which was very violent here, brought that down; and I believe the present zemindar is going to erect a temple for the goddess, who at present has to put up with a mere thatched hut.

Kopileshwari's temple.

5. In celebration of Kopileshwari a grand méla is held at Kopilmuni every year on the Bárani day, *i.e.*, the day of the 13th mansion of the moon, in Cheit. To this méla come people from all directions, as it is a very celebrated one. According to local belief the river Kabadak at this place acquires for

The méla.

that day all the virtues of Ganges water ; and though the higher castes do not trust it, the lower castes all bathe in the sanctifying stream on the day in question. It is of course to the virtues of Kopilmuni, or of Kopileshwari, that this sanctifying influence of the river is due.

6. More about Kopilmuni is not known, and the absence of tradition is probably due to the fact noticed before, that these places have not been continuously inhabited except in modern times. When, a hundred years ago, advancing cultivation reached this point, the place and the sage were new to the new settlers, and they have handed down to their posterity only the little tradition they picked up themselves.

7. In some other ruins close to this place, there is evidence of this want of continuity of habitation. At a place called
The mounds at Agra.   Agra, a mile away, there are two or three mounds. One of these has been excavated, and it is found that it covers some ancient brick houses, the walls and the windows of which are easily seen by descending into the excavation. There is not a doubt that the other mounds contain the same sort of ruins. I am informed that these mounds exist not only here, but occasionally all along the way between Talla on the north and Chandkhali on the south, a distance of some fourteen miles.

8. How old these mounds are, and when the houses which they cover were inhabited, it is impossible to say. The house I saw was only about the size of a well-to-do ryot's house ; but for all I know there may be some larger. There are some hollows, the apparent remains of tanks that once existed near the houses, but there is no mark of wall or ditch round the mounds that I examined.

9. Of the inhabitants of the dwellings which once existed here,
Ancient settlers.   there is at present not even a tradition. They were not unlikely some ancient settlers in the place, who had disappeared with all their work before the present race of settlers came into this part of the land. The present race dates from about a hundred years back, and the older race must therefore have dwelt in the place and disappeared long before that.

VIII.—*History of the Rajas of Naldanga.*—*From A.D.* 1500.

THE oldest family in the district, or at least the one which traces its descent farthest back, is that of the rajas of Naldanga. They have furnished me with an account of their origin and family history, an account which I can supplement from other sources of information.

2. It must have been about four hundred years ago that there lived

Bishna Dás Hazra, the hermit. in Bhabrasuba, a village in the Dacca district, a man named Haladhar Bhattacharj, whose profession was religion. His descendant of the fifth generation, a man named Bishna Dás Hazra, who had by practices of austerity acquired superhuman powers, left the house of his fathers and occupied a lonely abode at a place near Naldanga, then named Khattrasuni, but now named Hazrahati, which place was then all jungle.

3. One day the nawab, or other governor, whoever he was, returning from a visit to Dacca, passed by the river which was under the hermit's abode. His supplies had run short, he was in the middle of an almost uninhabited jungle, and he and his men were in great straits. Accordingly he sent a party ashore to see whether they could find anything. They could find nothing, but at last came across the hermitage of Bishna Dás Hazra, a poor enough place, from whose appearance they could hardly derive any hopes. The hermit, however, called them, and when he learnt their wants, he asked each person to name what he desired, and by the power of his devotion was able to produce all they wanted, causing it suddenly to appear out of the ground before them. The nawab, enabled thus to continue his journey, bestowed upon Bishna Dás five adjacent villages, and these formed the first beginning of the zemindari.

4. This man had a son named Srimanta Ray, who, from his great

Ranabir Khan's prowess. prowess, obtained the name of Ranabir Khan. One does not exactly see how, living alone as a hermit in the jungles, he could well have produced a son, unless, indeed, he used the same autochthonic process by which he supplied the nawab's men with provisions; but the legend does not descend to particulars. This son, less distinguished for piety apparently than his father, set about aggrandizing himself from a worldly point of view. The lands in this part of the country were then in the possession of Afghan zemindars, of whom one family resided at Sazup-pur (near

Founds an estate. Kotchandpur). This family Ranabir exterminated by the power of his arm, possessing himself of all their lands. Their zemindari from this extended till it occupied the whole circle of Muhammadshahi.

5. The legend just related probably has for its foundation the acquisition of the zemindari by some military chief when the Afghans were driven out of the country, an event which occurred about the middle of the sixteenth century.

6. The title of "raja" was first possessed by Chandi Charan Deb
Titles of "raja" and "Deb Ray." Ray, the third in descent from Ranabir Khan; and the family name "Deb Ray" appears to have been borne by every descendant since Ranabir's time, Ranabir's son being Gopinath Deb Ray.

7. Mindful of their brahminical origin, this family has always been distinguished for its liberality in erecting and endowing idols and in making grants of land to brahmins, and even to Mahomedan saints. Ram Deb Ray, the fourth raja, was especially celebrated for these virtuous acts. His date was 1105 to 1134 (1698 to 1727).

8. His successor, Raghu Deb Ray,. disobeyed a summons of the
Deprivation and restitution of the zemindari. nawab of Moorshedabad, and the nawab, as a punishment, deprived him of his zemindari, bestowing it upon Raja Ram Kant Ray, the then raja of Nattore. This occurred in 1144 (1737), but three years later the nawab restored it to the family.

9. The next raja, Krishna Deb Ray, died in 1180 (1773), leaving
Partition of the zemindar. two natural sons, Mahendra and Ram Sankar (who retained each two-fifths of the inheritance), and an adopted son, Gobinda (who held one-fifth of the inheritance). Gobinda got his share separated off shortly afterwards, and for a time was known as the "Teani Raja," that is, the three annas raja. The other two also, at a subsequent period, had their shares separated. The property of Mahendra chiefly lay on the western side, and was called the "western circle;" that of Ram Sankar being called the "eastern circle."

10. In a subsequent chapter it is related how the estates became
Ruin of the family. to a great extent lost to the family. The Teani Raj was taken possession of by a mortgagee, and remained in his and his purchaser's hands from 1800 till about 1840, when it was .purchased by the Naral Baboos. The western circle, similarly, was sold up by the sheriff in 1796, but the heirs of the Raja Mahendra brought a suit against the purchaser, which ended in their obtaining, by compromise, seven annas of the estate they had lost. About 1840 their seven annas was sold up, for arrears of revenue as I believe, and the Naral Baboos bought it in. They subsequently purchased also the nine annas portion of this circle.

11. Thus at the present day the Naral family has succeeded to the possession of the Teani, and of the western circle portions of the

Muhammadshahi estates; and the representatives of the two branches of the family to which they once belonged, live in comparative poverty in the old Naldanga family house, upon the proceeds of some pension lands, which did not pass to the purchasers along with their estates.

12. The middle branch of the family are still in possession of the "eastern circle," a result due in a great measure to the fact that their estates have repeatedly come under the court of wards. After Ram Sankar, Sasi Bhusan Deb Ray was proprietor; after him his adopted son, Indu Bhusan Deb Ray, who held by sannad the title of raja. He has now died (1870), and his adopted son, Pramoth Bhusan Deb Ray, is now proprietor. These three proprietors were minors when they succeeded.

The present raja.

13. The estate formed for a short time the nucleus of a separate collectorate, which was in 1787 swallowed up in that of Jessore. The seat of the collectorate was Jhenida, where the rajas appear to have had their cutcherries. At present the rajas' part is managed from Naldanga, and the Naral Baboos' part is managed from their "Chakla" cutcherry near Jhenida.

Collectorate of Muhammadshahi.

IX.—*History of the Rajas of Jessore (or of Chanchra).—From A.D.* 1590.

THE history of Bengal relates that in 1580 a rebellion broke out in Bengal, and that first Raja Todarmal, and afterwards Azim Khan, were sent by the Emperor Akbar to suppress it. Azim Khan arrived in 1582 and had finished his work by 1583.

2. One of the warriors who came with him was Bhabeshwar Ray, and he was rewarded by being put in possession of the pergunnahs of Saydpur, Amidpur, Muragachha, and Mallikpur—part of the territories which had been taken from Raja Pratapaditya. He enjoyed these possessions till 1588 (995 B.S.), when he died.

Bhabeshwar Ray, a soldier.

3. His successor, Mutab Ram Ray, held possession of these pergunnahs from 995 till 1026 (1588 till 1619). During Raja Man Singh's war with Pratapaditya, he gave assistance to the former, and that being the successful side, he retained possession of the four pergunnahs. During the last seven years of his tenure it is recorded that he had to pay revenue on account of his lands, which apparently had not before been assessed.

H

4. The next successor was named Kandarpa Ray, and he held pos-

Kandarpa Ray extends the zemindari. session from 1026 to 1056 (1619 to 1649), during which time he acquired, by what means is not stated, the following pergunnahs:—Dâtia, Khaliskhali, Bagmara, Selimabad, Shajialpur, extending his zemindari south-westward from Saydpur.

5. Manohar Ray was his successor, and he appears to have held

Manohar Ray, the chief founder of the family. possession for a long time. He apparently obtained from the nawab an authority over all the surrounding estates, which were to pay their revenue, not directly, but through him. Now, it is a fact that a large number of these estates began at once to default in revenue, and, in accordance with the then revenue system, Manohar Ray, by paying the arrears due on them, and engaging for the future, obtained possession of them as part of his own zemindari. I think the circumstances are such as to make one suspect that Manohar Ray brought about the default in order to attain his own ends. However this may be, we find that during his possession of the zemindari the following pergunnahs were acquired, mostly after this manner:—

Ramchandrapur, in 1682.	Isafpur, in 1696.
Hassenpur, in 1689.	Mallay, Sobnal, Sobna, in 1699.
Rangdia and Rahimabad, in 1691.	Sahos, in 1703.
Chingutia, in 1690.	

Some other smaller pergunnahs were acquired at the same time, namely Talla, Phalua, Sripadkabiraj, Bhatla, Calcutta, &c.

6. I should mention that I find Dâtia and Khaliskhali given in an ancient list of the acquisitions of Manohar, but in the lists recently put into my hands by the family, these two are, as already stated, enumerated among the acquisitions of Kandarpa.

7. Manohar Ray may thus be regarded as the founder of the

Old pergunnah zemindars. family. The zemindari, when he obtained it, was only a moderate one, but when he left it, it was by far the largest in the neighbourhood. The list, and the manner of his acquisitions, shew that at that time the pergunnahs were for the most part in the possession of different persons; and it is possible that these persons had acquired them in much the same way that Manohar's ancestor had: namely, on account of military service. As to the names of these zemindars, I find Kalidás Ray was the zemindar of Isafpur pergunnah. I do not know any of the other names. We will subsequently also find that there were a few pergunnahs which remained unabsorbed by these great estates (Hogla, for example, and Sultanpur), and that these were similarly each in the possession of different families. The estate of the rajas of Jessore is therefore founded upon the gradual acquisition by the possessors of one of these estates of the pergunnahs belonging to their neighbours; the aggrandizement, at the expense of the rest, of one out of several not unequal zemindar families. Their history differs in this respect from that of the Naldanga family, who appear, from almost their earliest residence in the district, to have held, with respect to their neighbours, pretty much the same position of pre-eminence that they held at the time of the permanent settlement.

8. The term "raja," which both these families adopted, means
The title "raja." nothing, and does not indicate any nobility of origin. Every great zemindar assumed the title of raja; and in the early correspondence of the district, the heads of the families of Jessore, Naldanga, and Nattore, are sometimes termed rajas and sometimes not. Their own petitions and representations as often omit as insert the appellation.

9. Manohar Ray died in 1112 (1705) [I think that is the date],
Krishna Ram Ray. and was succeeded by his son, Krishna Ram, who held the zemindari up till 1136 (1729). During his time the pergunnahs of Maheshwarpassa and Raymangal were acquired in the same way as Manohar had acquired his neighbours' estates, and some smaller and less known pergunnahs were added to the zemindari. Part of these, Bazitpur for example, were acquired by purchase from the raja of Krishnanagar (Nuddea).

10. After him came Sukh Deb Ray, and Manohar's widow
Partition into twelve annas and four annas. induced him to make over four annas share in the estate to his brother, Syam Sundar, and thus the estate became divided into two parts, and so for a short time it continued to be held. In the twelve annas share Sukh Deb was succeeded by his son, Nilkant, in 1152(1745); but the four annas share became untenanted in 1163 or 1165 (1756 or 1758); Syam Sundar and his infant son both having died.

11. At that time the East India Company received from the
The Saydpur estate founded. nawab a grant of certain land near Calcutta, and one of the zemindars whom the nawab dispossessed in order to make this grant was named Salah-u-din Khan. This man, representing that Syam Sundar's property had no heirs, requested its bestowal upon himself in requital for the loss of his previous zemindari,

and the nawab, not unwilling to give what was not his own, bestowed upon him the four annas share of the raja's estates.

12. I cannot tell at what precise period the 'specific' partition of these two shares was accomplished; but it was probably soon after the division was made. Had Syam Sundar not possessed a separate 'specific' share, a stranger could never have come in to arrest possession.

13. The four annas share lay mostly within the pergunnah of Saydpur, and was therefore known as the four annas estate, or as the Saydpur estate, both of which names exist to this day. The twelve annas share used to be called the Isafpur estate, that being the chief pergunnah in it.

14. In the possession of the Isafpur estate Srikant Ray succeeded Nilkant Ray in 1171 (1764), and it was this man who had possession of it all through the permanent settlement time. We shall recount in connection with that settlement how he lost it pergunnah after pergunnah, until his family, having nothing left, lived upon the bounty of Government.

Srikant Ray—his ruin.

15. Rajah Srikant died in 1802, and his son, Banikant, then became the head of the family, who were then, as just stated, only pensioners of Government. In 1808, by suit in the Supreme Court, Banikant Ray recovered, by having the sheriff's sale cancelled, that part of his ancestral property which lay within pergunnah Saydpur, and then he gave up the pension and once more became a zemindar.

The family recover.

16. Banikant having died, Baradakant, then a minor, succeeded in 1817, and the estate was managed by the court of wards, who considerably increased the value of it. Moreover, the pergunnah Sahos, one of the ancient possessions of the family, was restored to the family by Government, who had confiscated it in 1823, it having been proved to have been bought under a false name at an auction sale for arrears.

17. There are some other smaller estates in the family besides these two pergunnahs.

18. Raja Baradakant Ray, the present representative of the family, obtained from Government a sannad as Raja Bahadoor, in recognition of his position and of the assistance which he had rendered during the mutiny. His family residence, whence also his estates are managed, is close to Jessore; but he himself has been of late years rather an absentee from the district.

Raja Baradakant Ray.

19. So much for the twelve annas share of the Isafpur estate; we must shew now what became of the four annas share which was

bestowed on Salah-u-din Khan. At the time of the permanent settlement it was in the possession of a Mussulman lady, Manu Jan, his widow, and she is noted as having been a very good manager of her property. She brought it in safety through the critical time that succeeded the permanent settlement, and saved it from the dangers which overwhelmed almost all the other zemindars.

20. In 1814 we find the estate in the possession of Manu Jan's

The trust estate.

half-brother, Haji Muhammad Mahsin, who in that year died. Having no heirs, he by will made his estate over in trust for the benefit of the imambara at Hooghly, which has since that time enjoyed its revenues. A small part of the estate, namely Taraf Sobnal, had before the permanent settlement been granted to this imambara. (See Collector's 13-12-90). The estate now forms the Saydpur trust estate, and it will be noticed in a separate chapter. By the natives it is usually denominated the four annas estate.

X.—*History of the Rajas of Nattore.—From A.D. 1750.*

I HAVE not got from the Nattore family any account of themselves,

Their estates.

but I have collected some information regarding them from tradition in those parts of the district which were once within their zemindari. Last century their estates formed the largest, or nearly the largest zemindari in the country, and tradition calls it an estate of fifty-two lakhs of rupees. The pergunnah of Sahujial, in the west of the district, the zemindari of Bhusna in the west, including the pergunnahs Naldi, Mokimpur, Sator, &c., were within this zemindari; the latter apparently having been bestowed upon the rajas of Nattore when Sitaram's rebelliousness caused it to be taken away from his family.

2. In the last half of last century the Nattore zemindari was in

Rani Bhabani.

possession of Maharani Bhabani, who was widow of Raja Ramkant Ray, son of Raja Ramjiban Ray. This lady's fame is spread far and wide, and especially is it noted that she was a most pious lady, continually spending her money in the endowment of idols. She established in Benares alone 380 temples, guest-

Her piety.

houses (atíthalay), and other religious edifices, some of which are still kept up; but some have ceased to be kept up, probably because the family, by the loss of its estates, became too poor to support them.　Religious edifices were erected by her also in other parts of the country, and endowed with money and with land.　There are many of these at Nattore, the seat of the family, and there is one well-known one at Moorshedabad, which is named Sham Ray.　It is endowed with large lands, its principal endowment being Dihi (or "estate") Phulbaria, which lies between Chaugachha and Kaliganj, and has its cutcherry at Shibnagar, opposite Kaliganj.

3.　Either in consequence of her death, or in consequence of his coming of age, the zemindari was transferred from her hands into those of her adopted son, Raja Ram Krishna Ray.　He was also an exceedingly pious person, and spent his whole time in performing religious duties.　Unlike his mother, he forsook all care of worldly affairs, and left them to manage themselves as they best could, provided he only could carry on his religious duties. His zemindaris began to go to ruin, and his servants began to plunder him on every side, and to amass fortunes for themselves.　Then came the permanent settlement. With the best management it became very difficult, as will be subsequently explained in detail, to meet the demands made upon the estate, and the bad management of the raja only precipitated him the sooner into ruin.　His estates defaulted on every side, they began to be sold, and many of them were bought up by the servants, who should have looked after their due management with the very money which they had withdrawn from the coffers of the raja.

Raja Ram Krishna Ray.

His ruin.

4.　Before the permanent settlement had been ten years in force, the raja of Nattore had been stripped of his estates one after another ; and he who had obtained an inheritance of a zemindari of fifty-two lakhs, transmitted to his heir one which produced only three lakhs.　Apparently, the only part of the once magnificent estate which the family managed to retain was the part which had been devoted to the service of the many deities the family had set up.　I do not know if the family have any property in the district now except the Dihi Phulbaria which has been mentioned above.

5.　Of the estates of this once wealthy house, the Bhusna portion was sold up, being divided into many large pergunnahs.　One purchaser got Naldi, one Sator, one Mokimpur, and so on ; each of the portions forming in itself a respectable landed estate.　Sahujial was apparently broken up into dihis, or "small estates," each of which was composed of several

Disintegration of the estate.

villages lying in the same tract of country and paying revenue under one head. The largest of these was Dihi Arpara, which was purchased by Kelaram Mukharjya of Gobradanga, the grandfather of the late Sarada Prasanna. Two others, Dihi Kaneshpur and Dihi Saruppur, were purchased by Gopimohan Thakur, the ancestor of the great Thakur family.

6. The largest purchasers of these estates were Kalisankar Ray,

The Naral and Digha- the ancestor of the Naral family, and Dayaram
pati families. Ray, the ancestor of the Dighapati family. The former was dewan of the Nattore raja, and it was partly, if not chiefly, by unjust stewardship that he managed to acquire the estates which he ought to have managed for another. The latter was also dewan of the same family, and most of his purchases are near Nattore, in the Rajshahye part of the ancient zemindari. I have heard it stated, though I know not with what truth, that the history of their acquisitions is similar to that of Kalisankar Ray's.

PART III.—THE FIRST THIRTY YEARS OF BRITISH ADMINISTRATION—1781-1811.

COMPILED CHIEFLY FROM THE DISTRICT RECORDS.

XI.—*State of the District prior to* 1871.

BEFORE passing on to the narration of the establishment and progress of local administration on the part of the British, it will be well to state some leading facts connected with the condition of the district at the time when it passed out of Mahomedan into English hands. These matters are not categorically stated in any part of the records of the district, but especially in the very early ones there are so many allusions to them, that it is not difficult from the perusal of the records to divine much of the circumstances in which the first English district officers found themselves.

2. The district, as we have already seen, was divided chiefly among

GREAT ZEMINDARIS.
1. The Isafpur zemindari.

three or four great zemindaris. Raja Srikant Ray was the zemindar of all that part of the country which lay between the Bhairab and Pasar on the east, almost up to the Ichamati on the west. His northern limit, stated in the same general way, was the region through which the imperial road from Calcutta to Jessore and Dacca subsequently ran. This estate was called the Isafpur estate.

3. We have also seen that this zemindari was only a twelve annas

2. The Saydpur zemindari.

share of the original zemindari, for four annas of it had been separated off and conferred upon a Mussulman zemindar. This separated part was composed principally of lands in the pergunnahs of Saydpur and Sahos, and the estate derived its name from Saydpur.

4. Beyond the boundaries just specified, and to the north of them,

3. The Muhammadshahi estate.

was the estate of Muhammadshahi, which was at that time possessed by the Naldanga family. Its boundaries may be described as coincident with those which are now allotted on the map to pergunnah Muhammadshahi.

5. The next great zemindari was that of Bhusna, which was part

4. The Bhusna zemindari.

of the territory of the raja of Nattore. It included not only the present district of Furreedpore, but also the pergunnah Naldi, which is at present the north-eastern quarter of the district, and which, in its most extensive meaning, includes such pergunnahs as Sator and Mokimpur. Although Bhusna was only part of the domains of the raja of Nattore, yet it was a separate zemindari, and was all along treated as such.

6. Besides these great zemindaris, there were a few others of less

A few minor zemindaris.

extent within the district. Pergunnahs Hogla and Belfulia formed the largest of these minor zemindaris, and belonged to one Krishna Singh Ray, of whose family I know nothing, except that his heirs, at a subsequent period, were for a long time engaged in disputing about their shares.

7. Another minor zemindari which, along with the one just

Nature of zemindari right.

mentioned, and with Selimabad, filled up the south-eastern corner of the district was pergunnah Sultanpur. Kasinath Datt was the zemindar of it, and he obtained the zemindari in a manner which is sufficient of itself to show how little the idea of proprietorship in the soil, which was at the foundation of the permanent settlement, originally entered into the conception of a zemindar's rights. In 1774 the committee of revenue reported to the president and council that the then zemindars of Sultanpur were in arrear and would not pay up. They recommended that they should be turned out of possession, and stated that one Kasinath Datt was ready to pay up the arrear, and to engage for the payment of the future revenue accruing on the estate, if it were transferred to him. The Governor General approved the proposal on 16th May 1774, and some days after the committee again wrote stating that Kasinath Datt had paid up the arrear and had entered into engagements for the future revenue.

8. In consequence of this he was put in possession of the estate, or rather of thirteen annas of it, for that was all that was affected by these proceedings.

9. In the history of the family of the raja of Chanchra, I have noted several instances where proprietorship of an estate was transferred by the ruling power from a defaulting zemindar to a stranger merely on the latter's undertaking to pay up arrears, but the present is the only instance I have come across where the principle was adopted by the British Government. There are no doubt other instances, as I met this one only because it was referred to in a letter of the judge's of 19th October 1790, where he reports proceedings which had arisen out of it. The old zemindars had sued to have it declared that Kasinath Datt was only a farmer for life, and not zemindar in his own right. They claimed this, not by denying that Government had power to make such transfers as had been made in this case, but by alleging that this was the intention of the Government, because, when it accepted the committee's recommendation that Kasinath Datt should be admitted to engagements, it omitted to specifically declare that the old zemindars should be turned out of possession. What the decree in the suit was I do not know, but Kasinath certainly retained the zemindari.

10. The zemindaris I have mentioned included almost the entire area of the district, but there were other smaller ones scattered over the country. The total number of zemindaris at the time of the permanent settlement was just over 100; but the character of the large ones, which I have noted in detail, and the position of the proprietors of them, were so different from what obtained in the case of the smaller ones, that one is almost led to infer that these smaller zemindaris were rather fragments of

Distinction between great and petty zemindars.

I

the large ones which had been separated off by purchase or grant of some sort, than estates which had always had a separate existence. The owners of the larger zemindaris had a part in the administration of the country, to which these pettier zemindars were not admitted.

11. That which I have just stated with respect to the origin of

Zemindars were mere contractors for revenue. Kasinath Datt's title affords a strong argument to shew that the zemindars were rather in the position of contractors for land revenue, than of owners of landed estates paying revenue to Government. This view of their position is further supported by a fact which appears in the history of the Chanchra family, namely, that Manohar Ray, one of the Chanchra line, not only engaged with the nawab to pay the revenue of his own estates, but also to collect and pay over the revenue accruing on the smaller estates in his neighbourhood, with which previously he had had nothing to do.

12. But the zemindars were contractors not only for land revenue,

Their administrative powers and irresponsibility. but for other revenue also: in fact, contractors for the general administration such as it then was. They paid, as we shall see, a certain sum by way of excise revenue, and managed excise within their limits just as they pleased. They also handed over to Government a certain sum as duties on internal trade, and were allowed in turn to make almost any exactions they pleased on traders. The duties of police were in their hands, and they had to keep up police establishments. They were also held liable to reimburse any one who had been despoiled by robbery within their limits; though it is doubtful whether, at the time at least when the British obtained possession, they were ever called on to fulfil this condition of their contract, or even whether the Mahomedan Government was strong enough to enforce it. We shall find also that the zemindars, or rather their subordinates, had a good deal to do with the adjudication of petty disputes, whether of a criminal or of a civil nature.

13. The daroga, as he was called, appears to have been almost the

The daroga the only Government officer. only Government officer in the district who had anything to do with civil administration. It was his duty to receive from the zemindars the dacoits, robbers, and murderers whom they had to apprehend, and to try them. He might also receive complaints direct from complainants. His authority was, however, very limited, for, except perhaps in petty cases, he had to submit his proceedings to the Government (the naib nawab) in each case, and to receive from the Government the order passed on each individual accused; and neither in theory nor in practice had he any supervisional authority over the zemindars.

14. In such a system it may be said that the only object of the
Abuses resulting from the system. Government was revenue. Almost all the functions of administration were heaped upon the zemindars, and they might do pretty much as it pleased them so long as they discharged their revenue. Supervision was a mere name, if it was even so much as that.

15. The consequences of such a state of things may be easily imagined. The best and most energetic men in the world would be sure to fail as administrators if they found themselves left, without control or supervision, to rule over people whose interests in almost every matter were opposed to their own. How much worse must it have been when the rulers were Bengali zemindars, a class notorious, at that time at least, for their habit of handing over all their duties to too often corrupt subordinates, and who even now, after nearly a century of enlightenment, are often apt to postpone the interests of justice to their own private ends! The zemindars followed the example of Government and transferred the task of administration to subordinates selected by themselves, not with reference to their ability or uprightness, but solely with reference to their readiness to secure their masters' interests. The people were oppressed that the zemindar might have his rent, and they were plundered in order that the zemindar's servants might become rich. The zemindars, who performed all their police duties on contract, kept up the most wretchedly inefficient establishments for the purpose; and dacoits and robbers plied their profession with vigor, finding little hindrance from the police, and often in league with them, and even with the zemindar himself, or his higher officers.

16. Complaint against wrong was useless; the zemindar or his officer had it entirely in his own option whether he should listen to it or not: and the complainant had very little chance of relief, for the oppressor was often the zemindar's servant, and the plunderer, even if they took the trouble to trace him, would not find it difficult to make friends with his captors.

17. The collection of revenue was at this time, and for long after,
Collection of revenue. a matter entirely distinct from the rest of the internal administration. The first district officer came to administer the government and not to collect the revenue, and

for several years the revenue of the districts which he administered was
paid partly in Calcutta and partly in the Rajshahye district (Nattore).

18.   There had been a collector of Jessore for a year or two, from
1772 to 1774, but that was an experiment which Warren Hastings tried
in many districts of Bengal, and after a short time discontinued on the
ground of expense.   It was the first attempt at direct collection, but
was made to give way to a system much less expensive, but much less
efficient.   Had the English collectors been retained, and kept stationed
at the many places in the interior where they were in 1772 to 1774, it
is not unlikely that the British Government would sooner have had its
eyes opened to the monstrous injustices of the Native Government
through zemindars, and would long before 1781 have considered itself
obliged to take a direct part in the internal administration of the country.
I am aware that the direct government is usually dated from 1772, but
what the British did before 1781 can hardly be dignified by the name
of internal administration.   The maintenance of half a dozen provincial
civil courts in the whole of the wide territory of Bengal can hardly be
said to constitute an active government.

19.   The collection of the revenue had been in the hands of the
company for some years before they undertook the administration
proper of the country; and when our history of the administration
opens, the Mussulman system of collection had already given way to
a more regular one.   We can, however, see a little of its nature
from the accounts that have already been given of the old zemindars.
These zemindars were a turbulent lot, much too independent and not
very punctual in the payment of their revenues. .They might, however,
fight among themselves and swallow up their smaller neighbours, much

The faujdars.

as they chose, so long as they paid their revenue;
and to ensure their paying, the nawabs kept
a military governor with a small force in each of the districts.   This
officer, the faujdar as he was called, retained on the part of the nawab
sufficient appearance of power to make it the interest of each zemindar
to secure himself by continuing to pay his revenue, or as much of it
as would satisfy the nawab.   Beyond that point probably the faujdars
did not care to go, as the system of the nawabs was rather a military
occupation of the country where the zemindars, their tribute bearers, were
the potentates, than the administration of the country as their own.

20.   When the British undertook the collection of the revenues,
however, the faujdars appear to have been charged with duties somewhat

different to those they performed under the Mahomedan Government. The British idea of administration was not military occupation, and the faujdars became purely high officers of police. They formed part of a police system established by Warren Hastings, and had under them thanadars, or officers in charge of smaller jurisdictions. As there had been under the Mahomedans two faujdaris, one at Bhusna and one at Mirzanagar, so both of these appear to have been retained in the first police system of Jessore.

* * * * * * *

21. Such, then, was the condition of the district prior to 1781, when English administration was first established. More of the details will appear as we go on ; but the general view given in this chapter will aid materially in the apprehension of what comes after. It is as it were the starting point in our history of the administration of the district.

XII.—*The Establishment of British Administration in the District*, 1781.

In April 1781 the Governor General increased very greatly the number of civil courts in Bengal. There were only half a dozen before, and now twice that number were added. One of the new adawluts (as they were called) thus established was the adawlut at Moorly, and its jurisdiction included the whole of the present districts of Jessore and Furreedpore, and that part of the 24-Pergunnahs which lies east of the river Ichamati. Moorly was selected as the head-quarters of this district (or province, as it used then to be denominated), because it was the head-quarters of the Mahomedan Government, such as it was. The proximity of Chanchra, the seat of the raja of Jessore, was probably the reason why Moorly originally had become the head-quarters of the district. The adawlut or civil court thus established was indifferently termed the adawlut at Moorly or the adawlut of Jessore. The latter name of course superseded the former when ten years later the head-quarters of the district were removed from Moorly to their present location.

Court established at Jessore.

2. The same Government order declared that the judges of these courts were to exercise also the powers vested in the faujdars and thanadars, a system which was thus abolished all over Bengal. The faujdars were, as has been said, high officers of police, and the thanadars were the police officers who had charge of police stations. Their abuse of power, and the oppressions

The magistrate.

they committed, had become notorious.; and it was this chiefly that led
to their abolition and the transference of their functions to an English
officer located in the district.

3. In respect of these police functions the judge was denominated
also magistrate. He took the place of the faujdar, being a pure officer
of police, and the thanadars who still remained in existence were made
subordinate to him as magistrate.

4. This origin of the district magistracy will account for the
name of "faujdari," applied up to the present day

The faujdari.   to the magisterial jurisdiction. The functions of
the "faujdari court" have, however, entirely changed; for whereas it is
now an almost purely judicial institution, it was at its first establishment
in 1781 a purely police jurisdiction. The duty of the magistrate was
then only the management of the police: he had to apprehend offenders,
but with their trial he had nothing to do. .

5. The duty of trying accused persons was performed by an officer
called the "daroga;" and within the Moorly

The daroga.   .   jurisdiction there were two darogas, one at Jessore
and one at Bhusna. The daroga was subordinate solely to the nazim
of Moorshedabad, and the Government was very particular to instruct
the magistrate that he had over the daroga no authority whatever.
The nazim had, in fact, never conceded to the British Government the
power of trying and punishing criminals. (G. 3-7-81.   M. 22-1-82.)

6. The British Government also had no authority over the darogas,
although, desirous to keep itself acquainted with the details of the
administration of criminal justice, it induced the nazim to direct the
darogas to submit to it through the magistrates a monthly statement of
their criminal proceedings. (G. 9-10-81.)

7. The daroga's powers were exceedingly limited; in fact, he was
rather an officer who reported cases for the order of the nazim (or rather
the naib nazim, an officer appointed for this and other duties), than a
judge empowered himself to deal with criminals. Petty cases he could
deal with by inflicting small periods of imprisonment; but these cases
were very few compared with the number he had to refer for order to
the nizamat. (M. 17-10-81.)

8. The daroga also had charge of the jail and of the records.
So far as regarded the execution of sentences

The jail.   pronounced by the naib nazim, the magistrate
had a certain supervision. We find the magistrate occasionally making

to the British Government proposals regarding the treatment of convicts, a subject on which more will be said hereafter. Also it was through the magistrate that the darogas received the orders pronounced by the naïb nazim, and the magistrate on one occasion submitted to Government a complaint that the daroga of Bhusna would not receive an officer whom he had sent to see the sentences carried into execution. In respect of the jail also we find that the daroga was obliged to get the magistrate's approval of his estimates for repairs before he sent them up to the nizamat. (M. 8-3-84; 3-10-81; 31-12-88.)

9. Such then was the system of criminal administration when first established in 1781. The judicial part was performed by the daroga, a Mahomedan officer acting under the Mahomedan Government, and the executive part was performed by the magistrate, an English officer acting under the English Government. (Board's Reg. 6-4-81.)

10. The Governor General, when he established the court at
Moorly, appointed Mr. Tilman Henckell to be judge and magistrate, and Mr. Richard Rooke to be his register. The judge got Rs. 1,300 a month at first, but on 27th February 1784 his salary as judge was raised to Rs. 2,000, and he got Rs. 600 more as magistrate. A reduction was afterwards made, for on 9th May 1786 his pay as judge is stated at Rs. 1,120. Besides pay he got also a proportion of the institution fees deposited with civil court plaints. The register's salary was only Rs. 300.

Mr. Henckell, judge.
Mr. Rooke, assistant.

11. These two men, Tilman Henckell and Richard Rooke, remained a long time connected with Jessore. They were both men of more than ordinary ability. Mr. Henckell's name is still remembered in some parts of the district, and we shall observe in the history of his administration how admirably he did his work. His acquaintance with every subject affecting his district was most intimate; and no wrong was too remote for his energy to grapple with, no advantage too distant for him to strive after. The idea of his administration was, that it was the duty of Government to procure the peace and comfort of the mass of the inhabitants, though it might involve some harm in respect of the Company's commercial interests. These views were a little too advanced for his age, for there was then too great an inclination on the part of Government officials to look upon the natives as born only to be a means of profit to the Company. Mr. Henckell was never unmindful of his employers' mercantile interests, but he always set this before him as his duty,— to guard the then almost helpless natives from the oppressions to which

they were subjected by the commercial officers of the company as well as by their own zemindars.

12. Mr. Rooke apparently began his service in 1781 in Jessore. While he was Mr. Henckell's subordinate, he always carried out Mr. Henckell's views, and when he succeeded him in his office, he continued his policy. In fact, the fruits of Mr. Henckell's administration are for a long time visible in the history of the district; and it is certain that its early records derive great interest from the fact that it was two such men as Henckell and Rooke who were at the head of affairs, during the time which intervened between its first establishment in 1781, and the completion of Lord Cornwallis' reforms, which by 1793 had changed the first crude attempts at district government for a system substantially the same as that which ever since has prevailed.

XIII.—*The Police Administration.*—1781-90.

MR. HENCKELL arrived at Moorly in the middle of May 1781, and shortly afterwards submitted his proposals for the
Police system reformed. remodelling of the police force. The faujdars of course had already been recalled, to the great satisfaction of the people whom they grievously oppressed. In fact, the whole police system appears to have been one of oppression and corruption. There had been four thannahs—Bhusna, Mirzanagar (near Trimohini), Noabad (now Khulna), and Dharmpur, and subordinate to these thannahs were several chaukies. A thannah at Shahujial is also in one place referred to. There were paid officers at the thannahs, but the chaukies worked by means of *goïndas* or informers, who received no salary, and were, as a natural result, obliged to obtain a livelihood by capturing innocent persons and extorting money from them—a system which the faujdars and thanadars, their superiors, certainly made no endeavour to prevent, and perhaps even partook in the guilt of. (M. 24-5-81; 18-6-81.)

2. How far these faujdari police were a terror to evildoers, it is not easy to say. There were certainly a considerable number of people in jail, though one is disposed to think that the innocent were hardly safe from being mixed up with the guilty. Mr. Henckell goes so far as to say that the establishment of the four thannahs above mentioned "rendered it next to impossible for dacoits and robbers to commit depredation without meeting with their deserts." But this is hardly consistent with

what he states about the oppressions of the faujdars, and the collusion of their subordinates with robbers, or with the undoubted fact that at the time when he joined the district there were bands of robbers, fifty strong, roaming about it. The faujdars, no doubt, did something to check robbery and dacoity; but people were contented in those days with results that would now be considered disgraceful. (M. 24-5-81; 18-6-81.)

3. What Mr. Henckell proposed was rather a change of *personnel* than a change of system. Assuming himself the position and authority of the two abolished faujdars, he proposed to station at each of the four thannahs a girdwar, or head police officer, whose business it would be to apprehend dacoits and forward them for trial to Moorly. Their subordinates were not to be informers, but to be foreign sepoys, as native barkandazes were so apt to collude with offenders. His police were to possess more of the military than of the detective character, and this seems to have suited the then work. For the aim then proposed was not the prosecution of minor offences, but the checking of great ones—dacoity and murder, and such like. When a dacoity occurred the investigation consisted chiefly in following up the gang to their homes; and as the gang relied rather upon their strength than upon the secrecy of their proceedings, this was simply a *quasi*-military expedition. When the pursuing detachment reached the lair of the gang, the zemindar through his servants (who had always a semi-police character) was expected, and usually compelled by pressure on the part of the Government officers to deliver up the men.

4. The zemindars, it should be noted, are not talked of as having separate police establishments. They were ex-

Zemindari police.

pected, by means of their ordinary servants, to protect property from plunder and hand over offenders to the authorities; and when Mr. Henckell's girdwars and thanadars were appointed, they were to help in and to see to the performance of these duties, and could always claim co-operation on the part of the zemindar's servants. Mr. Henckell in an early letter complains that the zemindar's naib at Bhusna had refused to give paiks and nakdis (armed footmen) to assist the regular police. (M. 29-9-81.)

5. It will be observed that the establishment of a thannah at Moorly was no part either of the previously existing system of police or of Mr. Henckell's proposals. I presume Mr. Henckell himself intended to do the work which in other places was done by the thanadars. When his proposals were accepted by Government, a

K

force of fifty sepoys was established at Moorly, besides thirty each at
Mirzanagar and Bhusna, and four at Dharmpur, which was a small
thannah. Noabad is not mentioned as having any such force; the force
stationed at Khulna in connection with the salt department was probably
considered to afford sufficient military strength. (M. 2-4-82.)

6. This system of police, which cost perhaps Rs. 800 or 850 a month,
Police duties entirely
transferred to zemindars,
1782. turned out far too expensive for the commercial
ideas of the Government. The Government began
by ordering, in opposition to Mr. Henckell's
remonstrances, the substitution of barkandazes for sepoys; and before
this was carried out they ordered the entire abolition of the police
establishment, except that the force at Moorly was to be retained.
(M. 2-4-82. G. 29-6-82.)

7. The Government order which directed this step declared that
" all zemindars, chaudhris, and taluqdars, conformable to the original
and fundamental tenure on which they hold their zemindaris and other
lands, are to take effectual care that no robberies, burglaries, or murders,
be committed within their districts." They were to do their utmost
to bring all offenders to justice; they were to erect thannahs wherever
the magistrate should direct, to appoint officers for them, and to be
answerable for the good conduct of the people they stationed at them,
and for their obeying the orders of the magistrate. Persons suffering
from robbery were to be reimbursed for their losses by the zemindar of
the lands where the robbers lived, or of the lands within which the
robbery was committed; and if any zemindar committed or connived at
murder, or robbery, or other breach of the peace, he was to be punished
with death. He was liable also to punishment for other misconduct
according to the nature of the case. (G. 29-6-82.)

8. Under this tremendous order the zemindars were obliged to
give recognizances to carry out the duties required of them, and the
following places were selected for thannahs:—

Mirzanagar, Moorly, Lakindi, Khajura, in the Isafpur and Saydpur
zemindaris.

Muhammadpur, Batiapara, and Talma, in the Bhusna estates.

Kaliganj and Jhenida in the Muhammadshahi estate. (These and
Batiapara had been chaukies under the Bhusna thannah.)

Samargdia in Shahujial.

Noabad Haveli (pergunnah Hogla), Maheshpur (pergunnah
Sultanpur). (M. 1-12-82.)

9. The number of thannahs was thus increased from five (including Moorly) to thirteen—a decentralization necessitated by the change of system. The zemindars naturally objected to having to bear all this expense, but I cannot find that any answer was vouchsafed to their remonstrances.

10. The magistrate, as I noted above, was allowed to retain at head-quarters a certain force which was considered to be available for an expedition to any place whither the perpetration of any offence might render it advisable to despatch them.

11. The number of thannahs appears to have been changed from time to time by the magistrate; for in 1791 the magistrate gives the following list of then existing thannahs :—

In charge of the zemindars :—Dharmpur, Ichakada (one of the old chaukies four miles west of Magurah), Jhenida, Taragonia, Maheshpur.

In charge of Government :—Jhenida and Noabad.

This list (which by some error contains Jhenida twice) shows less change than at first sight might appear; for in 1787 Bhusna and Shahujial had been transferred to Rajshahye with all their thannahs, and there had been some rectification of boundaries also on the 24-Pergunnahs side. (M. 16-9-91. J. 5-9-87.)

12. This system, by which the zemindars bore the burden of the police establishments, continued in force from 1782 until 1791 or 92, when Lord Cornwallis reformed the administration. The magistrates were however allowed, for temporary purposes, to employ girdwars and thanadars; and under this permission the magistrate of Jessore managed practically to keep up two Government thannahs (Jhenida and Noabad) as noted above; but with this exception the whole burden lay on the zemindars. With an active and energetic magistrate like Mr. Henckell, the evils that would naturally spring from such a police system had less chance of development; but still the utmost that could be said for it, after some years of trial, was, that the police was better than it had been in the time of the faujdars, that is, before any European officer was stationed at Jessore. What there was of good in it, arose from the circumstance that the Government and its officers practically took upon themselves, and away from the zemindars, the supervision and management of the police work. (M. 16-9-91.)

Not fully carried out.

13. The peremptory declarations of June 1782 had, in fact, become a dead letter. The zemindars' liability to give compensation for robbery was never enforced except in extreme cases. The only part of the

order that remained in force was that which laid upon them the obligation to keep up and pay for the thannah establishments; and even this part of the order was, as we have seen, not enforced in the case of Jhenida and Noabad. No other result was possible where a sort of joint responsibility and authority was given to the magistrate—a man of energy who entered on these matters from motives of duty—and the zemindar, who no doubt did always as little as he could, and whose only motive was the fear of consequences.

14. The plan of managing the police through the zemindars had broken down. For the Mahomedan Government, careless of details, and desiring nothing but the most superficial results, it might answer; but when English administration was carried into the districts, the new idea arose that the world was not made for the enjoyment of a few great families, who might manage everything as they chose. It was impossible to hope for the due performance of public duty from individuals who had nothing to gain by doing their work, and little or nothing to lose by not doing it; and zemindars could hardly be expected to co-operate zealously with the magistrates, who had come to deprive them of their previously almost irresponsible authority. And thus the magistrates ignored the zemindars, who were little more than obstructives, and expected from them only obedience to specific orders addressed to them. From that time till now the public duties of zemindars have continually diminished, and their responsibilities are always changing from actual to nominal.

15. A few words must be said here regarding the establishment of patrol boats in the Sundarban rivers. The route from the eastern districts to Calcutta was very much what it is now; boats entered at Kôchua and passed along by Fakirhat, Khulna, across the Kabadak near Chandkhali, and so on past Kaliganj. There was also, as there is now, an outer route; but this seems to have been used only when the inner one could not be, that is, by large boats of 1,500 to 2,000 maunds during the dry months. (M. 31-5-89.)

The Sundarban police.

16. These routes were naturally the resort of robbers; and not only did people go there for the express purpose of committing robbery, but many persons, pursuing ordinarily the occupation of fishermen in the rivers, made experiments at dacoity when a favorable opportunity occurred. Frequented thus by robbers, the rivers must have been exceedingly unsafe, for the route did not then lie, as it now lies, amid

cultivated lands and settled villages, but the rivers then flowed through forest, and uninhabited jungle lay on both sides of them. (M. 31-9-89.)

17. The Sundarbans were always the resort of robbers and dacoits, and their depredations at length attracted the attention of Government, who called on the magistrate to propose means for its prevention, and, adopting his recommendation, established six guardboats to patrol the rivers and escort the ships. This was in 1788, and a year did not pass before Government began to repent so lavish an expenditure, and to consider that, in accordance with the usual plan, the burden might be advantageously laid on the zemindars. There was at that time stationed at Backerganj an officer termed "commissioner for the suppression of robberies in Backerganj," and Government thought they could do through him and the zemindars all they were bound to do. Against this Henckell remonstrated strongly, and in consequence of his representation the force of guardboats was retained. (M. 18-6-81. G. 1-2-88. M. 1-5-88; 31-5-89. G. 10-6-89.)

* * * * * *

18. A few incidents, gathered from the correspondence of Mr. Henckell, will serve the purpose of shewing the state of the district as regards crime and as regards police.

Instances of crime.

19. In the letter written immediately after his arrival in 1781, he states that a most noted dacoit, one Hira Sirdar, was at a place forty miles off; that he had often committed the "most horrid depredations on ryots." The nawab of Moorshedabad had frequently sent orders to have him arrested, but the zemindars, to screen him, had always declared he was dead. Five months after we hear of this Hira Sirdar in jail; but even there Mr. Henckell did not think him safe. Having just been promised a military force, of which, as narrated before, fifty sepoys were to be stationed for the protection of Moorly, he writes urging their being sent up quickly, because some 300 men had assembled at Khulna with the intention of attempting to rescue Hira Sirdar from confinement. (M. 24-5-81; 30-9-81; 2-4-82.)

Hira Sirdar's band.

20. In January 1783 a body of dacoits, about 3,000 in number, made an attack upon an escort conveying Rs. 40,000 from Bhusna to Calcutta. They murdered part of the escort and carried off part of the treasure. I do not think

Plunder of Government treasure.

the dacoits were captured; fifty men were arrested at Tumlook (Midnapore), but they turned out to be the wrong people. (G. 22-1-83; Salt
Controller 25-3-83.)

21. Kali Sankar Datt or Ray, the ancestor of the Naral family,
Kali Sankar Ray, of a man with whom we shall have more to do here-
Naral. after, makes his first appearance in Mr. Henckell's
letters as "a dacoit and a notorious disturber of the peace." I repeat
here simply what I find written in the letters, but Kali Sankar appears
to have been much more of a 'lathial' zemindar than a dacoit.

22. On the night of 8th June 1784, Kali Sankar, with his brother,
Nandu Datt, and an armed band, attacked and plundered a rice boat
and wounded the manjhi. To arrest the plunderers Henckell sent out
a band of sepoys under a girdwar, Kutbullah, who came up with the
enemy at Naral. Kali Sankar, however, had 1,500 men there, and
prepared to give battle, forming his men into four divisions. The fight
lasted three hours, and Kali Sankar gained the day, having killed two
and wounded fifteen of the magistrate's force; Kutbullah himself was
among the wounded.

23. On receiving tidings of this defeat, Henckell sent out
reinforcements, and succeeded by their means in capturing Nandu Datt
and other ringleaders, but Kali Sankar himself could not be found. He
had fled to the protection of the zemindar of Nattore, who, when ordered
to deliver him up, let him escape to Calcutta, where he was again
concealed by the zemindar's Calcutta agent. After much trouble and
delay he was finally apprehended and was brought into Moorly under
an escort of forty men, a measure which "tended to restore peace and
tranquillity to the province." (M. 27-6-84; 19-7-84; 30-8-84; 4-1-85;
13-4-85.)

24. The case is not further noticed in the correspondence, but I
am informed Kali Sankar was tried by the daroga and got off. The
particulars I do not know, but I was told that the offence he committed
was not a dacoity properly speaking, but a "lut-taraz" intended to
annoy a wealthy mercantile family who had offended him. Still he
surely ought to have been punished for his armed resistance to his appre-
henders.

25. The conduct of the raja of Nattore in this case is a fair
Collusion of zemindars specimen of the manner in which he performed
with criminals. the police functions expected of him. Mr.
Henckell complains, on 30th August 1784, that the raja does not properly

keep up the Bhusna thannah, and certainly there was much dacoity going on in Bhusna. About the same time that Kali Sankar's case occurred, an attack was made on the Bhusna thannah by a body of armed men, who rescued eight dacoits in confinement there; and at the same time another body also was out in Bhusna, committing depredations. (M. 27-6-84.)

26. The raja of Nattore was not the only zemindar who connived at the escape of great offenders. It appears to have been far too common a practice; and the natural result was an increase of crime, which shewed itself markedly in 1785 and 1786. In the end of 1786 both the collector of Muhammadshahi and the resident of Sonabaria (cloth factory) wrote to the magistrate, complaining of the frequent robberies and the numerous bands of dacoits, and desiring the landholders to be called on to do their duty. Mr. Henckell's answer to the latter is noteworthy. He wrote that he had sent a force to seek out and apprehend the delinquents, and had warned the zemindars to give him information of all robberies; and he sent to the resident a dacoit whose sentence of death had just arrived, requesting him to hang him in a conspicuous place near the factory, and thus "strike terror into the dacoits." (M. 5-3-85. C. Muham. 24-12-86. Res. Son. 28-12-86. M. 4-1-87.)

Increase of crime, and its remedy.

27. An event in 1788 will afford an example of the boldness of dacoits in those times. In October of that year a body of dacoits attacked a boat which contained eight sepoys, commanded by a naik, and of the sepoys three were thrown overboard and drowned. The dacoits for a time got clear off, but a party was sent after them to capture them. They effected the capture of twenty-two, but only after two or three of their party were wounded. (M. 23-10-88.)

28. More information under this head will be found when we notice the relations between the magistrate and the commercial departments, and the fights between them. But it is necessary first to make some remarks on the judicial arrangements.

XIV.—*The Administration of Criminal Justice.*—1781-90.

WE have already stated that the magistrate had no judicial criminal powers; all that he did was to receive cases from his police subordinates and send them on, if he thought fit, for trial before the daroga, an officer entirely subordinate to the nazim.

2. In 1785 the Government empowered magistrates to hear
Magistrate empowered to hear petty cases. petty cases of assault, abuse, and pilfering, and to inflict in them punishments not exceeding four days' imprisonment or 15 stripes. Beyond this no interference was made with the daroga's authority until the establishment of Lord Cornwallis' system. (G. 15-4-85).)

3. The delay in the hearing of cases seems to have been very
Great delays. great. From the statements of 1790 it appears that the accused took, on an average, a month to pass out of the magistrate's hands into the daroga's, and there they remained for months. The magistrate, reporting on the system after ten years' trial, says that if confession is obtained from the accused, or if proofs are speedily produced, sentence may be pronounced within seven or eight months; and in cases where there is no such plain sailing, he gives instances where the accused have remained under trial for four, and even for six years. It is certainly one small set-off against this that persons who had been tried and were waiting for the sentence to come from the nazim were sometimes let out on bail, and even murderers and robbers were so treated. (M. 19-12-89.)

4. For this tremendous delay there was no reason in the amount of work to be done, for the average was only about one case each day between the magistrate and the daroga. The reason lay in the absurd system by which almost every trial in Bengal had to be laid before the naib nazim for order, instead of being decided on the spot.

5. It is impossible to judge now of the quality of the justice
Lenity. administered in the darogas' courts. The darogas seem to have tended to lenity, for the magistrate complains in one place of the small sentences awarded in cases of robbery and murder, and suggests that the magistrate should be allowed to station a man in the darogas' courts to see to the proper conducting of cases. In the return of April 1791 I find some cases of murder and robbery punished with 39 stripes, or with four months' or one year's imprisonment. (M. 19-12-89.)

6. The punishments awarded were death, imprisonment, stripes,
Punishments or the loss of a limb. The imprisonment was often perpetual imprisonment; and frequently sentences of imprisonment were passed without specification of period, or during pleasure, or until the prisoner made reparation of the injury he had inflicted, or until he found security for good conduct. When the

British Government assumed charge of the jails, in the beginning of 1792, it was found that of 300 prisoners in the Jessore jail, there were 108 cases in which the imprisonment was thus unlimited. Some of these cases were of murder, but most of them were of robbery; one case was a case of assault. There can be no doubt that the men so imprisoned were simply forgotten. (M. 11-2-92.)

7. One peculiar proceeding deserves note. When a man was arrested his property was also at the same time seized. If he was finally condemned, his property was confiscated; if he was released, the property was returned to him, minus the deductions privately made by the police officials, whose duty it was to return it. It was certainly very unreasonable for the criminal courts in the same breath to confiscate a man's property and sentence him to make reparation for his offence and stay in prison till he did so. (M. 16-9-91.)

8. The jails were in charge of the darogas, and not of the magistrates; and the treatment of prisoners was a subject that received

Treatment of convicts.

no proper attention at the hands of the Mussulman Government, so that the magistrates were always pointing out the insufficiency of the means adopted for punishment. The discipline enforced among convicts was so lax, that the prisoners were hardly debarred from free intercourse with outsiders. They remained perfectly idle, and in some cases at least, if not in all, were allowed to go to make bazar for themselves. Imprisonment could therefore hardly be very efficacious as a deterrent. Loss of a limb one would think to be a deterrent punishment, but the magistrate says that prisoners are often brought up under new charges who have already lost one or even two limbs. Death itself even had few terrors to men who were fatalists so far as they had any creed at all. (M. 2-4-82. C. 20-7-87. M. 19-12-89.)

9. So early as 1782 Mr. Henckell pointed out this, and suggested that notorious prisoners might be sent to sea, as so many captains of ships were then looking for native sailors and could not get them. The sending prisoners to sea would make them lose their caste, and thus add a new and effective element to the punishment. The ordinary prisoners Mr. Henckell proposed to employ in such public works as were then going on at Budge-Budge. (M. 2-4-82.)

10. Nothing came of this proposal, but Mr. Henckell afterwards

Convict colony proposed.

proposed a new scheme, which for some time bore the name of the "Sundarban plan." It was a scheme for the reclamation of the Sundarbans partly by giving grants to

L

zemindars and taluqdars, partly by means of convicts. We shall treat of this plan subsequently, and notice it now only so far as regards the proposal to establish a convict colony by allotting small grants of lands to all but the most atrocious offenders. With regard to these last, Mr. Henckell was consistent in his opinion that there was only one way with them—namely, to send them out of the country. (M. 4-4-84. C. 20-7-87.)

11. The Board of Revenue, who were then the authorities also in criminal matters, approved the scheme, and Mr. Henckell applied for long-term prisoners from all the districts round about to be sent to him, that his convict colony might be commenced. Nothing, however, was done in the way of so disposing of prisoners. (Bd. 30-9-85. M. 22-11-85.)

12. Again Mr. Henckell submitted another proposal for the treatment of convicts. It was that long-term prisoners should all be transported, and that those of shorter terms should be made to work on roads. This proposal was approved by the Governor General, who recommended its adoption to the naib nazim. I do not know if it was then carried into effect, but the system of employing prisoners in road works was in operation shortly after the criminal administration was transferred from Mahomedan to British hands. (G. 21-5-88. C, 7-2-98; 17-2-00; 21-9-00.)

Transportation and forced labor proposed.

XV.—*The Administration of Civil Justice.*—1781-90.

So far we have been writing solely of Mr. Henckell's duties as magistrate; but his principal designation and his principal duty was that of civil judge. There is naturally very little of interest attaching to this branch of his duty, for almost all the correspondence refers to particular cases which have long ago lost all their interest.

The judge.

2. Of other and subordinate civil judges no mention is made till after the code of 1793 permitted the appointment of moonsiffs; but before that date a great deal of the petty work used to be done by the zemindars and naibs, to whom the judge referred cases for disposal. He did not so refer cases above Rs. 100 in value, but such cases were very few.

Petty cases referred to zemindars.

3. This system of reference did not work well. Almost all the suits were suits regarding land, or disputes about bramhuttar (or rent-

free) land, or claims in respect of excessive demand of rent. In all these matters the zemindars and their naibs had a direct interest, opposed generally to the complainants, and reference usually meant denial of justice. Mr. Henckell was so well aware of this, that less than half a year after his arrival at Jessore he appointed ameens, or subordinate judges as it were, at Bhusna and at Shahujial, to whom cases might be referred. This however was, on grounds of economy, disapproved by the Government. (J. 2-10-81. M. 18-6-81. S.D.A. 6-4-82.)

4. We must not award to the judge of 1781 the same paramount jurisdiction which the judge of 1870 exercises, for he had little to do with the acts of other public officers. Each department was, as it were, complete in itself; the judges were, for example, prohibited entirely from interfering in questions about rent and revenue, these being solely within the collector's jurisdiction. Their relations with the commercial departments, which were similar, we shall presently discuss in full. So also, in matters entirely within their authority, they were to consult the convenience of other departments. Ryots engaged in the Company's manufactures they could not summon otherwise than through the Company's manufacturing officers; and they were enjoined to be specially careful in summoning any one during the season of heavy revenue collections, that is, the months immediately following the autumn and cold-weather harvests. (G. 5-12-81; 16-4-82; 26-7-82. J. 27-11-82.)

Limited power of the judge.

5. The civil jurisdiction at that time was ruled rather by the defendant's residence than by any other consideration: a complainant had to seek redress at the hands of the judge to whom the defendant was subject. We consequently find cases of transfers of suits from one district to another; and sometimes, when two or three zemindars having their residences in different districts are fighting about a piece of land, we find the judges of the different districts corresponding about the case.

Inter-district relations.

6. Similarly, we find the various magistrates treating each other somewhat like potentates of adjacent countries. The one tells the other of some offender taken refuge in this other's district, and requests him to capture him; the other having effected the capture, calls on the first to give evidence of the offender's guilt, in order that he might hand him over. (M. 21-4-88.)

XVI.—*The Salt Department and its Fights with the Magistrate.*—1781-90.

BESIDES the departments that had to do with the administration of justice
and the collection of revenue, there were the com-
The salt officers.
mercial departments. There was a salt department,
whose jurisdiction extended all over the south of the district, and whose
local chief was a salt agent, a Mr. Ewart. Mr. Ewart had two or three
assistants, and an unlimited number of subordinates, including a small
military force at Khulna. The head-quarters of the salt department were
at Khulna (for the so-called Raymangal provision of salt) and Jaynagar.

There was also a cloth factory at Sonabaria, and another at
Buran, now both within the limits of the 24-Per-
The cloth factory.
gunnahs.

2. If the Government were now to establish any commercial
transactions in the districts, it would render all
Their independence.
its servants and all their transactions amenable
in the ordinary course to the established courts of judicature. But
such was not the system in force in 1781. The judicial departments
were expected to consult the convenience of the salt department, just as
much as the salt department was expected to yield to that of the courts
of judicature. Not only were disputes arising out of salt transactions
declared to be decidable by the salt officials, and not by the ordinary
courts, but the courts were even to avoid sending for persons engaged in
the Company's salt manufactures during their working season.

3. The salt officials were in the district long before there was
any civil court established within it. They had therefore all along
exercised uncontrolled authority in their own matters, and when a judge
came to Jessore they were disposed to resent his interference. On the
other hand, the judge, when he came to the district, came without any
particular instructions as to his relations with the salt authorities, and
was disposed to think he had jurisdiction in matters in which they were
concerned as well as in other matters.

4. There can be little doubt that the salt system was founded upon
the most grievous oppression. The plan followed
Salt system.
in the manufacture was that the salt agent, or his
assistants, contracted with certain persons called malanghies for the engage-

ment of people as salt-boilers. To these malanghies large advances were made, and they in their turn made advances to salt-boilers or maihandars. The contract with these maihandars was that they were at a certain season of the year to proceed to specified places far south in the Sundarbans, and there to give their personal labour in the manufacture of salt.

5. Now, the malanghies were an unscrupulous race of men. Bound by their contracts to produce a certain number of salt-boilers, they cared little how it was done, and it was directly to their interest that the maihandars should get as little as possible for their labour. The maihandars were impressed and compelled by force to take advances. Having taken advances, they were compelled to leave their homes and go to work like slaves at the salt-pans. If they refused, the malanghies complained against them to the salt officials, who, being directly interested in the extension of salt manufacture, were sure to find the maihandars to be in the wrong; if they complained against the malanghies, they could complain only to the salt officials, who were sure to side with their oppressors. The malanghies were vested also with certain powers to enable them to drive the maihandars to work, and to recover their advances from them. These powers were dreadfully abused by the malanghies, who strove to make money by their exercise, sure always to come off best when any complaint was made against their doings.

6. When, therefore, the judge came to the district, it was natural that the maihandars should apply to him for protection, and he spent a great deal of trouble in adjusting matters between the maihandars and the malanghies, who were determined to receive back Rs. 20 for every Rs. 4 they had advanced. The deputy salt agent resented this as poaching upon his preserves, but Henckell responded by condemning the oppression of the malanghies, and the subordinate salt agents who were in collusion with them, and said he should provide against their repeating their conduct. (J. 8-9-81.)

7. This was only the first note in the war that broke out between

War between Henckell and the salt officers. Henckell and the salt officials, who now for the first time had an observer of their deeds. Mr. Henckell continued to hear and determine disputes arising from salt transactions, till one day in 1784, when Mr. Henckell's peons had gone to arrest and attach the property of a judgment-debtor who owed some money on account of salt advances, Mr. Ewart, the salt agent, arrested the peons and complained to Government against Mr. Henckell's interference. A second time he did the same thing, arresting a body of peons sent by Henckell. The result of these proceedings was, that the Board of Revenue directed the salt agent to withdraw his protection from the judgment-debtor. Mr. Ewart did so, but took care first to let the debtor abscond. (J. 12-10-84 ; 29-10-84 ; 14-11-84 ; 5-3-85.)

8. A short time after this, Mr. Henckell submitted to Government a complaint regarding the proceedings of the salt agent and his subordinates, of whose conduct he gives some examples. First he narrated the case of a man named John Peters, a subordinate of Mr. Ewart's, who had impressed fifteen boatmen who were quite unwilling to serve. To reduce them to obedience Peters employed such force that four of them disappeared, and were supposed to have lost their lives; others of them were put in confinement. Henckell receiving intelligence had sent out men to release these latter, but Mr. Ewart met them in person, and by force prevented their executing their intention. (M. 12-5-85.)

Oppression by the salt officers.

9. Another case he represented, where Mr. Ewart had sent an agent, one Jagmohan, to a village with an order upon the villagers to deliver up whatever maihandars they had. If they did not obey, Mr. Ewart threatened to send a military force (which he had under him) to seize the first persons they came across. When the agent Jagmohan came with his escort, the people remonstrated with him, saying that they had never been subject to the salt manufacture; but this excuse he would not hear, and he seized and beat their headmen. This exasperated the villagers, who attempted a rescue, but four of them were shot down by the agent's men. Mr. Henckell, when he received information of this outrage, issued a warrant to arrest the agent, but, as in the other case, Mr. Ewart had protected him, and would not let him be arrested. (M. 12-5-85 ; 23-5-85.)

10. The Board called on Mr. Ewart for explanations in these matters, and though these were not satisfactory, they merely warned Mr. Ewart against them in future. The Board seem to have been aware that the salt manufacture was not founded on the good will of the ryots engaged in it, but accepted this condition of affairs as unavoidable. (B. 26-10-85.)

11. The warning of the Board had little effect upon Mr. Ewart. Within a month after he received it, we find him pursuing the same line of conduct. It was about this time that Mr. Henckell had begun his Sundarban plan, giving grants of lands in the Sundarbans to taluqdars who engaged to reclaim

Further oppressions.

them. Mr. Ewart saw danger in this, for it would create a competition on the part of the grantees for the labour of the ryots whom he sought to keep for salt manufacture. So one day, accompanied by an armed force, he went to call on a zemindar's gomashta to produce those of his ryots who were subject to salt manufacture. He met with some resistance, that is, the gomashta declined to himself give up any ryots, and upon this Ewart proceeded to seize some of them; at that moment he saw some ryots who appeared to be coming in his direction, and thinking they were intending a rescue, he fired on them, killing one and severely wounding another. (M. 20-11-85.)

12. Within a month after this another precisely similar affray took place, when Mr. Ewart's men proceeded to one of the Sundarban grants to seize some ryots employed there, whom they alleged to be subject to salt manufacture. On this occasion one man was killed and two were wounded. (M. 15-12-85.)

13. Jessore was not the only district where there was feud between the judicial and the salt departments, for we find Conflicts of authority. the salt controller, in April 1785, complaining to Government of the interference in salt matters exercised by the judges both of Moorly and of 24-Pergunnahs. He proposed to Government certain rules of procedure intended to prevent the clashing of authority. These rules, as was natural when they emanated from the salt department, were upon the basis of non-interference by the courts in questions arising out of salt proceedings; the courts were to have no cognizance in cases of claims upon malanghies or maihandars. Mr. Henckell objected to letting the salt authorities act without control in these matters, saying that not only the malanghies, but their sub-contractors (called tafalis), were guilty of the greatest abuses of their authority, and continually seized men by force to make them work as salt-boilers: he alleged also that when complaints were made to the salt agent he refused to pay attention to them, and when people complained in the regular courts, the salt agent punished them for it. (G. 10-5-85. J. 31-5-85.)

14. The rules of 1785 were, however, settled in nearly the same terms as they were proposed. The judge was to Rules of 1785. have no cognizance in purely salt disputes, and in the case of claims of a different nature made against any one engaged in salt manufacture, the judge was, if they were petty, to refer them for report to the agent; and if they were not petty, to decide them himself, summoning the parties through the salt agent and

adjourning the cases if they were brought at a time when the presence of the defendant would cause inconvenience in the salt manufacture. The agent was also to exercise certain criminal powers, subject to a report to the judge. These rules did not obviate the danger of collision between the departments; they rather put it in the power of the salt department at any time to delay proceedings to which they were opposed, by alleging them to interfere with their work. The Government, I am afraid, was more careful of its salt manufacture than anxious that even-handed justice should be done to all persons connected with it. The rules made the salt officers still the arbiters of their own proceedings, and in no way controlled them in their arbitrariness.

15. These regulations were laid down during the occurrence of the events, examples of which I have just been giving; but as some of the incidents referred to occurred after the promulgation of the rules, it is pretty evident that the rules had failed to attain their object. At length Mr. Henckell's repeated complaints induced the Government, in January 1786, to send down Mr. Evans, the deputy salt controller, to inquire regarding them, and he fixed his station and held his inquiries at Manirampur. I could not find whether the result of the inquiry was or was not favorable to the salt department. So far as I infer, the report was, as regards their conduct, rather apologetic than exculpatory, for the result was that the Board of Revenue again desired the controller to propose rules that would prevent the clashing of authority. (M. 7-1-86. B. 30-3-86.)

They fail to check the oppressions.

16. The authorities, however, had not ceased to clash, for we find two notable instances in the same year. In the first case Mr. Ewart, suspecting one of his European employés of committing embezzlement, held him in confinement at Khulna. Mr. Henckell received information of it, and released the man from confinement on the ground that the charge was not satisfactorily made out. The second case was connected with the man John Peters, whom we have before mentioned, as guilty of using great barbarity towards a boat's crew whom he had impressed. In October 1785 we find this same John Peters accused of wantonly maltreating a man simply because his father had been guilty of the grievous offence of seeking redress at the judge's hands for some injury he had suffered in respect of a salt matter. Now, he was accused by one Mr. Povery, apparently a trader at Chupnagar, of committing assault upon him, and Mr. Henckell sent out a warrant to arrest him; but Mr. Ewart sent a force of

Further disputes.

men, and prevented the warrant being executed. Subsequently, however, the Government compelled Ewart to deliver up Peters. (M. 27-9-86; 25-10-85; 26-11-86; 19-12-86.)

17. In the beginning of 1787 we find Mr. Henckell renewing his complaints against the salt subordinates. He alleges that the malanghies extort money by seizing people's children, and that the salt agent's people commit extortion also by seizing boats on pretence of searching for salt and detaining them till payment is made. In the latter case Mr. Henckell himself tested the truth of the statements made to him by hiring and sending a boat along the route where these depredations occurred. His boat was seized and detained for three months. (J. 4-2-87; 20-4-87.)

Complaints renewed.

18. At length, in 1787, Mr. Henckell submitted a proposal for the reform of the salt department. Tracing most of the evils in it to the employment of malanghies as go-betweens, men who had no interest in acting honestly, and who only abused their powers for purposes of extortion, he proposed that they should be abolished, and an attempt should be made to work by advancing direct to maihandars. He stated that there was no real unwillingness to work in the salt manufacture, provided the maihandars could be convinced they would receive just treatment. The advances ought to be made at an earlier season, zemindars should be informed of the number of maihandars required of them, and places should be fixed for their assembling. Cutcherries should be established for the regular hearing of complaints, and to ensure the maihandars receiving proper pay. Also that the stores should be provided by the agent's people. The manufacture required the maihandars to leave their homes to proceed far south of the inhabited parts of the district; no food was of course obtainable there, and the ordinary plan of leaving the maihandars to provide for their own food left them at the mercy of malanghies and others, who were able to import their supplies from the north.

The salt department reformed on Henckell's plan.

19. Above all, to give the system a fair trial, Mr. Henckell offered himself to undertake the duties of salt agent. The plan would, he said, have this advantage, that it would unite in the same individual, namely himself, the dealing with the claims for rent on the maihandars, and the dealing with the claims on them that arose out of salt transactions. The former was part of his duty as collector, and Mr. Henckell had now been collector for a year, and in that capacity also had had

M

difficulties with the salt department, who were too ready to protect from demands for rent maihandars engaged in salt manufacture. (C. 20-7-87.)

20.   The Governor General approved the proposals of Mr. Henckell, and directed him to take charge of the salt agency so far as regarded the Raymangal division, Mr. Ewart having to confine himself to the Backerganj side.   Mr. Henckell accordingly put out a proclamation inviting maihandars to offer themselves at certain specified places, assuring them that there would be no impressing of labour, and that the former theory would be abandoned, whereby a man engaging himself for one year was held liable to impressment every succeeding year.   To this proclamation the Board expressly added a clause, stating that, if Government found that the salt manufacture could not be carried on on the basis of the good-will of the ryots, it would abandon it altogether.   (G. 3-9-87.   B. 21-9-87.)

21.   This new policy probably entailed a little loss to begin with; and, in fact, we find Mr. Henckell anticipating some diminution in the salt provision for the first year.   But the Government adhered to the resolution they had adopted, to carry on their salt department without any system of impressment.   Lord Cornwallis's salt department rules of December 1788, subsequently codified into the Regulation 29 of 1793, contain almost all the elements of reform proposed by Mr. Henckell. The salt-boilers were to be perfectly free to engage or not as they liked, and steps were taken to ensure liberty of action on their part and to secure them from ill-treatment.   The salt agent, in fact, was made to be a protector to them instead of a slave-driver ; and, wherever possible, the system of direct dealing with them was to be adopted instead of the system of intermediaries, from whom, as Mr. Henckell had pointed out, and as the regulation expressly admitted, the abuses which previously existed had chiefly originated.   (C. 25-10-87.)

22.   These proceedings, being as they were an implied condemnation of the salt department, were not very well received by the salt officers.   Mr. Ewart first objected to the proclamation, that it would prevent him getting men for his part of the work, which still proceeded on the old plan; but Government avoided this objection by specifying distinctly the limits within which the proclamation was to have validity.   Mr. Ewart then trangressed those limits and invaded Henckell's division, his malanghies threw advance-money into the maihandars' houses and seized the maihandars on pretext that they had taken advances.   He would not give over

The salt officers refuse to submit.

charge, but had summoned the malanghies and was conducting his operations as before. Mr. Henckell naturally complained of all these proceedings as tending to impair all the good effect of his proclamation and ruining his scheme, and the controller in reply, while he made Ewart give over charge, directed that the advances already made should be worked out, a stipulation to which Henckell of course objected, insisting that the pergunnahs affected by the advances should be separated off from his division. The salt department got up also another squabble, for when Mr. Henckell, taking charge of the Raymangal division, desired to occupy the offices and godowns at Khulna, Mr. Ewart objected to give them up, declaring that they were, in part at least, his own property, and desiring Mr. Henckell to occupy the houses at Jaynagar, which, though sufficiently centrical for Mr. Ewart when he had charge of the salt agency as far east as Backerganj, was far from centrical so far as regarded the Raymangal division, of which alone Mr. Henckell had charge. The salt controller, who was biassed in favour of his own department, decided this point also against Mr. Henckell. (C. 30-10-87; 4-12-87; 13-12-87; 29-12-87.)

23. However, the change was in the end effected, and it put an end for the time to the constant quarrels between the departments. The records say nothing for some years of salt matters, probably because all the books and papers bearing on salt were made over to the salt department when the salt agency was re-transferred. I cannot say therefore whether Henckell was or was not successful as salt agent; and the fact of a re-transfer taking place, which it did about three years after, proves nothing, for it was far more likely attributable to Lord Cornwallis's re-organization of all departments than to any bad success of the new system. Some time after the re-transfer there again broke out quarrels between the departments, the history of which we will see when the time comes.

XVII.—*The Cloth Factories.*—1781-90.

THE disagreements between the judge and the Company's cloth establishments were similar in nature, but were not so violent as those with the salt establishments. The system of the cloth manufacture was, that the residents or superintendents of the factories, of which there were two, Sonabaria and Buran,

System.

within Jessore, made advances through their subordinates to the native weavers, who were bound to give their woven cloths to the factory.

2. The judge began receiving and listening to complaints made

The judge asserts his authority. by weavers against the commercial residents' men, that they made an excessive demand upon them and were forcing them against their will to receive advances; and he entertained also demands for sums due from people engaged in the cloth manufacture. The superintendents of both the factories wrote to him in 1786, complaining of this as an infringement of their authority, saying that the matters were for them to decide and the judge had no business to summon persons engaged in their department. In Mr. Henckell's answer to these complaints, he says that he had been in the habit of referring these matters for disposal to the commercial officers, but he found that justice was not done, and he was obliged to decide the cases himself. There were apparently some cloths of which the Company had declared themselves to have a monopoly, for Mr. Henckell says in this letter that he never interfered in cases where monopoly cloths were concerned, but only where the gomashtas had been making illegitimate demands on the weavers in respect of other cloths. He stated also that the gomashtas were using their authority to commit oppressions on the ryots, and that they were not properly controlled by their own officers. (Superintendent, Buran, 22-7-86. Superintendent, Sonabaria, 14-9-86. M. 27-7-86; 31-8-86.)

3. About the time that this correspondence was going on, the

Rules of 1786. Government published certain regulations to prevent the clashing of authority between the civil and commercial authorities: probably the difficulty had arisen in other districts also. These regulations were to this effect. The resident was to keep a list of Company's weavers, and he was empowered to summon any weaver he chose to ask him whether or not he would consent to weave for the Company. Zemindars were forbidden to imprison Company's weavers in case of their defaulting in rent (a rule which assumes they had the power of imprisonment in other cases), but they were bound to give them pottahs, and then if they defaulted, they were to apply to the commercial resident. When a criminal charge was made against any weaver, if it was not a serious one, it was to be referred to the resident for inquiry and report; and in case of a charge against an agent, redress was first to be sought from the resident, and if not satisfied with his judgment the complainant might apply to the collector. (14-9-86.)

4. These rules still left the commercial department uncontrolled, and a year later we find Mr. Henckell complaining of the evil-doings of the gomashtas or agents.

Henckell represents the evil-doings of the department.

He says, they impress weavers in all directions, even though they are not regular Company's weavers; that many of the latter had, since the establishment of the court in the district, sought redress from it, and had their engagements cancelled; that the resident got his cloths cheaper than the men could sell in the market, by which I presume he means that the weavers would not, unless compelled, sell to him; and that he impresses all the weaving labour in the district on the plea that the Company's investment requires it all. He argued that these questions of impressment should be decided before the civil court, and not before the resident, who was too apt to favour his own men; and desired also that the weavers should be under the same regulations as all others were, so far as regarded realization of arrears of rent. They were so easily able to delay payment, when in case of their defaulting so many references were required, and other people could and did cause similar delays by falsely pleading the protection of the factory. (C. 27-6-87.)

5. No change, however, appears to have been made in the regulations, for next year again Henckell repeats his complaint; this time addressing the residents themselves regarding the misbehaviour of their native agents. He says also that one man, not a regular agent, was following in their steps, and he had had him strapped up and had given him a punishment of ten shoes and Rs. 3 fine—a punishment which, judicially at least, he had no power to inflict. But these were times when people were not so bound by rule as now they are. (C. 2-63-88.)

6. The collector indeed, for many years after, continued to refer to the residents complaints against the agents they employed.

7. It must not be inferred from these proceedings that Mr. Henckell set his face against the commercial part of the Company's transactions. A single instance will prove the contrary. Beyond the north of the district was the silk factory of Comeroolly, which, however, made advances for silk within the district. In 1788 Mr. Henckell, of his own motion, took steps to encourage the mulberry cultivation which the floods of previous years had much diminished. He proposed favorable terms of holding for ryots bringing lands under mulberry cultivation, his position as collector giving him much to do with the assessment of the lands. (C. 5-10-88. Res. Comeroolly, 31-10-88.)

8. Mr. Henckell, therefore, did not oppose himself for any mere
Subsequent carrying out of his views. personal reasons to these commercial departments, but acting on the theory which he set before himself, that the people of the district were under his protection, he was never tired of guarding them against the oppression which the practical irresponsibility of the departmental officers permitted to exist. He continued to urge upon Government the necessity of abolishing the system which made the heads of departments final judges in all matters affecting themselves. It was one of the many matters in which he was in advance of his time; and as it is plain from the correspondence that the Government always listened to him as to one whose opinions were of some authority, I have little doubt that the facts he brought forward in his remonstrances, and the arguments he urged for the subordination of departmental matters to the judicial authority, conduced in some measure to the reforms which Lord Cornwallis in this respect carried into effect.

XVIII.—*Establishment of the Collectorate of Jessore.*—1786.

On 4th April 1786 Mr. Henckell, writing to Government, pointed
Mr. Henckell proposes a collectorate at Jessore. out the inconvenience which the district, of which he was judge and magistrate, suffered in revenue matters from having its revenue head-quarters fixed at a place so remote as Calcutta. Not only had the revenues of all the estates, except those which, being in Bhusna, were under the Rajshahye collectorate, to be paid in Calcutta, but as the civil court was prohibited from interference in revenue matters, all questions arising in connection with revenue (and these included demands by zemindars for arrears due from their ryots) had to be heard and decided in Calcutta. This caused so much inconvenience and difficulty that the results were often unsatisfactory.

2. Mr. Henckell proposed, therefore, that the collectorship should be added to the judgeship, and offered himself to undertake the duty without additional salary, "actuated," as he said, "by motives of publick good, and the enhancement of his own credit and reputation."

3. The Government responded at once by creating Jessore a col-
And is made collector. lectorship; it was to comprise Isafpur and Saydpur (which had apparently been under the collector of Rajshahye and Bhusna), the estates lying between the Ichamati and the

present Backerganj district (then part of Dacca), which had previously been paying revenue at Calcutta and at Hooghly, and also some estates separated off from Moorshedabad. Muhammadshahi was at that time, or had before been, constituted a separate collectorate; and Naldi and Furreedpore (adopting the names at present applied), though within the judgeship of Jessore, remained attached to the collectorship of Rajshahye. The land revenue of the Jessore collectorship, thus defined, amounted to nearly six lakhs. (C. 7-5-86; 22-7-86; 27-12-86. M. 2-7-83.)

4. The duties of a collector at that time were almost entirely

Collector's duties.

confined to matters directly connected with land revenue. He had every year to make settlements of all the estates within his collectorship, and he had to realize as he best could the revenues so settled. He had also a judicial function, namely, the decision of disputes about rent and about land arising between zemindar and ryot.

5. The whole district had been settled in 1178 (1772) by the com-

Collection of land revenue.

mittee of revenue, who had deputed to this district a Mr. Lane, in order, by extensive local inquiry, to reach a proper estimate of the zemindars' assets. This settlement was varied from time to time as circumstances rendered fit, but there had been little change in the entire assessments since they were first made. The collector, in making his yearly assessment, had few regular principles and little detailed information to go upon. A sort of rough calculation was made, and the collector got the zemindar to undertake to pay as much rent as he could be got to consent to. If the collector and the zemindar could not come to terms, then the collector temporarily ousted the zemindar and tried, by direct collections, to get the revenue he had estimated for. (C. 15-12-86; 5-3-92.)

6. This process was gone through every year, and the settlements for each year appear never to have been completed till about Bhadoo or Assin, the fifth and sixth months of the year.

7. To enforce the payment of revenue, the collector appears principally to have used strong pressure. Continual demands were made upon defaulters, and these had some weight, since the collector had power to use harsher means. He had a defaulter's jail, into which recusants might be made to go, and he might also attach and realize directly the rents of any estate. This attachment involved to the zemindar a greater penalty than at first sight appears; for, as we shall see, a zemindar's demands upon his ryots were by no means confined to what was

justly realizable, and the collector's demands being thus so much less
than the zemindar's, a zemindar could not but lose when he had
nothing placed to his credit but what the collector realized. Sales of
zemindaris for arrears of rent do not appear to have been thought of at
that time, and I find only one reference even to the theory that the
zemindars had saleable rights; for, as I have shewed before, they were
rather regarded as contractors for the collection from the ryots of the
revenues belonging to Government. The reference is contained in
Board's 27-7-87, and referred rather to future plans than to existing
relations.

8. The collector had also the management of the treasury, that is,
he had to make a monthly remittance to Calcutta
Treasury.
of all the sums he collected; only he was allowed
to send, in lieu of cash, bills for the fixed allowances, such as his own
and his establishment's pay, and for contingencies. In the matter of
expenditure, he was treated rather hardly, being occasionally called on
to refund certain expenses which were no doubt both legitimate and
necessary, though incurred without previous sanction; on one occasion,
too, he was fined Rs. 300 for not having sent in his accounts within
the prescribed limit of time.

9. These are the matters which fill up the bulk of the collectorate
correspondence about 1787, and might have filled it up for some years
had it not been that the permanent settlement was being brought on,
and was the cause of much correspondence of the most interesting nature.

XIX.—*The Permanent Settlement Proposed.*—1788.

WHEN Lord Cornwallis came out from England, instructed by the
Court of Directors to effect a permanent settlement of the land revenue
of Bengal, he set about collecting information from the local officers,
who were naturally best able to give it. Mr. Henckell was one of the
more prominent of these, and the information which he and his successor
have placed on record in their reports regarding the permanent settlement afford most valuable indications of the then position of affairs.

2. In writing about these matters, one thing above all is necessary;
we must separate ourselves from the ideas which
Ignorance of exact rights.
subsequent legislation has engrafted upon the
country. We have now given the zemindar a certain position as owner

of the soil, and we have laid down exactly the status of the ryot; know when to call him a tenant-at-will, and when to look on him as having joint interests in the proprietorship. In 1787 these were still undecided questions, and they were also rather obscure ones. Indeed, it is exceedingly doubtful whether the permanent settlement did not proceed upon a mistake when it regarded zemindars as being proprietors of the lands whose revenues they collected from the ryots and paid to Government.

3. The first question which the Government referred for report regarded the assets of the zemindars; the collectors were asked whether the zemindars realized from the ryots any sums over and above the nominal rent (jumma) which they paid, and on what principle the zemindars acted in the imposition of these additional demands. Henckell answered that the zemindars were in the habit of constantly imposing cesses upon the ryots. There was a cess for collection expenses, a cess for "faujdari," a cess to be paid on all occasions of marriage, birth or death, which, from being a casual cess, had become a regular one, and a tax had to be paid upon all things taken to the hât for sale. Zemindars had to give security for the revenue they undertook to pay until the Board abolished it in 1787, and this security formed another excuse for a cess upon ryots. These and other less definite cesses added to the ryot's jumma usually about 60 per cent., but sometimes as much as 90 or even 120. Henckell recommended that all these cesses should be consolidated with the jumma, by increasing the latter 50 per cent. and securing the ryots from future increment by giving them written pottahs. (C. 14-3-87. B. 13-7-87.)

Cesses on ryots.

4. According to our present notions, these are matters which the authorities should leave to be regulated by the zemindar and the ryot themselves. But it was otherwise then: the ryots had no permanent fixed tenure, and when the collector settled what the zemindar should pay to Government, he settled also what the ryot should pay to the zemindar. True to the contractor theory of the zemindar's position, the collector, as we shall see throughout the correspondence of the permanent settlement period, acted as if he had all right to impose upon the mutual relations of zemindar and ryot such conditions as he thought fit. The abolition and consolidation of the cesses was only carrying out on a larger scale what he had already done when he abolished the one-anna security cess in the Isafpur zemindari. We shall find other similar instances as we proceed. (C. 14-3-87.)

Relation of ryot to Government.

N

5.   In this report the collector points out a fruitful source of evil in the zemindar having uncontrolled liberty to appoint as naib, or as farmer, of any pergunnah, any one whom he thought fit.   The zemindar did not seek for such appointments the people who would best discharge their duties towards the ryots, or towards the estate; and Henckell urged that the collector should have a distinct power of interference in these matters.

6.   In the year after these matters were under discussion, the Government called upon the collectors to submit their opinions as to the possibility of a settlement of the estates for a period of years, and directed them also to report upon the question with whom, ryot or zemindar, such settlement ought to be made.   It should be stated that throughout all these discussions no permanent settlement was talked of, but only a settlement for a period of years.   The settlement, as finally concluded, was nominally one for ten years, and it was only when everything was settled for ten years that the Government proclaimed the ten years' settlement perpetual.

Settlement to be with zemindars or with ryots.

7.   At that time the idea of settlement which the Board had before them, and the idea which Mr. Henckell also had, was that settlement should be made with the ryots, and arrangements made for the collection, through the zemindars, of the rents settled with them.   Mr. Henckell, in his answer, avoided entering into the question of the exact status of the zemindar, passing it over with an acknowledgment that the zemindar had *some* right, though he could not say what it was.   The zemindar of course had *some* right since he was entitled to have, in preference to others, the settlement of his own zemindari, but Henckell regarded him rather as a servant of the State, employed to collect the rents from the ryots and rewarded for his trouble by a grant of rent-free lands. *All* zemindars, he said, had these rent-free lands, but as they were not sufficient to satisfy their requirements, they made up the deficiency by making a profit out of the collections.   The ryots had some of them tenures at low rates, such as gantidars and jotedars; but others had tenures of less profitable nature.   The Board entertained the idea of increasing the rates in these low-rated tenures, esteeming that the zemindar had no business to grant them; but Mr. Henckell pointed out that these tenures did not, as a rule, diminish from the revenue of the estate, because the gantidar or jotedar was usually also the farmer of the lands adjoining his own holding, and having a profitable tenure in his own lands was expected to remit to the zemindar the entire realizations of his farm.   The

"Ganti" tenures—their nature.

abolition of the system might increase the revenue of the ganti lands, but would diminish the revenue of the rest by adding to the expense of collection. (C. 25-6-88.)

8. Whether the origin of the tenure called ganti was or was not that indicated by Mr. Henckell in this report, namely, the giving certain lands on a low rent to an individual who undertook to collect and pay in, as farmer, the revenues of other lands adjacent, it is certain that in many places this sort of connection still exists between ganti and farming. In many places the gantidar of the whole or part of a village is stilled looked upon as the person who naturally occupies the position of farmer in some adjacent lands. The theory of this connection is supported by the terms which Mr. Henckell's successor uses in a letter (12-1-93), where he says that almost all the cultivating ryots pay rent either to a farmer or a gantidar.

9. Of course it is not meant that this theory is applicable to all gantis at present existing, for many, if not most, of these date their origin from periods subsequent to the date of which I am writing, and have more to do with the zemindar's desire to fill his purse than with the land system indicated above. The raja of Chanchra, for example, when in 1796 he was getting into difficulties, created in the Isafpur estate a large number of ganti tenures, receiving of course a premium from the tenant. (C. 12-1-93; 8-6-96.)

10. Continuing his report, Mr. Henckell writes that it might be possible to increase the revenues of the land, but it would require extensive local inquiries, as the settlements then made from year to year were made upon very imperfect data; even the zemindars and their officers remained ignorant of the actual resources of their estates. The ryots nominally held a few biggahs at a very high rate, but actually cultivated an area twice, or even three times, as large as their nominal holding, the excess land enabling them to bear the very high rates. But this position of affairs gave rise to continual bickering between the zemindars and the ryots. The latter were continually striving to conceal their actual holdings, and the former, aware that excess existed, continually attempted to enhance the rent, and imposed upon the ryots all sorts of cesses, which, as their imposition assumed what was far from being the fact, namely, that the incidence of the original rent or jumma was equal upon all the ryots, were the source of great oppression and hardship. Mr. Henckell thought that the ryots would be willing to accept pottahs for

Can the revenue be increased? [marginal note]

their holdings, even at an increased rent, if these pottahs secured to them the whole of their lands, and granted immunity from additional demands by way of cess on the part of the zemindars.   (C. 25-6-88.)

11. Another matter to which the Government directed their attention with reference to the proposed settlement was the question of lakhiraj or rent-free tenures: how far they were to be recognized, and how far they should be disregarded. The Government proposed to resume all tenures which had not been granted, and possessed by the grantees before the cession of the Dewany (1765), and no grant was to be considered hereditary which was not distinctly so created. Rent-free grants had been directly prohibited only in 1178 (1772), when the British undertook the direct management of the collections, and therefore all invalid grantees of an earlier date were to be permitted during their lifetime to retain half of their grants. Native officers were to be appointed to hunt out invalid grants, and were to be rewarded by obtaining the first year's assessment, and to be punished, if they concealed invalid grants, by a fine of three times the amount of the assessment.   (B. 5-9-88.)

Question of rent-free tenures.

12. Mr. Henckell, while admitting the extent of the evil which the Government sought to suppress, considered it almost impossible to move in the matter without inflicting great injustice. There was no doubt that immense amounts of land had been alienated by zemindars giving rent-free tenures, and Mr. Henckell estimated the whole within the district at about 350,000 biggahs, about a twentieth or more of the whole area, cultivated and uncultivated, of the lands within the district; and of this he considered two-thirds would be resumable if the orders of Government were carried into effect. The grants made before the British possession were to be respected, but the carelessness of natives in preserving documentary evidence, and the impossibility after a lapse of time of procuring oral evidence of any reliability, would place insuperable obstacles in the way of valid grantees proving their title and possession as far back as 1766. As for the grants between that date and 1772, Mr. Henckell stated that the zemindars had so long enjoyed, by custom, the right of creating lakhiraj tenures, that it was hardship by a retrospective rule to declare them invalid; and as to disallowance of hereditary right to ordinary grants, he urged that precision of language was not customary in such grants, and that many grants intended to be hereditary were not distinctly declared so. The prohibition to zemindars to create rent-free tenures had not made

Difficulty of resumption.

them cease from giving grants, but only made them antedate the sannads they gave; and forgery and fraud had been so rife in the district, that it would be impossible to avoid confounding the genuine with the false. As for the proposed establishment it would be useless, for it would only give the proposed native officers a grand opportunity for extortion and bribery. No doubt native officers have, in point of official morality, immensely improved since Mr. Henckell's time, but I can hardly accept his wholesale condemnation of them when he says, " rapacity and oppression are, I believe, the ruling passion of the generality of natives, and very few of them have sufficient fortitude to resist the temptation of a bribe." (C. 5-12-88.)

13. The above discussion contains the nucleus of the resumption *Final resumption provisions.* provisions of the code of 1793. In their ultimate form they were a little more favorable to the grantees than the first proposals of Government. It was not till long after that they were to any considerable extent brought into operation, and we shall subsequently see the beginning of the agitation about them. But when the resumptions were effected, I am afraid Mr. Henckell's fears were realized; and though perhaps the strictness of the law prevented many fraudulent grants from escaping, still the difficulty thrown on grantees caused the non-acceptance of many grants which no doubt were valid according to the standard the Government laid down.

XX.—*State of Things Prior to the Permanent Settlement.*—1785-90.

IN 1787 the collectorship of Muhammadshahi, whose head-quarters were *The Muhammadshahi zemindari, an example.* at Jhenida, was abolished, and the Muhammadshahi zemindari, and the few others that were attached to that district, were transferred to the collector of Jessore. Of the state of this zemindari before and up till the time of the permanent settlement we have abundant information; and with this reservation that it was in rather worse circumstances than the other zemindaris, I set it forth as an example of how matters were managed under the temporary settlement system. (C. 8-10-94.)

2. This estate was settled in 1178 (1772) upon the basis of a local inquiry made by Mr. Lane, and at the same time it was divided into two shares, of four-fifths and one-fifth respectively, the first instance of batwára in the district. (B. 22-5-87. C. 29-9-91.)

3. Shortly after this settlement, the proprietor of the four-fifths share
being considered, either on account of his minority
Farmed out.
or for some other reason, incapable of undertaking
the settlement, the estate was given in farm to one Pran Bose, who held
it in 1186-87-88 (1779-80-81), and after him his son (which of course
only meant himself in the name of his son) had it for 1189-90-91
(1782-83-84). (C. 12-3-90; 13-12-90.)

4. Now the estate had already been assessed to the very utmost;
the rates had been fixed very high, and the
The estate was over-as-
sessed.
margin allowed to the zemindar was very small.
The assessment of 1178 was, for the whole estate, Rs. 2,87,614, and the
zemindar's allowance was Rs. 18,000, besides his briti or stipendiary
lands, which were very small, only about Rs. 1,800. There were several
circumstances which rendered the estate incapable of yielding the revenue
imposed upon it. First of all the fundamental rate was assumed at too
high a figure; secondly, the estate was liable to continual inundation from
the big rivers which then flowed through it; and thirdly, the zemindar
had already granted away huge amounts of land either rent-free or
on almost quit-rent tenures, called taluqs. These taluqs require to be
explained. They were of two sorts: pattai, i.e.,
Taluqs.
founded upon a lease or pottah, and kharida, that
is, purchased. They were created by the zemindar, who, on receiving
sufficient present consideration, made over to the taluqdar almost his
entire rights in a small portion of his estate, subject to the payment to
the zemindar of an annual rent. The creation of taluqs was therefore
a very easy way of realizing money at present by drawing upon
future resources. The distinction of "leased" and "purchased" taluqs
was probably rather one of name than of substance, as they all, no
doubt, involved to some extent both present payments and future rent.
Now, between taluqs and rent-free tenures, half of Muhammadshahi
(i.e., 310,000 out of 700,000 biggahs) had been partially alienated by
the zemindar and rendered incapable of contributing to him the revenue
assessed upon it by the Government. (B. 4-5-86; 22-5-87. C. 13-12-90;
25-2-91; 12-5-91; 6-8-90.)

5. Pran Bose had, however, undertaken the farm with the intention of making it pay, and a system of oppression
The farmer's exactions.
and exaction followed. The ryots were made to
pay numberless cesses and imposts, and were so reduced in circumstances that they gave up extending their cultivation, and sometimes

fled altogether. The taluqdars, too, were ordered to pay an increase of rent, and turned out of possession until they did; many of them abandoned their taluqs altogether, leaving their ryots the alternative of quitting their lands or paying the farmer his exorbitant demands. The farmer finding, in consequence of his own oppression, greater and greater difficulty in realizing the revenue, imposed upon those who remained that part of the assessment which had been previously paid by those who had fled and given up their lands. (B. 22-5-87. C. 28-4-89; 12-3-90; 13-12-90; 25-2-91; 12-5-91.)

6. The consequence of all this was that a large amount of land

Impoverish the estate. fell out of cultivation, and the estate became impoverished. The Government had so far to participate in the loss, that when in 1192 (1785) they settled the four-fifths share with the zemindar himself, they reduced the assessment to Rs. 2,44,223 (on the whole estate), whereas in 1178 (1772) it had been Rs. 2,87,614. (C. 5-10-91. B. 4-5-86.)

7. But even this reduced assessment was an exorbitantly rated one.

The estate falls into arrear. The basis of it was a biggah rate of Rs. 1-8 for ordinary land, and Rs. 3 for homestead or garden land. There was also consolidated cess (called tax) at 5 annas per rupee, and newly reclaimed land even had to pay 12 annas per biggah. Mr. Rocke writes of these rates that they are a third more than those prevailing in the rest of Jessore, and that the land upon which they are assessed is not nearly so fertile as the rest of the district. It was no wonder therefore that the zemindar of the four-fifths portion, after holding his estate for the two years 1192-93 (1785-86) found himself hopelessly in arrear. His annual payment was Rs. 1,85,000, and he was Rs. 27,000 in arrear the first year and Rs. 1,05,000 the next. (C. 12-3-90 B. 22-5-87.)

8. Part of this was of course owing to bad management; the zemindar was young and inexperienced, and in the hands of rapacious amla. He had received from the ryots in 1193 Rs. 32,000 more than he had paid into Government, a greater amount than was necessary for his expenses of collection and his allowances. Still, even with paying over this Rs. 32,000, he would have fallen far behind the Government demand. (C. 12-3-90. B. 27-7-87.)

9. The estate being therefore hopelessly insolvent, the Board

The Board oust the zemindar. directed the collector to take it out of the zemindar's hands and to settle and manage it directly. They had already, when they consented to reduce the assessment, cancelled the zemindar's proprietary allowance, and demanded on the part of Government the entire revenue realized from the ryots, giving the zemindar only his very meagre stipendiary lands to support himself with. They now threatened him that unless he paid up the Rs. 32,000, referred to in the last paragraph, they would take from him also these stipendiary lands. (B. 4-5-86; 27-7-87.)

10. The Board's instructions to the collector were these: He was to abolish the numerous cesses levied on the ryots and re-settle their lands on the basis laid down in 1178. He was to inquire into the large alienations of land by way of rent-free or taluq; and where he found taluqs had been given at a very small rent, or that they included more land than the taluqdar nominally paid rent for, he was to re-assess and re-settle them at a fairer rent. The taluqs, as I have stated, had fallen fearfully in arrear, and many of them were ruined; but the collector was to turn out the taluqdars and collect direct from their ryots unless they paid up the arrears they owed. (B. 22-5-87.)

11. The collector entered upon these inquiries and meantime The estate re-settled in settled the estate for the year 1194 (1787), which farm. had just commenced. He divided the whole estate into parts, and gave each part in farm, the aggregate assessment being Rs. 1,65,390, being about Rs. 20,000 less than last year. Even this could not be collected; the farmers found great difficulty in getting in their rents ,and after they had paid Rs. 9,000 out of their own pockets, they were still Rs. 7,200 in arrear. This arrear the zemindars were held responsible for, albeit they had had no connection with the estate during the year; and the Government reserved to itself the option of collecting the arrear from the zemindars or collecting it from the farmers and leaving them to recover from the zemindars. This was a particularly harsh order, as the estate during the year had suffered severely from an inundation and a cyclone. (C. 5-7-78; 16-6-88. B. 12-9-88. C. 25-6-88.)

12. The collector was not successful in tracing the alienated lands. The collector's manage- Farmers and taluqdars colluded to conceal the ment fails. tenures which were in danger of being re-assessed: the zemindari papers were unreliable, and exhibited rather the state of things that existed before 1178 (1772) than the position of matters in 1788. He pointed out, however, the causes of the insolvency of the estate, and proposed its re-settlement at somewha tlower rates; that is, instead of Rs. 1-8 and 7½ annas "tax," it was to be Rs. 1-6 and 6 annas tax. The rent of the ryots he did not propose to reduce,

but intended to give them new land to reclaim within their old rent. He proposed also favorable terms for ryots bringing new land under cultivation. The amount of uncultivated land appears to have been enormous. The collector, estimating it apparently from figures in the zemindari office, gives the following as the amount of cultivated and uncultivated land in the alienated taluqs: cultivated, 76,558 biggahs; uncultivated, 140,611. (C. 28-4-89; 12-3-90. B. 22-3-90.)

13. The above terms were not successful in causing reclamation of land, and in 1791 the collector (then Mr. Rocke) proposed still more favorable terms, namely, three years' rent-free and then increasing rent. But by this time the permanent settlement had been effected, and the Board therefore, while approving Mr. Rocke's proposals, pointed out that by the terms of the settlement it was for the zemindar to arrange such matters. (C. 5-10-91. B. 17-10-91.)

14. So far as we have gone, we have been referring almost entirely to the four-fifths share of Muhammadshahi, and have not dealt with the one-fifth share. This estate, however, suffered to a certain extent from excessive assessment; but being in the hands of its zemindar, and not in the hands of a man like Pran Bose, it did not suffer nearly so much. As in the case of the larger estate, the assessment of the smaller one had also to be reduced about 1192 or 1193 (1785-86), and the zemindar even then refused to undertake the settlement, as he considered it excessive. It was given out in farm, but the farmer fell in arrear by Rs. 9,000; and the Board refused, as in the case of the larger estate, to give the zemindar that part of the farmer's payments which represented his proprietary allowance. At the time of the permanent settlement the assessments on both the estates were, temporarily at least, farther reduced. (B. 4-5-86; 27-7-87; 21-9-87.)

The other share also over-assessed.

15. Although of course the estates of Muhammadshahi come under special notice, because they were exceptionally badly circumstanced, still almost every estate under the temporary settlement system shewed the same features to a greater or less extent. We have seen Mr. Henckell reporting it as almost impracticable to obtain from the zemindaris greater revenue than they paid; and his successor based the permanent settlement calculations on those of 1179 (1772), on the express ground that there had been little or no progress since that time. The zemindars, he said, were then assessed to their utmost, and had so little to spare for

Other estates also in evil plight.

o

themselves, that they eked out their revenue by oppression and exaction on their ryots, and caused loss to their estates. Of the extent of jungle we have seen one instance; and a letter of Mr. Henckell's mentions, as existing in many estates, "gurkati" chaukies established for the collection of *forest* revenue. In another letter, too, the collector states it as a well-known fact that "cultivation everywhere, in every district, had decreased since 1179 (1772), and there was a difficulty then (1790), which there was not before, in collecting the rents from the ryots." (C. 13-12-90; 27-12-86; 26-3-90; 5-3-92.)

16. There is, I think, no doubt that all this was the direct and the necessary result of the annual settlement system. To make full inquiry each year was impossible, and the settlements were made on admittedly imperfect data. The power was on the side of the collector, and where the data were imperfect, he was too apt to interpret them in his own favour. The zemindar not only began in 1179 (1772) with a very high assessment, but we can easily understand that the collector would only on the strongest grounds ever admit a decrease, and always was ready, where he had only slight grounds, to demand an increase. The annual revenue being, in fact, fixed on each zemindar without any detailed assessment, but rather by a sort of haggling between the collector and the zemindars, the latter must go to the wall. That the zemindars did go to the wall, and that they were irretrievably plunged in debt, is a fact, as we shall see hereafter.

The result of annual settlements.

17. It might be thought that the zemindar, if he found his assessment too high, could simply refuse to settle and allow the collector to settle with a farmer. Apart from the consideration that this would not remedy matters so far as regarded the ryot, I have to observe that the zemindar could hardly, without incurring great loss, refuse the settlement, however high it was; for, by being ousted, he parted with one great source of his profit—irregular collections. We have seen, too, in the case of Muhammadshahi, that the zemindar, even after being ousted, was held responsible for the shortcomings of the farmer, and was called on to pay up the latter's arrears; and this, though perhaps an extreme instance, shews the ideas according to which matters were then managed. Besides this, a zemindar would always rather incur a loss than see his zemindari in another's hands; and this tendency, observed even now, must have been still more strong before the permanent settlement, when, according to native ideas, a zemindar was held in very high honour, and

yet in law had a most indeterminate position—a position which might be endangered by an act resembling relinquishment.

18. The unsettled state of affairs must have produced, and did pro-
Want of security, and its results. duce, the worst consequences. Neither zemindar nor ryot had any assured position. The act of a collector, or the order of Government, could entirely change the position of affairs; no standard had been established, but, as must have been seen from instances that have come under our observation, the opinion of Government was the chief source of executive action. And Government had, it must be acknowledged, given the zemindars little encouragement to rely on its generosity: it had acted far too much in the character of a landlord determined to get the utmost out of his lands.

19. The zemindars, therefore, uncertain of to-morrow, and having little enough for to-day, fell back on the ryots and determined to get the utmost out of them; they were pinched in their turn, and progress of any sort was rendered impossible. No ryot would improve his land or extend his cultivation when he knew that the zemindar would at once demand all the advantage that might accrue; and no zemindar would attempt improvement of his estate when he knew the certain result would be an increased demand, and an *indeterminately* increased demand, on the part of the collector. The mutual distrust between Government, zemindar, and ryot—the natural consequence of an annual settlement system, especially where no principles were laid down as a basis to work upon—barred all progress, and a remedy was loudly called for.

20. It may be said that the system was no new one introduced by
How far the English system was responsible the English, but one handed down from generation to generation. But the truth is that the English added to the native system precisely those elements which produced all the evil; namely, watchfulness to seize any opportunity for new demands and power to enforce the demands they made. Under the native Government the power was in the zemindar's hands, and he no doubt easily retained sufficient for himself: and when a zemindar is his own master, he usually places somewhere a limit to his oppressions on his ryots. But when the British came, they began by increasing the revenue by the 1772 assessment; and while they made the zemindar more than ever dependent for his revenue upon the excessive exercise of his power, they set it before them as one of the objects of their administration to limit and control that very exercise of power on which the zemindar had to depend. (C. 18-1-90.)

XXI.—*The Permanent Settlement.*—1790.

IT may appear strange that after so many years of settlements it should still have remained in doubt whether the forthcoming decennial settlement ought to be made with the ryots or with the zemindars. But really the question had never yet come up for decision. For each previous settlement the assets of the estate were estimated, and the zemindar, retaining as his reward the produce of his rent-free lands, and a "suitable" but not accurately defined allowance, handed over the whole to the Government. There was no margin to be distributed, as the assets were estimated year by year, and it was only when a settlement for a period of years was about, as it was hoped, to create an excess of assets over the Government demand, that it became necessary to consider beforehand whether this margin should be considered the property of the ryot or of the zemindar.

Settlement with ryot or with zemindar.

2. In the end it was decided that the settlement should be made with the zemindars, they being bound in their turn to make a similar settlement with their then existing ryots. Thus the profits from extension of cultivation and from the settlement of new ryots would fall to the zemindar, while the profits from the improvement of each ryot's holding would be obtained by the ryot himself. The detailed orders for the settlement were issued in 1790, and are now grouped together in Regulation VIII, 1793. (G. 10-2-90; 25-6-90.)

A mixed plan adopted.

3. A year before the settlement came on, viz. on the 14th October 1789, Mr. Henckell had left the district to become collector, judge, and magistrate of the larger district of Rajshahye, and Mr. Richard Rocke, his assistant, was his successor. On him therefore fell the duty of making the settlements.

Mr. Rocke, collector.

4. The permanent settlement involved a good deal more than a mere settlement of the revenue to be paid by zemindars. First of all the zemindar's allowance was settled. It had been indeterminate before—a "suitable competency;" and now it was decided to give them ten per cent., that is, not ten per cent. of the assets, but only ten per cent. of the Government share, which left them only one-eleventh in all. The first orders had

Proprietary allowance settled.

directed five per cent., and when Mr. Rooke submitted his first settlement proposition, he allowed only five per cent. "He was reluctant," he said, "to spend so much revenue on them," as the later orders required; but of course the Board directed him to give the ten per cent. (G. O. 10-2-90; 25-6-90. B. 31-1-91. C. 25-2-91.)

5. Before this ten per cent. was calculated, however, all those non-revenue-paying lands the profits of which under the old system were enjoyed by the zemindars were resumed and grouped up with the rest of the estate. A reservation was made in favour of lands dedicated solely to religious purposes, but this reservation was very narrowly construed. For example, one of the ranis of Muhammadshahi had devoted one of these religious grants to the payment of her debts, and so the Board directed its inclusion in the ordinary assets, though they awarded her a little compensation by giving her Rs. 3,000 a year with which to maintain her position. So also there was a long correspondence between the collector and the Board about the revenue to be fixed on the Isafpur estate; the question being simply whether certain lands and allowances given by the raja for the worship of idols should or should not be included within the assets of the estate. The raja's assessment, as it was finally made, included as assets Rs. 13,674, which the raja spent on temple service. This was included because it was a *money* grant; but had the raja devoted to the temples, not that sum of money, but lands yielding as much in the form of revenue, the grant would not have been considered an asset in the calculation of the assessment. (C. 12-5-91. B. 24-6-91.)

6. Whether the zemindars, under this new plan, got allowances as great as those they enjoyed under the old system, depends very much upon the extent of the stipendiary lands resumed. The resumptions do not appear to have been very small; and it must be remembered that it was the practice among great families (as indeed it even now is) to retain certain lands as stipendiary lands, not only for the zemindar himself, but also for some of his closest connections: for example, his mother and his wife. These stipendiary lands were now also for the first time included as assets of the zemindars' estates: for example, the calculation of the Isafpur assessment includes Rs. 5,043, the rani's lands. (B. 24-6-91.)

7. Another important change of system consisted in the separation of dependent taluqdars. These, as before explained, were a class of minor zemindars created by, and paying their revenue through the regular zemindars. Some of

them had obtained their taluqs by purchase from the zemindars, and
thus held them at a somewhat low rent, and some of them also appear
to have done something in the way of improving their lands. Being,
therefore, many of them men of some little substance, they were grand
objects for the extortions of the zemindar; and as either the zemindar
or some of his ancestors had granted to them rights which, so far as they
went, were in opposition to the zemindar's own rights, they were particularly obnoxious to the zemindars. We have already, in the case of
Muhammadshahi, seen instances of the manner in which the taluqdars
were treated by the zemindars; and in consequence of the bad treatment
they received generally, the Government ordered that they should be
separated; that is, instead of paying their revenue to the zemindar,
to be included in the assets of his estate, they should pay it direct
to Government, and be placed on the footing of other zemindars.
(G. 6-7-90. C. 13-12-90.)

8. A number of taluqdars were bound by their engagements to
pay revenue through the zemindars only, and these, it was held, were not
entitled to separation. But it was directed that their rent, and its
future increase, should be accurately laid down, so that exaction in future
might be prevented. (B. 6-8-90.)

9. These orders were received with great joy by the taluqdars, and
not only were many separated taluqs settled along with the decennial
settlement of the rest of the district, but even after that the taluqdars
frequently came forward and got the collector to separate their taluqs.
The zemindars opposed the separation as far as they could, and occasionally (especially about 1802-03) made complaints against the collector
when he granted it. .It must be said, however, that, apart from the
lost opportunity of exaction, the zemindars suffered a direct loss by the
separations, as they ceased to obtain from the taluqdars such items as
kharcha (expenditure cess) and salámi (the present a dependent makes
to his superior). (C. 13-12-90; 5-7-91; 7-9-91.)

10. The abolition of the sayar duties was another great change

Abolition of sayar duties.

effected at the same time. These were duties
levied at háts or markets upon the goods brought
there for sale. The duties were of two sorts: first, "chandni," which
meant the sum paid for the occupation of a place in the hát; and second,
"tolahs," or rates paid upon the various articles, partly going to the
proprietor, partly to the maintenance of the daroga or keeper of the hát,
the "jarubkash" or sweeper, and the caller of the hát. These taxes the

Government determined to abolish as prejudicial to the interests of trade ; payments for permanent occupation of land on the hâts, being of a different nature, were alone to be retained. (G. 28-7-90 ; 6-8-90. C. 24-6-90.)

- 11. These sayar collections were just as much part of the revenue of the zemindars as their rent collections from their ryots; and upon the principle which Government laid down for itself, one-eleventh part of them was the property of the zemindar and ten-elevenths was what he had to pay to the State as its share.

The Government therefore reduced their demand upon the zemindar by the ten-elevenths of the sayar collections which otherwise would have formed part of it ; and, by way of compensating the zemindars for the one-eleventh which they were prohibited from collecting for themselves, they made a further deduction equal to this one-eleventh, a procedure which of course was tantamount to putting the sum into the zemindars' pocket and reimbursing to them the whole loss they sustained.

12. The zemindars of course consented to receiving these deductions, The zemindars continued but they did not, for all that, cease to collect the to collect it. sayar duties. The policy of Government was not carried out, and the result was not an abolition of the sayar duties, but simply a handing over to the zemindars of the entire amount of them. They continued to collect them, and appropriated not only their own share (for the loss of which they had received compensation from Government), but also the share which belonged to Government. The collector reported in 1798 that the sellers in the hâts still voluntarily paid it, and it is notorious that now-a-days the collections in the hâts form a most valuable part of the zemindar's revenue, albeit they are not only not included in their settlements, but expressly against the conditions of them. (C. 22-9-98.)

13. The amount of revenue in Jessore which was thus lost to Government without any advantage was about Rs. 10,000 or Rs. 12,000. In Muhammadshahi alone there was a net collection of Rs. 4,371, and in the Isafpur zemindari there was Rs. 4,493. (C. 13-12-90.)

14. Apart from these and a few other modificatory circumstances to be presently noticed, the basis of the settlement was the settlement of the previous year. In all but the largest estates the collector's calcu-Settlements were at high lations, so framed, were accepted. In the case of rate. the largest estates the Board went into details and somewhat modified them. That the terms were not very favorable

to the zemindars, will be seen from the figures of the settlements of the
large estates. Isafpur was settled at Rs. 3,02,372, about Rs. 5,000
more than the demand of the previous year (taking sayar deductions
into account). The Saydpur estate was made to pay Rs. 90,583,
or Rs. 2,000 more than the previous year. Muhammadshahi, four-fifths
share, an estate which had been almost ruined, as before described,
had its revenue increased from Rs. 1,34,665 to Rs. 1,37,697, and a
further increase of Rs. 12,634 in five yearly additions was to accrue
to this demand. The one-fifth share obtained better terms, for whereas
its revenue in 1789-90 was Rs. 50,737, that for 1790-91 was to be
Rs. 46,642, and Rs. 1,750 was to be added by increments extending
over five years. (C. 13-12-90. B. 10-10-91.)

15. Some of the zemindars fought hard for a reduction of the
terms first proposed, the zemindar of Isafpur especially; but finally
almost every one of them accepted the terms which the collector and
the Board in the end determined upon. They appear to have had
little idea of the rigour with which the terms were to be enforced,
and probably thought that the old hand-to-mouth system, by which
they paid up only when the collector's dunning drove them to it, and
in which it was a matter of no great consequence to be half a year in
arrear, would still apply to the new settlement. Such was not, however,
the system now to be introduced; and the zemindars, as we shall see, in
accepting the settlements, set the seal to their own ruin.

16. The permanent settlement, it will be observed, was based
partly upon knowledge of the details of the zemindari accounts. This knowledge was preserved by
the kanungo officers. These kanungoes were officers deputed on the
part of the ruling power to the offices of the zemindaris. Their duty
was to authenticate transfers and leases, and to see that the zemindari
accounts (the basis of the various settlements) were truly and properly
kept. According to a very ancient custom, they were paid by a sort of
cess called "nim-taki" or "pao-taki," according as it was half or quarter
per cent. of the collections. Besides the kanungoes at the sudder office
of the zemindari, there were similar subordinate officers at the mofussil
cutcherries, but these were paid either in cash or by a piece of land by
the zemindars. Some of the zemindars did not like this supervision,
and did what they could to oppose the kanungoes; but some of them,
for their own sakes, liked to have one as a check upon their own amla.
The raja zemindar of Isafpur, for example, actually applied that a

kanungo might be appointed to watch over the transactions in his own office, so little confidence had he in his servants. (C. 15-12-90; 13-12-90.)

17. When the settlement was made, the kanungoes' allowances were included in the assets of the estate, and they were in future to be paid from the Government revenue office. After a short time, however, the kanungo system either died away or was formally abolished—the natural consequence of the relinquishment by Government of all interference in details, and the creation, by the terms of the permanent settlement, of an absolute proprietorship in the zemindars. (C. 15-12-90.)

18. One other matter peculiar to Jessore had to be dealt with. The Boho Begam's allowances. During the Mussulman rule the Nawab had granted to the Boho Begam, one of the Moorshedabad family, the right to levy certain allowances from some of the estates in Jessore. It was partly an allowance in money, and partly an allowance of guards, which had been commuted for a money payment, and the whole amounted to Rs. 6,300, as admitted by those who had to pay it, besides Rs. 2,900 which was disputed by them. The Begam had to collect these amounts by her own officers, and both in consequence of its interference with the regular revenue demands, and in consequence of the misconduct of the officers employed to collect it, the levying of it was the cause of great trouble and disquiet. When the permanent settlement was made, it was ordered that the amount so paid to the Boho Begam should be added to the revenue leviable from the estates, and the Government should hand over the amount, by way of pension, to the Begam. This was done for a few years; but the Begam died in January 1794, and the pension accordingly lapsed to Government. (C. 15-12-86; 13-12-90; 31-7-91; 5-3-92; 30-8-94.)

19. There were certain other allowances that were similarly dealt Zemindari pensions. with, namely, certain pensionary allowances granted by the zemindar. These had formerly been deducted from the assets, but now the deduction was disallowed, and Government took over the burden of the pensions, instituting, however, an inquiry regarding them. (B. 24-8-91. C. 15-5-92.)

· 20. I come now to the last feature of the permanent settlement— Permanent settlement of ryots' holdings. the condition imposed upon zemindars of granting pottas to their ryots, that is, of making a permanent settlement with them. This is a condition which seems to have been entirely forgotten by the zemindars of the present day, who

P

deem it hardship that they should not be allowed to enhance the rent of ryots dating from the permanent settlement; yet the condition is one that is distinctly laid down in the regulations, though it is not said in so many words that the rent fixed by the pottas was to be unalterable. We have seen, however, how the condition arose, namely, that the Government at first half-intended to make a permanent settlement direct with the ryots, but subsequently altered its intention and devolved this duty upon the zemindars. And to enable them to carry it out on the same terms as the Government itself acted upon in dealing with the zemindars, the regulations gave to the zemindars the liberty of revising their rent-roll, even in respect of persons holding on fixed terms, *i.e.*, mukararidars and others. (Reg. VIII, 1793. G. 23-11-91. B. 23-7-92.)

21. That this was the intended interpretation of the then rules, I shall further shew by quoting certain declarations of Government. On 17th September 1792, a date subsequent to the promulgation of the settlement, a general order of Government encouraged the ryots to undertake the cultivation of sugarcane. Very high prices were then ruling, and Government impressed upon the ryots the profit they might make from it. The order distinctly declared that the profits that arose from the introduction of this cultivation should go to the ryots, and the zemindars were not permitted to enhance the rents on account of it. Again, when in 1804 several zemindars were desirous of revising the holdings of their ryots, and making new contracts with them, they were informed by the collector that they could not annul the previous settlement unless they could shew that it was brought about by fraud, or was made at rates which were improperly low according to the then standard. The very object of the regulations was, as the collector said, to guard the ryots from demands of this nature. Again, when a dispute arose between the collector and the judge, whether the former had liberty, under the regulations, to re-settle, at new rates, the lands of fixed tenure-holders in Bhusna, the Government, to whom the matter was referred by the collector, declared that the collector had that power, and that fixed tenures were, under the regulations, revisable. The Board had declared a somewhat similar opinion at an earlier date. (C. 5-5-04. G. 3-11-97. B. 17-10-91.)

22. The order was that the pottas should be given before the end of 1198 (April 1792), and after the time was up the Board called for a report as to whether their intentions had been carried out or not. Mr. Rooke said that though

Pottas had to be given.

many zemindars had given pottas to their ryots, there were some,

Difficulties in the way. especially the larger zemindars, who found it impossible to carry out the order in consequence of the peculiar system on which they managed their lands. The ryots mostly held under a farmer or gantidar, who was bound to pay a fixed sum to the zemindar, and it was the farmer or gantidar, and not the ryot, who was borne upon the zemindar's books.

23. Now, the farmer or gantidar had no regular rates, and no regular amount of land under cultivation, so that he could not get a potta specifying his rates or his quantity of land. The farmer collected the rents from the ryots who remained (hazira), and re-settled the lands of such as ran away (ferari), and it was the farmer also who disposed of unappropriated lands. The zemindar had nothing to do with the ryots' contracts, but always, whatever the actual state of the land, or whatever the amount paid by the ryots, shewed an unvarying sum, viz. the farmer's rent, in his books. In these cases it was clearly impossible for the zemindar to give pottas to the ryots. There were also, however, upon these estates, ryots who paid their rents direct to the zemindar, and it does not appear from Mr. Rooke's report that they got pottas. Of the ancient ryots—the persons whose tenure it was the chief object of this part of the regulations to revise and permanently settle—Mr. Rooke remarks that they do not hold upon a potta, but get an adjustment paper at the end of the year. His meaning I conceive to be that their not getting pottas under the new regulations was of less consequence on that account. (B. 23-7-92. C. 12-1-93.)

24. The Board, in their orders upon this report, directed that in

Not actually carried out. cases where the ryots paid through a farmer, the farmer and the zemindar should measure the ryots' lands, and that according to that measurement the farmer should give a potta to the ryot, valid for the period during which he should retain the farm. It is extremely doubtful whether this was ever carried out. When the collector, a few years later, took charge of the Bhusna estate, he found that no re-settlement had been made with the ryots; and he found also that the ryots were unwilling to receive pottas, as they considered they thereby lowered the nature of their tenures, which were founded, not upon document, but upon ancient custom. I conceive that a ryot would still more strongly object to receive a potta valid for a period only from a farmer. No attention was paid to the subject after this last-quoted order of the Board; and from this fact, and from the fact that no notice is anywhere taken of the difficulties and disputes which would have attended a general re-settlement with the ryots (except in the case of Bhusna, where the collector himself undertook the re-settlement), I conclude that the provisions of the permanent settlement code, so far as they regarded settlement between zemindar and ryot, remained almost a dead letter. (B. 19-6-93. Com., Bhusna, 16-10-97. C. 21-1-99.)

XXII.—State of Things Following the Permanent Settlement.—1791-1802.

I TOOK Muhammadshahi as a type of the evils which had to be dealt with prior to the permanent settlement, and I now take Bhusna as the type of the evils that had to be dealt with after it. This estate was a large part of the great zemindari of Rajshahye, and though not in Jessore at the time of the settlement, was added to it in the beginning of 1793. It comprised the greater part of the present Furreedpore district, together with pergunnah Naldi (including Sator), in Jessore. Its assessment, apart from separated taluqs, was Rs. 3,20,000 or 3,30,000. (G. 11-1-93. C. 21-5-93 ; — 1-96.)

Bhusna an example.

2. Two years after this the estate was very seriously in arrear, so that the Board placed the whole estate under attachment, with a view to its sale, and appointed a special officer, with collector's powers, to manage the matter. This arrangement, however, was set aside for some reason or other after a very short time, and nothing was then sold of the estate. (B. 14-4-95 ; 17-4-95 ; 22-8-95.)

It falls in arrear.

3. The arrear was partly the result of bad management, but for the most part it arose from the opposition made by the ryots to the zemindar and his farmer. The greater part of Bhusna was held by a class of ryots called jotdars, who occupied pretty much the same position that gantidars did on the west of the district. They had obtained their tenures on very inadequate rents, partly, no doubt, from having received the land at a time when, by inundation or through oppression, it was very much depreciated in value, but mostly through the collusion of the zemindar's amla and the farmers. Acquiring, through their wealth, a certain amount of power, they could easily obtain the rents due to them by the ryots who were settled within their tenures ; but they seized upon any excuse for

Recusancy of the jotdars.

not discharging their own rents (a recusancy for which they are still notorious), and, above all, they made the most strenuous objections to having their rental revised and increased under the terms of the permanent settlement. (Com., Bhusna, 21-6-97; 16-10-97; 16-1-98.)

4. Kalisankar Ray, the ancestor of the Naral family, whom we have seen, ten years before, involved in proceedings on the criminal side, had purchased from the raja of Nattore the pergunnah Telihâti, and was farmer under the raja of the rest of Bhusna. His farm commenced with 1200 (April 1793), and he proceeded at once to enhance the rents of the tenures. The rent-roll was at first Rs. 3,24,000, hardly sufficient to meet the assessment (which had, of course, been calculated on the theory that the rental could be and would be increased). Kalisankar increased it the first year to Rs. 3,48,000, and, by taking very strong measures (violence and oppression, as they were called by the commissioner), he succeeded in realizing it in spite of the opposition made by the jotdars. Next year, 1201 (1794-95), his demand was Rs. 3,88,000; but the opposition had now become too strong for him. Some ryots led the way by making formal complaint of excess demand, and obtained in the court a decree authorizing them to a refund of three times the amount taken, and this success greatly encouraged the opposition. Then a charge of murder—apparently an ill-founded one—was brought against the farmer, and though he got off in the end, he had been four months in confinement, during which time all operations upon his side were stopped. When he came out of jail, about April or May 1795, the opposition had become so strong that he hardly got in any collections. (Com., Bhusna, 21-6-97; 16-10-97; 16-1-98. C. 10-3-95.)

5. It is at this time (April 1795) that, as just stated, the estate was so very heavily in arrear, and it will be seen it had very little chance of recovery. The raja had, no doubt, made over the estate in farm to Kalisankar, in the hope that he would be able by strong management to preserve it; but his power was now broken, and nothing was to be hoped for in this way. The raja was himself a thoroughly bad manager; he dissipated his whole wealth and spent his whole time in religious exercises, and let people do what they liked with his estates so long as he could get money for his devotions. Such at least is his character as it is handed down in the district. Apart from Kalisankar's management, therefore, he had no resource; and unless Kalisankar managed to collect the revenue and pay up the assessment, the estate must go. But one device was left, and that was tried.

Devices to save the estate.

About December 1795 the raja transferred his property in Bhusna to his minor son, Bishnanath, and the estate, becoming thus the property of a minor, had to come under the management of the court of wards, and would therefore, according to law, be ordinarily exempted from sale for arrears. Bhusna was not the only instance where this trick was brought into operation. (Cunningham, collector, charge letter, 2-7-96.)

6. At the same time that this transfer was made, a secret deed was executed by the raja to Kalisankar, by which the raja suspended, till Jeyt 1203 (June 1796), the demand upon Kalisankar for Rs. 50,000 of the rent then due by the latter. The object of this was, no doubt, to enable Kalisankar to keep the collector for six months from realizing that amount of money, though it was already due from the estate; for the collector, now that the estate was brought under the court of wards, collected the revenue of the estate from the farmer, and met the Government demand out of his collections. As it turned out, however, Kalisankar was able by this document to gain even greater advantage than this.

7. The above deed was not yet known, and the collector had not yet become acquainted with Kalisankar. So when he had to appoint a manager for the estate just come under the court of wards, he appointed Ram Narayn Ray, Kalisankar's son. This was an injudicious appointment; for, as Kalisankar still remained farmer, it was not likely that Ram Narayn would perform with zeal his duty of demanding from his own father punctual payment of his rent, now so much in arrear. When, therefore, Kalisankar's payments were falling still more behindhand, the collector proposed to imprison him as a defaulter, but Ram Narayn managed to throw obstacles in the way, and this was not done. Ram Narayn also helped to conceal the secret deed, the ignorance of which led the collector to believe that the zemindar had already collected the money before he transferred the estate. Finally, he was suspected of misappropriating money belonging to the estate, and was removed from the managership in April or May 1796, only two or three months after he got it, being superseded by a man whose chief recommendation was that he was a deadly enemy to Kalisankar. (C. 18-1-96; 9-4-96; 24-5-96. B. 1-4-96.)

Estate under court of wards.

8. For the year 1202, expiring in April 1796, Kalisankar owed the estate Rs. 55,000, and after two or three months he had run up an additional debt of Rs. 43,000 for the year 1203. The collector therefore imprisoned him as

Estate in arrear—the farmer imprisoned.

a defaulter, and the Board subsequently cancelled his lease, appointing a sazawal or manager to collect the revenues from the ryots and under-farmers. The collector attributed Kalisankar's failure to thorough dishonesty, and he applies some very bad language to him. But what the commissioner of Bhusna subsequently found, proves that there was much truth in Kalisankar's own plea, that the ryots would not pay him. (C. 13-8-96; 30-8-96; 7-9-96. B. 4-11-96. C. 23-12-96.)

9. It must be remembered that there were two totally distinct Difficulties in collecting debts now under management by the collector; rent. namely, the debt due to Government by the estate on account of its assessment, and the debt due to the estate by Kali-sankar, and, after the cancelment of his farm, by the ryots. That part of the first debt (that due to Government on account of assessment) which had accrued before the transfer of the estate to the minor and the interference of the court of wards was realizable by sale of the zemindar's property, and it was partly recovered by sale held in June 1796; but that part of the Government demand which accrued after the estate came under the court of wards could be realized only by recovering from Kalisankar and the ryots the rent they owed to the estate. This it was found most difficult—almost impossible—to realize. Kalisankar made away with, or concealed, his movable property, and certain forms had to be gone through before his immovable could be brought to sale; nothing therefore could in the meantime be got out of him: and as for the ryots, we shall presently see what it was that prevented collections being made from them. (C. 7-6-96.)

10. Besides this, the Government were guilty of a piece of great mismanagement in adjusting the demands upon the estate and upon the farmer. They declared that the zemindar would be held responsible, not for the whole amount of the *assessment* due up to the date of the transfer, but for the amount of his collections up to that date less expenses and proprietary allowance. From that date up till 27th June 1796, when the sale had changed the circumstances of his farm, Kalisankar was to be liable according to the conditions of his farm, and after that date Kalisankar was to be liable for his gross collections less reasonable expenses. This would have suited very well had the first part of the demand, viz. that upon the zemindar, produced a sum equal to the assessment upon his estate; but, unfortunately, his collections were so far behindhand, that a demand calculated upon the basis of these collec-tions could not produce an amount approaching that of the Government

revenue due upon the estate. The collector pointed out to the Board
the deficiency that would result from their method of calculation,
but the Board did not see it, and reprimanded him for objecting. The
commissioner of Bhusna also urged the same points, but was told by the
Governor General that his views were "obviously objectionable." The
Board found out the mistake soon enough, when they came to put their
demands in force, and found themselves, as shall presently be described,
checkmated by the 50,000 rupees document already alluded to.
(G. 29-7-96; 2-12-96. C. B. 21-6-97; 16-7-97. B. 13-1-97.)

11. When Kalisankar's farm was cancelled, and the court of
wards undertook direct collections from the ryots
through a sazawal or collector, they might have
realized part of the debt due from Kalisankar by collecting the
accumulated arrears due by the ryots to Kalisankar. But in this also the
collector altogether failed; no papers could be got from Kalisankar and
the under-farmers, and the collector was quite at sea, knowing neither
the demand nor the arrear.

Failure of attempt to collect direct.

12. At last, in May 1797, after nearly a year had passed without
getting in any money, Mr. Ernst was appointed
commissioner of Bhusna (a new and special office),
with powers to settle and act in the whole matter. He began by
restoring the old amla, whose knowledge of affairs enabled him to work
on some basis, and he put out a proclamation stating that he would
abolish the whole of Kalisankar's second increase of rent and half of
his first. Even then the jotdars would not come forward to settle; but
by dispossessing a few of the refractory chief ones, and by a general
distribution of threats and entreaties, he succeeded in settling the
pergunnah. But with all his tact the opposition very nearly overcame
him too. His strongest means of compulsion was threat of dispossession, and this worked very well until, in November 1797, some of the
ryots brought it to the test in the civil court, and found that the judge
held the ryots could not be dispossessed by Mr. Ernst unless he first
shewed his title to do so in each case. With 2,000 jotdars to deal
with, this simply forbade dispossession. Mr. Ernst held that he was
entitled to revise the settlements of the jotdars, and that involved
dispossessing them when they refused fair terms; and in this opinion the
Board and the Government upheld him. But the judge, Mr. Parr,
practically held that the jotdars were entitled to hold on at their old rates.
Then the ryots naturally had no objection to continue the previous

A special commissioner appointed.

disordered state of things, since it saved them the trouble of paying rent. They beat Mr. Ernst's peons when they went to collect rent; they refused rent as long as they could; they brought frivolous cases against Mr. Ernst's amla, and were continually citing them as witnesses to the courts. However, after some time, and with much trouble, Mr. Ernst managed to settle everything, and the jotdars consented to the slight increase he demanded, merely stipulating that it should be entered separately in their pottas. The whole revenue as fixed in this settlement was Rs. 3,27,800, allowing a Government assessment of Rs. 2,84,118, and a zemindar's allowance—*provided he could collect it all*—of Rs. 26,654. (Commissioner, Bhusna, 21-6-97; 16-10-97; 16-1-98. G. 3-11-97.)

13. We have now to see what was done about collecting the arrears; and first those due by Kalisankar. First of all, a summary inquiry was held under Regulation XXXV of 1795, while Kalisankar was yet in custody. In this he first brought forward the 50,000 rupees document, and obtained a deduction to that extent from the calculated debt. For the Rs. 50,000 remission had been granted by changing it into the form of a personal debt due by Kalisankar to the zemindar, and therefore it could not be realized from Kalisankar by the Board, who succeeded to the possession of the estate only after the debt had accrued to the zemindar. The Board therefore found themselves by their own mismanagement cheated out of Rs. 50,000. They could not get it from the farmer, and they had already determined to hold the zemindar responsible only so far as he had actually made collections, so that they could not get it from him either. (B. 26-9-97.)

Great difficulty in recovering by legal means.

14. The rest of the arrear was however decreed against Kalisankar, but he appealed the case to the judge, and the judge ordered his release from confinement on security (the raja of Nattore becoming his security) pending decision. There was something wrong in the form of the case which led the Board to imagine the appeal would go against them; and, besides, the case was only a summary one, which enabled the debtor to be imprisoned, but did not help the Board towards selling his property. They therefore determined to withdraw the case and institute a regular suit; but before they did so, the judge had rejected the appeal as inadmissible. Kalisankar, meantime, released by the judge, went off to Calcutta, to be out of the jurisdiction, and made away with his property, transferring Telihâti to his son and concealing the rest. When process was sent out to obtain his re-arrest, he had gone to Serampore,

Q

and it was found that process under Regulation XXXV of 1795 could not be served there. A short time after also Raja Ram Krishna, his security, died; so that Kalisankar was practically free, and the collector was not a bit nearer realization than before. (C. 17-9-97 ; 16-3-98.)

15. The collector had meantime attached Kalisankar's property, Telihâti, refusing to recognize the fraudulent transfer he had made to his son. The son had been trying to entrap the collector into a recognition by giving in accounts and paying in arrears in his own name, but had failed to gain his object. (C. 9-2-98.)

16. A regular suit was now brought against Kalisankar by the Board, but the suit was dismissed, on the ground that the minor zemindar had attained his majority, and though he had not taken over charge of the estate, he alone was competent to sue for arrears of rent; so a suit was again brought, this time making the zemindar a party, and at length, in September 1799, a decree was obtained for Rs. 62,000 and costs. The zemindar had caused much delay by refusing to act in the matter with the Government. (Commissioner, Bhusna, 8-4-98. G. 11-6-98. C. 17-7-99 ; 26-9-99.)

17. Some difficulty was experienced in getting hold of Kalisankar, but he was arrested about the middle of 1800 and put in confinement under the decree. He made several petitions from the jail, alleging his inability to meet the debt and offering partial payment. Telihâti was either suffered to fall in arrear and be sold up, or, at all events, the collector was afraid to, or did not sell it to pay Kalisankar's debt. He made occasional inquiries about Kalisankar's alleged benami property, but came to the conclusion that he had not any. The Government, however, refused for a long time to remit, as Kalisankar desired, either interest or costs, but finally, after Kalisankar had been imprisoned for more than four years, allowed him to be released on his paying down Rs. 10,000 and engaging with five securities to pay the rest of the principal (Rs. 35,450) by instalments. The interest was remitted, but Government apparently still held Kalisankar responsible for the costs. The instalment bond appears to have been honestly discharged. (C. 22-8-02. B. 16-11-02. C. 4-8-03 ; 5-7-04 ; 22-10-04 ; 22-11-04. B. 3-12-04. C. 1-12-08.)

The farmer, after some years' litigation, is imprisoned and made to pay up.

18. We come to see what means were taken to realize the rents due and accruing to the estate from the ryots. Mr. Ernst had settled Bhusna, in that he had given the ryots and jotdars pottas specifying their rent; but he apparently found

The ryots refuse to pay, and cannot be made to.

the greatest difficulty in inducing the ryots to pay their rents. A few months after the settlement he had already suits for Rs. 1,00,000 of arrears due by various ryots, who, as we have said, avoided by every means in their power the payment of their debts. He had power under the law to distrain, but that was useless, as he could never find anything to distrain, and he was met by forcible opposition. The law was, in fact, quite inadequate. All that the zemindar could do—all that even the collector could do—was to bring suits against the ryots, and these suits were so numerous that great delay occurred in disposing of them. But what sort of remedy was a suit? The zemindar had to pay much money to carry it on, and it was a chance if he got the money back; the suits naturally took some time and the ryot gained his object by gaining delay. And it was one thing to get a decree, another to execute it. The ryot got out of the way, removed his property, and even combined with others to forcibly resist the execution. In short, if the ryots banded together to keep the zemindar out of his money, forcing him to bring suits against them by hundreds as his only remedy, they could postpone almost indefinitely the payment of their rent. (C. B. 14-4-98; 13-6-98. C. 21-1-99; 2-4-98.)

19. Mr. Ernst accordingly found himself laden with a mass of suits against his ryots. The ryots, bent on opposition, denied their engagements, and Mr. Ernst had to prove them—a task of great difficulty when there were so many; and even then he did not gain his full object, for the judge held the increase, which was separately specified on the jotdar's engagements, to be an "abwab" or cess, and refused to decree it. The witnesses also could not be got at—another difficulty. Mr. Ernst, however, obtained in the end a lot of decrees; but the delay in obtaining them, and the difficulty in executing them, were ruinous to the estate. When, in February 1799, he handed over the management to the collector, he handed over decrees aggregating Rs. 84,000, and about a hundred current suits, aggregating Rs. 45,000 more; but the collector declared that the decrees were of no use, and could not be enforced. (J. 3-11-97. C. 6-5-99; 15-4-00.)

20. The judge (Mr. Melvill) had, at Mr. Ernst's request, put out a sort of proclamation that he would execute decrees against defaulters in Bhusna by dispossessing them of their tenures. The sudder court, whom he informed of it, told him his law was bad and the jotdars could not be dispossessed. Mr. Melvill argued they could, on the ground that though there was no specific provision of law to the effect that ryots

might be dispossessed in case of non-payment, yet such was the law as to zemindars, and the custom of the country applied it to ryots also: moreover, the laws specially spoke of their retaining possession *so long as they paid rent*. But dispossession even was not a sufficient means of execution, for the lands in the various tenures were so scattered, that none but the ryots themselves knew them, and though the first tenant might be formally dispossessed, a second tenant could not be put in possession. (J. 30-7-98; 31-8-98. Sud. Ct. 22-8-98.)

21. We therefore find these ryots' and jotdars' arrears outstanding for a very long time. In February 1799, we have already said, there were Rs. 1,29,000 outstanding, decreed or being sued for. In 1804 the collector writes of several of the Bhusna defaulters of 1797-98 being still in jail, though many had been arranged with. There were 3,471 defaulters in all, and very little was realizable. In 1809 there were still Rs. 92,701 of the arrears of Mr. Ernst's time due, most of it perfectly unrealizable. (C. 20-6-04; 3-12-04; 15-8-09. B. 2-3-11.)

22. The zemindar had come of age in the latter half of 1797, but,

The zemindar refuses to receive back the estate.

as Mr. Ernst was then engaged in settling the estate, the Government continued, with the zemindar's consent, to manage till the end of the year (*i.e.*, till April 1798). But when that time came, the zemindar refused to receive the estate, as the Government had themselves proved it to be impossible to realize from it anything equal to the assessment. I do not find, in fact, any notice of his having received back charge of the estate at all; but as the Board held the estate to be responsible for its revenue, whether he took charge of it or not, they proceeded to sell it up piecemeal for the arrears that had accrued

The estate is completely sold up.

upon it through their being themselves unable, by realization from the ryots, to meet the assessment. One large slice of it had already gone in June 1796, a sale on account of arrears which had accrued before the transfer to the minor, and Telihâti had been already privately sold.

The following sales for arrears due on Bhusna took place in 1799 :

Pergunnah.	Assessment. Rs.	Date of sale.	Purchaser.
Haveli ...	32,613 ...	15-2-1799 ...	Ram Nath Ray
Mokimpur ...	25,347 ...	25-2-1799 ...	Ditto
Nasibshahi ...	16,937 ...	25-2-1799 ...	Bhairabnath Ray
Sator ...	39,968 ...	28-2-1799 ...	Shibprasad Ray
Naldi ...	66,760 ...	23-3-1799 ...	Bhairabnath Ray

and the smaller parts of it were almost all sold away also in 1799. (G. 13-10-97. Commr., Bhusna, 30-4-98. C. 6-5-99; and towjee books.)

23. The Bhairabnath Ray who bought Naldi was really a pseudonym for Rani Bhawani, the grandmother of the zemindar, who apparently strove in this way to save the family estate, to some small extent at least. Her endeavours were, however, fruitless. Two years later, in March 1801, the pergunnah was again deep in arrears, and was again sold up for arrears and bought by Pran Kishto Singh. (C. 21-3-01; 17-5-02; 9-1-02.)

Again in arrears and again sold.

24. The case of Sator was similar. It was found to be really the property of the zemindar Bishnanath Ray, who had bought it in in another's name. So the Board in 1803 ordered it to be sold up for arrears still due by him. (C. 27-5-03.)

25. Some others of the purchasers fell in arrears and had their estates put up for sale. It was apparently very difficult to find new purchasers, for no one would bid for estates that were such sure sources of ruin; the law being utterly inadequate to enable zemindars to get in their rents and so discharge the Government revenue due on their estates. (C. 18-6-99; 9-7-99.)

XXIII.—*The Ruin of the Old Zemindars.*—1795-1802.

WE have now seen one of the great zemindar families of the district lose all their estates one after another, through no fault of their own, but from causes directly referable to the action of Government. First of all, the assessment fixed at the permanent settlement was too high; it assumed as its basis less the rate which actually existed than the rate up to which the zemindars might increase. But when the zemindars tried to increase, they found the ryots too strong and the law too weak to help them. Next, it assumed the realizability of the entire assets, but the zemindars found it impossible to realize without a system of oppression and violence which not only ruined the estate, but drove the ryots into opposition and made them speedily discover·how weak the law was against them. Next, while the law insisted upon the immediate payment of all the assessments due by the zemindars, it placed in their hands the most insufficient means of collecting their dues. The zemindar was sold up in a moment if he failed to pay his assessment, but if any

Causes of the ruin of estates.

ryot failed to pay him, he had to go through a dilatory, expensive, and by no means certain process of suing the ryot in court and executing a decree against him—that is, if the ryot had not meantime taken advantage of the delay and run away with his money in his pocket.

2. All this we have seen in the history of the Bhusna estate; but it was plain also wherever the collector had to collect from ryots direct. The collector complains on 2nd April 1798 that he finds it most difficult to collect in Government estates; and again, on 21st January 1799, he writes that the ryots refuse to pay and utterly disregard his orders. Suing them is useless, as the expense does not pay; and he urges that he should be vested with powers to imprison defaulters in Government estates. In the same year (13th March) he writes that people are actually refusing to purchase estates when put up for sale, so great is their fear of ruin through the contumacy of the ryots.

3. But besides the contumacy of the ryots, there was another, though a less effective, cause operating to procure the ruin of the old zemindars. The permanent settlement, in declaring the lands to be the property transferable by sale of the zemindars, had made them available to the creditors of the zemindars for the realization of their claims. The zemindars before the settlement were many of them in debt, and now they had occasionally to part with their lands to meet their creditors' demands.

4. We will trace the ruin of some of the families, and first the raja the zemindar of Isafpur. The Raja Srikant Ray had been greatly in debt long before the settlement and the committee of revenue interfered in his affairs in 1784. His debts are thus enumerated in a letter of the judge's: Rs. 9,979 due to his household servants, Rs. 17,376 due on bonds, and Rs. 3,101 miscellaneous; about Rs. 30,000 in all. That the committee of revenue thought fit to interfere in the case of such a small debt, shews how little margin they knew had been allowed to a zemindar whose estates paid a revenue of three lakhs. Three years after this the collector describes the raja as having been reduced "through bad management" to "beggary." From all this it is clear that the raja did not exactly start upon fair terms at the time of the permanent settlement, and could do little to bear up under the hard terms then imposed upon him. (J. 16-7-84. C. 5-1-87.)

The Isafpur estate.

5. The raja's zemindari appeared in the sale list in 1795, but as the debt was somehow paid up in time, the sale did not take place. Again, in February next year, it was in arrear, and in May it was placed under attachment. The

Is sold up.

zemindar himself applied for permission to sell part of his estate privately and thus liquidate the demand, but the Board refused to do that, ordered sale of part, and released the rest from the attachment. Pergunnah Mallai (Assessment 22741) was accordingly sold in November. (B. 14-4-95. C. 10-2-96; 10-5-96. B. 5-7-96.)

6. In the commencement of next year (1797) the raja petitioned the Board, that as some of his property was already gone by sale (Rasulpur Assessment 27649—having been sold by the civil court in 1796 also), and as the rest of it was under attachment by the sheriff at the instance of his creditors, the whole might be sold by the Board, when he would get a better price than in the civil court, and he might thus, after meeting all claims, have something left to him. This, however, was not done, for we find in that year some other large sales of the property :—

Pergunnah.			Assessment. Rs.		Date of sale.	
Rangdia	...	...	7,452	...	11-1-97	For arrears.
Jatia	...	...	44,364	...	24-1-97	Ditto.
Ramchandrapur		...	17,300	...	22-4-97	Ditto.
Chengutia	...	...	19,522	...	14-5-97	Ditto.
Emadpur	...	...	6,428	...	5-9-97	Ditto.
Saydpur	...	...	43,296	...	17-6-97	By civil court, for realization of debt.

Sahosh had also been sold privately in 1796-97, and part of Isafpur had been sold by the sheriff. (C. 31-1-97; 9-8-97; 4-8-97; towjee records.)

7. The raja, now driven apparently to his wit's end, adopted

Fraudulent attempts to raise money.

more objectionable means of making money. He and his brother Gopinath made some private partitions of the remains of the estate, and while the raja sold, or realized money by mortgaging parts of his lands, Gopinath came in to claim that the parts so mortgaged or sold were not the raja's but his, and refused to deliver possession. Then he created taluqs, receiving purchase money; and afterwards refusing possession and collecting the rents direct from the ryots, he caused the taluq to fall in arrear and be sold up. Finally, he transferred his lands to his minor son, expecting thereby to save them from being sold; but, apparently, the Government had now refused to recognize this device. Another plan by which he tried to get money was by suing the Government for a lakh of rupees on account of the resumption, at the time of the settlement, of his briti or stipendiary

lands; but this suit of course he lost. (C. 19-8-97; 9-11-97; 24-10-97; ·
5-7-98; 26-9-98; and 30-11-98.)

8. The rest of the estate was sold up one way or another

The family entirely ruined. in 1798-99, and then the raja died leaving a
widow and a minor son. They had sold up
everything and were reduced to destitution—even their jewels had
gone. So the collector, at the instance of the widow, applied for and
obtained for them a compassionate allowance of Rs. 200 a month.
(C. 2-9-02; 20-2-04.)

9. After enjoying this for four or five years, the widow died in
1807, and Gopinath, the brother, applied that it might be continued.
They had in the meantime been suing, and had gained a decree
against one Durga Charn Mukharjya, the effect of which was to set
aside the sale of a large estate and restore it to the family. But the
case was appealed to England, and so the pension was still required.
The pension was continued with a deduction of Rs. 14, and Rs. 186
continued, up till 1812 at least, to be paid to the family. (C. 9-7-07;
12-7-08; 30-12-11. Bd. 3-1-12.)

10. We come now to trace the fortunes of another family, viz.

The Muhámmadshahi the Naldanga, or Muhammadshahi family. Their
estates. estate was at the time of the permanent settlement already divided into two parts; Raja Gobind Deb Ray having the
smaller share, one-fifth, and Mahendro Deb and Ram Sankar holding
in common the four-fifths share. In 1797 we find Gobind Deb's lands
heavily in arrear and exposed for sale, but for some reason they were
shortly after released. A year later they are in the sheriff's hands, and
he is about to sell them on the part of Gobind Deb's creditors. The

The youngest branch sale, however, did not then take place, for we find
ruined. them in 1800 again put up for sale in the same
way, and this time they were actually sold. (C. 31-5-97; 6-7-97;
16-7-98; 27-8-00; 22-10-00.)

11. The sale had been brought about in this way. Gobind Deb

Partly the result of their had sold to one Gharib-ullah Chaudhri a taluq
own fraud. within the limits of his estate, and Gharib-ullah
was proceeding, in opposition to the zemindar's wishes, to have it
separated. So Gobind Deb colluded with one Rupnarayn Ghos, to
whom he had long owed a lot of money, to get this taluq set aside. He
executed to Rupnarayn a mortgage of all his directly held property, as
well as of the large taluqs that stood in the name of his sons. The

mortgage was made in the name of Baranasi Ghos, Rupnarayn's father, and it was antedated by seven or eight years. The raja, whose sole object in this was to set aside Gharib-ullah's taluq by proving that he had it not in his power to create it, took an agreement from Rupnarayn that he would never actually foreclose the mortgage, but Rupnarayn forsook this agreement and sold up the estate. A relative of his, Pitambar Bosu, bought it, and sold it to one Krishna Mohan Banarjya; and Gobind Deb found himself possessed of nothing but his briti or stipendiary lands, and the religious lands attached to his family. The fraud was not successful so far as regarded Gharib-ullah, for he not only saved his taluq but got it separated next year. Gobind Deb's heir subsequently instituted a suit for the recovery of the estate, but he was cast. (C. 22-10-00. B. 24-11-00; 5-6-01. C. 26-8-01. See S. D. A. Reports, II, p. 18.)

12. Of the larger share of the estate a partition was commenced shortly after the settlement. Ram Sankar desired

The eldest branch sold up.

it, and Mahendra Deb opposed it by all means in his power. The partition in its first form (1794) was rejected by Government, but was afterwards properly done and approved by Government (1796); it is noted, however, at the time of its completion, that both the zemindars were in arrear. Before a year had passed, Mahendra Deb's share had been attached by the sheriff and sold on account of debts due by Mahendra. The purchaser, who was also the creditor, was Radhamohan Banarjya. Even this sale was not without an attempt at fraud, for Mahendra attempted to save his estate by gifting it to his son Anand. (B. 26-9-92; 26-7-94. C. 19-1-96; 30-3-96; 4-8-97; 1-9-97.)

13. Thus two branches of the family lost their estates within ten years of the permanent settlement, and were

The middle branch scarcely saved.

reduced to poverty. The remaining branch (Ram Sankar) with difficulty escaped the same fate; their estate was saved, but only by the interference of the collector. We have seen it in arrear in 1796, and next year it was exposed for sale along with Gobind Deb's, but was released in the same way. Again, the estate is noted in 1799 as being heavily in arrear, and next year it was under attachment by the collector. The zemindar, however, managed to have it released by paying up the debt; but in 1801 we again find it in arrear by Rs. 25,000. Part of this was due to severe losses caused by the inundations of the previous year, and the collector, representing this fact,

R

and representing also that the whole of the rest of the estates of this ancient family had now gone, and only this branch was left, induced the Board to consent to holding over Rs. 10,000 of this debt. The amount was regularly paid up by Ram Sankar as it fell due. (C. 31-3-97; 6-7-97; 4-4-99; 21-7-00; 20-6-01; 11-3-02.)

14. Again, three years later, the collector had to interfere to save the estate. For the raja, to pay up the arrears he owed, had run into debt, and had given his creditors farms in his estate with which in part to repay themselves. These creditor-farmers withheld their rent in the hope that the estate would thus be brought to sale and they might then buy a more permanent interest. Further, there had been a little fraud; for the raja, by way of providing against ultimate sale, which he apparently thought must come sooner or later, had alienated, in the names of servants and relations, certain portions of his estate, attaching to them an inadequate assessment, and by consequence to the remainder an excessive assessment. This time the collector attached the whole of the estate for arrears, but as the arrears were paid up it was released. (C. 3-10-04; 28-10-04; 14-11-04.)

15. I cannot say whether the estate afterwards passed through any more similar difficulties. But zemindaris were by this time beginning to improve, and that fact, together with the death of Ram Sankar, and the consequent assumption of the estate by the court of wards about 1813, finally saved the estate for the family. Ram Sankar's descendants are now the rajas of Naldanga, and the other two branches of the family are in comparative poverty. The sons of Mahendra managed for a time to regain partial possession of their father's estates, for about 1216 (1809) they brought a suit against Radhamohan, the purchaser of the estate, and compromised it by receiving seven annas, while Radhamohan retained nine annas of the estate. After a time, however, they again lost their lands, the Naral family purchasing them. (C. 16-1-13; 30-5-14.)

16. A short glance, in chronological order, of the sales for arrears of the other estates in the district will shew how general was the ruin of the old zemindars. From a letter in 1799 it appears that Belfulya pergunnah had been several times under sale. Hogla had also been sold in 1203 (1796), and it had been bought in the name of a minor, a relation of the previous proprietors. This was a device to save themselves the profits of the estate; for as soon as the estate was brought under the court of

Minor estates equally ruined.

wards, the previous proprietors got themselves appointed managers of the estate, and then of course defaulted with impunity, as the estate could not, being under the court of wards, be sold for arrears. In a letter of 1800, which was probably the height of the difficulties, the collector writes that there were 1,000 estates in arrear. In 1801 Belfulya was again sold, twice over. In fact, as the collector wrote in 1799, in reply to a call from Government, "The landholders were ruined by the insufficiency of the regulations, and there was hardly a single large landholder in Bengal who had not been reduced to ruin through the inefficiency of the regulations affecting the ryots." (C. 15-2-99 ; 11-3-99 ; 21-4-00 ; 13-5-01 ; 15-7-99.)

17. These matters at length pressed themselves upon the attention of Government, and Regulation VII of 1799 was the result. But the mischief was already done, and the new regulation could not give back to the old zemindars the property they had lost; it could only give the new zemindars stability in the estates they had purchased, by giving them greater facilities than the old ones had for realizing their rents. (C. 8-10-99 ; 3-7-00 ; 9-1-02.)

Regulation VII of 1799.

18. Although the ruin of the old zemindars cannot but be looked on as matter for regret, yet it was not without many great advantages to the district. Hampered on every side by debt, they could do nothing for the benefit of their estates, having absolutely no capital to work on. The new purchasers of the large zemindaris were for the most part men of business from Calcutta. They had often, like Radhamohan Banarjya who purchased Muhammadshahi, got their first footing through having lent large sums to the zemindars, and at all events they were men who had by their own exertions amassed some degree of wealth. They had consequently, so early as 1801, acquired the reputation of managing their estates well; they began looking into the old sub-tenures, they extended the cultivation, and ceased to oppress the ryots, from whom alone in the end improvement must begin. In 1802 the collector notices the extension of cultivation, and again in 1811 he writes that there is a general reclamation of waste lands, and that the regulations are now strong enough to ensure a speedy realization of the public dues. The regulation of 1799 had, in fact, so much changed the position of affairs, that whereas the collector and the zemindars had up to that year been continually complaining that they could do nothing with the ryots, the collector wrote in 1800 that he found the ryots absconded

Zemindaris begin to improve.

bodily when pressed by the powers the law had given him. (C. 9-1-02; 15-9-01; 3-7-11; 23-4-00; 5-5-04.)

19. Of all the considerable zemindaris in the district, only two appear to have withstood the ordeal of the first ten years under the permanent settlement. The one was the Saydpur estate, now known as the Trust Estate. It was then in the hands of a Mahomedan lady, and is mentioned as being so very well managed by her, that interference on the part of the court of wards was deemed quite unnecessary. The other estate was Sultanpur, which had been acquired by Kasi Nath Datt in the manner I have before alluded to. At the permanent settlement the collector did not consider himself at liberty to revise the settlement of this estate, as its assessment had been fixed some time before by the Governor General. He consequently allowed the old assessment to remain, although he declared it was inadequate. To this fact the estate no doubt owed its immunity from arrear and from sale. (C. 13-12-90.)

XXIV.—Creation of a New Class of Zemindars.—1795-1802.

WHEN all these large estates began to fall in arrear, it was not the practice to sell up each estate bodily, but only to sell a sufficient quantity of each estate, so that the purchase-money might cover the arrear. In the case of large estates including within their limits several pergunnahs, this was easy enough, as the assessment borne by the large estate was the aggregate of the assessments calculated separately upon the pergunnahs, and thus any single pergunnah might be sold, liable only to the distinct assessment upon it. But in the case of smaller estates it was different. When it became necessary to sell a portion of such an estate, it was specified only as a certain fraction of the whole, and thus the purchaser and the old zemindar became joint proprietors, and their relations were not likely to be very amicable. In some of the large estates, also, specific portions were sometimes sold upon which the assessment had not been separately calculated: they were, in fact, sold subject to assessment to be calculated after sale. This last-mentioned practice, however, was very early found to be a bad one; it was manifestly so so far as regarded the chance of getting a good purchaser, and even when a good purchaser was found, great difficulty was experienced, through the want of proper data, in apportioning the assessment. The Board therefore

The large estates were broken up into portions.

directed that the assessment should in all cases be apportioned before selling any part of an estate. (C. 11-9-97; 18-1-98.)

2. The selling of a specific portion subject to a specific assessment was attended with no difficulty. The portion *Joint-estate system.* sold simply formed a new estate, and the rest of the zemindari was brought on the books in the place of the entire estate thus broken up. But there were difficulties in respect of the other practice, that of selling a non-specific share subject to a share of the entire assessment. In that case no new estate was created, but the old and new proprietors continued to hold jointly the common estate. But they were so far separate that they might separately fall in arrear. If the old zeminder fell in arrear, then another share of his estate was similarly sold up and a new proprietor introduced; if the new zemindar fell in arrear, then a share of his share was sold up and another separate liability created. A confusion of rights threatened, which would cause great insecurity to the revenue; and the collector, when in 1799 he wrote pointing this out, proposed treating all the proprietors as possessed of a joint undivided estate, that is, rendering them liable for each other's arrears. This was not done; but there was a practice not very different from it. For the various proprietors were obliged to appoint a single manager for the estate, and if they could not agree on one, the collector might make the appointment. This, however, was a practice which hardly suited the proprietors, and people became very chary of buying estates so circumstanced. The collector, writing in 1801, says there are about 100 such estates in the district, and that it is difficult to find purchasers when they fall in arrear. (C. 12-1-99; 5-6-01.)

3. The Board, on this last letter, recommended the partition of the estates among the various proprietors—a plan *Frequent partitions.* which already had been largely availed of, for the records of these years contain many notices of such partitions. In this manner, therefore, there also arose much multiplication of estates.

4. But by far the most fruitful source of increase in the number of estates was the separation of taluqs. All who *Frequent separation of taluqs.* held taluqs at the time of the permanent settlement were entitled to have them separated then, that is, considered as a separate estate. But the separations made then were nothing in proportion to the large number that were separated afterwards, and a great part of the collector's work was in connection with the separation of these taluqs. The zemindars, as I have said before, frequently opposed

the separation of the taluqs; but in many instances they created
taluqs, receiving purchase-money, and knowing perfectly that they
would be separated. There was one danger in the separation, namely,
that a large slice of land being separated off with an inadequate
assessment, the remainder of the estate might be insufficient to secure
the remainder of the assessment; but with this exception the work
presented no difficulty. In fact, the taluqs were sometimes, as in the
case of Muhammadshahi, created by zemindars for the express purpose
of bringing about this insecurity of revenue, and so forcing on the
Government a reduction of assessment. (O. 9-1-02 ; 28-10-04 ; 26-9-98.)

5. The increase in the number of estates caused by these measures
Increase in number of   may be estimated from the following figures :—At
estates.   the time of the permanent settlement there were
just over 100 mahals (estates), and there were also a few—but I cannot
say how many—separated taluqs. When Bhusna was added to the
district, besides the estate itself there were 2,155 taluqdars ; but
whether these were all separated or not, I cannot say. In 1799, the
collector writes that there are in the district 6,000 estates, of which
more than 1,000 bear a revenue less than ten rupees. But the number
is in 1809 given at 3,444, so that I cannot say whether the 6,000 is a
mere rough guess, or whether any change had taken place between
1799 and 1809. Mr. Wintle, the collector, however, writes in 1798
that since he had joined, that is, since two years before, 1,000 estates
had been added to the register by separation of taluqs. (C. 13-12-90 ;
4-7-93 ; 8-10-99 ; 9-11-09 ; 3-12-98.)

6. Except during the fifteen years which succeeded the permanent
settlement, and during the resumptions which long subsequently took
place, there was no considerable addition to the number of estates on
the roll.

7. This breaking up of the large estates, and the creation out of
Advantages derived from   them of many small estates, was therefore one of
it.   the effects, though perhaps an indirect one, of
the permanent settlement. Of the great advantage brought about by
it there can be no doubt. That state of society is always the most
prosperous where the wealth is distributed over many individuals,
instead of being massed in the hands of one or two only. Powerful
and wealthy zemindars, even now, are too apt to abuse their position
and consider themselves beyond the pale of the law. The ryots and
the poorer classes fail to receive due consideration at their hands, and

their power and the number of their dependants enable them easily to carry everything before them. It is different, however, when we find moderate wealth and a certain independence of position possessed by a large body of people. No one of them is powerful enough to injure with impunity any of his neighbours, and a certain amount of mutual consideration and forbearance is forced upon all. People can live at peace with each other, instead of living in perpetual dread of superior power.

8. Another great advantage resulted from it in this way. The management of landed property is not the *forte* of Bengali zemindars, and a zemindar who possesses an immense tract of country naturally finds greater difficulties in management. The best managed estates are almost always those which are not too large to become unwieldy. A proprietor whose estate is measured by tens of miles may easily be frightened away by the difficulties that lie before him; and with his prominent position, too, he has less motive to apply himself with energy to the task of improvement. But a man whose lands are not too large for him to remain perfectly acquainted with everything affecting them, and whose property is not too large to make him despise the slow but sure increment which the improvement of landed estates brings with it, is likely to manage his lands with success, and in improving them, to improve also the position both of himself and of his ryots.

XXV.—*Early Attempts to Reclaim the Sundarbans.*—1784-1800.

MR. HENCKELL, at an early period of his magistracy, turned his attention to the Sundarbans, and he was the founder of the system of reclamation which is now converting these great forests into immense rice tracts.

2. The route from the eastern districts to Calcutta passed at that time by nearly the same river-courses which it follows now—by Kochua, Khulna, Chandkhali, and by the river leading past Kaliganj. But this route was then south of the cultivated tracts, and for the most part lay through forest, no habitations being on either side. Cultivation had in some places been carried farther south—for example, in the pergunnahs of Hogla and Chirulia; but the above description for the most part held good. (M. 31-5-89.)

The Sundarban route.

3. Apparently about 1782 or 1783 Mr. Henckell established,
for boats passing through this inhospitable tract,
Three ganjes established. three ganjes, that is to say, places where travellers
might meet with traders and provisions might be obtainable. One of
these was at Kochua, on the eastern side of Jessore; one was at Chandkhali, now on the western side of the district, but then in the centre of
the passage through it; and the third was at Henckellganj, then the
western side of the district. This latter place is close to Bangalpara, a
little west of Kaliganj, in the 24-Pergunnahs, and it was named after
Mr. Henckell. When Mr. Henckell's agent was clearing the place
(for it was jungle when first occupied), he was very much disturbed by
tigers, who would make attacks upon his people, so he affixed to the
place the name of Henckell, expecting that the tigers, dreading that
name, would no more molest him ; and the name adhered to the place
ever after, until at last the survey authorities went round and,
picking up the name only from native pronunciation, wrote it down
"Hingulgunge" in their maps, and blotted out the history it contained. (C. 29-7-89.)

4. In all the three places, in fact, clearings of jungle had to
be made before the ganj could be established, for they were all in
the Sundarban forest; at each of them also some tracts of land
were brought under cultivation. From some correspondence in the
beginning of 1794, it would appear that Mr. Henckell paid in a great
measure out of his private purse for these reclamations. Possibly he
had his outlay afterwards reimbursed to him. (C. 26-3-90.)

5. On 4th April 1784 Mr. Henckell submitted to the Board his
Henckell's reclamation scheme for the reclamation of the Sundarbans.
scheme. He proposed granting plots of land, on favorable
terms, to people undertaking to reclaim them. The terms where these :
the grantee or "taluqdar" was to retain 200 biggas of land for
himself; upon the rest he would be chargeable with Government
revenue, according to the amount he brought under cultivation. The
revenue was to be for the first three years nothing ; fourth year, 2 annas;
fifth, 4 annas ; sixth, 6 annas ; seventh and succeeding years, 8 annas.
It does not appear that the grantee was bound to bring under cultivation
any specified amount within a fixed time. Mr. Henckell urged the
scheme both because it would bring in a revenue from lands which
then were totally unproductive, and because the cultivation would,
by its peculiar nature, form a grand reservoir for rice against seasons

of drought or famine, as the crops grown in the Sundarbans were little dependent upon rainfall. (M. 4-4-84. C. 20-7-87.)

6. Another part of the scheme, which we have alluded to before, was the establishment of a sort of convict colony in some part of the Sundarbans, but that part of it was never carried out. (M. 22-11-85.)

7. The Sundarban plan, as it was then called, was approved by the Board and was speedily brought into operation,
At first successful.
Mr. Henckell being made " superintendent for cultivating the Sundarbans" (it must be remembered he was not then collector). In 1787 Mr. Henckell already looked on the scheme as a " great success," and reported that many zemindars had come forward and taken grants, and that 21,000 biggas were already under cultivation. He had largely interested himself in the plan, and had even personally advanced money to taluqdars to carry it out. (B. 30-9-85. G. 21-12-85. C. 20-7-87.)

8. Mr. Henckell had foreseen the probability of disputes arising
Opposition of the old zemindars.
with the zemindars who possessed the lands adjoining these grants, and accordingly, in August 1786, he caused the whole of the boundary between the zemindars' lands and the Sundarbans to be marked off with bamboo stakes. This boundary was, of course, far from easy to determine. The zemindars held their lands not by specific boundaries, but by pergunnahs, and as they extended their cultivation southward (as no doubt they did in some measure), they of course attached the newly cultivated land to the adjacent pergunnah. But as the pergunnahs were divisions which bore reference to the land revenue system, they did not extend southward of the cultivation, and land which was yet unreclaimed belonged to no pergunnah at all and therefore was within no zemindar's settlements. (C. 7-8-86 ; 16-5-88.)

9. Mr. Henckell was not wrong in his anticipations regarding disputes, and in 1788 he writes almost despairingly to the Board. The zemindars were making claims to the lands which had been granted to the taluqdars. The zemindars would not assert any specific boundaries to their estates, but whenever any land was brought under cultivation, they would make the demand that it was within their limits. They were taking up and bringing under ryottee cultivation small patches of land here and there in the interior in order to show, by bringing the land upon their rent-roll, that it was theirs. And not only were they making claims, but they were enforcing them; the Selimabad zemindars especially were interfering with the cultivation and

s

forcibly opposing the taluqdars. Mr. Henckell for two years repeatedly urged the Board to interfere to protect the taluqdars, and wished an order to be issued upon the zemindars that within three months they should declare their boundaries, so that he might have them finally determined. The present unsettled state of affairs was ruining the whole scheme. The taluqdars in possession had for some time continued to pay their revenue, in the hope of having matters settled, but were latterly falling in arrear; and though Mr. Henckell held applications for 200,000 biggas from new proposing taluqdars, he delayed making the grants until he could be quite certain whether the lands were his to grant. (C. 16-5-88; 24-7-88; 26-8-88; 31-7-89; 26-3-90; 12-4-90.)

10. In a letter of 26th March 1790 a statement is made of the progress of the scheme. The grants which had been made were—

Year.	English year.	No. of biggas.
1192	.. 1785	.. 21,000
1194	.. 1787	.. 13,094
1195	.. 1788	.. 8,113
1196	.. 1789	.. 1,603

The grants were being made latterly in smaller numbers for the reason given above; but Mr. Henckell said that were matters only settled, he would likely grant 100,000 biggas in 1197 (1790).

Revenue became payable first in 1195 (1788), the demand for that year being Rs. 2,625; by 1200 (1793) there would be a demand of Rs. 20,540 on grants already made, besides the revenue of the 100,000 biggas he would be able to give in 1197 (1790), which would be Rs. 12,500 in 1200 (1793), and Rs. 50,000 in 1203 (1796).

The names of the grants are given in the same letter; they almost all have names derived from those of the grantees—"Kalidaspur," "Muhammadabad," "Bhairabnaggar," and so forth. The first two of these were apparently the most prosperous, but in some others much land had been brought under cultivation. In most of the instances, however, the disputes originated by the zemindars were keeping matters in a backward state.

11. The Board, however, were not persuaded by these facts and figures, and were not nearly so keen about the scheme as Mr. Henckell. They had already withdrawn, on the score of expense, the establishments which had been placed at the three ganjes (Kochua, Chandkhali, and Henckellganj,) to promote and manage the scheme and to manage the small Government

The scheme begins to fail.

estates formed by the clearings at these three places.* The present
expenditure and the prospects of litigation apparently were not to their
minds justified by the chances of future revenue, and in 1790 they practically abandoned the scheme to take its chances. (M. & C. 31-5-91.)

12. Next year the collector writes the scheme had begun to fail
from the above causes, and some zemindars had succeeded in showing
that the taluqdars' lands were within their settlements and in having
them dispossessed. So a new settlement was made of all such grants
as were affected by these considerations, namely, the old terms were
applied to that part of the lands which remained after the exclusion of
what belonged to the zemindars, and a certain amount of revenue
continued still to be realized from them. But no more grants were
made, and we find the Board even in 1796 refusing to entertain an
application on the ground that the extent of the zemindars' claims was
not yet decided. The question, in fact, was whether the permanent
settlement proclamation had not vested in the zemindars the proprietary
right over the whole Sundarbans. (C. 28-5-91; 4-2-94. B. 30-9-96.)

13. The old grants, too, began to decline. Kalidaspur and
Muhammadabad, once the most prosperous, fell so far into jungle
that they were unable to bear their assessment. They were relinquished by the grantees in 1798 and became Government estates.
When Kalidaspur was thus bought in by Government, there was hardly
an inhabitant on it. Chandkhali, too, which was a Government
clearing, began to relapse about 1796; but apparently it was redeemed,
for we find it in 1808 in the hands of a farmer. (C. 2-1-98; 15-2-98;
5-8-01; 12-6-96; 29-2-08.)

14. However, after a season of adversity matters began to look

It afterwards recovered.

brighter, and in 1802 the improvement was so
great, that the collector proposed to send ameens
to measure how much land had been brought under cultivation, in
order that the assessment might be increased. Nothing was done then,
and the collector again in 1808 urged upon the Board an inquiry of
this nature. He said that the amount cultivated by people who have
no grants, or cultivated by grantees in excess of their assessment,
might be 40,000 biggas. About 1814 a measurement was made by
native ameens, but it was pronounced unreliable, the grantees having
bribed the ameens to understate the cultivation. And finally, in 1816,

---

* These establishments had police duties also, being intended to act, as occasion required,
against robbers. (M. 31-5-91.)

a measurement was being carried out by a Mr. Smith, apparently an
assistant collector. (C. 16-10-02; 24-2-08; 3-9-14; 20-7-12.)

15. About 1807, also, applications for grants, which had for a long
time ceased, began to come in. (C. 23-6-00; 17-6-07; 2-1-08; 25-1-08.)

16. Of Henckellganj the subsequent history is this. After remaining a long time the property of Government,
the raja of Nuddea claimed the reclaimed land,
on the ground that it was part of the village Parbatpur, or Bangalpara,
which was within his permanent settlement. The judge of Jessore,
finding that it was so, decreed possession to the raja as zemindar, but
as Government had spent so much money on its reclamation, the judge
declared they might continue to possess as ryots, paying rent to the
raja at pergunnah rates. When the case was appealed to Calcutta,
the Government got still harder terms: it might retain the ganj alone
(the place where the houses and market grounds were), paying rent of
course to the raja, but would have to give up the cultivated land. The
rent of the ganj was then about Rs. 550. But a brilliant idea struck
the Board. If the raja was entitled to become a proprietor under the
permanent settlement of Henckellganj, the revenue he would get from
it must be added to the other assets of his zemindari (which it had not
been of course), and his assessment must be increased by the assessment
on Henckellganj, that is, ten-elevenths of the net revenue. The collector
was accordingly directed to assess this addition to the raja's zemindari.
These proceedings lasted from 1802 to 1804. (C. 29-4-01. B. 26-5-01;
13-8-02. C. 9-11-02; 30-8-02; 23-4-03; 29-6-04.)

17. The raja was not at all prepared to find that he had to
render to the Government ten-elevenths of what he had gained by his
decree, and he steadily refused to take the settlement which the Board
offered to him at Rs. 531. The estate was consequently continually given
out in farm, the zemindari allowance being kept for the raja. The
raja finally sold all his rights for Rs. 8,001 to one Radhamohan
Chaudhri, who in 1814 accepted the settlement, which had then
increased to Rs. 872. (C. 12-5-09; 24-9-14.)

18. Chandkhali I have not much information about. When at
the place I made some inquiries, and was told it was reclaimed by
Mr. Henckell; whether for himself or on the part of Government, was
not stated. After that it was sold (probably by Government) to one
Rupram Mazumdar, and he transferred it to its present proprietor,
Umanath Chaudhri of Satkhira.

History of Henckell-
ganj and Chandkhali.

19. Kochua was at a very early period claimed by the Selimabad zemindars, but whether given up to them or not I do not know.

20. The subsequent history of Sundarban reclamation is beyond my present intention. It is sufficient to notice that, starting from the beginning I have described, grants have continually increased and cultivations continually extended. A belt of Sundarban land, about twenty miles wide, has been reclaimed from forest and brought under cultivation since the time when Mr. Henckell established his outposts at Kochua, Chandkhali, and Henckellganj.

XXVI.—*The Sub-Division of Chandkhali.*—1786.

IN 1786 we have said that Mr. Henckell, desirous of procuring an accurate definition of the lands that were available for his Sundarban reclamation scheme, marked off by bamboo stakes the line which he considered to be the northern boundary of the Sundarbans and the southern of the zemindari lands.

A sub-division erected at Chandkhali.

2. A boundary being thus defined, Mr. Henckell provided, for the trial of claims made by zemindars with respect to their boundaries, a "cutcherry of reference," as he termed it; that is, he established a cutcherry at Chandkhali under Mr. Foster, one of his assistants. Mr. Henckell, in his instructions to Mr. Foster, directed him also to take cognizance of civil and criminal matters (except when they were of importance, when he was to refer them to himself,) arising within a radius of thirty miles from Chandkhali; he was also to give passports and collect the Government dues on wax and honey taken from the Sundarbans; and there was one rather characteristic injunction laid on him,—he was not to issue summons during the four heavy collection months Bhadro, Aswin, Agun, Pos. (J. 13-10-86. C. 7-8-86.)

3. This was a regular sub-divisional jurisdiction, and it was probably the first sub-division in Bengal. It was no doubt extremely useful, for Mr. Foster remained at Chandkhali, till after two years his health obliged him to leave it, and on his leaving the establishment was all brought into Jessore (Moorly). (C. 5-8-88.)

4. Almost immediately on its establishment this sub-division furnished an instance of the advantage to be derived from carrying authoritative supervision into the interior of the districts. Shortly after arriving Mr. Foster

System of blackmail.

found that the zemindars had all set up tolls upon the rivers to collect money from the trading boats. "Not even those protected by the custom house pass were allowed to go free." There were eighteen of these tolls within a circuit of fourteen miles from Chandkhali, so it may be imagined what a hindrance to trade they were. The Board, when they were told of it, were very irate, declared it was contrary to repeated orders, and directed Mr. Henckell, in all cases of levying tolls, to cause immediate restitution and to inflict corporal punishment on the offender on the spot where the exaction was made. The zemindars were included in this order of corporal punishment, but if they were minors, females, or incapables, their manager was to bear the punishment for them. Mr. Henckell suggested a more thorough method, viz. the abolition of the "gurkati" chowkeys, that is, the zemindari tolls, where, on pretence of collecting tolls on their forest produce, the zemindars levied dues upon all traffic. But this would have cost Government the loss of its then forest revenue, about Rs. 5,000. (C. 29-19-86. B. 28-11-86. C. 27-12-86.)

5. This method of making zemindars obey orders by threatening them with flogging was not in those days altogether unknown to the Board, or Committee as it was called, of Revenue. The Preparer of Reports was an officer who in those days exercised part of the functions of the present Board; and on one occasion, arising out of a case where some landholder had refused on his order to give up possession of some lands, he submitted a complaint on the subject to the Board. The Board's orders were, that on proof of disobedience by parties to his orders, he should inflict on them corporal punishment. (Committee, Revenue, 30-12-84.)

6. The remains of the days when Chandkhali was occupied by the collector are still to be seen there. There stands Remains of the sub-division. on the river's bank a little brick-house composed of three rooms ranged longitudinally and an arched verandah in front of them. The masonry is still quite good, but the roof, which was supported on beams, has fallen in. A masonry wall once surrounded and enclosed the building, but in these more civilized days this has ceased to be necessary, and it has long disappeared. The gate-way alone remains, standing roofless in front of the building. It was Mr. Henckell who put up this building, and it was used as a cutcherry not only in his time, but even in that of Rupram Mazumdar, a subsequent zemindar, who bought it of Government. The river now threatens to carry it away.

A tank, situated south-eastward from the cutcherry, whose antiquity is attested by large banyan trees growing on three of its sides, is also attributed by the residents to Mr. Henckell. It has now almost silted up, but at the time of my visit (January 1870) the zemindar was about to redig it, as a tank he had dug close by failed to give sweet water. (P.E.)

XXVII.—*The District and its Head-Quarters.*—1781-1810.

I ENUMERATE under this head the changes that took place during the time over which my examination of the old records extends in the officers of the district, in the boundaries of it, and in its head-quarters.

2. Of the short period, 1772 to 1774, when Warren Hastings established a European collector in Jessore, I find no records. It was only a temporary measure, for the collectors (who had also civil court powers) were abolished in 1774 and provincial councils established. One of the collectors of Jessore of that time was named Samuel Charters. (M. 2-6-86.)

3. In May 1781 Tilman Henckell arrived as judge and magistrate, and in April 1786 he added to his appointment the functions also of collector. He was tranferred to Rajahahi, and made over charge of his three offices, on 14th October 1789, to Mr. Richard Rocke. In 1793 the offices were again separated, and after this date the judge and magistrate remained different from the collector.

4. As for the office of magistrate and judge, Mr. Cosby Burrowes was appointed to it on 29th March 1793. He left in December 1794, and after Mr. H. Strachey had acted for a short time, Mr. A. Heselrige joined on 10th February 1795. Then Mr. Melvill appears as judge in September 1797; but as some of the correspondence is wanting just before that date, I cannot say when he joined.

5. Of the collectors the following is the list, taken for the most part from notices of their making over charge :—

20th May 1793.—Mr. Arthur Heselrige succeeds Mr. Rocke, who becomes judge of Nuddea.

23rd January 1795.—Mr. Samuel Hasleby succeeds Mr. Heselrige, who becomes judge of Jessore.

12th January 1796.—Mr. Thomas Parr, collector. Mr. Hasleby had left on leave on 21st November, and Mr. Cunningham, the assistant, had been acting since that time.

22nd March 1796.—Mr. Parr is made judge and Mr. Cunningham again acts as collector.

2nd July 1796.—Mr. James Wintle, collector.

12th January 1801.—Mr. Wintle left for Backerganj, the site of which was then being changed for Barisal on account of its unhealthiness. Mr. F. Balfour succeeded him temporarily. (C. 27-12-00.)

20th April 1801.—Mr. W. Parker, acting collector.

11th January 1802.—Mr. R. Dick, acting collector.

12th April 1803.—Mr. W. Armstrong, collector.

19th January 1805.—Mr. R. Thackeray, acting collector. (This Thackeray is the father of the novelist of that name.)

12th June 1805.—Mr. A. M. Willock, collector.

8th November 1806.—Mr. Willock having suddenly left in bad health, Mr. H. J. Travers arrives to act for him.

24th December 1806.—Mr. Willock returned.

13th October 1807.—Mr. Willock having died in Jessore about 18th or 20th September 1807, Mr. E. Parker is made collector.

23rd December 1807.—Mr. Parker being ill, Mr. J. Digby acts as collector.

9th June 1808.—Mr. Parker returns.

20th December 1808.—Mr. Parker was obliged to go to Calcutta in bad health on 8th December, and Mr. H. Shakspeare acts.

8th February 1808.—Mr. Parker returns.

10th June 1809.—Again Mr. Parker goes away in bad health and Mr. E. Barnett acts as collector.

18th July 1809.—Mr. Parker returns.

30th September 1809.—Mr. Parker having died on 18th September, Mr. E. Barnett becomes acting collector.

29th January 1810.—Mr. Thomas Powney, collector.

19th October 1812.—Mr. W. H. Belli, acting collector for a short time during Mr. Powney's temporary absence.

17th May 1813.—Mr. J. Littledale, acting collector.

8th February 1814.—Mr. W. Fane, acting collector.

9th May 1815.—Mr. C. W. Steer, collector.

6. As for the boundaries of the district, I have already said that when first constituted it extended over the present districts of Furreedpoor and Jessore, and included also that tract which lies south of the present Bongong and Jessore road and east of the Ichamati river. This was the boundary of

Boundaries of the jurisdictions.

the magistracy jurisdiction ; for the collectorate jurisdiction, when first established, did not include Muhammadshahi, nor Bhusna, which latter name includes Naldi with its sub-pergunnahs and all Furreedpoor. In 1789 Bongong was the boundary of Nuddea, and Bhusna and Shahujial were both under the collector of Rajshahye. In 1787 these last-mentioned tracts were excluded from the magistracy jurisdiction, and as Muhammadshahi was at the same time added to the collectorate jurisdiction, the two jurisdictions became all but identical, extending over the present district of Jessore (except Naldi and Shahujial) and the tract, described above, lying east of the Ichamati. (C. 30-10-89. J. 5-9-87.)

7. In 1793 Bhusna was added to the Jessore district, but the addition to the magistracy jurisdiction was slightly different from that made to the collectorate, and in that and the subsequent year some further changes took place. On the north-west the district marched with Moorshedabad, and Naupara and Kushtia were transferred from Moorshedabad to Jessore. Pergunnah Jaodia, just south of these, was transferred from Jessore to Nuddea. In the beginning of 1794 there was a rectification of boundaries between Jessore, the 24-Pergunnahs, Nuddea, Moorshedabad, Rajshahye, and Dacca. The chief result, so far as Jessore was concerned, was the transfer to Nuddea of all that tract of land through which the Bongong and Jessore road runs, so that Jingagachha now became the boundary of Jessore in that direction. Jessore still retained the lands farther south lying between the Ichamati and the Kabadak rivers, but with that exception its western boundary was nearly what it remained till 1863. On the north the district ran up to the great river, including that part of Muhammadshahi which now lies within the Pubna district, and including the whole, or nearly the whole, of the Furreedpoor district. These two districts did not then exist, and in fact, where Pubna and Furreedpoor are named in the records, they are explained by saying "Pubna, near Comeroolly," "Furreedpoor, near Hajiganj." (G. 11-1-93; 29-3-93. C. 5-6-93; 11-1-94. M. 24-1-94. B. 7-1-94. C. 14-1-94; 22-10-00. Col., Nattore, 24-12-93. Col., Nuddea, 4-12-93. C. 3-12-05.)

8. The next great change in the boundary was the creation of the Furreedpoor district. For a long time there had been a civil jurisdiction there, and at Backerganj, under a registrar at each place; and in 1814 the Board made these registrars *ex-officio* assistants to the collector of Dacca, and directed the collector of Jessore to report what estates, bearing

Creation of Furreedpoor district.

T

assessment of less than Rs. 5,000, could be transferred from his district to them. The collector sent up a list, and a considerable transfer took place. Furreedpoor was at that time only an assistant-collectorship, but it had a treasury where revenue could be paid, and as it was subordinate to Dacca, the transfers of estates to it reduced the boundaries of Jessore. The boundary between the civil jurisdictions of Jessore and Furreedpoor appears to have been at or near the Madhumati river, but the collectorate boundary, that is to say, the definition between the estates paying revenue at Jessore and those paying revenue at Furreedpoor, seems to have been at all times very indistinct. When in 1863 the rectification of boundaries took place, the number of estates inter-transferred was very large indeed, while the change in the geographical boundary was very small. The reason of this probably was that the collector, in giving his list of estates to be transferred to Furreedpoor, regulated it less by geographical position than by other considerations. (B. 19-4-14. C. 16-7-14.)

9. In fact, the collector was himself rather opposed to the transfer, and gave his support to a representation put in by several of the transferred zemindars, who, having bankers and agents in Jessore, and many of them having also estates still paying revenue in Jessore, objected to the inconvenience of paying revenue at two places. This objection does not seem to have received much consideration from the Board. Another objection which the collector made was more of a personal nature. It was the custom that collectors should receive a certain percentage upon the sale of stamps within their jurisdiction, and now that Furreedpoor was in its collectorate jurisdiction entirely under Dacca, the Jessore collector lost the percentage upon those stamps which were sold in that part of Furreedpoor which had been under the Jessore collectorate. This difficulty was, however, arranged by giving half the commission on Furreedpoor sales to each. A similar objection and a similar arrangement was made about the excise revenue. (C. 20-5-15; 8-8-15; 14-9-15; 5-10-15.)

10. The head-quarters of Jessore were at first at Moorly, two

Head-quarters at Moorly. miles from the present station; and when Mr. Henckell came there, he found one house, "the factory" belonging apparently to the British Government. This house he repaired and extended, and if the value he himself puts on it (Rs. 18,650) is a true value, it must have been a fine house. He afterwards built a cutcherry for dewani and faujdari for about Rs. 2,500,

one for the collector for Rs. 450, a registrar's residence and office for
Rs. 1,000 or Rs. 2,000, a record-building for Rs. 850, and a small
treasury building. A short time after Mr. Rooke became collector, the
head-quarters were transferred from Moorly to
At Kusba.
Kusba, or Sahibganj, their present locality. The
reason of this change I do not find anywhere stated; but Sahibganj
appears already to have attained some prominence as a trading place,
and this may have been the reason for the change. The name Sahibganj, I may mention, is now obsolete. (C. 14-1-94; 8-10-94; 26-2-88.
M. 2-10-81. C. 20-8-93. M. 1-3-93. C. 19-5-93. J. 19-3-95.)

11. At the time of the 1179 settlement the raja zemindar of
Isafpur had relinquished 500 biggas of land for the occupation of the
Government officials in Jessore. Whether this land was originally in
Moorly and was afterwards exchanged for a quantity in the new site,
or whether the 500 biggas were originally near Kusba, I cannot say.
About 1800 we find a notice of their being measured out near the
new site, but they had, it is stated, been much encroached upon on all
sides, and only 362 biggas were then found. The bazar had been
built, and apparently continued to be built, over part of this land, and
so little care was taken to preserve it that, in 1803, 29 biggas of this
land were by oversight sold for arrears due upon pergunnah Imádpur,
the pergunnah within which geographically it was situated. Part of the
station land of Jessore is still the property of Government upon this title,
and it goes by the name of "Sahibdakhl." (C. 30-11-98; 15-8-00.)

12. By old residents in Jessore a site is still shown, on the bank
of the "lal-diggi," or principal tank, where it is
Old sites.
said the cutcherry was situated when first the
head-quarters were removed to Kusba; and the malkhana or treasury
house was, it is said, on the west side of the present police station.
The cutcherry is noted in a letter of 1805 as being situated in the
middle of the bazar, and being a small house with masonry sides and
a thatched roof, the records and papers in it had more than once
suffered damage from fires and from storms; it was therefore deemed
advisable to remove it, and the old building was sold with the land
upon which it stood, which was to bear a revenue of Rs. 15-8. Mr.
Armstrong had built a house upon the site which the present building
occupied, and this house was, in part at least, rented for a new
cutcherry. When Mr. Armstrong left he sold it to a native, but
Government subsequently purchased it, and after using it a long time

built another, the present cutcherry, upon the same site. (C. 2-8-05.
M. 5-3-98. C. 2-4-06; 20-2-06; 23-2-09. P. E.)

13. The station appears to have been a somewhat unhealthy one.
We have enumerated already two collectors who
Unhealthiness.   suffered very bad health there and subsequently
died at the place. One of these writes about the "damp situation of
the place." The station too was badly kept. In 1800 it is described
as all jungle trees and bamboos, the bazar and the roads covered with
unhealthy vegetation; and letters of other periods say the same. The
Bhairab river too was then, as now, a source of malaria, for it was
almost dry in the hot season. The place, in fact, retained for a very
long time a reputation as an unhealthy station; but its character in this
respect has been entirely changed since Mr. Beaufort, the magistrate,
about 1854, supplied it with an efficient system of drainage, the first
great step in its sanitary improvement. (C. 24-5-09; 21-8-00. P. E.)

14. There was in 1795 a proposal to remove the head-quarters
of the district to Muhammadpur. This would certainly have been
more centrical than Jessore as the district was then constituted; but
nothing came of it, and compared with Jessore, Muhammadpur had
a great disadvantage in its inaccessibility. (C. 30-3-95.)

XXVIII.—*Famines and Remedial Measures.*—1787-1801.

In 1787 there occurred an inundation and a cyclone, and there was
much consequent suffering among the people.
Famine of 1787.   2. In writing of the inundation of that year,
it must be remembered that the northern half of the district was then
watered from the north-west; the Kumar, the Nabaganga, the Chitra,
and other rivers had their heads still open, and brought down large
streams of water, so that embankments had to be kept up, especially
along the first two, to keep out the waters of even ordinary floods.

3. On 5th September it first became known that an unusual
rise was to be expected, and by the 14th the water had burst the
embankments and submerged part of the country. It still rose, and it
attained its highest point during the first few days of October (21st Assin).
Had the calamity ceased at this point, it would have been bearable.
An abundant aus harvest had been reaped, and the second harvest,
though much injured, was not entirely ruined. Though the water rose

in some lands seven or nine feet above the surface, yet the long-stemmed rice kept pace with it, and always kept its head above water. After all not all the land was submerged; the collector estimated the submerged portion at one-seventh, but this, by his own facts, I judge to be an under-estimate. But again about 20th October (10th Kartick) the waters begain to rise, and a few days after came a cyclone. This destroyed the crops; the heads of the long rice, which the ryots during the inundation had been floating upon twigs, were broken off, or were submerged and became rotten. Large quantities of rice floated away in masses, and great disputes arose about the property in them. The til crop was completely destroyed; the date trees, and the mustard and dâl crops, were much injured. Prices speedily rose, and the ryots after a short time began to sell their implements of husbandry (the early period at which they began doing so shews how badly off, as a rule, they were), and after exhausting these, flocked into Jessore, offering their children for sale. (C. 25-6-88.)

4. Before the cyclone had come,—before even the highest rise of the inundation—the Government informed the farmers of Muhammadshahi (this was the year when it was given out in small farms by the collector) that the demands upon them for the months of Assin and Kartick would not be levied till the following months; and later on a general order was issued to collectors to make full inquiry and report upon any claims that zemindars might make to suspension of revenue (the Board believed it would not be necessary to entirely remit any revenue), and collectors were also directed to inform the zemindars that unless they shewed some indulgence to their ryots, they could expect none from the Government. (B. 21-9-87; 27-10-87.)

Suspension of revenue demand.

5. The scarcity and dearness of food extended over other districts besides Jessore, and it attracted the attention of the Governor General. The first step was adopted in December, when the Governor General temporarily suspended all transport duties on grain. Then, two months after, orders were issued to collectors that they were to send in fortnightly price-currents, and to see that all duties and other obstacles to the transportation of grain were removed. This refers to the sayar duties; the zemindars having a right to collect, as part of the revenues of their zemindaris, certain small duties on articles which were being conveyed through their territories. Monopolies were prohibited, and the collectors

Remedies proposed.

were to watch the importation of grain in order to detect and punish them. The collectors were directed to pay particular attention to complaints that traders refused to sell grain, and if they found any one retaining a stock more abundant than seemed to them to be reasonable, they were to sell the surplus by public auction, and either hand over the proceeds to the proprietor or distribute them for the relief of the distressed, whichever course they deemed proper. These orders were, two months later—that is, in April—followed up by a direction to the collectors to send out an assistant on tour to inspect stocks and see how much grain was procurable. (B. 14-12-87. G. 1-2-88. B. 17-4-88.)

6. Henckell saw the folly of these orders, and made a remonstrance against them. He pointed out that their effect would be to increase the alarm by making people believe the scarcity much greater than it was; that the traders would only conceal their stores or send them out of the district; they would be afraid to sell or to advance grain to the ryots; and not only would the latter starve, but the Government would lose its revenue through their having no seed to sow their lands with. The Governor General on this withdrew the orders and directed that no sort of interference should be exercised in the purchase, sale, or transportation of grain. (C. 29-4-88. G. 4-6-88.)

7. A more effectual way of meeting the distress was pointed out by Mr. Henckell. He had already induced the raja the zemindar of Isafpur to advance nearly Rs. 5,000 to his ryots, and the "boro dhan" (late cold-weather rice-crop) which they had cultivated with this, some 30,000 biggas of rice, had materially improved the situation. He proposed to the Government to give Rs. 15,000 in takavi advances to the ryots, many of whom had sold their implements of cultivation and could not recommence agricultural operations, and he wanted also money to place the broken embankments in a sufficient state of repair. It was, he admitted, the duty of the zemindar to keep embankments in repair; but the Muhammadshahi zemindar was deep in debt and could do nothing. On this request the Board granted the Rs. 15,000 for takavi advances, and gave Mr. Henckell Rs. 6,000 with which to repair the embankments. (C. 25-6-88; 9-5-88; 7-2-88.)

8. It is worthy of notice that even in this famine year the collector got from the zemindars the whole of his demand upon them; and we have already seen how, in the case of Muhammadshahi, he made the ousted zemindar pay up the arrears which the farmers appointed by himself failed to realize from the estate. (C. 25-6-88.)

9. In 1790 there was some temporary distress, but not sufficient to
call forth any action on the part of Government.

Distress in 1790.

In August of that year an inundation threatened
in the Saydpur and Isafpur estates, and some embankments were burst:
the collector got about Rs. 1,200 from Government and successfully
repaired them. He apparently did it himself for the same reason as in
Muhammadshahi—because the zemindar was too poor to do it. At the
same time a severe drought in the south of the district caused some loss
of crops, and from this cause apparently sprung a pestilential disorder
which carried off a third part of the inhabitants there, and another third
of them ran away. Strange to say, nothing appears to have been done in
this case, and the collector mentions it only incidentally. Perhaps it did
not endanger the Government revenue. (C. 30-8-90; 10-1-91; 28-9-91.)

10. But a new calamity was impending—the drought and famine
of 1791. On 20th October the collector reported

Famine of 1791.

that no rain had fallen for 38 days and the crops
were in a most critical condition. He recommended the postponement
of the Assin and Kartick instalments of revenue, on the ground that
they were usually paid by the ryots out of the advances they received

Suspension of revenue.

from their mahajans on the security of the aman
(cold-weather) rice, and that the mahajans were
refusing, under present circumstances, to make any advances. The
Board granted this suspension. A month later the collector reported
that all hope was gone, the drought having continued, and the ryots
were coming in to represent their distress. He proposed to hold over
three annas of the rent in the distressed tracts until the next aus crop
should come in. The Governor General approved the suspension of
Rs. 85,500 in all, about the same amount which the collector had applied
for, but he directed that the sum remitted to each zemindar should not
be in equal proportion, but be in proportion to his necessity. Only
Rs. 69,000, however, was actually suspended. A little later the
Government, with the view of guarding against scarcity of food, urged
the execution of an order which it had three years before made public,
forbidding the exportation of grain by sea, and even the lading of grain
in vessels fit to go to sea. (C. 20-10-91. B. 31-10-91. C. 19-11-91.
G. 25-11-91. C. 10-6-92. B. 17-3-89. G. 13-1-92.)

11. As a measure of the intensity of the distress, it may be
mentioned that the price-current of 31st December 1791 shews the price
of food had even then risen to twice or three times its usual figure.

12. Besides the above measures taken for the relief of the ryots, another measure was directed by the Government, one which tastes of its then usual arbitrariness. As soon as he heard of the serious drought, the Governor General issued these orders to the collectors. They were to open all reservoirs and tanks (except such as were in private enclosures), and thus to water the crops; the owners of the tanks were to have no compensation, only they had the privilege of having their fields watered first. Except regular grain dealers, no one was to keep more than a year's consumption of grain in his possession under penalty of deprivation of land or of office. Dealers were to bring forward and sell their stocks of grain; else the Government would seize them. The collectors were told to assure the traders that there was no intention of interfering with their profits, and he was to bring to the notice of Government those mahajans who were prominent in doing the duty Government expected of them. (G. 21-10-91.)

Opening of tanks.

13. A characteristic incident occurred in connection with this matter. The collector of Nuddea inquired whether under these orders, which were perfectly general, he might open the tanks attached to the Government commercial factories; and so the Government issued orders that these tanks should not be opened without the permission of the commercial resident. (B. 31-10-91.)

14. The opening of the tanks did little or no good. In the level plains of Bengal the tanks are not above, but below, the surface of the soil, and the water could never of itself flow from them over the surrounding fields. (C. 16-2-92.)

15. Stimulated by these calamities the Government turned its attention to taking precaution against future ones, and first of all proclaimed that since the zemindars could not yet be expected to have amassed capital from their permanently settled estates, the Government was prepared, on the security of their estates, to make advances to them to enable them to keep up tanks and reservoirs as a protection against drought. Not a single applicant, however, appeared. (B. 13-1-92. C. 27-4-93.)

Advances offered to zemindars.

16. In 1794 there was a very abundant harvest, and the Government, seizing the favorable opportunity, directed the establishment of large granaries, where rice might be stored by Government against seasons of scarcity. In Jessore two were to be established, one at Babukhali (near Magurah), the other at Shorganj, adjoining Phultalla, on the Bhairab. (G. 8-10-94. (C. 13-12-94.)

Public granaries established.

17. Never was a venture more unfortunate. Misfortune pursued these granaries from the first, and they were final-

Failure of the plan.

ly abolished without having ever come into use. The first year a flood nearly carried away the Babukhali granary, though the site of it had been selected precisely because it had never at any time been flooded over. Then, in May 1796, Government decided to abolish the Babukhali granary, and directed the collector to sell off the stores of grain there, of which there were about 50,000 maunds. A fair price, however, could not be obtained, the stores having probably deteriorated very much. This deterioration determined the Government to sell off all their grain, that is, the 40,000 maunds at Shorganj, besides the 50,000 maunds at Babukhali, and to lay in newer rice. The prices obtained were so bad that the collector recommended an abandonment of the system on account of the loss it involved, but after much trouble and delay everything was sold by October 1797. (C. 4-9-95 ; 7-4-96 ; 3-5-96 ; 21-1-97 ; 15-2-97 ; 29-10-97.)

18. But the golahs at Shorganj were in a bad state and required extensive repairs before they could be made fit to hold the new stores of rice, and it was accordingly determined to build new golahs of brick, and about fifty were so built. But neither were they more fortunate. There was first a great loss and waste in building them, and in May 1798, a few months after they had been finished, one of them was struck by lightning and burnt down. They were at that time engaged in re-filling the golahs, and the same storm that burnt down the golah sank a shipload of the new grain, which was at Senhati coming up the river. Then the Government found they had selected for their purchases a very dear season, and stopped the work for a time. The gomashtas engaged in purchasing had been charging high prices, and their honesty was suspected. One of them, indeed, in that same year embezzled a large amount of money. (C. 13-2-97; 5-7-97; 6-3-98; 16-3-98 ; 31-5-98 ; 6-12-97; 29-9-98.)

19. So Government, in 1801, came to the conclusion that this sort of work had better be left to traders, as it was only a source of loss. The establishments cost a good deal (for a year or two they had a superintendent on Rs. 300 for the two granaries in Jessore alone) ; the wastage was very great; there was no end to the pilfering ; it was found impossible to prevent embezzlement ; and great loss was entailed in the occasional renewals of stock. So in the middle of 1801 the granary system was abolished ; it was considered better to rely on the

U

ordinary mercantile stores than to interfere with the market by Government operations. (G. 23-3-01. C. 7-4-96; 26-11-99; 4-6-01.)

20. It may be mentioned here that the making takavi advances to the ryots was not a measure which Government adopted only in the case of local distress, but before the permanent settlement it appears to have been frequently adopted, as an ordinary consequence of the position of Government as proprietor of the land : for example, in the cold weather of 1790-91, when there was no particular distress, the collector applied for advances to enable the ryots to cultivate their "boro" rice crop, the application being based simply on the ground of its being the practice. He undertook to distribute it to the ryots himself, as the farmers were in the habit of applying the money, when distributed through them, to the payment of the rents owed by the ryots—a declaration which also assumes the practice of advancing to have previously existed. The advances of the season 1791-92 I have referred to above. I do not find notice of any in 1792-93, but in the year after that the collector again applied for advances, on the ground that the zemindars, to whom the permanent settlement had transferred this duty, were not yet in a position to undertake it. (C. 16-1-90. B. 21-1-90. C. 30-12-90; 26-1-91; —1-94.)

Advances to ryots.

XXIX.—*Floods and Embankments.*—1787-1801.

I HAVE already noted the bursting of the Muhammadshahi embankments in 1787 and the repairs which were effected in consequence; but as the keeping up of embankments formed part of the collector's work in those days, a few more similar incidents remain to be noticed.

2. In 1790 there was another considerable rise of water, and the embankments in the Isafpur and Saydpur zemindaris were somewhat damaged. The collector effected their repairs at a cost to the State of about Rs. 1,200. From this inundation very little loss was experienced. (C. 30-8-90; 10-1-91.)

3. But the embankments in Muhammadshahi, which were principally along the banks of the Nabaganga river, were not in an efficient state, and the collector required Rs. 13,649 to put them in good order. On this demand the question arose whether the zemindar was not bound to keep up the embankments without help from the State; but as no provision had been

Muhammadshahi embankments.

made for this liability in the terms of the permanent settlement with the Muhammadshahi zemindar, the Government granted the amount. (C. 24-1-91; 9-2-91. G. 16-3-91.)

4. Much money continued to be spent upon the embankments, and about 1794 a superintendent was appointed to have charge of both the Muhammadshahi and the Bhusna embankments; for the south bank of the Padma river apparently was all embanked, as well as the south bank of the Nabaganga. In this year also the embankments were, at considerable expenditure, put into an efficient state of repair. (B. 1-2-93; 4-3-94. C. 8-3-94.)

5. Except a slight inundation in 1795, which caused little harm,
Flood of 1796. no further inundation after 1790 is noted until 1796, when not only was considerable injury sustained from the flood, but a storm, apparently a cyclone, added to the destruction. No steps were taken to alleviate the calamity, such as it was, and it was apparently not considered necessary to use the granaries which Government was then keeping up as a resource against distress. (C. 4-9-95; 13-1-96; 9-11-96; 12-8-96; 26-8-96.)

6. In a report upon embankments, written in 1798, the collector states that he considered no proper system was carried out. Much money, he writes, is spent on embankments, the only object of which is the protection of swamps and low grounds; and he recommends that such cases as these should be left by the State to take care of themselves, and Government should exert itself only to prevent inundation of more general extent. A certain difficulty had begun to show itself, which gave much trouble afterwards; namely, the ryots, for fishing purposes, continually cut the embankments in order to fix fishing cages in them, a practice which injured them exceedingly. (C. 11-4-98.)

7. At the time that the collector wrote this, the embankments had
Series of floods—1798 to for some years been of little use, but that very year
1801. an inundation occurred, stated to be the highest in the memory of the oldest inhabitants. The embankments were surmounted, but they protected the country from general devastation, and the collector acknowledged their usefulness. This inundation of 1798 was apparently the prelude to a series of floods, for next year again there was an unusually high rise of the rivers, which, however, was prevented by the embankments from causing much injury. The districts adjacent to Jessore had apparently suffered much more from it than Jessore had, for they began to come to Jessore for their supplies of grain.

Next year again, that is in 1800, there was an "unexampled rise of the rivers," but again the damage was very small and the harvest was very good.   (C. 22-9-98; 14-11-98; 13-11-99; 6-1-00; 14-1-00; 20-10-00.)

8.   These threatened disasters caused the embankments to be
The embankments ren-   looked on as possessing some value, and the
dered efficient.   Government sent one Captain Mouatt to make a
professional examination of them and have them put into complete order.   A Mr. Jennings had up till now been in charge of them as superintendent, and it was apparently not without reason that Government suspected that they had not been receiving at Mr. Jennings' hands sufficient attention.   Captain Mouatt recommended certain considerable improvements both in the way of repairing the then existing embankments and of combining them, by a few additions, into a more complete system.   (C. 2-3-01; 31-3-01; 14-4-01.)

9.   These improvements were not sooner made than required, for in 1801 there was again an unusual rise of the rivers, and, especially near Naldi, there was considerable loss of crops.   The embankments also were so much injured by undermining, that Rs. 10,000 were required for their repair, and the ryots had done much harm to them by cutting them in order to catch fish.   (C. 18-9-01; 9-1-02; 16-3-02; 4-5-02; 2-8-02.)

10.   The following will give an idea of the large sums that were spent upon embankments under the collector.   The yearly expenditure during the five years 1798 to 1802, inclusive, was Rs. 1,400, 15,000, 6,999, 28,000, and 27,287.   The Board rather reluctantly sanctioned this high expenditure, and it led to a proposal to transfer the burden of the embankments to the zemindars; giving them, of course, a certain reduction in their assessment.   It was, however, in the end determined to keep them under a European superintendent; and now that they were put into a thoroughly efficient state, there appears to have been less expenditure upon them.   We do not find any further notices of inundations; but that much attention was paid to the embankments, is plain from the fact that the collectors frequently went out to examine their condition, up till 1811 at least.   (C. 28-11-03.   G. 24-11-03. C. 30-11-02; 5-4-04; 16-7-10; 21-1-08; 30-12-08; 30-1-11.)

11.   From the facts I have noted, I think it impossible to avoid
Cause of these frequent   the conclusion that inundations were much more
inundations.   frequent in these times than they are now.   In
Jessore there was an inundation in each of these years—1795, 1796, 1798,

1799, 1800, and 1801; a series of floods unexampled in more recent times. Besides this, however, we find the road from Jhenida to Comercolly described as being annually inundated, and a large part of Bhusna is described as being regularly flooded from Assar to Assin of each year, and all this is much different from the present state of affairs. For this change several reasons may be given. First, there is no doubt that the general reclamation of jungle and extension of cultivation has tended to change the rainfall all over the country; but besides this there are local reasons. The district was then more subject to inundation because it lay more directly on the line of the rivers which discharge the water of the Ganges. The Nabaganga, which was then fortified with a regular series of embankments, is now closed at its head and brings down hardly any water; the same may be said of the Kumar, the Chitra, and other rivers, but it is a subject which I have already written of. It is natural that the district should be more subject to inundation when all these rivers ran across it than now, when they are closed at their heads and only discharge the water that accumulates in them from local sources. But from the way these floods of 1798 to 1802 are written of, it is plain that there was then a period of inundation such as had not been known before for a long time. I am inclined to think that this had something to do with the opening of the Madhumati river. It was certainly about that time that the Madhumati opened, and the tract of country which appears to have been most liable to inundation was the north and north-east of the district, precisely those parts whose present drainage is into the Madhumati. I think therefore that the unusual inundations of 1798 to 1801 mark the period when that change was taking place in the river courses of the district which I have written of in describing the topography of Jessore, namely, the change by which the district, which had been watered from the north-west, came to be one watered almost entirely from the north-east. (C. 18-7-94.)

12. I am strengthened in this opinion when I find, after the dates I have mentioned, a sudden cessation both of inundation and of heavy expenditure upon embankments. When the Madhumati river opened a large channel by which the floods found an exit to the south, the water ceased so continually to pour itself over the north and north-east of the district, and the embankments, so well repaired in 1800-1801, being less attacked by the floods, demanded less continual attention and repair.

13. The embankments of the Nabaganga even now, after half a
Remains of old embank-   century and more of neglect, are still easily trace-
ments.   able for some miles upon both sides of Magurah.
Ordinarily they are very low, being in most places raised only about two
feet, and there they have, of course, been to a great extent washed away.
But where a lower part of the river-bank has been embanked, or where
the embankment has been carried inland in order to be brought round
some inlet or creek leading in from the river, the old embankments still
stand some eight feet high, and are still quite strong enough to resist
heavy floods. In some places, however, the old embankments have
served indigo planters as a foundation for newer and better ones required
by them: near Hazrapur, for example, there is a large embankment,
which is, I believe, the old embankment rebuilt into a new one.

XXX.—*Establishment of Excise.*—1790-1810.

UNDER the government of the Moguls spirits were at first entirely
          prohibited, but afterwards it was permitted to distil
Ancient system.   them upon payment of a small tax. The collector
writes that in 1032 B.S. (1625) the distillers paid "a tax of Re. 1-10."
When the English Government came they found the matter entirely
in the hands of the zemindars.' The zemindars fixed the terms upon
which persons might distil spirits, and the taxes they levied in this way
formed one of the assets of their zemindaris. Some zemindars who
personally disapproved of spirit manufacture entirely forbade it within
their limits, but in most estates there was a small annual tax levied
upon distillers, so small indeed that spirits were very cheap and
drunkenness was rife. From what the collector writes about the stills
stopping work in the month of Ramzan, it would appear that the use
of spirits was confined to Mahomedans; and, in fact, in one place he
says that the Hindoos do not consume spirits. (O. 6-9-94; 8-11-90;
27-12-92.)

2. Lord Cornwallis, among his other reforms, proposed a regular
          licensing system in 1790, up to which time the
Lord Cornwallis' system.   zemindars had had the control of the matter.
The collector, in his answer, enumerates 48 stills, almost all in the
Isafpur zemindari; and estimating the produce of each at 40 maunds
per annum, he proposed a tax of Rs. 20 per annum per still. The

Governor General upon this and other reports prescribed the levy of a license fee upon all distillers and all vendors, leaving the amount of it to be fixed by the collector. (G. 12-4-90. C. 8-11-90. G. 14-1-91.)

3. Next year the Board, adopting a suggestion made by the collector of Behar, changed the system of taxation. The distillation was to be confined to certain places, and stills were to be arranged in two classes, taxed 12 annas and 6 annas per day respectively. Vendors were to remain untaxed, and the tax upon taree was to be one-fourth of the rent paid for the taree trees. (B. 3-8-92.)

4. In Jessore the settlement for excise for 1201 (1794-95) was Rs. 567 for 151 stills, the rates apparently having been increased. In 1202 the high rates were adhered to, and the settlement fell to Rs. 147. But in 1203 an improvement took place. The tax was re-modelled in 1800 by Regulation VI of that year, and the estimated revenue for 1801-02 (i.e. for 1208) was Rs. 5,000. The rates appear to have been again increased in 1809. A sudder distillery system had been started by 1814, but it was apparently far from successful. One fault in it was that it recognized no distinction between vendors and distillers, and thus placed in the hands of a few distillers the monopoly of the trade. (C. 26-6-94; 3-8-95; 22-6-96; 31-3-10; 6-10-14.)

5. A small establishment was kept up, both to collect the tax and to guard against illicit distillation. The establishment was only Rs. 66 a month, and being so small it was little effective in preventing contraband trade. Even Rs. 66 was considered too much, and it was reduced to Rs. 46 in 1811. (C. 19-4-05; 26-4-07; 27-3-09; 6-4-10; 8-4-11.)

6. The exciseable drugs consumed in Jessore were maddat, ganja,
Drugs.—Jessore a ganja district.
sabji, bhang, majúm, bákar, charas. Ganja was largely cultivated within the district, principally about Keshabpur, in pergunnahs Ramchandrapur and Taragonia, but also to a small extent in the north-west corner. The duty was collected upon it at the time of its purchase or export from the producing districts, of which Jessore was then a principal one. The collector, writing in 1809, estimates that 50,000 or 60,000 maunds are prepared within the district and are bought up from January to April by byapáris (or traders) at Keshabpur, Fakirhat, Noapara, and Kushtia, the price being then about Rs. 4 or 5 per maund. (B. 21-11-92. C. 3-5-00; 17-4-06; 25-4-09.)

7. There was some difficulty in collecting the tax in the manner just mentioned, for the byapáris might come, make their whole transactions in a single night, and clandestinely export large quantities of

ganja without paying tax. The collector proposed to remedy this by making ganja a monopoly, but this was not consented to. He also wished to make the byapáris pay a license tax, but the Board was opposed to this also. (C. 25-4-09; 1-6-09.)

8. Opium was sold in no small quantities within the district. The Government, who had, or rather imagined

Opium.

they had, a monopoly of opium, and desired to work it on very moral principles, called upon the collector in 1814 for an estimate of the quantity of opium which would be required in his district for *medicinal* purposes. The collector astonished them by answering that opium was sold in every haut and bazar in the district, and that the vendors got it elsewhere than from him. Under instructions from the Board, the collector appointed four persons as opium vendors in the four principal towns of the district, but he warned the Board when he did so that these vendors would not restrict themselves to collectorate opium. (C. 2-6-14; 28-4-15; 19-5-15.)

XXXI.—*Coinage and Currency.*—1793-1807.

THE coinage regulation in the 1793 code, naming as it does many varieties of current coins and the rates at which

No proper currency.

each of them were current, is sufficient to indicate the difficulty that was felt at the time in the matter of coinage. There was in fact little coinage properly speaking, but silver coins of various denominations passed from hand to hand at the value of the silver they contained. The regulation just quoted directed the delivering up these coins for re-coinage at the Company's mint; but it was not a sufficiently obligatory law, and as late as 1802 there were five or six different sorts of rupees used in the district, which were not only current at their standard values, but even when depreciated passed from hand to hand at their depreciated value. The standard Company's rupee—the "19 year sicca rupee" as it was called—was also in use in the district. (C. 9-1-02; 8-3-00; 17-1-00.)

2. Gold was a very frequent form of currency at that time. In 1793 half the revenue was paid in gold, and in

Gold abundant.

1802 it is stated that one-third of the currency is in gold. At the time of the permanent settlement all remittances of money from the treasury at Jessore to Calcutta were made in gold, and for a long time after gold preponderated in them. The treasury also, whenever we find a statement of its contents, contained a very much larger amount of gold than of silver. In 1799 silver began to be more largely remitted, and for two or three years about one-third of the value of each remittance was silver, the rest being mohurs, half-mohurs, and quarter-mohurs. In 1805 silver had become so comparatively abundant, that the bulk of remittances was now in silver, and five years later gold entirely disappears from the lists of treasure remitted to Calcutta. (C. 30-11-93 ; 27-9-94 ; 16-1-98 ; 25-1-99 ; 9-1-02 ; 29-1-05 ; 6-8-08 ; 16-10-08 ; 23-12-08 ; 13-10-09 ; 15-9-11.)

3. It must be noted that in the earlier years at least the proportion of gold in the treasury was always greater than that current in the district. The Government received goldmohurs at 16 rupees value, while their value as current in the bazar was only Rs. 15-6 or 15-4. People who wished to buy them for purposes of remittance might give Rs. 16, but their ordinary value was less than that at which they were received at the treasury, and the consequence was that people preferred paying their debts to the treasury in gold when they could. There appears, in fact, to have been a regular trade in mohurs, for native bankers bought them in the Calcutta bazar and sent them up to Jessore to be used in discharging revenue. In all this there was less loss to Government than at first sight appears, for facility and cheapness of transport were more valuable qualities then than now. (C. 30-11-93 ; 31-7-93 ; 28-5-94 ; 9-1-02.)

4. There was no copper coin current, up till 1814 at any rate, cowries alone being used for small change. The
Copper.
space for "copper pice" is always blank in the cash returns, but the existence of a space for it shews that either pice existed somewhere, or it was in contemplation to supply them. (C. 22-10-07 ; 10-8-14 ; 1-8-09 ; 1-9-09 ; 1-10-09.)

5. Notes are first mentioned in the cash balance return of August 1st 1809, when there were Rs. 420 in
Notes.
notes in the treasury, which contained about Rs. 75,000 in all. But as it was only in this month of August 1809 that regular cash balance reports began to be sent up, I have not the means of finding whether there were bank-notes in the treasury before or not. Notes, however, were then only begun to be used in Jessore, as is manifest from the small value in the treasury. On 1st September there were only 50 rupees notes out of one lakh of treasure, and on 1st October Rs. 360 out of two lakhs. But an order of Government of two

years' earlier date assumes the possibility of their being introduced into circulation in the districts, for it directs that when in any treasury they reach in value Rs. 5,000, they are to be remitted to Calcutta in halves. (G. 23-6-07.)

XXXII.—*The Collector's Duties.*

WE have dealt with most of the branches of the work which during the period immediately succeeding the permanent settlement had to be performed by the collector; it remains to recount them, and to make a few notes regarding them in passing.

2. There was, first of all, the collection of the land revenue by attachment and sale of defaulting estates. The first
Collection of land revenue.
sale for revenue in Jessore took place on 19th November 1792. The zemindars in these times frequently opposed by force the attachment and sale of their estates; they turned the collector's attaching ameen out of their lands, and refused to permit the purchasers to be put in possession. (C. 19-10-92 ; 28-11-97 ; 18-1-97 ; 12-12-97.)

3. The Board had also a certain authority with respect to sales of estates in the civil courts. The sheriff could not sell an estate without reference to them, and all sales, such as private sales by the zemindar, were invalid so long as there remained upon the estate any unpaid arrear. (C. 9-8-97.)

4. The collector, writing in 1802, estimates thus the profit derived by purchasers from the estates, referring particularly to the Calcutta purchasers of the large estates. The purchase money is usually slightly more than the amount of the assessment. By lending out their capital they can get about 24 per cent. profit on it ; therefore, concludes the collector, their profit being about the same when they lay out their money in land, the profit in a landed estate must be about 20 per cent. of the assessment. (C. 9-1-02.)

5. The collector had also to manage Government estates and estates brought under the court of wards, of
Khas management.
which Bhusna has been mentioned as one instance.

6. Then there was the work of assessment arising out of sales of portions of estates, and separations of taluqs, and
Assessment.
partitions of estates. The partitions were not such very formidable matters then as they have now become through

the multiplication of interests in the land. The partition of Muhammadshahi, for example, took only about two years to complete. But there were then also examples of very long protracted partition cases. One, of an estate called Nowara, lasted at least from 1801 till 1808, principally on account of the opposition made and the difficulties raised by opponents. (B. 26-7-94. C. 19-1-96; 27-4-08.)

7. The collector's work under the heads of excise revenue and of embankments has been separately noted. Treasury remittances have also been noticed, and the work that arose from famine and the precautions taken against it. It remains only to say a word about stamps.

8. From the indents for stamps there appears to have been a
considerable sale of them. They were sold
through agents appointed by the collector and
paid by Government, stationed at various parts of the district. In 1814, for example, there were about eight stamp vendors stationed mostly at thannahs. Upon the amount of stamps sold the collector got a commission in addition to his salary. (C. 3-5-14; 8-8-15; 5-10-15.)

Stamps.

9. In 1813 there was a grand forgery of stamps. The agent who had charge of the head-quarter stamp-store was the chief person implicated, and he had for a long time been selling stamps of his own manufacture instead of Government stamps. He must have made much money by it, for both in that year and the next the civil court was continually sending over deeds bearing the false stamp, which had been there presented, to have the proper stamp impressed upon them on payment of penalty. The stamp agent was tried criminally, but I do not know what came of him. (C. 26-7-13; 16-7-14.)

10. The resumption laws of the 1793 code do not appear to have
given any work at all to these early collectors,
though there was no doubt then that a huge
amount of invalid grants existed. The prescribed registers were opened in which people might register their grants, but notwithstanding penalties set forth, many people refused to come forward. No attention was directed to the matter until Mr. Steer became collector in 1815. He states that there had been 35,000 statements filed in the office involving in the aggregate three lakhs of biggas, and that of the grants referred to in these statements, a great number were invalid on the face of them, and many of them were declared

Resumption.

with manifest falsehood to have been lost or destroyed by fire.   He asked
permission to inquire regarding these cases.   Subsequently, extending
his inquiries, he found many other suspicious and plainly invalid
grants.   By the ordinary process of going through the courts, the
Government, he said, could do nothing under ten years, so great were
the delays of civil justice, and he desired that he might be empowered
to adopt more summary measures.   The direction his inquiries
took apparently frightened many grantees, and they began devising
counter-measures.   The favorite plan was to collude with the zemindars
to convert the tenure into a holding under them at a merely
nominal rent, thus depriving the land of its character of rent-free.
Of these representations, however, no particular notice was taken,
but it was the beginning of the agitation which led to the grand
resumption operations of fifteen or twenty years after.   (C. 4-11-15 ;
30-11-15 ; 12-1-16.)

11.   The pûnya festival is an annual institution in every zemin-

Pûnya, or first-fruits. dari.   A little expenditure in fire-works, sacrifice,
and festivities, is made at the zemindari cutcherry,
by way of inaugurating the collections for the new year.   Before it no
collections of current rent are made; and it is a sort of advertisement
that collections are begun.   Mr. Henckell in his time held a pûnya
at Moorly, and commenced from the date of that celebration to make
his collections, advertizing in the customary manner to the zemindars
that the pûnya was to be held upon a certain day.   We have in
the books a list of the expenses incurred by the collector at his pûnya
in 1790.   It contains these expenses: fire-works, Rs. 65; tom-
toms, Rs. 7; dancing-girls, Rs. 35; dancing-boys, Rs. 15; and others
of like nature.   The Government did not admit these charges, on
the ground that they had never done so before; but the holding of
pûnya is referred to repeatedly in the correspondence between the Board
and the collector.   Possibly they meant something less expensive.
(C. —2-91 ; 16-9-11.)

12.   Collectors were required to make annual tours by an order of

Annual tours. the Board in 1789.   They were not, however, by
any means regular in making them, as in some
years the collector went out and in some he did not.   In fact, the
collectors appear to have thought there was no work to do in the interior,
except such as inspection of embankments.   (B. 17-12-89. C. 22-11-06 ;
5-1-07. B. 13-1-07.)

XXXIII.—*Reform in the Administration of Criminal Justice.*—1791.

THE attention of Lord Cornwallis, shortly after his arrival, was turned to the reform of the administration of criminal justice. He called for reports from the magistrates upon the different matters bearing upon the question : the adequacy of punishments, their efficiency as deterrents, the treatment of criminals, the delays in procedure, the efficiency of the police system, and such other matters. The substance of the reports on these subjects which were submitted from Jessore we have already given in the chapter concerning the administration of criminal justice.

2. The reforms which he effected in judicial matters were these.

The magistrate replaces the daroga. the jurisdiction of the daroga was abolished, and the magistrate did all petty criminal work ; courts of circuit were established, before whom the more heinous offenders should be tried ; the nizamat adâlat took the place of the nazim as the chief criminal court (as indeed its name implies) ; and in police matters, a number of police stations were established all over the district.

3. It became necessary, in changing the system, to pass some orders on those matters which the old system had left to be handed over to the new. There were

Pending cases. many cases pending before the naib nazim in which he had not yet passed orders ; these the Governor General wrote to him asking him speedily to decide. All pending and unexecuted sentences of the naib nazim were to be carried out ; but as the punishment of mutilation was not admitted by the British Government, that was not in any case to be carried out. Cases remanded by the naib nazim the magistrates were to take up for trial and decision under the new system. (N. A. 14-2-91 ; 28-2-91.)

4. With regard to old prisoners, it became necessary in many cases to reconsider the orders under which they

Old prisoners resentenced. were suffering imprisonment. Convicts whose imprisonment had no specified duration, or who had been imprisoned till they could find sureties (which many of them, being strangers, could never do), and people imprisoned till they made reparation for

their offence, which their very imprisonment rendered impossible—
all these cases were reported upon by the magistrate or examined by
the nizamat adâlat, and the orders were re-framed.   There were, at
the time that these orders were passed, about 300 individuals in the jail
at the Jessore, and the greater number of these were confined merely
"during pleasure."   Many of them were now summarily discharged;
the remainder were sentenced to various stated periods of imprisonment.
The revision of sentences was made still more efficient by the magistrates
being permitted to offer remarks upon any of the revised sentences
which from circumstances locally known they might deem capable of
improvement.   The magistrate of Jessore availed himself of this permission in a few cases, procuring the release of one or two boys who were
too young to be considered capable of any offence, and the detention of
a few prisoners whose character was so notorious in the district that
their release would have been an evil to society.   (M. 30-6-91.
N. A. 27-6-92 ; 15-9-92. M. 13-11-92 ; 1-12-92.)

5.   The new system had been introduced on 1st January 1791,
and these revisions were all completed by the end of 1792.   The
benefit of the revision was afterwards extended also to the "perpetual
imprisonment" convicts, as apparently the Government came to the
conclusion that under the old system that form of sentence had been
too lavishly applied.   The magistrates were directed to submit for
revision any of the perpetual-imprisonment cases in which they deemed
the punishment excessive.   (N. A. 3-4-93 ; 17-4-93 ; 20-8-95.)

6.   The execution of these orders was apparently not well received
by those of the convicts who did not benefit by them but had still to
remain in jail.   They became very discontented, and the magistrate at
one time feared an outbreak among them.   (M. 25-5-95.)

7.   Together with the punishment of mutilation, another old
system was abolished—the "pernicious practice,"
as the court called it, of attaching the effects of
persons arrested.   Some customs were retained which we have now
abolished: for example, the nizamat adâlat, in passing sentence of death
in a case of 1795, directed the body to be hung in chains after execution.
The punishment of stripes appears to have been a very frequent one in
those days, and in 1795 the nizamat adâlat distributed to the various
magistracies "cats" to be used in their infliction, and directed the
magistrates to apply for new ones when these were worn out.   A short
time after, the judge of Dacca invented, and the nizamat adâlat

Punishment code re-modelled.

recommended, a leathern coat, which was made so as to protect from harm all parts of the body except those where it was intended that the stripes should fall. (Ct. Ct. 20-4-95. N. A. 8-4-95.)

8. The jails had of course attracted Lord Cornwallis's attention, and reports were called for; so thorough indeed was the reform proposed, that the magistrates were desired not only to report upon their condition, but to submit plans and estimates for new jails, if in any case they were deemed necessary. The report then submitted from Jessore declared the jail to be in a satisfactory condition, but apparently it was so only because the standard of judgment was a very low one. The debtors' part of it, at least, was in a very bad state only a year or two after. (G. 3-2-92. M. 26-3-92. C. 25-2-94.)

Jails.

9. However, the reports which Government received were of such a nature, that it was determined that jails built of brick should be substituted for the then existing erections; and steps were immediately taken to have a jail built at Jessore. The jail that was then in use was upon the south side of the river Bhairab, and it was intended at first to build the new jail on the same side. But Mr. Heselrige proposed, and the judges of the circuit court approved, a site on the other side of the river. The jail was under construction in April 1796, under charge of an engineer, a Mr. Stephens being contractor. In 1797 Mr. Melvill, the then judge, proposed to build a bridge across the river by convict labour, a step which was long subsequently carried into execution. (G. 5-4-93; 8-4-96. M. 1-12-95; 30-9-97; 3-12-95.)

New jail.

10. The land required for the jail was apparently occupied without asking the consent of the proprietors. But some years afterwards compensation was applied for by the owners, who were a remote branch of the Isafpur zemindar's family, and a rent was paid for the land. The whole land is still in the occupation of the jail; half of it had been taken away from the jail by the collector about 1840, but it was restored in 1869. (M. 30-9-97. C. 10-7-04.)

11. About the employment of the prisoners I do not find much information. The magistrate, in 1791, proposed to employ them in making and deepening tanks in places where water was wanting, but they do not appear to have been actually so employed. Large numbers of them were used in the making of roads, and a very common form of sentence was "so many months' labour on the public roads." (M. 11-2-92; 19-3-95.)

Employment of prisoners.

12. The jail passed from the charge of the daroga to that of the magistrate on 1st January 1791, and it was guarded by burkandazes specially entertained. (G. 15-12-90.)

13. In matters of police a system of thannahs was again introduced.

Police stations.

The idea of Government was that police stations should be so placed as to be about twenty miles apart from each other. In Mr. Rooke's first proposal he considers ten thannahs to be sufficient for the district, but the earliest actual enumeration I find in 1794, a year or two after their first establishment. There were then nineteen stations in all, of which the Jessore station cost Rs. 56 a month, and of the rest, one cost Rs. 90 and seventeen Rs. 56 per month. Besides this, the establishment of guard-boats, which had never been entirely given up, was maintained, and the total cost, guard-boats and all, was Rs. 2,028 per month. (J. 26-8-93; 3-5-94. M. 12-4-94.)

14. It is worthy of notice that all the darogas of the thannahs were Musulmans, with the exception of one, who was a Hindoo. In 1843, on the other hand, out of twelve darogas, ten were Hindoos and only two were Musulmans. (M. 1-3-93.)

15. To meet the expense which these establishments involved, an assessed tax was directed, to which merchants

Police tax.

and traders and shop-keepers were to be liable; and this tax was to be assessed by ameens working under the collector. They had to estimate, not the income, but the capital of those who were liable to the tax, and when the total was known, a rate was fixed, so that the whole sum required might be collected. The ameens assessed the capitals of the merchants and traders at an aggregate of Rs. 8,90,000 for the whole district, and the amount to be collected was Rs. 25,000 or 30,000. This sum it was exceedingly difficult to raise in Jessore, for, either on account of the then poverty of the district, or, more likely, on account of the corruption of the ameens employed, the number of persons returned as liable to the tax was somewhat small. The tax, moreover, being raised in each district for the expenditure of that district alone, fell very unequally on the different districts. In Burdwan, which was then a comparatively wealthy district, the amount required was only one per cent. on the merchant's capital, while in Jessore it was, according to the collector's calculation, $8\frac{1}{4}$ per cent. The merchants saw this inequality, and one of their objections to the tax was that people of other districts benefited as well as they by the establishment they kept up. The guard-boats notably were more useful for the through traffic from other districts than for the Jessore traffic. Besides, they objected to direct taxation altogether, and would much rather have had the required amount collected in the form of sayar duties, or of tolls. The collector, indeed, proposed to supplement the direct taxation by these indirect sources, so heavily did the burden fall upon those who had to pay the direct tax; and the experiment of direct taxation was apparently so far unsuccessful, that Government withdrew it after it had been in operation for a few years. (G. 7-12-92. Reg. 23-93. C. 6-6-94.; 7-1-95; 28-9-96. M. 1-3-93.)

16. In the administration of civil justice there was naturally

Civil courts.

less of change than in the administration of criminal justice. The former remained, as it had before been, under the charge of the judge (who was also in his other capacity magistrate). But moonsiffs now appear for the first time in the district. The notices of these and of their duties are rather scanty. They had small jurisdictions all over the district, and the fighting between zemindars and ryots gave them, for the first ten years of their existence, quite enough work to do. In 1798, 4,000 or 5,000 suits in every month had to be decided by them, almost all of them being rent-suits. (J. 29-9-97; 3-12-97; 23-5-98; 18-8-98.)

XXXIV.—*The Civil Judge's Authority Extended.*—1793-1800.

LORD CORNWALLIS gave to the judges a jurisdiction which embraced

Judges' jurisdiction paramount.

within its limits also the departments upon the executive side. They were no longer forbidden, as they were before his time, to interfere in matters which more properly belonged to other officers of Government, but people might sue the executive officers before them as they might any other individual.

2. This position was apparently a little too high for some of the

Their overbearing style.

judges, and they were apt to take up a position of opposition to the other authorities as if they had been appointed to protect the public against the misdoings of the collectors and others. Mr. Parr, as we have seen, was inclined, in matters connected with Bhusna, to take strained views of the law in opposition to the collector; and Mr. Melvill, who came after him, though in these matters he did not oppose the executive, got up a quarrel with them in some other matters.

Y

3. He used occasionally to issue purwanas to the collector couched in language which no officer in a collector's position could tolerate ; and so much did he favour this overbearing style, that even his register—a very junior officer indeed—adopted the same style in writing to the collector, telling him in very curt terms to adopt a more humble tone in writing to him, and threatening to fine him for his impertinence. (C. 18-2-00 ; 11-9-00.)

4. The nature of Mr. Melvill's doings may be understood from an example. Some ganja traders had been prosecuted by the collector for selling ganja without a license. Mr. Melvill held that such traders as they were (byapáris) were not obliged by the law to take out a license, a matter about which there was at least room for question. So, in dismissing the case, he fined the " Honorable Company" five rupees as compensation to the traders on account of false accusation. The collector was unwary enough to present a petition asking for a review of this judgment, and Mr. Melvill at once fined him Rs. 200 for doing so. It was apparently the second occasion of the collector's offending, for once before, when in some disputed matters he informed the judge that he had referred the question to the Board of Revenue, the judge had fined him Rs. 100. (C. 28-4-00 ; 14-5-00.)

5. On another occasion we find Mr. Melvill releasing from custody Government defaulters and others upon their liquidating the original debt, and refusing to hear the collector's plea that they should remain in confinement till they liquidated also the legal expenses incurred in collecting the debt. Another case also in which, I think, there can be no doubt that the civil court was wrong in interfering, but in which the sudder court upheld the judge, was this. Pergunnah Dantia had been settled with the raja zemindar of Isafpur for a lump sum, and having been sold for arrears subject to this revenue, had been purchased by certain persons. The purchasers brought a suit to reduce the assessment, upon the ground that there was a clerical error in the calculation of it, and the judge gave them a decree. The error no doubt existed, for one village had been reckoned twice, but still it is plain that the purchasers had no claim to reduction on account of it, before the civil court at least. (C. 25-4-00. B. 29-10-99. C. 22-7-00.)

6. These instances will suffice to shew the tendency of the civil court at that time to take up an attitude of opposition to the executive, or at least to arrogate to themselves an extent of power which they did not possess.

7. I make a few remarks on the relations between the judge and the

The salt department again misbehaving.

salt department, by way of continuing my previous narration of their disagreements. The salt had again become a separate department in 1790, but it was not after the permanent settlement so independent of external interference as it was before. It was now rather in the position of a mercantile body acting subject to the ordinary laws—a position which the agents did not like so well as their previous one. The salt department had apparently re-adopted the old system of malanghis and maihandars with all its iniquities, and in 1793, when a number of maihandars had, as usual, failed to appear at their place of work, the agent wrote to Mr. Burrowes, the judge, asking him to deliver them up. Such one-sided proceedings Mr. Burrowes refused to adopt, and while he was willing to summon and hear the alleged defaulters at his own court, he refused to deliver them up on mere requisition. He wrote that the most illegal and oppressive stratagems had been practised to force advances on unwilling maihandars, and that many complaints had been made before him. In these cases, when he summoned the accused— who were, of course, either malanghis or servants of the salt department —the agent refused to let them go, and accused the judge of illegally interfering and of stopping the salt manufacture. (J. 21-12-93; 3-1-94. Slt. Ag. 7-2-94.)

8. In 1795 Mr. Heselrige came as judge, and the salt agent wrote to him hoping he would stop the practice of the civil court interfering in salt matters; but he does not appear to have obtained much satisfaction thus. In fact, the misdoings of the salt department, and the opposition which the judge in the course of his duty had to offer to them, had well nigh stopped the salt manufacture altogether; and we find in 1795 that the Government is again considering the matter, and is about to issue regulations on the subject of salt manufacture. (Slt. Ag. 20-1-95. G. 27-2-95.)

9. These were the beginnings of affairs before matters had settled down under the new *régime*. There appears to have been less of quarrelling and of clashing of authority after these first few years.

XXXV.—*Early Notices of Trade and Agriculture.*—1788-1805.

IN two or three places we get a list of the hâts and ganjes, where most

Hâts and ganjes.

of the trading of the country was carried on; and the lists which are given shew that in respect of these places considerable changes have occurred during the last half century. The principal features of these lists I recapitulate.

2. In 1790 price-currents were returned for the following places:—
Kusba, Moorly, Sen's Bazar, Faqirhat, Keshabpur, Kochua, Manohar-ganj, Khulna, Tala, Kaliganj, Inchakada, Jhenida, Gopalpur, Solkopa.

Except Moorly, these are all of them still places of local trade, from which price-currents might be sent; but it is noticeable that several large hâts of the present day, such as Kotchandpur, Chaugachha, Jinga-gachha, Trimohini, Nimei Ray's Bazar, Basantia, Rajahat, and Naral or Rupganj, are all omitted from the list. Khajura does not appear either, but its mention in a contemporary letter shews that it then existed. (C. 1-7-90 ; 24-6-90.)

3. When the police tax was levied in 1793, the following was the order of the various ganjes with reference to their productiveness :—
Sahibganj, Faqirhat, Kaliganj, Jhenida, Keshabpur, Sen's Bazar, Manoharganj, * * Moorly, Tala, Khajura.

(Sahibganj and Manoharganj are both parts of the town of Jessore.)

Again we note the absence of all the above names; they are clearly names which have become important only since 1793. (C. 1-3-93.)

4. A year later we get the following list of places where grain would be abundantly procurable for the granaries :—Alinagar (now called Naupara, on the Bhairab), Kumarganj, Faqirhat, Chandkhali, Henckellganj, and one or two others. The first two are still consider-able hâts, though not for grain; the others are the Sundarban hâts, where the traffic in grain had thus early developed itself. (C. 18-10-94.)

5. In a letter written in 1815 we find the following given as the four most considerable places in the district :—Jessore, Mirzanagar, Faqirhat, Chaturabaria. Mirzanagar is now a village near Trimohini, which has usurped whatever importance Mirzanagar once had; Faqirhat is only a second-rate ganj; of Chaturabaria, I do not even know the situation. Kotchandpur, which is now the greatest commercial place in the district, is about the same time mentioned as " a place called Kotchandpur at which a thannah is established, in appearance a town of some importance and magnitude, about ten cos from Naldanga." (C. 28-4-15 ; 3-11-15.)

6. From a list of produce and of exports and imports prepared by the collector on 14th March 1791, we obtain the following information regarding local trade.

Trade in rice and grain, &c.

Of paddy the produce is estimated at 900,000 maunds, of which half was exported westward. Besides this, 150,000 maunds passed through the district from Backerganj. The trade is still in the same direction. Of kallai and of masuri (both vetches) also considerable exports were, as now, made to Calcutta. Cocoanuts were then, as now, largely cultivated in the south of the district, and a large quantity was exported. Betelnuts also were a characteristic trade, being exported from the southern pergunnahs, as they are now. Tobacco appears to have been exported in much greater quantities than now. Thirty thousand maunds are stated to be grown in the north-west part of the district, and of these 10,000 were exported to Calcutta."

7. Of cotton a detailed account is given in 1789. The production
Cotton.
of cotton at the present time is extremely limited, but then 2,400 maunds were produced and 3,600 maunds were imported for local manufacture. A very small quantity of thread was also imported from Bhusna for the weavers in Jessore. From all this 148,100 pieces of cloth were yearly manufactured. The cotton was purchased from the cultivating ryots and then it was cleaned. After that it was spun by women for weaving; one very fine sort being spun, not on a wheel, but on a wire on the fingers. The cotton crop was sown sometimes in May, sometimes in October, and May was the reaping time for both sowings. It was a rather expensive cultivation. (C. 31-5-89.)

8. Sugar, which is now so important a manufacture, distinguished
Sugar.
Jessore in those days also. It is mentioned as one of the evils of the 1787 inundation that it would diminish the date-sugar manufacture. In the table of 1791 we find the sugar produce put down at 20,000 maunds, of which half was exported to Calcutta; and the greater part of this was date-sugar. (C. 25-6-88; 24-11-92.)

9. From the absence of indigo in the 1791 list of exports, we may
Indigo.
justly conclude that no indigo was then manufactured. In fact, we can trace the rise of this manufacture; for, as it was introduced by Europeans, and Europeans were not permitted to rent even enough land for a factory without the Company's permission, we trace the history of the manufacture in the applications for land.

10. The first mention is in 1795, when Mr. Bond, "a free merchant under covenant with the court of directors," erected a factory at Rupdia and wanted to put up another at Alinagar (or Naupara). Then, in the beginning of 1796, came a Mr. Tuft, who obtained permission to start indigo works in Muhammadshahi. In 1800 a Mr. Taylor

is mentioned as having indigo factories in the direction of the great river; and in 1801 Mr. Anderson, the civil surgeon, erected works at Barandi and Nilganj (both suburbs of Jessore), and at Daulatpur. (C. 14-4-95; 4-2-96; 17-2-00; 23-4-01; 20-11-01.)

11. Against these last factories Mr. Jennings, who had factories at Jingagachha, and Mr. Bond, who had factories at Rupdia and at Nrisinghapur, made a protest. The proposed factories would be too near theirs, and would encroach on the lands where they cultivated. The collector also considered that now that so many works had been set up over the district (for there were evidently many more than I have named), some rule should be laid down to prevent their clashing with one another. Apparently nothing was then done with this object. But applications for new lands still continued to come in, and in 1811 Jessore and Dacca are stated to be both crowded with indigo factories, and the then collector again pointed out the frequent disputes and jealousies, and recommended that no new factory should be established within ten miles of any old one. (C. 20-11-01; 3-7-01; 20-2-09; 1-5-11.)

12. A list of Europeans resident in the district in 1805 mentions the names of the first indigo cultivators in Jessore.
Europeans.   Europeans used frequently to be called on to send in their names on pain of forfeiting the Company's protection, which, to judge from their remissness in complying with these requisitions, they did not so highly appreciate. The list quoted contains the following names:—

Deverell, Hazrapur; Brisbane, Datiakati; Taylor and Knudson, Mirpur; Reeves, Sinduria; Razet, Nohatta; and several others. (3-12-05.)

13. It may be noted as a measure of the progress of commerce and the advance in administration since the time to
Progress of commerce.   which the statements made in this chapter refer, that while for the police tax of 1795 the trading *capital* of the district was assessed at Rs. 8,90,000, for the certificate tax of 1868 the trading *profit* of the district was estimated at Rs. 32,00,000. (C. 7-1-95.)

XXXVI.—*Public Communications—Civil Surgeon—Census—
Miscellaneous.*

Public Communications.—A little information under this head is obtained from the old letters. The public road,
Roads.   as it was called, from Calcutta to Dacca, which passed through Jessore, is noticed in a letter of 1791; but though it

was designated by this name, it appears to have been rather a track kept up by country traffic than a road maintained as such. The part of it which lay between Calcutta and Jingagachha is described in 1794 as being in fair order, and that which lay between Jingagachha and Jessore was a year or two later, by means of convict labour, put into fair repair. But as in 1800 we find the collector proposing to carry on the road towards Dacca, that part of it can hardly have been before that year a regularly maintained route. (C. 28-7-91; 18-7-94; 7-2-98; 21-9-00.)

2. There was in 1794 also a road from Jessore through Jhenida to Comercolly and a road to Chaugachha and one to Khulna. These last two were in a very bad state at that time, and as the collector, in 1800, proposed to renew both the Chaugachha and the Comercolly roads, they can have been paid very little attention to up to that time at least. They were probably little more than uncared-for tracks, for in 1802 there were only twenty miles of road properly so called in the district. (C. 18-7-94; 21-9-00; 2-1-02.)

3. These twenty miles appear to have included only the Jingagachha road and the following "station roads," which had been for the most part made and maintained by prison labour: Rupdia to Kasba, Churamankati to Kasba, Moorly to Chanchra. These roads all still exist, and the last named, though much damaged by recent cyclones, has still the character which is implied in the epithet "avenue" applied to it in 1800. The Churamankati road was not, I believe, planted with trees till a much later date. (C. 21-9-00; 2-1-02.)

4. None of the considerable rivers on the roads were bridged. (C. 21-9-00; 2-10-10.)

5. There was little cart traffic in the district, the consequence probably of the state of the roads. The collector, in 1794, says there were not one hundred carts in the whole district, and in 1810 he writes that at the head-quarters there were only six procurable. Water carriage was adopted in almost every case in preference to land carriage. Treasure was for special reasons sent by land to Calcutta, but officers joining the district appear to have done so mostly by the river route. (C. 18-7-94; 2-10-10; 9-5-15.)

Traffic.

6. A regular postal line was kept up between Calcutta and Jessore, going by land, and besides these there were minor cross-lines managed by the collector. In 1790 the following cross-lines were kept up:—Jessore by Jhenida to Comercolly; Jessore by Khulna to Jaynagar (a salt-station); and

Post.

another line in the same direction, perhaps the same route, on to Backerganj. (C. 15-7-90.)

7. *Civil Surgeoncy.*—There was no civil surgeon in Jessore till 1786, when, on Mr. Henckell's proposal, the appointment was created. A Mr. Henderson was the first appointed, and after him a Dr. Anderson held the appointment for a long series of years. This Dr. Anderson went largely into indigo and erected small factories, among other places, at Nilganj and Pulu Ghât, both close to Jessore. (J. 12-4-86.)

8. *Census.*—On two occasions, first in 1789 and afterwards in 1802, the collector submitted an estimate of the number of inhabitants in the district. In the first case the region to which the enumeration extended included the parts east of the Ichamati now within the 24-Pergunnahs, and it included also the whole of Muhammadshahi, but it excluded Naldi and Bhusna. The collector reckoned 547,250 males and 508,859 females; total, 1,056,109. On the second occasion the limits of the enumeration were nearly those of the present two districts of Jessore and Furreedpoor, and the estimate was 1,200,000. On the first occasion I do not know on what the collector based his estimate; but as he gives the figures in somewhat of detail, and says they are as accurate as without minute inquiry they could be, he must have had some sort of basis for his estimate. In the second case the collector had no details; he writes simply "there are about 12,000 villages, and they contain on an average 1,000 inhabitants a-piece." The figures are not very valuable, except in so far as they shew that Jessore was a very populous district at the time of the permanent settlement. (C. 30-9-89; 9-1-02.)

9. *Miscellaneous Notes.*—Slaves are mentioned in a casual notice of
Slaves.
"Cæsar, Mr. Osborne's slave-boy," in connection with the death by accident of Mr. Osborne, who was in the salt department. (Letter to magistrate, 14-3-85.)

The Government, in 1789, forbade the exportation of natives as slaves. It appears to have been a regular trade, however illegal it may have been. (M. 14-8-89. C. 12-8-89.)

The Government, in 1792, that is shortly after the establishment
Lynch law. ·
of the new system of criminal justice, prohibited the practice of private individuals confining people of their own authority in stocks and in irons. This practice appears to have been a common one, for it is called a "custom." (C. 6-11-92.)

A reward of Rs. 10 sicca for each tiger destroyed was proclaimed in 1788. (B. 18-6-88. C. 24-6-88; 10-6-08.)

The French revolution even turns up among these old letters; for the Government, on 14th September 1791, communicated to all collectors the intimation he had received from the French Government of the abolition of the old "fleur-de-lis" flag and the adoption of the tri-color.

XXXVII.—*The Saydpur Trust Estate.*—1814-23.

In our history of the rajas of Chanchra it has been mentioned that at one period four annas of their estates came into possession of a Mahomedan family, and that that family had, before the permanent settlement, made over one portion of their estate, namely "Taraf Sobnal," for the benefit of the imámbára at Hooghly.

2. The possessor of this estate, Haji Muhammad Mahsin, died in

Trust created. 1814, and having no heirs he bequeathed his estate in this manner. It was to be kept in trust in the hands of two trustees, who were each to have one-ninth of the profits as their share; they were to spend three-ninths upon religious observances at the imámbára at Hooghly, and the rest was to be employed in discharging the salaries of certain officers appointed at the imámbára, and in keeping up the imámbára and the tomb of Salahuddin, which is also, I believe, at Hooghly.

3. The two trustees into whose hands the property came very

Government takes possession. soon quarrelled among themselves, and the affairs of the estate got into dreadful confusion. So in 1816 the collector took possession of the estate under a recent law (XIX of 1810) devised to enable Government to prevent trustees of property devoted to religious and charitable purposes from appropriating it to their own use or abusing their trust. The two trustees were relieved of their functions, and the Board of Revenue (5-3-16) adopted the following method of regulating the estate.

4. The Government, acting by the collector of Jessore, was to be one trustee, who was to look after the management of the property; and for the second trustee a member of the Shia sect of Mussulmans was to be appointed by Government, his function being to see to the due expenditure of the funds at the imámbára. With this second trustee Government concerns itself very little, leaving to him and to the religious community interested in the imámbára the care of their own matters.

z

5. The collector accordingly undertook the management of the
Improvement of the   estate, and has ever since carried it on. A
estate.   general measurement and settlement was made
during the first few years of the collector's possession, and about 1823
almost the whole of it was given out in patni tenure. By these
operations not only was the annual revenue of the estate increased
from Rs. 1,25,000 to Rs. 1,70,000, but Rs. 5,70,000 was realized as the
premia paid on the patni taluqs. The surplus available for the
purposes of the endowment was increased in this way from Rs. 25,000
to Rs. 70,000, which is the present net annual value of the endowment.

6. The share which, under the terms of the will, would belong
to Government as trustee, is granted by Government for the maintenance of the Hooghly College, and the rest of the Rs. 70,000 goes to
the trustee, Sayd Karámat Ali, in charge of the imámbára; the endowment being, in fact, the chief source of its wealth.

7. The estate is known as ".The Saydpur trust estate," and its
more familiar name in the district is "The four-anna estate." Its
cutcherries were once at Moorly, and it was managed from Moorly
while the collectorate was in Jessore. There are one or two European
graves in Moorly, which are said to be those of Europeans engaged in
the management of this estate.

8. The lands attached to the estate are of considerable extent, and
Situation of the lands.   include a large part of the pergunnah Saydpur,
                            with much of the land surrounding Jessore, part
of the pergunnah Isafpur, considerable lands on the north-west of Khulna
and on the right bank of the Bhairab, much of the land near Keshabpur,
and an estate in the south, near Sobna. The pergunnah Sobnal, which
is also within the estate, is within the geographical limits of the 24-Per-
gunnahs. The lands are almost all given in patni; pergunnahs Khalispur
and Maheshwarpassa, on the north-west of Khulna, are given in farm;
and a number of scattered portions, paying rents of from Rs. 5 to 150, are
also given nominally in farm, but practically in a short of ryotti tenure.

XXXVIII.—*The Origin of Cholera.*—1817.

In one respect Jessore has acquired a very evil reputation; for it was
the place where began that first great outbreak of cholera which,
spreading up the valley of the Ganges, attacked and decimated the army

of the Marquis of Hastings, then engaged in operations against Scindia, in Central India, and afterwards extended itself, in a north-westerly direction, over the whole of the civilized world.

2. Cholera had been known before as an endemic disease prevailing more or less in almost every region in the plains of Lower Bengal, but before 1817, the year of the outbreak now referred to, it had not that dreadful form which we now associate with its name. Medical men have in recent researches shewn that at various dates between 1503 and 1756 there had been violent outbreaks of cholera, but these had been confined to India, and apparently none of them spread beyond narrow limits. Before, therefore, the outbreak which began in 1817 carried the knowledge of the disease far and wide over India, and then over Europe, cholera was known only in its milder endemic form; and it had previously attracted little attention, being apparently not more fatal, and not more dreaded, than the fevers which usually exist in the districts of Lower Bengal. The Medical Board, when, on 22nd September 1817, they reported on the outbreak of that year, identified the disease to a certain extent with that which " generally prevails in greater or less extent at the present season of the year," remarking, however, that " it has of late proved far more fatal than at any former time within recollection."

Previous form of cholera.

3. The first case of cholera, then, occurred at Jessore on 20th August 1817, and a day or two after that the whole town was seized with panic. And no wonder—the disease seems to have been exceedingly sudden in its attack. On August 25th Mr. Chapman, the then judge and magistrate, writes of it as a "most alarming and fatal disorder;" and in a letter of the same date the collector, Mr. Tucker, calls it "an inveterate and fatal disease." Several persons were suddenly seized with it when walking along the roads in the bazar: an instance is mentioned where a sepoy had been attacked with it about midnight, while on guard at the jail, and was dead before morning. In most cases in fact, at the beginning of the outbreak, the suddenness of the attack almost precluded the application of medical aid. (M. 25-8-17. C. 25-8-17. C. S. to M. 23-8-17 and 30-9-17.)

Outbreak in 1817.

4. The alarm in the town was general, and everybody left the place who could do so. The judge shut up his court, for the vakeels declared they would all resign their offices if he insisted upon their remaining at work. The

Panic.

collector also stopped work; he had some sales fixed for August 25th, which he writes that he put off on account of the absence of bidders; and he warned the Board that he might find it necessary to let his clerks and writers leave the station for a time, and said that one or two of them were already dead. This, however, was not ultimately necessary, for three days afterwards the disease was decreasing; but the magistrate and the collector both of them attributed this effect to the desertion of the town by its inhabitants. (M. 25-8-17. C. 25-8-17. M. 28-8-17. C. 28-8-17.)

5. A few days after it appeared in the town, cholera also appeared in the jail. The prisoners of course were more closely looked after than was possible in the case of the town, and there was no case of cholera proper in the jail after September 2nd. In the town and its vicinity the disease was dying away in the beginning of September, for it is its nature never to stay long in one place. It had, however, broken out in a few other places in the district, but the magistrate, on October 3rd, reported that even from these it had by that time almost entirely disappeared.

6. Of the mortality in the town the records omit to supply infor-
Mortality.   mation. The magistrate sent up some statistics on
                                February 5th, 1818, but no copy has been preserved.
In the jail there were over 800 prisoners. Of these, during the few days of August during which cholera was present in the jail, 36 were attacked and 7 died. This is, however, probably no measure of the mortality outside the jail walls.* (C. S. to M. 17-9-17.)

7. The epidemic attacked chiefly the lower classes. Its symptoms, as described by Dr. Tytler, the civil surgeon, were these: excessive purging and vomiting; great thirst; a sensation of great heat, without any actual increase of temperature. The treatment Dr. Tytler used and recommended to others was the exhibition of calomel and opium, and he records that these medicines were always successful when given at a sufficiently early stage of the disease,—a rather indefinite qualifi-cation. (C. S. to M. 23-8-17 and 30-9-17.)

8. Dr. Tytler at first attributed the outbreak to "a vitiated
Cause of the outbreak.   state of bile" caused by the hot weather, to the
                                increase of jungle, and to the great collections of
water caused by the unusually heavy rainfall of the season.   The

---

* In a recent pamphlet by Dr. D. B. Smith, it is stated that 10,000 people died in two months in the district of Jessore.

Medical Board stated the cause more generally as lying in the "extreme humidity of the atmosphere, occasioned by the long-continued and incessant rains of the present season." (C. S. to M. 23-8-17. Med. Bd. 22-9-17.)

9. Dr. Tytler also records some interesting information regarding a special cause, to which he attributes a somewhat exaggerated importance, calling it "a great Truth which has under the favour of the Almighty been disclosed at this station, where the disease first broke out." The heat and humidity of the season had not only brought to early maturity the autumn crop of rice, but had imparted to it an unusual richness of flavour. The supply of new rice was abundant and cheap, and it was eagerly sought after; even before being fully ripe, it was "devoured with avidity by natives of all descriptions." To this extensive use of immature rice Dr. Tytler ascribes the outbreak, and from what he says it is clear that it was a predisposing cause. He mentions this as an opinion generally received and openly declared by the natives. He states that in many places attacked by cholera, though nothing had been done to cut the jungle and drain the pools of stagnant water, the mere prohibition by the magistrate of the sale and use of new rice had been effectual in causing an immediate decrease in the disease; and he mentions one instance coming under his personal observation. On 2nd September the use of new rice was absolutely forbidden in the jail, and on that day cholera disappeared from the jail. One case occurred after that, namely, a case of a female prisoner who, having surreptitiously obtained and eaten a small quantity of new rice, was attacked by cholera a short time after. (C. S. to M. 30-9-17 and 1-10-17.)

10. One measure adopted to meet the disease I have already noticed—the general prohibition, or rather warning, against the use of new rice. Besides this, native doctors were entertained, and worked in Jessore under Dr. Tytler, who himself obtained great credit for his personal exertions. Of all the native doctors entertained only two remained at their post; they were attacked themselves with the disease, but recovered and continued their work. To some planters residing in the interior, instructions were forwarded how to deal with the disease if it appeared in their vicinity. (C. S. to M. 1-10-17.)

Remedial measures.

11. All that was done to meet the cholera at Jessore was done by the local officers (Mr. Chapman and Dr. Tytler) on their own

responsibility. The Medical Board were informed, but their first letter, which was little more than a general approval of the steps taken by the local officers, did not arrive till the disease had begun to disappear. It was the first time the Medical Board had heard of this new form of cholera, and they were of course not in a position to take on themselves the direction of matters at Jessore in the same way that they afterwards did when the epidemic appeared at their own doors in Calcutta (the next place it came to after Jessore), or when it commenced its journey up the valley of the Ganges. (Med. Bd. 6-9-17.)

12. The vice-president in council also approved the proceedings of the local officers, and especially commended Dr. Tytler's exertions; and to each of the two native doctors mentioned above a gratuity of Rs. 50 was awarded. (G. 14-10-17.)

     *   *   *   *   *   -   *

13. Though not immediately connected with Jessore, the magistrate received copies of the correspondence relating to the subsequent progress of the epidemic, and from these papers I gather the following notes about the epidemic in Calcutta.

Subsequent progress of the disease.

14. On 15th September 1817 Mr. Elliot, magistrate of the suburbs of Calcutta, reported to Government the presence of " an epidemic disease" in Calcutta and its vicinity, and Government sent on the report to the Medical Board. Previously to this the Medical Board, in their letter of 5th September regarding the cholera at Jessore, alluded to the existence of a similar epidemic in Calcutta and its vicinity, but the quietness of their language, and the fact that no steps whatever were then taken, or even advised, with regard to Calcutta, shews that the cholera, as it existed there in the beginning of September, was the older and milder form of the disease, and not the new form it had assumed at Jessore.

Calcutta.

15. When, on 16th September, they received information of the new and more alarming outbreak in Calcutta, they at once took steps to provide remedies. Native physicians were employed, and were supplied with medicines from the Government stores, and detailed written instructions were given to them. They numbered in all forty or fifty, and more would have been employed had they been available. These steps were approved by Government, who gave the Medical Board permission to meet any expenditure they might deem necessary. (Med. Bd. 22-9-17. Gov. 23-9-17).

16. The Medical Board appear to have even then hardly understood the intractable nature of the disease. They write, when reporting regarding the Calcutta outbreak, that "it is fortunately a disease which admits of a speedy remedy." Those who had more immediately to deal with the disease found it far otherwise. We have seen that the Jessore officials found it difficult even to apply medicines in time, and the Board themselves admit that in Calcutta it "threatened to sweep off a large portion of the native population," and consider a slight reduction in the number of funerals one passes in the streets a matter for congratulation. (Med. Bd. 22-9-17.)

17. The disease, as it appeared in Calcutta in the middle of September, is described in very much the same words which Dr. Tytler used in describing its symptoms at Jessore. It attacked its victims without any warning. While walking in the roads, or engaged in their ordinary pursuits, they suddenly fell down, and immediately began vomiting; a cold, clammy sweat broke out, and the patient became so weak as to be unable to move, feeling a painful sense of heat and weight in the stomach and bowels.

The Medical Board record that in Calcutta the disease tended towards the lowest and worst drained parts of the town. (Med. Bd. 22-9-17. Enclosure to G. 23-9-17.)

18. Copies of the instructions which had been drawn up by the Medical Board were sent to Jessore, where, however, the epidemic had ceased before their arrival; and to Burdwan, where it had broken out at nearly the same time as at Calcutta. Cholera had already started on that fatal journey which was to take it over half the civilized world. (G. 23-9-17.)

* * *

PART IV.—LANDED PROPERTY.

XXXIX.—*The Distribution of Landed Property in the District, and the History of the New Zemindars.*

IT has been described as a consequence of the permanent settlement
The old and the new zemindars. that small zemindaris and small zemindars came to be substituted for great zemindaris and great zemindars. It was, however, natural that of these small zemindars

some should increase their substance above others, and by buying up zemindari after zemindari, and tenure after tenure, aggregate in the end a very large estate. Such estates differ entirely in their nature from the old zemindaris; they are not compact and single estates extending over some tract of country where their owner is prominent as the great zemindar, but they are an accumulation of separate and separately held tenures, acquired in different ways and at different times, held under all sorts of different rights, and scattered here and there over the country. Zemindari, in fact, has become more of a profession and less of a position.

2. Of these newly arisen great zemindar families only one, the Naral family, belongs properly to the district of Jessore. But there are several others who, residing in other districts, have lands within Jessore. Of the Naral family I narrate the history in a separate chapter, but the other great families need not have their history recorded at such length. I shall make some notes regarding them in connection with the lands they possess.

3. I propose therefore going round the district and narrating in order such remarks as I have to make regarding zemindari holdings and zemindars.

4. *Sub-division Jessore.*—A considerable part of this sub-division is the lands included in the pergunnah Saydpur,
Saydpur.
which are distributed for the most part between two zemindaris, that of the raja of Jessore and that of the Trust Estate. The history of each of these has been separately given. The lands in both are given out to a great extent in patni.

5. Another considerable part of the sub-division is pergunnah Shahujial, which in ancient times belonged to the
Shahujial dismembered.
Nattore raj, but was sold up a short time after the permanent settlement. It was sold up, not as a whole, but in small parts called "dihis," each of which contained a few villages, not necessarily adjoining each other.

6. One of the largest of these dihis, dihi Arpara, within which Chaugachha is, was bought by Kelaram Mukharjya,
Gobradanga family.
of Gobradanga, in the name of his son-in-law, Ram Kishor Chattarjya. From Kelaram it descended to his two sons, Kali Prasanna and Baidyanath, and the latter having died heirless, the son of the former, Sarada Prasanna Mukharjya, obtained the estate. He died in 1869, and the estates came under the court of

wards. The Gobradanga family have a much larger estate than this in the south of the district; they have also considerable estates in Nuddea, and a little in the 24-Pergunnàhs.

7. Another of the dihis is dihi Phulbaria, which had been long before the permanent settlement devoted to Shyam Ray, an idol in Moorshedabad. It was retained when the rest of the Nattore estates were lost, and is still held on the part of the Nattore family, its proceeds going to the idol.

8. Dihi Kaneshpur (within which is part of Kotchandpur) and dihi Sarup-pur were, in the sales of the Nattore estates, purchased by Gopimohun Thakur, the principal founder of the Thakur or Tagore family.

Thakur or Tagore family.

9. The Tagores come of a family of tainted brahmans, called Pir Ali Brahmans; and they originally belonged to Narendrapur, near Rajahât, in the Jessore district. The story of the tainting is not by any means a distinct one, but it runs somewhat in this fashion. A controversy had arisen as to whether smelling was half-eating or not, and Pir Ali Khan, a Mahomedan, who was doing some work in the district, connected either with the Government or with the raja of Jessore's zemindari, invited to his house a number of brahmans. When they came, he caused them, against their will, to smell flesh, which was to them forbidden meat, and the pandits deciding that their smelling it amounted to half eating it, declared those tainted who had smelt. Two persons named Ray Chaudry, who sat next the ameen, were declared to have really eaten the food, and were therefore ordered to become Mussulmans. They took the names Jamal and Kamal Khan, and their descendants are still alive in Basantia (near Jessore). They bear the Mahomedan surname Khan Chaudhry, and a Hindoo first name.

10. The name of the first Tagore ancestor who became tainted was Purushuttam, but it is undetermined whether he was tainted directly by being present on the above occasion at Pir Ali's, or whether it was by his being afterwards seized by the Khan Chaudhries and compelled to marry their daughter.

11. For six generations after Purushuttam the Tagores lived in Jessore, and then, about the beginning or middle of last century, Panchanan, leaving Jessore, settled and built a house on what is now the site of Fort William: He entered the service of the British, and received, as his descendants have retained, the surname of " Thakur," which was then given to all brahmans by the English.

12. His son Jayram had to give up the site at Fort William, and no doubt received for it ample compensation.

13. Jayram's son Darpanarayn acquired great wealth by commercial dealings and by money-lending, and also by serving the French at Chandernagore ; and when the Nattore estates began to be sold up, he purchased a large pergunnah in Rangpur, and his son Gopimohun, who also served the French, added other estates, partly purchased from the disintegrating Nattore raj.

14. The Tagore family have many estates all over Bengal, being one of the large land-holding families; they have not much in Jessore. Besides the two dihis near Kotchandpur which have been mentioned, and which are given in patni, they hold also a half share in the zemindari of taraf Rusulpur, which contains many villages along the north side of the Bhairab, between Jessore and Afra, and on both sides of the khal between Afra and Gobra.

15. The east and north-east of Jessore sub-division are occupied by pergunnahs Imadpur (a small one close to Jessore) and Isafpur (a large one extending over a large tract of country). Originally part of the Chanchra raja's zemindari, these were sold up at the time of the dispersion of his property. The lands are now held by many zemindars, but the chief of them are these : Baboo Anandchandra Chaudhry of Bagchar (who will be noted under Magurah sub-division) holds a good deal of land in the southern part of it, his zemindari cutcherry being at Taraganj. In the northern part of it the Naupara Baboos (whose history will be recorded in a note to this chapter) have some zemindaris and some patnis. In the south-east of it taraf Rusulpur is the patni of the Naral Baboos, the zemindari rights being held, I believe, by the raja and by one branch of the Tagore family.

Imadpur and Isafpur.

Naupara family.

16. In the vicinity of Jessore itself the raja has some property, and a good deal belongs also to the Trust Estate. The Ramnagar Baboos (who come under Khulna sub-division) hold land lying between Ramnagar and Chanchra, partly in patni of the raja and partly in patni of the Trust Estate. They have also some property in the direction of Manirampur. Anandchandra Chaudhry, just mentioned, has also some property close to Jessore, and so have his cousins, the heirs of Ray Radhacharn, whose father was Anandchandra's father's brother.

17. On the whole, it cannot be said that within the sub-division of Jessore there are any large accumulations of property in the hands

of one individual. The Saydpur estates, both the raja's and the Trust Estate, are of course excepted, but all the rest of the sub-division is divided among many proprietors.

18. *Sub-division Jhenida.*—The sub-division is almost entirely within the pergunnahs which form chakla Muhammadshahi, whose boundary on all sides is some ten miles or so outside of that of the sub-division. Its zemindari history therefore is the history of Muhammadshahi. It has already been said that Muhammadshahi was the patrimony of the rajas of Naldanga, and it has been narrated how the Naldanga house split into three branches, and only one of these three, that represented by the present raja of Naldanga, managed to retain its property, while that of the other two branches, being three-fifths of the whole, passed into other hands, and finally into the hands of the Naral Baboos.

[margin note] Muhammadshahi.

19. The property in the sub-division, apart from the small estates scattered here and there, is therefore divided between the Naral Baboos, most of whose land lies in the western part of it, and the Naldanga raja, most of whose is in the eastern part of it. The Naral Baboos for the most part manage their lands direct, while the raja of Naldanga's is mostly given in patni. The indigo concerns have large tenures within the pergunnah, many of them, and perhaps most, being held of the Naldanga raja. There are many small lakhiraj holdings in Muhammadshahi.

20. The Naldanga raja's place of business is at Naldanga, while the Naral Baboos manage their lands from the chakla cutcherry, two miles west of Jhenida. Until they obtained the pergunnah the chakla cutcherry was in Jhenida, on the same site, I believe, where the sub-divisional cutcherry now is.

21. *Magurah sub-division.*—Of Magurah the extreme west and north falls within the Muhammadshahi pergunnah which has been described above.

22. The eastern part of it, that is, the land round about Muhammadpur, is pergunnah Sâtor, which pergunnah crosses the river and runs well into Furreedpore district. This is one of the pergunnahs which were sold on the break up of the Nattore raj, and the purchaser of it was Krishnachandra Pal, the founder of the Pal Chaudhry family.

[margin note] Sâtor.

23. Krishna Pal was originally a petty trader at Ranaghat, and there lived at that time a certain mohant (a brahman priest) who had a considerable trade or

[margin note] Pal Chaudhry family.

cultivation at Aranghatta, a little north of Ranaghat. This mohant
had some very large stores of the grain called "chola," but the insects
got at it and spoiled it all—at least so it seemed. The mohant determined to cast it all away, when Krishna Pal offered him some small
price for it, and subsequently by selling it realized an enormous profit,
for it turned out that the insects had destroyed only a little of the
surface grain.

24. Krishna Pal was now a merchant of great capital, which he
further greatly increased by trading in, and almost monopolizing the
trade in salt, which at that time was sold by auction at the Board of
Revenue, as opium is now (so at least say the narrators of the history).
At last he resolved to establish a zemindari, and pergunnah Sâtor was
the first purchase which he made.

25. The family afterwards made other very large purchases,
especially near Ranaghat and Bongong in Nuddea; and after enjoying
for a time a very prominent position, they began to lose their estates.
There were several descendants of Krishnachandra Pal, and, as is the
usual history of zemindar families, they fell out among themselves.
The story is that the first falling-out was a dispute about a goat,
worth four annas, required for some family sacrifice. They disputed
about the goat, then separated as a family, then fought against each
other in the courts and lost all their wealth in litigation. There was
one great suit which lasted from 1821 till about 1850, and which in its
course (so I am told) went to Europe four times in appeal. By it an
ousted member of the family, Baidyanath by name, sued for and
obtained possession of his share. Then a Mr. Mackintosh, who had
advanced large funds to the Pal Chaudhries with which to carry on this
litigation, obtained a large decree against them and proceeded to sell
up their property in satisfaction of it. Then a four-anna share in Sâtor
had been pledged as security to Government, and by this means
subsequently became lost to the Pal Chaudhry family.

26. The result of all these suits, and of the executions of decree,
and compromising, was that Mr. Mackintosh became possessor of half of
pergunnah Sâtor, and Thakur Dass Gosain of the other half—one by
compromise, the other by purchase—about 1861-62. The two halves
are specifically separated, that is, separate villages belong to each.

27. Mr. Mackintosh sold his half a year or two since to Gobind
Shaha, a merchant of Dulur, in Furreedpoor, who seems to be establishing at present a zemindar family such as the Pal Chaudhries once were.

28. Thakur Dass Gosain, who still possesses his share, is a member
The Gosains of Serampore. of the Serampore family of Gosains. This family lived at first by the practice of their profession (religion), till Ramnarayn Gosain, Thakur Dass's grandfather, abandoned the ways of his fathers and gave himself up to commerce. He made much money by trading with the Danish merchants at Serampore, and purchased various zemindaris in Burdwan, Purnea, and Midnapore. His son Kamallochan, who acquired money by serving Government as a commissariat agent, purchased further lands in Hooghly. And Thakur Dass, son of Kamallochan, made money in the same way, and with it purchased Sâtor when the Pal Chaudhries got into difficulties and were obliged to part with their estates. Muhammadpur is the site of his cutcherry.

29. Of the Pal Chaudhries, Srigopal, son of Nilcamal, son of
Srigopal Pal Chaudhry. Sambhu, brother of Krishnachandra, is the only one who by good management saved himself from the ruin that overtook the other branches of his family, and he is now adding to his zemindaris and has regained the position of a large zemindar. His estates are principally in the Ranaghat and Bongong sub-divisions of Nuddea, and they just enter Jessore on its western boundary.

30. Taraf Nohatta is a considerable estate within Magurah, and
Anandchandra Chaudhry of Bagchar. its proprietor is Anandchandra Chaudhry of Bagchar, close to Jessore. His family comes originally from Burdwan, whence a hundred years ago his grandfather, Kâbal Ram, migrated to Jessore. He was a merchant, and in that capacity he and his sons acquired wealth and purchased some lands in Isafpur and Imadpur, two pergunnahs near Jessore. Anandchandra, the principal member of the family, is the younger son of Guruprasad, the youngest son of Kâbal Ram. He served as treasurer to the raja of Jessore for six years, and as the treasurer's function was to lend the raja money, he obtained some wealth in this way, and more by his own commercial dealings which he carried on at the same time. After that, from 1847 to 1865, he was treasurer of the Jessore collectorate—a position which, then at least, gave considerable prominence, and brought considerable business, to a merchant. The treasurer of the collectorate is the man to whom needy zemindars naturally apply when they have no money to meet the Government demand, and their necessity being very urgent, the treasurer can make his own terms.

31. Anandchandra therefore, by his commercial and money-lending dealings, has become a wealthy man, and has acquired from time to time various landed estates. Taraf Nohatta was purchased by him in 1844, and he owns also some lands in Isafpur pergunnah. Taraf Nohatta is given in patni to Mr. Savi, of Nohatta factory.

32. The south-west part of Magurah sub-division comes within the pergunnah Isafpur, mentioned under the sudder sub-division. The lands are divided among many persons, the Naupara Baboos being perhaps the most prominent, and Alangmohun Deb Ray, of Chandra, being also a leading proprietor.

33. *Naral sub-division.*—The northern half of Naral sub-division is pergunnah Naldi, which runs a good way into Magurah also, and this pergunnah (apart from smaller estates and "khariji" or separated taluqs scattered through it) belongs to the Paikpara family, whose ancestor, Prankrishna Singh, purchased it about 1798, at the disruption of the Nattore estates.

Naldi.

The Paikpara family.

34. Prankrishna Singh came of a family which had for some time been eminent in the politics of Bengal, its founder being one Harkrishna Singh, who acquired great wealth under the Mahomedan government. This man's grandson Behari had two sons, Radhagobind and Gangagobind. The former was a high revenue officer under Alivardi Khan and Suraj-ud-daula, nawabs of Bengal, and when the British undertook the management of the revenues, he rendered great service by putting at their disposal the necessary settlement and collection papers, for which he was rewarded by a grant of a "sayar mahal," or right of collecting octroi, in Hooghly. The family still draw Rs. 3,698 per annum from Hooghly, the compensation given them for the resumption of this sayar in 1790.

35. Gangagobind, the other brother, held high employment under Warren Hastings; but as he spent all his wealth in charity (spending, for example, twenty lakhs on his mother's shradh) he left his family destitute, and bequeathed his son Prankrishna to his brother Radhagobind.

36. Prankrishna was apparently the acquirer of the zemindaris, which, added to by subsequent members of the family, extend now into more than half the districts of Bengal. In Jessore, however, they have hardly anything else besides their Naldi estates.

37. Prankrishna's son was Krishnachandra Singh, who is better known as Lalla Baboo. He became a religious pilgrim and took up

his residence in the north-west, where his immense liberality rendered him famous. At Brindaban he built a temple of Rajputana marble, and he was involved in some political complications in Rajputana when he went there to purchase the marble. There is a large tank in the Muttra district, called "Radha Kunda," and this tank was by Lalla Baboo faced on all sides with steps.

38. His widow, Rani Khatyany, who is still alive, has signalized herself also by various acts of liberality.

39. Lalla Baboo's son was Srinarayn, and Pratapchandra Singh was Srinarayn's son. He died about 1866, and his large estates came under the court of wards. They lie chiefly in the districts of the Burdwan division, and in Noacolly.

40. The Naldi pergunnah, their property in Jessore, used to have its head-quarters in Muhammadpur; but when that place was plague-stricken and deserted, the pergunnah cutcherry was removed to Lakshmipassa. The lands are partly directly managed and partly given in patni, the patnidars being the Naupara Baboos, the Naral Baboos (both branches), Mr. Savi, and others.

41. Within the Naldi pergunnah there is a peculiarity of tenure,

Mukarrari tenures in Naldi. in the existence of many large mukarrari tenures. A good deal of the history of these will be found in a previous chapter about the Bhusna zemindari, for the tenure was one which existed from before the permanent settlement.

42. One finds in almost every part of Jessore that the lowest class of tenant claiming an interest in the soil is the ryot who holds a "jumma" and actually cultivates the soil himself, or gives it out in part to a man, half-laborer half-ryot, who cultivates with his own hand some little piece of ground, but never claims to have any right in the land he cultivates. Immediately above this jumma-holder there is another class of ryot whose holding extends over a village or half a village, who never cultivates with his own hand, but sometimes has fields under cultivation by his servants. This class is, in Naral and Magurah, called "jotdar," and in the west of the district is called "gantidar," and their tenures are, whatever the law may say, understood by the people themselves to be fixed.

43. These jotdars, or mukarraridars as they are called from the fixed nature of their tenures, are spread in great numbers over all Naldi. They are for the most part very well off, the rent they pay being small in comparison with what they realize, and the zemindars find them

a most refractory set. They have substance enough to resist, and they decline paying their rents as long as they can possibly hold them back.

44. These tenures are, I think it probable, founded upon rights acquired or granted at the time of the reclamation of the land—not necessarily its original reclamation, which may be very ancient, but the extension of cultivation which is of more modern date. This is an opinion which arises from the perusal of the descriptions of the tenure in the Bhusna records of 1798. At that time the lands of each "jot" were apparently scattered here and there, and were far from compact, and each jot contained apparently lands that were being reclaimed, or had been reclaimed, by the jotdar; for Naldi and Telihâti especially were far from completely reclaimed at the end of last century.

45. To the ganti tenures of the west of the district I have ascribed a different origin, regarding the arrangement rather as one made by the zemindar for the collection of his rents. But the gantidar there also had much to do in the way of promoting cultivation and settling land.

46. Within the geographical boundaries of pergunnah Naldi are these three estates :—

Taraf Naral, held by the Naral Baboos, elder branch.

Tarafs Khalia and Gobra, held by the younger branch, Guru Dass Ray.

47. Both branches of the Naral family have many patnis, and farms, and jummas, and gardens, and all sorts of tenures, in various places within the Naral sub-division; in fact, they are very often the ryots of their own ryots.

48. Pergunnah Mokimpur is a large zemindari in the east of Naral sub-division, and extending also across the river into Furreedpoor district. Its head-quarters are at Chandpur, a small place four miles south-east of Lakshmipassa.

Mokimpur.

49. Of the family who at present possess Mokimpur, the first member was Prit Ram, who, with his brother Ram Dhan, acquired wealth by trade and bought the zemindari when it was sold up, or shortly after it was sold up, as part of the Nattore estate. Of their acquisition of it I have received the following story, for the truth of which, however, I cannot vouch.

History of its acquisition

50. In olden days, when the East India Company were great merchants, they had an extensive cloth godown in Calcutta, which was in the charge of two sircars—Sibram Sanyal and Dulal Sircar. The godown was one time burnt down, and the Government officials who

examined the burnt cloth condemned it and ordered it to be sold to the highest bidder. The sircars alone bade, and they got it for Rs. 16,000. When they came to sell it, they found that beneath a surface of burnt goods there was much very good cloth, and they realized seven or eight lakhs of rupees by the sale.

51. With his share of the proceeds Sibram purchased one or two pergunnahs of the Nattore raj, then being sold—Nasibshahi, Mohimshahi, and Mokimpore. The latter, however, was a losing zemindari. The inundations at that time happened to be exceedingly great, as indeed we have found that they were, and in the whole pergunnah there was only one holding or jote which could pay its way, and that was Prit Ram's holding of Rs. 1,000. Sibram Sanyal, therefore, seeing no hope of meeting the Government revenue of Rs. 19,000, sold the pergunnah to Prit Ram for Rs. 19,000, which was to be paid in annual instalments of Rs. 1,000 each.

52. Prit Ram had a great trade with Calcutta; he used to export thither large quantities of reeds, bamboos, wood, and fish—the produce of the marshy region about him, and from the proceeds of this trade he met for a year or two the Government demands.

53. Just at that time the great river opened out, the inundations decreased, and immense quantities of silt brought by the river began to raise the land. The pergunnah became more and more fertile, and the estate became a valuable one.

54. Prit Ram was succeeded by his son Rajchandra, and he by his widow Rasmani Dasi, commonly known as Rani Rasmani. She died a few years since, and the zemindari is now held by Padmamani Dasi and Jagadamba Dasi, daughters of Rasmani, whose interest, however, only lasts for their lives. The family possess large estates in Rangpore zillah, and also in the 24-Pergunnahs, and they are known, from the place of their residence, as the Jan Bazar zemindars.

55. Prit Ram and Rajchandra, both of them built several houses in the English quarter of Calcutta, which their descendants still own. Rani Rasmani built and endowed at great expense a temple called the "Navaratna" (nine jewels), which is a mile or two north of Calcutta.

56. A small zemindar family in the west of Naral should be mentioned, the Bosus of Shridharpur, two brothers.

Bosus of Shridharpur.

They are a family of recent origin, so far as their present zemindari goes. They made money by commercial dealings, and Ishwar Bosu, one of the two brothers (Panchanan being the name of the eldest) was treasurer in the collectorate before 1847. They have a little zemindari near Shridharpur, and also in Backerganj. Their house at Shridharpur and its grounds are remarkably nicely kept, and they have established there a school and a dispensary,· both very success-ful, and have also at some outlay made a good road to Shridharpur from the banks of the Bhairab opposite Naupara.

57. *Khulna sub-division.*—In the Khulna sub-division we have first in that part of it which lies north of Khulna and on the west of the
Khalispur.
Bhairab, the lands of Khalispur and Maheshwar-passa, which belong for the most part to the Trust Estate, and are given out partly in farm, partly in patni. The great bhils of Dacatia and Pabla which lie here belong to this estate.

58. On the other side the river we have the pergunnah Belphulia.
Belphulia.
This pergunnah is mentioned in 1799 as having been sold up in bits, and having been repeatedly sub-divided; but the various bits seem to have been gathered up again, for, omitting those scattered estates which one everywhere finds, the bulk of it is possessed by the family of Datt Chaudhry, living in Calcutta, who are also possessors of Sultanpur, by the Prasad Rays who have many lands also in Hogla, and by the Ramnagar Baboos. These three sets of zemindars call themselves possessors respectively of six annas, six annas, and four annas shares; these shares being specifically divided.

59. Down the east bank of the Passar river lies the pergunnah of
Hogla.
Hogla, which derives its name from the great reed called "hogla" which grows among the Sundar-ban rivers. Of this pergunnah eight annas share is possessed by the family of Prasad Rays just mentioned. They are the same family who held it about the time of the permanent settlement, but I cannot say whether they had then a larger share in it or not. Different branches of the family were then perpetually fighting about their shares, refusing to accept settlements, and so forth. Of the family there are at present two branches, each holding four annas of the pergunnah, and the three people who represent them all hold their lands in the names of their mothers. The family is a non-resident one, and their zemindari cutcherry is at Mansha, on the Bhairab.

60. The Ramnagar Baboos next have four annas share, which
The Ramnagar Ghoses.
consists of lands quite distinct from the remaining shares. This family, belonging at first to Burdwan, where they have some very small property, came to the district about

the time of the permanent settlement, when Krishna Dulal Ghose was dewan of the collectorate. In this position he acquired sufficient money wherewith to purchase some zemindaris, and his son Radhamohun made great additions to the landed estates of the family. He left five sons and they or their heirs now hold the zemindari. Besides four annas share in Hogla, and four annas in Belphulia, as just noticed, they have some considerable tenures in the Jessore sub-division, and in the part of Naral which is nearest Jessore. Their chief zemindari cutcherry is at Mansha, but their estates are at present under the collector's management.

61. Hogla, the remaining four annas share, also held separately, belongs to the Rainey family, who live at Khulna. Mr. Rainey, their father, acquired it with the primary object, I believe, of indigo planting. He then lived at Nihalpur, four miles east of Khulna, but that house is now in ruins.

62. Sahos is another large pergunnah in Khulna, and it is the estate of the raja of Chanchra, as mentioned in the history of his family. The Trust Estate have also a large estate in Sobna, which is within the geographical limits of Sahos.

Sahos and Sobna.

63. The extreme west of the sub-division is Ramchandrapur on the north, and Mallai on the south. They both originally belonged to the raja's estates, but were, as already narrated, sold up at the time of the permanent settlement. Ramchandrapur is now possessed by a family called the Taki family, of whom I know little else than their name and residence, Taki being within the 24-Pergunnahs, not far from Basirhat. Mallai is held by another 24-Pergunnah family, the Chaudhries of Satkhira, who have large estates all over the Satkhira sub-division of the 24-Pergunnahs.

Ramchandrapur and Mallai.

The Satkhira Chaudhries.

64. This family comes from Bishnaram Ray, who was a servant of the raja Krishnachandra Ray of Krishnanagar. When the Nuddea estates were sold up, as many of them were, this Bishnaram purchased the pergunnah Buran (24-Pergunnahs), and from that pergunnah, in the hands of Bishnaram, and of his son Prannath Ray Chaudhry, the zemindari extended. Prannath is at present the head of the family, a very old man and blind.

65. The zemindari of Mallai has been in the courts like most of the others, and was the subject of a long prolonged suit between the

raja of Jessore and the Chaudhries of Satkhira. The latter eventually won the case, and they have been in possession ever since 1848.

66. Besides the family properties, the separate members of the family own several lands in the same part of the country. Umanath Chaudhry, for example, owns the zemindari of Chandkhali.

67. *Baghahat sub-division.*—Of the Baghahat sub-division, the northern part, the triangle intercepted between the Atharabanka, the Madhumati, and the Bhairab, is the pergunnah of Sultanpur-Khararia, which extends also into Furreed-poor district. The proprietors are the Datt family living in Calcutta. They are the descendants of that Kasinath Datt who, as stated in a previous place, acquired the zemindari by a sort of grant from the Board of Revenue made in their early days of land management. The revenue fixed upon the estate at the time of the permanent settlement was very small, and the zemindars were easily able to pull through the crisis that succeeded it.

Sultanpur-Khararia.

68. Three branches of the family hold the pergunnah in equal shares, which they have partitioned among themselves. They are Nrisingha Datt, who recently succeeded his father Bisheshwar, Anand-chandra Mittra, and Kaliprasad Datt. Their zemindari cutcherries are at Mulghar, opposite Mansha.

69. The pergunnah of Chirulia, which is on the south side of the Bhairab, and is mixed up with Hogla pergunnah, is the property of the Gobradanga family, who are mentioned in connection with dihi Arpara in the sudder sub-division. The zemindari cutcherry is at Jatrapur, on the Bhairab. This property was purchased in 1813 of Raja Gopimohun Deb, the father of Raja Radhakanth Deb, and he got it, as I think, by purchasing it of Government. At the time of the permanent settlement, and for some time after, the pergunnah went a-begging. No owner could be found, and it was managed "khas." After some time the Government sold it, as no person appeared to have any good claim to it.

Chirulia.

70. The Gobradanga zemindars hold a patni also of the pergunnah Rangdia, which lies not far from Jatrapur, and is the property of the heirs of that Dulal Sircar who is mentioned in connection with the Mokimpur zemindari. This Dulal was a great miser, and he hoarded up the wealth he had accumulated, restricting his expenditure to eight annas a day. When he

Rangdia.

died his sons, who inherited his wealth, bought with part of it this pergunnah of Rangdia.

71. The eastern part of Baghahat, and the adjacent part of Backerganj district, is the pergunnah Selimabad.

Selimabad.

Of this pergunnah the southern part has been filched away from the Sundarbans, the Selimabad zemindars having brought many of the lands under cultivation and attached them to their pergunnah before Government became alive to its proprietary claims over the Sundarban lands. One part, indeed, was resumed by Government, namely, the triangular space opposite Morrellganj, which is called "The Four Mauzas," and was settled with the Ghosal family.

72. Of Selimabad pergunnah the chief proprietors are the Ghosal family (Raja Satyanand Ghosal) and the Deb family. The former resides in Calcutta, the latter in Backerganj district. The Deb family appear to have been the ancient possessors of Selimabad, and the Ghosal family have also held property in it for a very long time. The Ghosals acquired distinction through one of their ancestors, who was right-hand man to Mr. Verelst, one of the administrators of the East India Company about the middle of last century. I have heard, I know not with what truth, that a previous ancestor held a high position at the court of the nawab of Dacca, and got half of Selimabad from the Deb family as a bribe to induce him to gain at the nawab's hands a favorable hearing for the Deb family, who had got into difficulties through withholding their rents. I cannot say if this is anything but a mere tale.

The Ghosal family.

73. In the years succeeding the permanent settlement Selimabad did not regularly discharge its rents, and it began to be sold up piecemeal, as the custom of the time then was. This process created within its limits a number of separate estates, and there are many such estates, smaller or larger, scattered all over it, which have been further divided by inheritance and partition. The chief of the possessors of these extraneous estates is Baboo Mohimachandra Ray, of Bangram or Bangaon, in Selimabad.

74. A very ancient family, which claim descent by a female branch from Raja Pratapaditya, are the Rays of Karapara near Baghahat, the head of whom is Mohimachandra Ray (not the same as the above Mohimachandra). They have some zemindari in the pergunnah Khalifatabad which includes the land lying near Baghahat.

Karapara family.

75. Almost all the lands that lie south of Baghahat are Sundarban taluqs; some of these have, however, been sufficiently long under cultivation to have put off the appearance of recently reclaimed lands, but they have mostly been acquired subsequently to the permanent settlement.

Sundarbun taluqs.

76. We do not find in Baghahat, among the ryots of those lands whose reclamation is comparatively recent, the same tenures which prevail in places farther north. There are not here the ganti and jot tenures which we find in the west of the district and in pergunnah Naldi, but an entirely new series of tenures going by different names. Patni tenures and farms are almost unknown, as the zemindar does not ordinarily transfer all his rights to others, constituting himself a mere rent charge, but, on the other hand, he manages his lands himself. In the south of the district, in fact, it is the ryots, and not the zemindars, who take to creating tenures. The highest tenure is called taluq, the taluqdar holding and paying rent for a village, or half a village, sometimes cultivating himself, sometimes not. The taluqdar corresponds with the gantidar of the older tracts, where the word taluqdar has a totally different application, and refers, not to the ryot series but to the landholder series of tenures. The taluqdar's rent is looked upon as a fixed rent. Under him comes the "hawaladar," who corresponds with the jumma-holder farther north, and whose rent is also regarded as fixed. The hawala tenure may be created by the zemindar, if he has not already created a taluqdar, and in this case a taluqdar subsequently created will take position between the hawaladar and the zemindar. The right of a taluqdar, however, includes that of creating hawalas within his own tenure, and the hawaladar again may create a subordinate tenure called nim-hawala, and may subsequently create an asath-hawala, intermediate between himself and the nim-hawaladar. In these subordinate tenures the tenants are almost always of the pure ryot class, and engage personally in agriculture. They are always regarded as having rights of occupancy, but if they again let their lands, those who cultivate under them, who are called "charcha" ryots, have no such rights, and regard themselves as only holding the land for the time.

Peculiar tenures.

77. These tenures have their origin, I have no doubt, in rights founded upon original reclamation. A ryot who gets a small piece of land to clear always regards himself as having a sort of property in it,—

an " abadkari swatwa" or " reclamation right." As reclamations extend, he begins to sub-let to other ryots, and we have a " hawaladar" with his subordinate hawaladars in a few years.

78. The taluqdars above described are those who, in the pergunnah lands, come between the zemindar and the ryot proper or hawaladar. In Sundarban grants the word has another meaning, for the Sundarban grants are themselves called taluqs, and their possessors are taluqdars. Among these taluqdars we find, as we would naturally expect, several persons holding considerable zemindaris in Jessore, or Backerganj, or the 24-Pergunnahs, but a great number of them appear to belong to the comfortably circumstanced class of people residing immediately north of the Sundarbans. Many people there, who derive a competence either from a tenure in land or from commerce, have also some taluq in the Sundarbans, and they form for the most part successful reclaimers. They have just enough money to enable them to carry on Sundarban reclamation with success, and they are not rich enough to leave everything in the hands of agents, and by forgetting their direct interest, relax their enterprize; many of them also have ryots of their own in their older settled lands, and can use them for their newer lands. It is to the class to which these men belong that the greater part of the agricultural improvement and extension since the permanent settlement is owing; and the advantage of having men of this class as Sundarban taluqdars was strikingly shewn in 1869. The ryots lost very much indeed by the cyclones of that year, and the loss would have been sufficient to paralyze the whole reclamation scheme but that these taluqdars, immediately connected as they are with the grants, at once came forward to give their ryots the necessary assistance, drawing only upon the little surplus of money they had at their homes. Larger zemindars require to have these matters brought home to them, and even then expect their ryots to settle matters themselves; these smaller men at once appreciate the whole case, and step into the gap.

79. Of Sundarban taluqdars, the chief are the Morrells of Morrellganj, who have established a large and wealthy zemindari on what thirty years ago was a marshy forest. Their story, if I were at liberty to tell it, would afford an example of indomitable and patient energy such as is rarely found in the annals of enterprize; and their example and success, by encouraging others to engage in Sundarban reclamation, have done more towards the

formation of the great rice province which is there springing up, than any one not acquainted with the case can conceive.

80. Their zemindari, which is a model of good management, extends inwards, westward, and south-westward from Morrellganj, and lies also on both sides of the Baleshwar river below Morrellganj.

NOTE REGARDING THE HISTORY OF THE NAUPARA FAMILY.

THE founder of this family was Harideb Deb, who in the time of the Hindoo kings (some 500 years since) dwelt at Muragachha, near Saptagram (or Satgaon), an ancient celebrated city in Hooghly. Purandar Deb, the eighth in descent from him, held a high post under the Mahomedan sovereigns, and from them received the title of "khan." From the Kulin Kayasths he received the position of "gushtipati" (head of a clan), an honour which has descended to his posterity, whose chief representative is the family of which the late Raja Radhakant Deb was the head.

2. Seventh in descent from Purandar was Raja Ram Chandra Khan, who was a favorite of the great Raja Man Singh, and held high post under him. He acquired, probably by some sort of grant from Man Singh, the zemindari of Muhammadabad, in Nuddea, and established the seat of his family at Bára Bazar, ten miles north of Jessore. There are one or two tanks there (one a very large tank), and there are the remains of ancient buildings; these are attributed to the Raja Ramchandra by his present descendants; the people at Bára Bazar know very little about them.

3. When Ramchandra died he left a minor son, but the Mahomedan Government, on some pretext or other, confiscated all the estates and bestowed them on others. His grandson, however, Kamal Narayn Ray, appears to have held some zemindari at least, for we find him the head of a family. He removed the seat of the family to Bodhkhana, about twelve miles south-west. There are at Bodhkhana the remains of a ditch and ramp, the "garh" as the Bengalis call it, of an ancient zemindar's house, and probably the house is that of Kamal Narayn Ray.

4. Of Kamal Narayn's sons, one named Raja Kangsha Narayn Ray obtained part, or the whole, of the family estates, and removed to Ganganandpur, in Nuddea. His son Ratneshwar quarrelled with the Raja of Nuddea, who in the end dispossessed him of his estates, about 1735 A.D. He was unsuccessful in obtaining redress at the court of Moorshedabad, and retired to Naupara, close to Jessore, possessed of only a few taluqs and lakhiraj lands. From Ratneshwar to Kalikant Ray is four generations, and Kalikant Ray died about April 1870.

5. This history of this family deserves further elucidation; they appear to be one of those families who, in the time of the large zemindars, possessed the small zemindaris, single pergun-nahs, or similar estates, and were therefore a prey to their larger and more wealthy neighbours, as we have seen in the history of the raja of Chanchra. They are nowhere prominent in the history of the district, and in its records I find no mention of them. Their ancient history is, I am inclined to think, something quite apart from their modern history, and they are an instance where one of the zemindar families of modern days happens to be also a representative of a family that had possessions in olden times.

6. The raja of Jessore, in his account of his history, mentions that this Naupara family owe their present position to their connection with his house, Kalikant Ray's elder brothers having been naibs upon his estates. This is perfectly possible; for, as their entire property is composed of petty zemindaries, and patni and darpatni tenures, it is undoubtedly of modern acquisition, and is, in continuity of history at any rate, entirely separate from what their family originally may have possessed. Their lands are scattered in various parts of Isafpur pergunnah, and they have a good deal in the northern part of that pergunnah, from Khajura up to Salkhia. They have some small lands near Jessore, and some near Bára Bazar. Their principal estates are, however, patni tenures within Naldi pergunnah. Kalikant Ray was naib of Naldi pergunnah, and while in that position obtained many patnis within these lands. All these lands would form a respectable zemindari in the aggregate, were it not that the family is so deeply in debt that they can scarcely call the lands their own.

7. Kalikant Ray, in his account of the family, mentions that there exists at Ganganandpur a temple built by Ratneshwar, his ancestor, bearing an inscription with the date 1738 A.D.

XL.—*The Naral Family.*

THE family of Naral deserve the leading place in a history of the new zemindars of Jessore. Both branches of it have given me an account of their family, and besides that it is very fully detailed in a High Court case (22nd July 1861). There are also some notices of one of their ancestors in the records of the collectorate.

2. They derive their descent from a family bearing the name of

Ancestry.

Datt, who were descended from the Parashuttam Datt of the story of king Adisura, and who at the the beginning of last century dwelt at Bali, near Howrah. The Mahrattas at that time were disturbing the country by inroads, and the Datts retired to a more distant place, a village Chaura near Moorshedabad. The same reason induced them to retire still farther, and Madangopal Datt bringing his family with him settled at Naral.

3. Madangopal, while living at Chaura, had been in the service of

Madangopal settles at Naral.

the nawab of Bengal, and had by that means accumulated sufficient wealth wherewith to establish a merchant's business. He lived principally by merchandise, and possessed no land except twelve biggas, which he acquired for the purpose of building a residence for himself. In the High Court decision it is stated that both branches of the family admitted that he was a person in indigent circumstances, so that it is possible that his mercantile wealth may be an embellishment of a later age.

4. Madangopal had a son Ramgobind, who had a son named

Rupram acquires wealth.

Rupram, besides another son who died childless. This Rupram Datt became vakil or agent at the court of the nawab for the raja of Nattore, who was then one of the greatest zemindars of Bengal. By this means he acquired a certain amount of wealth, and he also obtained from the Nattore raja a lease of some lands at Naral, for which he paid Rs. 148. These apparently included the lands upon which the family residence, then a sufficiently unpretending building, was erected. This lease is dated 1198 (1791), and Rupram appears to have lived up till about 1209 (1802), when he died leaving two sons, Kalisankar and Ramnidhi.

2 c

5. The history of Kalisankar is the history of the family. The
foundation of its wealth was laid by him; when
Kalisankar.
he began life the family held only a few hundred
biggas of land near Naral, and when he died he left property whose
revenue was measured by lakhs of rupees.

6. Kalisankar was a man of wonderful energy and ability in
business, and—my regard for truth compels me to say it—he was perfectly
unscrupulous. Introduced, probably by his father, into the service of the
raja of Nattore, he became dewan to that raja, who was then the owner,
if tradition speaks true, of fifty-six lakhs of rupees zemindari. Kalisankar
afterwards became farmer under the raja of Nattore of his zemindari
of Bhusna. The raja probably placed this zemindari in his charge as
the only possible way of making anything out of it; and certainly if any
man could have made it a paying zemindari, that man was Kalisankar.

7. Kalisankar had already begun to amass wealth and to purchase
estates, and if we are to accept the account of it
Acquisition of estates.
which the High Court's decision gives, and which
is in part based upon the declarations of his descendants, the process
by which he acquired his wealth was simply this, that he abused his
position of dewan to transfer part of his master's wealth into his
own pockets. It was during his management that the Nattore raja's
estates began to default and to be sold up for arrears of revenue. I do
not go so far as to say that their default was wilfully brought about by
Kalisankar in order to gain his own ends. The default I have
traced to other causes, but still it might have been possible—nay easy—
for Kalisankar by good management to have staved off the evil time.
It is certainly the case, and it does not look well for Kalisankar that
a very short time after the permanent settlement the estates of Telihâti,
Binadpur, Rupapat, Khalia, and Pokhtani, were sold up, and were
bought in by Kalisankar in the names of obscure individuals who were
his dependants. According to the decision in the case referred to, the
only money which Kalisankar could have used in buying these estates
was that which by unjust stewardship he had acquired. These estates
were all large estates, and there were apparently some smaller ones also
sold up and similarly bought by Kalisankar.

8. These acquisitions were made in 1795 and 1799, and it was
about that time that Kalisankar got into trouble with respect to his
farm of Bhusna. The various proceedings of Kalisankar and of the
collector with respect to this farm have been already detailed (chapter

XXII). The collector then, and the current report now, would make out that Kalisankar collected his rents duly from his ryots, but wilfully and fraudulently kept them back from the collector who then managed the estate. I have previously stated the reasons I have for believing that Kalisankar, however guilty in other respects, did not entirely deserve the hard language which the collector constantly applied to him, in the belief that he only through sheer dishonesty kept back the rents of his farm. He might, of course, have paid them from his other property, but in Bhusna itself he could get hardly anything from the ryots, and it was for this reason that he failed to pay his own rent.

9. After much suing and disputing, Kalisankar finally was in 1800 imprisoned as a defaulter, and he remained in jail for four years. His property was all benami, part of it notoriously his own but standing in the name of his son Ramnarayn. Whether it was that he was determined to force a compromise upon the court of wards, at whose suit he was imprisoned, or whether it was that he hesitated to do anything to assert right of property over the lands, which he would thus make clear that he had acquired only by unjust stewardship, he refused for four years to do anything towards paying his debt, and remained in jail, constantly urging his insolvency and praying for release. He was finally released on a compromise, which remitted a small part of his debt.

10. Kalisankar had two sons, Ramnarayn and Jaynarayn, and Kalisankar retires to Benares. from the period when Kalisankar was released from jail up till 1820 these three lived as one family at Naral. The landed estates already possessed by them were considerable, and they continued to be added to. In 1820 Kalisankar retired to Benares in preparation for his death; he already had purchased some estates there, and when there the old man was still engaged in managing and in amassing landed property, both in Benares and perhaps also in Bengal. In 1822 Jaynarayn died; in 1827 Ramnarayn died; and finally, in 1834, Kalisankar died, being 85 or 90 years old, leaving to his heirs more than a hundred estates, some of them large enough to form singly a handsome property, and at least half a lakh of rupees in personal property. When Gurudass, one of his heirs, sued the rest for only a part of this inheritance, he valued his claim (including a few years' mesne profits) at more than forty-one lakhs of rupees.

11. Kalisankar had obtained from the nawab of Moorshedabad the title of Ray, and the family have ever since that time called themselves Ray instead of Datt.

12.   When Kalisankar died he left as his heirs two branches of the
Disputes between the family—the sons of Ramnarayn, who were Ram-
two branches. ratan, Harnath, and Radhacharn; and the sons of
Jaynarayn, who were Gurudass, and one or two who shortly after died.
The elder branch (Ramratan) set up a will by which they alleged Kalisankar had made a distribution of his property between the two branches,
giving the elder branch the lion's share.   This preference they accounted for on the theory that Kalisankar had never ceased to be grateful for
an act of piety performed by Ramnarayn, who in 1802 had for a short
time stood substitute for Kalisankar in the civil jail, when the latter
was anxious to go home to perform certain religious rites.

13.   Gurudass was a minor at the time the deed was set up, and
when he came of age he called it in question, and sued the elder branch
of the family for possession of one-half share in the whole of the
family possessions.   The grounds of the claim were double.   He alleged
that the deed itself was a forgery on the part of Ramratan, and he
alleged also that the distribution was beyond the power of Kalisankar,
he having long before made over all his property to Ramnarayn and
Jaynarayn and retired from worldly affairs to Benares, and all the
recent acquisitions having been made not by him, but by his sons in
common.   Gurudass made his first claim very early, but the Sudder
Court cast out the suit, as he had split his claim.   The great suit was
instituted on 5th October 1847.   The investigation was a most difficult
one; it involved an inquiry into all the transactions of Kalisankar and
his sons, and they had so overlaid all their proceedings with conceal-
ments, and benami, and all sorts of roundabout actions, that it was
no easy matter to unravel them all.   It is likely enough that many of
Kalisankar's proceedings could not bear the light of day, but apparently
the system of concealment and benami had been adopted by the
family as a regular system, perhaps without any definite ulterior object.

14.   In the lower court Gurudass' claim was cast (December 1858),
Gurudass victorious. but in the Sudder Court it was decreed, and it is
now under appeal before the Privy Council.   But,
meantime, the two branches of the family are in possession pretty nearly
according to the partition deed or will.

15.   In the elder branch of the family, when Kalisankar died,
Ramratan's management. Ramratan became the head.   He was a man of
remarkable ability, and he continued to extend the
zemindari in all directions.   In his time Muhammadshahi (three-fifths

share) was acquired, and this forms one of the largest zemindaris in possession of the family. According to the decision quoted above, and according to local rumour, it was paid for partly by money borrowed from Abdul Gani of Dacca. Under Ramratan's management, both Muhammadshahi and the other family estates increased very greatly in value.

16. Ramratan died somewhere about 1859 or 1860, and Harnath Ray became the head of the family, and when he died in 1868, Radhacharan Ray became the head; but no great acquisitions have been made by them, and the property is now substantially in the same condition as when Ramratan died. The chief part of it may be generally described as extending over the Jhenida sub-division and the western part of the Magurah sub-division, and running about ten or twenty miles into the districts of Nuddea, Pubna, and Furreedpoor, where they border upon these sub-divisions. In many other parts of Jessore, and in Hooghly and the 24-Pergunnahs, and to a smaller extent in other districts also, they possess estates, and the separate members of the family also separately possess many estates in Jessore, Furreedpoor, Backerganj, and elsewhere. They have property also in Benares and Mirzapore.

Extent of the estates.

17. The family house is at Naral, and they have another family house at Cossipore, in Calcutta. Both in Calcutta and at Naral they have large places of business, where they trade in agricultural produce, a sort of appanage to their zemindari. And they have several indigo factories situated in various parts of their Jessore, Pubna, and Furreedpoor estates.

18. The property in possession of Gurudass, the younger branch of the family, is not nearly so extensive. Khalia in Jessore, and Rupapat in Furreedpoor, are his principal properties, but he has many others scattered over Jessore and Furreedpoor. He has himself made no great additions to his estates. He has two family residences, Naral and Rupapat.

19. The family of Naral have never been backward in those works of piety and liberality which the Hindu religion recommends. From Madangopal's time to the present they have continually been establishing idols and endowing their temples, and it would require a long list now to include all the idols set up from time to time at Naral and in other places by the ancestors and the present representatives of the Naral family. These idols and their endowments, of course, afford sustenance to many of those persons whom the Shastras recommend to the care of the pious. They have also dug several tanks at various places within their estates,

Liberality of the family.

and among their good works may be enumerated a large bathing ghát at Cossipore (Calcutta) and another at Mirzapore. Kalisankar naturally spent some of his wealth in pious works after he had gone to Benares, and the chief of these works appears to be a religious edifice at Mirzapore, which is called the "Bhusi," and which cost two or three lakhs of rupees.

20. In more recent times the representatives of the elder branch of the family can certainly claim a position among the enlightened zemindars of Bengal. Harnath Ray began, and spent much money upon, a road intended to join Jessore and Naral; and for this and other acts of generosity he received from Government the title of Ray Bahadur. Both he and the rest have done, and continue to do, much to further the cause of education, and one most successful school at Naral is supported entirely by them. Last, not least, of their good works is their maintenance of a charitable dispensary at Naral. It is superintended by Dr. Anderson, and its expenses are entirely met by the Naral Baboos.

21. Their names may be here recorded, and they are these:

Radhacharn, the head of the family.

Chandra Kumar and Kali Prasanna, sons of Ramratan.

The minor sons of Umesh Chandra, and Kali Dass, the grandsons and son of Ray Harnath Ray Bahadur.

22. Gurudass, the representative of the younger branch, is quite a contrast to the members of the other branch,—one of those conservative old zemindars who think and act on the principle that the zemindar's will should be the one law of the land; a man who opposes authority whenever he has an opportunity; who looks upon every symptom of advancing civilization with distrust; considers every new road as a new calamity; and, when people talk of schools, thinks the world is coming to an end. I need not say that he is not to be depended upon for subscriptions or assistance towards any work of charity or improvement. He ought to have lived, not now, but a hundred years ago.

Gurudass.

PART V.—AGRICULTURE AND COMMERCE.

XLI.—*Sugar Cultivation and Manufacture.*

ONE of the most important industries in the district of Jessore is
the cultivation and manufacture of date sugar.
Its importance.
All over the north and west of the district, and to
some extent also in other parts of it, the ryots may almost be said to
depend more upon sugar cultivation than upon any other branch of
agriculture. Of course other cultivation demands their attention, and
forms no mean part of their livelihood; but there are so many people
who derive from sugar all that they have above the mere necessaries of
life, that it may be considered that the sugar cultivation and trade is
the root of all their prosperity.

2. Though the great activity of the sugar market is a creation
only of the last twenty or thirty years, yet the district has been for a
very long time prominent as a sugar-growing district. In 1788 the
collector enumerates, as one of the losses caused by the cyclone of 1787,
the injury to the date trees and the weakening of the sugar produce.
Later on, in 1792, he writes that "date sugar is largely manufactured
and exported" (24-11-92) ; and in a statistical table prepared in 1791,
we find it recorded that 20,000 maunds was the annual produce of the
sugar cultivation, and that of this about half was exported to Calcutta.

3. At that time, however, there was a considerable production of
cane sugar as well as of date sugar, while in these later years the date-
sugar has almost entirely driven away the cane sugar from the fields
as well as from the market.

4. I have said that it was only twenty or thirty years since the
sugar trade has became so prominent a branch of
Recent extension of the
trade.
industry. It was about thirty years ago that
European factories began to be set up in the district, and it was these
factories that gave such impulse to the trade.

5. The first sugar factory in the country was at Dhoba, in
Burdwan, a little below Nuddea, and it was
European factories.
erected by a Mr. Blake. When his success began
to diminish, he changed the business into that of a Company, from which
he gradually withdrew. This Dhoba Sugar Company established a

factory at Kotchandpur, in Jessore, setting up English machinery, and afterwards applied the English system to the Dhoba factory also. Besides Kotchandpur, they established a factory also at Trimohini; but I cannot say whether it was a mere agency for buying produce, or whether it was a place for manufacturing sugar.

6. This company failed after a very short time, about 1842, and of their factories in this district, Kotchandpur passed into the hands of Mr. Newhouse, and it is still in working order. Trimohini became the property of a Mr. Saintsbury, who worked it for three or four years and then broke it up.

7. The factory of Chaugachha was created about the same time (1842) by Gladstone, Wyllie, and Co. It was first under the management of a Mr. Smith and afterwards of Mr. McLeod, and it had out-factories for purchase at Keshabpur, Trimohini, Jingagachha, Narikel-baria, and Kotchandpur. It worked at a profit for only a year or two, and after that was discontinued. In fact, since 1850, there has been no regular sugar-refining going on in any of the factories. Chaugachha and Kotchandpur alone were in working order, and they only worked occasionally ; and Tahirpur, which was built about 1853 by Mr. Newhouse, was worked only two years, and was then sold and converted into a rum-distillery.

8. It will be seen therefore that the history of the English sugar refineries is not a record of success. The truth
Their general failure
was that when they gave a great impulse to the sugar cultivation, native merchants stepped in and appropriated all the trade which the factories had given birth to. English refining is good only for one market, the European market. The demand for sugar among natives is very great, but they do not care to have it so thoroughly refined. Thus, as the native market is now, and has been for very many years, the chief market for sugar, it follows that expensive methods of refinement are thrown away, and the methods used by native merchants impart to the sugar all the purity which is required by the consumers.

9. Had the European market remained open, the European factories might have competed with the native with some chance of success. But the duties levied in Europe appear to have been sufficient to prevent the development of the export trade, and the factories established at Cossipore and Bally, near Calcutta, appear, through the more favorable circumstances in which they were placed, to have monopolized the European market in Calcutta.

10. My object at present is to give an account of the cultivation and manufacture of date sugar, from the planting of the date tree to the exportation of the manufactured sugar. And first as regards the land cultivated :—

11. The ground chosen for date cultivation is the higher ground,
The planting of the trees.
that which is too high for rice to grow well, and the rent paid for such ground is at least three times that paid for rice land. One often finds date trees ranged round the borders of fields cultivated with cold-weather crops, and indeed in the west and north of the district almost every village is thickly studded with these trees; but a very large amount of cultivation is upon land especially set apart for it. The trees are planted in regular rows, each tree being about twelve feet from its neighbour. If so planted and left for seven years before being touched, good healthy trees may be expected. Those who cultivate dates keep the land, especially in the cold season, perfectly bare of any vegetation, ploughing up the turf, so that the whole strength of the ground may expend itself in the trees. Of course, there are people who cultivate other crops upon the land where the date trees grow, and there are very many who have not patience enough to wait for the expiration of the full seven years; such people, however, lose in the end by their trees failing to give the same richness in juice that is obtained from trees more carefully tended.

12. When the tree is ripe the process of tapping begins, and it is
Tapping.
continued each year thereafter. There are in the date-palm two series, or stories as it were, of leaves; the crown leaves, which rise straight out from the top of the trunk, being, so to speak, a continuation of it; and the lateral leaves, which spring out of the side of the top part of the trunk. When the rainy season has completely passed, and there is no more fear of rain, the cultivator cuts off the lateral leaves for one-half of the circumference, and thus leaves bare a surface measuring about ten or twelve inches each way. This surface is at first a brilliant white, but becomes by exposure quite brown, and puts on the appearance of coarse matting. The surface thus laid bare is not the woody fibre of the tree, but is a bark formed of many thin layers, and it is these layers which thus change their colour and texture.

13. After the tree has remained for a few days thus exposed, the tapping is performed by making a cut into this exposed surface, in the shape of a very broad V, about three inches across and a quarter or half inch deep. Then the surface inside the angle of the V is cut down, so

2 D

that a triangular surface is cut into the tree. From this surface exudation of the sap takes place, and caught by the sides of the V, it runs down to the angle, where a bamboo of the size of a lead pencil is inserted in the tree to catch the dropping sap and carry it out as by a spout.

14. The tapping is arranged, throughout the season, by periods of *Its periodicity.* six days each. On the first evening a cut is made as just described and the juice is allowed to run during the night. The juice so flowing is the strongest and best, and is called "jíran" juice. In the morning the juice collected in a pot hanging beneath the bamboo spout is removed, and the heat of the sun causes the exuding juice to ferment over and shut up the pores in the tree. So in the evening a new cut is made, not nearly so deep as the last, but rather a mere paring, and for the second night the juice is allowed to run. This juice is termed "do-kât," and is not quite so abundant or so good as the "jíran." The third night no new cutting is made, but the exuding surface is merely made quite clean, and the juice which runs this third night is called "jarra." It is still less abundant and less rich than the "do-kât," and towards the end of the season, when it is getting hot, it is even unfit for sugar manufacture, the goor made from it being sold simply as "droppings."

15. These three nights are the periods of activity in the tree, and after these three it is allowed to remain for three nights at rest, when the same process again begins. Of course, every tree in the same grove does not run in the same cycle. Some at their first, some at their second night, and so on; and thus the owner is always busy.

16. Since every sixth day a new cut is made over the previous *The notches.* one, it follows that the tree gets more and more hewed into as the season progresses, and towards the end of the season the exuding surface may be, and often is, as much as four inches below the surface above and below. The cuts are during the whole of one season made about the same place, but in alternate seasons alternate sides of the tree are used for the tapping; and as each season's cutting is thus above the previous season's, and on the opposite side, the stem of the tree has, if looked at from the side, a curious zigzag appearance. The age of a tree can of course be at once counted up by enumerating the notches and adding six or seven, the number of years passed before the first year's notch. I have counted more than forty notches on a tree, but one rarely sees them so old as that, and when they are 46 years old they are worth little as produce-bearing trees.

I have said that at first the size of the bared surface, previous to the notching, is about ten inches square; but it gets less and less as the notches come to the higher and narrower part of the trunk, and I have seen old trees where not more than four inches square could be found.

17. It is somewhat remarkable that the notches are almost always on the east and west sides of the tree, and very rarely on the north and south sides; also, the first notch appears to be made in by far the majority of instances on the east side.

18. As to the produce of one tree, one may expect from a good tree a regular average of five seers per night (excluding the quiescent nights). The colder and clearer the weather, the more copious and rich the produce. In the beginning of November tapping has begun. In December and January the juice flows best, beginning sometimes as early as 3 P. M., and it dwindles away as the warm days of March come. If the cultivator begins too early, or carries on too late, he will lose in quality and quantity as much as he will gain by extending the tapping season. But high prices begin in October, and I am afraid there are not many who can resist the temptation of running into market with their premature produce.

Produce of one tree.

19. During the whole of the tapping season a good cultivator will keep his grove perfectly clean and free from jungle or even grass.

20. So much then for the tapping: the next process is the boiling, and this every ryot does for himself, and usually within the limits of the grove. Without boiling the juice speedily ferments and becomes useless; but once boiled down into "goor," it may be kept for very long periods. The juice is therefore boiled at once in large pots placed on a perforated dome, beneath which a strong wood fire is kept burning, the pared leaves of the trees being used among other fuel. The juice, which was at first brilliant and limpid, becomes now a dark brown half-viscid half-solid mass, which is called "goor" (molasses), and when it is still warm, it is easily poured from the boiling-pan into the earthenware pots (small gharras) in which it is ordinarily kept.

Boiling.

21. As it takes from seven to ten seers of juice to produce one seer of "goor" or molasses, we can calculate the amount of goor which one ordinarily good tree can produce in a season. We may count four and a half months for the tapping season, or about sixty-seven tapping nights. These, at five seers each, produce 335 seers of juice, which will give about forty seers, or one maund of

Produce of goor.

goor, the value of which at present rates is from Rs. 2 to Rs. 2-4. A bigga of grove containing 100 trees will therefore produce from Rs. 200 to Rs. 225 worth of goor if all the trees are in good bearing.

22.   It is not all sorts of pottery which will bear the continuous hard firing required for boiling down the juice, and some potters have obtained a special reputation for the excellence of their wares in this respect.   The whole of the region about Chaugachha and Kotchandpur is supplied principally from a village, Bagdanga, a little west of Jessore, where the clay seems to be of an unusually good quality.   The southern part of the district, again, is supplied chiefly from Alaipur, a bazar near Khulna.

Pottery.

23.   A ryot, after boiling down his juice into goor, does not ordinarily do more; it is then sold to the refiners, and by them manufactured into sugar.   Near Keshabpur, however, a large number of ryots manufacture their own sugar and sell it to the exporters only after manufacture.   There are also in almost all parts of the district a class of refiners different from those who are refiners, and only refiners, by profession.   These are the larger ryots in the villages, many of whom combine commercial dealings with agriculture.   They receive the goor from the ryots in their vicinity, and sometimes also purchase it in the adjacent hâts, and after manufacturing what they thus purchase, they take their sugar to some exporting mart and sell it there to the larger merchants.

The refiners.

24.   These, however, are the outsiders in the sugar trade; for by far the greater quantity of the sugar is manufactured by regular refiners, and it becomes necessary to describe how the goor finds its way from the ryots' hands into theirs.

25.   Few of the sugar refiners purchase direct from the ryots, for the small quantities which each man brings would render this inconvenient; there are consequently a number of middlemen established, called byapáris or dallâls (the latter name prevails principally near Chaugachha), who collect the produce from the ryots and sell it at a small profit to the refiners. They do it sometimes by giving advances to the ryots to aid them in their cultivation, getting the advances repaid in produce; but the ryots are not, as a rule, dependent on such advances for their sugar cultivation, and the greater number of byapáris simply make excursions round the country, buying up the goor from the ryots and bringing it in to the merchants.

Their method of purchase.

26. On hât days also another class of byapâris will be seen (some of whom have a very large business) lining the roads by which the ryots bring their produce to the hât. They pick up the pots of goor by ones and twos from the smaller class of cultivators and profit by selling them in bulk to the refiner. Ryots who have extensive cultivation sometimes bring in quantities large enough to be sold direct to refiners, but by far the bulk of the goor comes through the hands of intermediaries, in the various methods just described. Of course, the earthen pot is transferred along with the goor that is in it; separation is in fact impossible, and the refiners always smash the pots to get out the goor. Hence there is a great trade in pottery during the whole of the sugar season, for every ryot must buy for himself as many new pots as he sells pots of goor. Those ryots who bring their own produce to the hât always buy and take away with them the new pots they require.

27. We have now traced the goor into the hands of the refiners, and we shall now see what the process of manu-facture is. But there are several methods of refining, and two or three sorts of sugar produced. We will take them in order, and describe first the method of manufacturing "dhulua" sugar—that soft, moist, non-granular, powdery sugar used chiefly by natives, and especially in the manufacture of native sweetmeats.

Manufacture of dhulua sugar.

28. The pots of goor received by the refiner are broken up and the goor tumbled out into baskets, which hold about a maund each and are about fifteen inches deep; the surface is beaten down so as to be pretty level, and the baskets are placed over open pans. Left thus for eight days, the molasses passes through the basket, dropping into the open pan beneath and leaving the more solid part of the goor, namely the sugar, in the basket. Goor is, in fact, a mixture of sugar and molasses, and the object of the refining is to drive off the molasses, which give the dark colour to the goor.

29. This eight days' standing allows a great deal of the molasses to drop out, but not nearly enough; and to carry the process further, a certain river weed, called syâla, which grows freely in the Kabadak especially, is placed on the baskets so as to rest on the top of the sugar. The effect of this weed is to keep up a continual moisture, and this moisture, descending through the sugar, carries the molasses with it, leaving the sugar comparatively white and free from molasses. After eight days' exposure with syâla leaves, about four inches on the surface of the mass will be found purified, and these four inches are cut

off and syála applied on the newly exposed surface. This and one other application will be sufficient to purify the whole mass.

30. The sugar thus collected is moist, and it is therefore put out to dry in the sun, being first chopped up so as to prevent it caking. When dry it is a fair, lumpy, raw sugar, and it weighs about thirty per cent. of the original mass, the rest of the goor having passed off in molasses. Dishonest refiners can get more weight out of it by diminish-ing the exposure under syála weed, so as to leave it only five or six days, instead of eight. The molasses is less perfectly driven out, and the sugar therefore weighs more. Of course, it has also a deeper colour, but that is in a measure remedied by pounding under a dhenki. There are also other dishonest means of increasing the weight: for example, the floors of the refineries are sometimes a foot or more beneath the level of the ground outside, the difference representing the amount of dust which has been carefully swept up with the sugar when it is gathered up after drying. Also, it is very easy so to break the pots that fragments of them remain among the sugar.

31. The "first droppings," gathered in the open pans in the
The droppings.   manner described above, are rich in sugar, and are
                used, especially in the north-west, for mixing up with food. It entirely depends, therefore, upon the price offered for them for this purpose, whether they are sold at once or reserved for a second process of sugar manufacture. In this second process the first droppings are first boiled and then placed underground in large earthen-ware pots to cool. Unless thus boiled they would ferment, but after being boiled in this fashion they on cooling form into a mass somewhat like goor but not nearly so rich. After this the previous process is again gone through, and about ten per cent. more weight in sugar is obtained. This sugar is, however, coarser and darker in colour than the first.

32. If the refiner is not very honest, and if he is sure of finding immediate sale, he will use a much more speedy process. Taking the cooled goor, he will squeeze out the molasses by compressing the mass in a sack, and then, drying and breaking up the remainder, will sell it as sugar. It does not look much different from that prepared in the more elaborate way, but it will likely soon ferment, and hence the necessity of finding an immediate purchaser.

33. The remainder, after all this sugar has been squeezed out, is molasses, "chitiya goor" as it is called. It forms a separate article of com-merce, being exported to various places, as will be subsequently mentioned.

34. The sugar produced by the method just described is called

Manufacture of "pucka" sugar.

dhulua sugar—a soft, yellowish sugar. It can never be clean, because it is clear from the process used that whatever impurity there may originally be in the goor, or whatever impurity may creep into the sugar during its somewhat rough process of manufacture, must always appear in the finished article. Another objection to it is that it tends slightly to liquefaction, and cannot therefore be kept for any considerable time.

35. The "pucka" sugar, whose manufacture I am now about to describe, is a much cleaner and more permanent article. It has also a granular structure, which the dhulua has not. The manufacture of it is more expensive than the other, and the price of it when finished is about ten rupees, whereas dhulua costs only about six rupees per maund.

36. In this process the goor is first cast upon flat platforms, and as much of the molasses as then flows off is collected as first droppings. The rest is collected, put into sacks and squeezed, and a great deal of the molasses is thus separated out. The sugar which remains behind is then boiled with water in large open pans, and as it boils all scum is taken off. It is then strained and boiled a second time and left to cool in flat basins. When cooled it is already sugar of a rough sort, and now syála leaves are put over it and it is left to drop. The result is good white sugar, and should any remain at the bottom of the vessel still unrefined, it is again treated with syála.

37. The first droppings, and the droppings under the syála leaves, are collected, squeezed again in the sacks, and, from the sugar left behind, a second small quantity of refined sugar is prepared in exactly the same way, by twice boiling. The droppings from the sacks are chitiya goor, and are not used for further sugar manufacture. About thirty per cent. of the original weight of the goor is turned out in the form of pure pucka sugar.

38. There is another method of manufacture peculiar to Keshab-

Keshabpur method.

pur, and slightly differing from that just described. I find it thus described in my note, but I am not sure if I have it correct. The goor is first boiled in large open pots, and into each potful is put a handful of "bíchh;" it is then left to cool, and in doing so it coagulates, and then it is treated with syála leaf and thus refined. The last droppings under the syála leaf are burnt, and this forms the "bíchh" used in the manufacture, the effect of which is apparently to make one boiling do instead of two.

The droppings from this first process (which, if I am correct in my description, must be very abundant, since the goor before undergoing it suffers hardly any purification) are collected, boiled with bichh, and cooled as before; then squeezed in sacks, mixed with water, boiled to drive off the water, and after cooling purified with syála leaf. The droppings now are exhausted molasses, or chitiya goor. The produce in sugar is twenty-five or thirty per cent. of the weight of the original goor.

39. There remains to be described the English process of refinement used in the factories at Kotchandpur and Chaugachha. In this the raw material is mixed with a certain amount of water and boiled in open cisterns, the boiling being accomplished, not by fire, but by the introduction of steam. The lighter filth now floats to the surface and is skimmed off, while the boiling solution is made to flow away through blanket strainers into another cistern. After this it is boiled to drive off the water. Now, if the mass were raised to boiling temperature, the result would be sugar, granular indeed in structure, but not differing in this respect from native pucka sugar. But if the water be driven off without raising the mass to boiling point, then we get the crisp and sparkling appearance which loaf sugar always has. Whether there is any difference in the substances, I do not know; but so long as people prefer what *looks* pleasant and nice, sugar of this sparkling appearance will command a higher price in the market.

English process.

40. The object is attained by boiling in a vacuum pan, that is to say, a large closed cistern from which a powerful pump exhausts the vapour as it rises. The lower the atmospheric pressure on the surface of the liquid, the lower the temperature at which ebullition takes place. The pump is therefore regulated so as to diminish the pressure on the surface to such a point that the mass will boil at about 160° Fahrenheit; and the apparatus being kept regulated to this point, all the water is driven off by boiling by means of introduced steam, without the temperature becoming higher than 160°.

41. It is out of place here to describe the mechanical devices for filling and keeping filled, and emptying and watching and testing the liquid within the closed cistern, or for regulating the supply of heat and the action of the pump, which is driven by steam. It is sufficient to pass at once to the end of the vacuum pan stage, which lasts eight hours, and to say that the mass in the pan is now run off into sugar-loaf moulds. It is already in a viscid state, and it is now left to cool in

the moulds, which are stood upside down, having a hole in their vertex, placed above a pot. The molasses by its own weight drops out by this hole and is caught in the earthenware pot beneath.

42. The last of the molasses is washed out in this way. The uppermost inch of the sugar in the mould is scraped off, moistened, and put back. The moisture sinks through the mass and carries with it the molasses. This is done some three times, and then, the sugar having now been twelve days in the moulds, the purification is considered to be finished, and the loaves may be turned out of the moulds. If the raw material used was the goor as it comes from the cultivator, the result is a yellowish, sparkling loaf-sugar; but if native-refined dhulua sugar is the raw material used, then the loaf is of brilliantly white sugar.

43. The process used at Cossipore, near Calcutta, is similar to that last described. The principal difference consists in this, that the sugar is at one stage additionally purified by being passed through animal charcoal, and that the molasses, instead of being allowed to drop out by its own gravity from the moulds, is whirled out by the application of centrifugal force.

44. Although sugar is manufactured to some extent all over the district, the principal sugar country is the western part, which may be considered as included between these places :—Kotchandpur, Chaugachha, Jingagachha, Trimohini, Keshabpur, Jessore, and Khajura; and these places are the principal marts for its production and export. There are two chief places to which export is made—to Calcutta and to Nalchitti. Nalchitti is a place of great commercial importance in Backerganj ; a sort of central station for the commerce of the eastern districts. The demand there is for dhulua sugar, as it is for local consumption ; and except from Kotchandpur itself, almost all the dhulua sugar produced in the district finds its way to Nalchitti or to Jalukati, which is near it. Kotchandpur also sends a good deal of dhulua sugar there, but most of its produce goes to supply the local demand in Calcutta, as it is favorably situated for land carriage to Calcutta. Calcutta has, in fact, two demands, namely, a demand for dhulua sugar for consumption in Calcutta and other places whither it sends the sugar, and a demand for pucka sugar for export to Europe and other places. This last demand is met by Keshabpur, and by most of the other places in the southern half of the district. The former demand is, as stated, already met by Kotchandpur.

The sugar market.

2 E

45. The distribution of manufacture and export may therefore be shortly stated thus. In the northern half of the sugar tract dhulua sugar is manufactured for native consumption and sent either to Calcutta or to the eastern districts. In the southern half there are two manufactures: dhulua is manufactured by the ryots, and is brought up and exported to Nalchitti and the eastern districts; and pucka sugar is manufactured by professional refiners and exported to Calcutta.

46. Now, the demand for dhulua sugar is increasing every day, especially the demand from the eastern districts, while the demand for pucka sugar is decreasing. The increase of the former is a natural result of the increasing prosperity, and the decrease of the latter is due to causes connected with the European market, for which, as I believe, most of the pucka sugar sent down to Calcutta is intended. For the Europe trade there are, of course, several competitors with Calcutta. Mauritius especially is a close rival of Calcutta; and as the Mauritius cultivation is now extending and prospering, and as it has greater facilities for entering the European market than Calcutta, it necessarily results that exports from Calcutta are diminishing.

State and prospects of the trade.

47. The sugar trade is therefore less lively in the southern half of the Jessore sugar tract (whence the export is chiefly to Calcutta) than in the northern half. Both at Trimohini and at Keshabpur there have been a large number of refineries closed. As for Keshabpur, the number of refineries has decreased in five years from about 120 to 40 or 50. Trimohini has for a long time been overshadowed by Keshabpur, being hardly more than an out-station of Keshabpur; it had some ten or twelve refineries about five years ago, and now it has not one. It must be remembered, however, that Keshabpur and Trimohini used to be not only refining, but also purchasing stations. I have stated that about these places a large number of the ryots manufacture the sugar they produce, and as the sugar they make is all sold to merchants who have agencies at these places, it follows that a very large amount of sugar trade goes on apart from the refineries.

48. While Keshabpur and the region near it have suffered especially from this cause, there is another cause for the decrease of the sugar trade which has influenced equally every one of the sugar marts, the northern as well as the southern. A short time after European enterprize gave the first stimulus to the cultivation of the date, the native merchants began to step in and take away from the European manufacturers the

fruits of their action. The demand for native-refined sugar was greater than that for the first-rate sugar manufactured by European means, and the consequence was, that the native merchants appropriated all the trade, to the exclusion of the English. But they came in too great a rush, and they competed with each other for the produce. Since a date tree takes seven years to grow so as to produce goor, the demand cannot in this case produce supply till after the lapse of some time. The price of raw material rose; the merchants' profits became more limited; and the consequence was that a slight depression in the trade had the result of driving away many traders from it. The ryots, meantime, profited

Recovery expected. largely by these high prices, and there has been of recent years a great extension of cultivation. This will tend to reduce the price of goor, and to give the traders a larger share of the profit; and if, as is most likely, the increase of demand from the eastern districts keeps pace with the increase of production, the sugar trade will soon recover from its present depression and extend even more widely than it did before.

49. It should be noticed that the depression has been of such a

Prosperity of the culti- nature, that while it affects the merchants and vators. refiners engaged in sugar traffic, it hardly, if at all, affects the ryots. They have all along got high prices for their goor, and have prospered so much, that, as already mentioned, new groves are starting up in all directions. Similarly, near Keshabpur and Trimohini, the many ryots who manufacture their own dhulua sugar have never felt the influence of the evil season that has caused so many merchants to withdraw from the trade. The demand from Nalchitti for the dhulua sugar has never fallen off, as has that for pucka sugar from Calcutta; and thus the ryots' manufacture has never diminished as the merchants' has. It is thus that the apparent paradox is explained, that while the sugar trade, so far as regards the cultivators, is in a most flourishing state, it is as regards the merchants in a somewhat depressed condition.

50. What I call depression is of course only comparatively so, for

Description of a sugar there can be few busier scenes than such places mart. as Kotchandpur or Keshabpur display during the sugar season. For four or five months the produce is seen pouring in every day from every direction; at Kotchandpur alone two or three thousand maunds is the daily supply of goor, and at Keshabpur probably about one thousand. Carts laden with jars, and ryots bringing in their own goor, fill the streets; the shops of the byapáris are crowded with sellers, and the business of weighing and receiving goes on without intermission. Larger transactions are going on at the doors of the refineries, where carts full laden stand to deliver their cargoes to the refiner. At Kotchandpur this occurs every day more or less, though on the regular hât days there is more business done than on others; at Keshabpur also there is a daily market, but at the other places the supplies are mostly timed, so as to reach on the hât day.

51. Let us enter a refinery: a large open square, shut in with a fence, and having sheds on one or two sides of it where part of the work, and specially the storing, is done. If it is a refinery of pucka sugar, we will find several furnaces within the yard, and men busy at each, keeping up the fire, or skimming the pots, or preparing them. If it is dhulua sugar, we will see many rows of baskets with the sugar, covered with syála leaf, standing to drop; rows of earthen pots with goor, or sugar, or molasses, according to the stage of manufacture, are seen on all sides; and in the same open yard all the different processes are at the same time going on.

52. The manufacturing season extends from the middle of December to the middle of May. In December the merchants and the refiners all congregate at the sugar-towns, and in May they finish their work and go home. Compared with their state during these five months, the appearance of such places as Kotchandpur and Keshabpur during the rest of the year is almost that of a deserted town. The refineries are shut up; no goor is coming in; nothing is going on.

53. Many of the manufacturers belong to Santipur, in Nuddea, and while they have their chief refineries in Kotchandpur or some other place, have also smaller ones in Santipur. Whether the Santipur factories derive any part of their raw produce from that part of the country, I do not know; but no inconsiderable quantity of goor is taken across from Kotchandpur, Jingagachha, and Jadabpur to Santipur for manufacture there. The merchants of Keshabpur and Trimohini have their connection rather with Calcutta than with Santipur and places in Nuddea.

54. Kotchandpur has, from its prominence, suffered more in the competition of the merchants than most other places, and it has got rather a bad name for the quality of its sugar. During that competition very many dishonest practices were introduced, some of which I have described before. The misfortune of such practices in this trade is, that as manufacturers have no such distinguishing marks for their own sugar

as indigo planters have for their indigo, a few dishonest men can cause a bad name to adhere to all the produce of the locality, and even honest men will find some additional difficulty in disposing of their wares. So much was this felt, that part of the goor which otherwise would have been manufactured in Kotchandpur was taken over to Santipur and manufactured there. Nay, in some cases the same persons who manufactured dishonest sugar in Kotchandpur, manufactured honest sugar in Santipur.

55. It remains to make a survey in detail of the chief sugar marts, so as to note matters which in our general survey have not found a place. I note first those places which are within what I call the chief sugar tract.

56. *Kotchandpur* is by far the largest of the sugar-marts, as both it and the adjacent village, Sulimanpur, are covered with refineries. Of the sugar manufactured most goes to Calcutta, but about a quarter or a third goes to Nalchitti and Jalukati in Backerganj. The proportion of the latter is steadily increasing. From Kotchandpur to Calcutta there are two routes, by water and by land. The bulk appears to go by land to the Kishnaganj and Ramnagar stations of the Eastern Bengal Railway, going by it to Calcutta. The same carts that take away the sugar frequently collect goor to bring back with them.

Kotchandpur.

The amount of sugar manufactured in and near Kotchandpur in each year must be near 1,00,000 maunds, worth about six lakhs of rupees. It is perhaps about a quarter of the whole manufacture of the district.

The principal merchants are Bangshi Badan, called Sadu Khan by title, and Gurudass Baboo, the great brassware manufacturer of Nuddea. Bangshi Badan, now an old man, is I believe one of those men who, starting from a very small capital, become, by the application of extra-ordinary business qualifications, leading merchants in their country. He has several refineries all over the district, and an agency in Calcutta.

57. *Chaugachha* is, like Kotchandpur, on the bank of the Kabadak river. The pucka sugar is manufactured here, as well as the dhulua. The refiners are chiefly residents of the place. Of the exports I have not obtained very much information, but apparently it is not very different from Kotchandpur. Part of the export goes by river, and part across country to Kishnaganj railway station.

Chaugachha.

So far as sugar goes, the place has been made by the factory erected here by Gladstone, Wyllie, and Co., a factory capable, I believe, of turning out 1,000 maunds of sugar in one day, but which has not been worked for years. This factory cultivated the date very extensively, and Chaugachha is now surrounded by forests of date trees. Goor, I am told, might have been bought at one anna a pot when the factory first came, a quarter of a century since, while now a pot is worth six or seven annas. The proprietor's revenue was then Rs. 118 from the whole bazar (probably about Rs. 5 per bigga), and it is now Rs. 40 per bigga.

58. *Jingagachha*, still further south, is rather a place for the purchase of goor than for the manufacture of sugar.
Jingagachha.   There are three or four refineries in the place, but the greater part of the produce brought to market is bought up by byapáris who take it across to Santipur for manufacture there. This part of the district is, in fact, the part most accessible to Santipur, being on the imperial road.

59. *Jadabpur* is a little to the west of Jingagachha, and like it
supplies goor to the Santipur refiners rather than
Jadabpur.   for local manufacture. It is simply a large goor hát, whither twice a week, that is, on Mondays and Fridays, the sellers bring their goor from all the places round about, and the byapáris come to meet them, purchase the produce, and carry it off to Santipur.

60. *Keshabpur.*—The business here consists in purchasing home-
made dhulua and in refining pucka sugar, most
Keshabpur.   of the former going to the eastern districts, but partly also to Calcutta, and almost all the latter going to the Calcutta market. The purchasers are for the most part agents of Calcutta firms, and give their name to the chief street in Keshabpur, "Calcutta-poti." The export is either by the river from Keshabpur itself, or by cart to Trimohini, and thence to Calcutta by river.

There is a very large pottery manufacture at Keshabpur, the pottery being required for the sugar manufacture. One large pára is full of potters.

Another pára contains coolies, the Kaorapára as it is called, who are employed during the sugar season in the sugar manufacture.

Keshabpur has one advantage over the other places in the sugar tract, in its proximity to the Sundarbans. The river Bhadra leads from it straight down towards the forest, and by this river large cargoes of firewood are brought up to be used in the manufacture of the sugar. It is probably to this circumstance that it owes its prominence as a sugar manufacturing place, for it is the second largest in the district.

61. *Trimohini* is now a sort of out-station of Keshabpur, for
Trimohini.
most of the merchants who have agencies here
have agencies also in Keshabpur. It is entirely
a place for the purchase of sugar, and not for its manufacture; and both
the dhulua sugar manufactured by the ryots and village factories round
about, and also the sugar manufactured in and near Jingagachha, are
bought up here and exported to Calcutta and other places by river.

Talla.
62. *Talla*, further south, is another large sugar
mart, also closely connected with Keshabpur.

Manirampur.
63. *Manirampur* has two or three factories which
do little more than supply local consumption.

64. *Khajura* is a place of very large sugar trade, its name being
Khajura.
derived from that of the date tree (khajur). I
have not visited it, and cannot give details of its
manufacture, but I believe I may say that its export is to Nalchitti
and Backerganj.

65. *Kaliganj* is farther up on the same river, and is only eight
Kaliganj.
miles from Kotchandpur. Most of the sugar
which is exported from Kotchandpur to Nalchitti
is brought here to be shipped.

Kaliganj is not itself a large manufacturing place, but there are
several refineries scattered in the villages round about it; for example,
in Singhia, Farashpur, and others. The sugar manufactured is almost
all exported to Nalchitti and Jalukati.

66. I have now gone round all the marts which lie within the
sugar tract proper, except one or two in the vicinity of Jessore itself,
such as Rajahât, Rupdia, and Basantia. These places and Narikelbaria
I have not had an opportunity to examine, but I believe I may state
that their export is to Nalchitti and Jalukati.

67. A few of the manufacturing places on the outside of the
Jhenida and Magurah sugar tract remain to be noticed. There is, first,
sub-divisions.
the line of the road between Jhenida and
Magurah, which passes through a date-producing region. There are not
here any regular sugar-refining towns, as the refineries are small ones
scattered here and there. Ichakada, a town upon the road at a distance
of four miles from Magurah, is the principal place where the goor is sold.
The ryots bring it there in considerable quantities upon the hât days,
Tuesdays and Fridays, and sell it to refiners. Part of the goor here
produced is also carried further east to Binadpur, six miles east of

Magurah, where there are one or two refineries established for the manufacture of the goor, not very abundant, which grows about these parts. The export is almost entirely to Nalchitti.

68. Further east still is Muhammadpur, where a little sugar is refined. The produce here is very scanty, but what there is manufactured goes to Nalchitti.

69. The Naral sub-division is for the most part of very low
Naral sub-division. situation, and is devoid of that high ground which is essential for the cultivation of the date. But at Lohagara there is some sugar manufacture, though of an abnormal sort. A few date trees grow near Lohagara, but on land so low that they produce no juice, and it is not from its vicinity that Lohagara derives its goor. But the sugar tract proper is, as we shall presently see, deficient in rice cultivation; and as Lohagara, a low region, has some rice to spare, it sends a little, laden in ships, to Khajura and other places. The ships which go laden with rice bring back cargoes of goor, and it is thus that the small amount of raw material required for the manufacture at Lohagara is supplied. The sugar manufactured in Lohagara is mostly pucka sugar, and its export is mostly to Calcutta. But some goes also to Backerganj.

70. We have another instance of this reciprocity between the
Khulna sub-division. sugar trade and the rice trade, for large quantities of rice pour up the Bhairab river, conveying the rice from the great cultivating regions in the south to Naupara, Basantia, and Khajura, the inlets on the eastern side, into the sugar tract. From these places, but especially from Basantia and Noapara, the ships carry down goor to be manufactured into sugar at Daulatpur, Senhati, Khulna, and Faqirhat. Near Faqirhat there is some high land producing date trees, but for the most part it is dependent for its supply of raw material upon the cultivation further north.

71. The places just mentioned, and also Phultalla (which is on the border land between the rice country and the sugar country, and can supply its own material for manufacture), produce for the most part pucka sugar. This is a natural consequence of their proximity to the Sundarban supply of firewood. Their export is chiefly to Calcutta.

72. I have already given instances of reciprocity of rice import
Interchange of sugar and rice. and sugar export, but the principle extends further than I have stated. Throughout the delta there is a general westward movement of rice. Calcutta attracts most of the

rice grown in the Jessore Sundarbans, and leaves the riceless districts in Jessore to be supplied from Backerganj. All over the sugar tract the cultivation of rice is very deficient, and rice pours in from Nalchitti all over Magurah and the south of Jhenida, and all over the sudder sub-division. The ships that come laden with rice therefore take back with them to Nalchitti cargoes of sugar. So also rice is imported by the Kabadak from the south, and through Jingagachha, Chaugachha, and Kotchandpur, is spread over the western part of the district. And the ships engaged in this import can carry away the sugar to the tracts whence they have come.

73. From Calcutta itself the principal import is salt, and the salt ships are employed in carrying away sugar to Calcutta.

74. It remains to mention a few facts, which should probably have found a place elsewhere. First, as to the refiners. Professional refiners are for the most part themselves exporters; that is to say, those who buy sugar to refine it in large refineries, scarcely ever sell it to other merchants to export. In fact, they frequently combine, with their refining trade, the trade of purchasing from the smaller or village refiners for export. This latter, however, is also a separate trade, and, especially at Keshabpur and Trimohini, there are merchants who, themselves doing nothing in the way of refining, purchase sugar locally refined and export it to Calcutta or to Nalchitti. Most of these are agents of Calcutta or Nalchitti firms. In fact, according to the native system of trade, it will be found that the same firms, or firms having, in part at least, the same partners, have establishments at many places, and carry on business at each place through different partners or agents. Bangshi Badan Sadu Khan, for example, has refineries at all the large sugar marts, and has besides that a branch in Calcutta to receive and dispose of the sugar which he exports thither.

Exporters.

75. I have not yet said what becomes of the "chitiya goor," the refuse of the sugar-refining process. It is to a very small extent locally used for mixing up with tobacco to be smoked. By far the bulk of it is however exported to Calcutta, Nalchitti, and Surajganj; but what ultimately becomes of it I do not know. An attempt has been made, once or twice, to utilize it by distilling it into rum at Tahirpur, where, as already mentioned, the old sugar factory was converted into a rum-distillery. The first attempts failed to produce any sufficient commercial return, and I do not know how the present attempt is prospering.

The chitiya goor, or refuse.

2 F

76. From what I have said, it will be readily understood how
Sugar trade a source of wealth. great a source of wealth to the district lies in the sugar trade. The cultivation involves little labour and it gives a productive return; and the manufacture also is such that many ryots can and do engage in it. I have above roughly estimated the outturn of the district at about four lakhs of maunds, worth twenty-five or thirty lakhs of rupees, and I conclude from independent sources that this estimate is not far above the truth. In the certificate tax year the sugar refiners were taxed upon an income of about Rs. 3,24,000, and this excluded some of the largest firms (who were taxed in Calcutta) and all the small home refineries which fell under Rs. 500 profit. The whole trading profit distributed among ryot and professional trader amounts, I am pretty sure, to at least six or seven lakhs of rupees. And there is throughout the sugar tract an air of substantiality and comfort about the ryots and their homesteads which testifies to the advantages they derive from engaging in sugar cultivation.

XLII.—*The Rice Trade and Sundarban Reclamation.*

THE second great trade connected with Jessore is the rice trade, and the subjects connected with it may be shortly stated thus. The south of the district, and especially the Sundarbans, form a great rice-producing tract. From the Jessore Sundarbans, and from the Backerganj Sundarbans through those of Jessore, there is a continual flow of rice to the westward towards Calcutta. Rice also goes northward, spreading itself all over the sub-divisions of the sudder and of Jhenida, which do not, as a rule, produce sufficient rice for local consumption.

2. The fitness of the Sundarbans to serve as a grand rice-supplying
The Sundarban rice-province. tract was pointed out by Mr. Henckell so long ago as 1784 and 1785, and the measures that were taken at his instigation have been already described. It is unnecessary also to repeat here what has been said in another place regarding the extension of Sundarban cultivation. I proceed rather to describe the nature of it.

3. The clearing of Sundarban forest is a most arduous undertaking.
Difficulty of clearing. The trees intertwine with each other to such an extent, that each supports and upholds the other; and some of the trees are of an immense size, one sort, the jín tree, of

which a good specimen is seen at Morrellganj, spreading and sending down new stems till it covers perhaps an acre of ground. Trees like these cannot be cut down and removed in bulk; they must be taken piecemeal, and the tree must be cut up into little pieces before an attempt is made to cut it down. But the trees are not the only difficulty, for there is a low and almost impenetrable brushwood which covers the whole surface. This brushwood has simply to be hacked away bit by bit by any one who attempts to penetrate into the forest.

4. And there is no small danger from wild beasts while all this is going on. Alligators one is not likely to come across, except on the immediate banks of rivers;

Wild beasts.

but tigers are not unfrequent, and occasionally break out upon the defenceless forest clearers if the latter approach their lair too closely. A great number of these accidents one never hears anything about, but the occasions on which one does hear of such depredations, through their occurring near inhabited places, are very frequent.

5. Sometimes a tiger takes possession of a tract of land and commits such fearful havoc that he is left in peace in his domain. I am not writing of things which may occur, but of things which have occurred. The depredations of some unusually fierce tiger, or of more than one such tiger, have often caused the retirement of some advanced colony of clearers, who have, through their fear, been compelled to abandon land which only the labour of years has reclaimed from jungle.

6. It is curious how single tigers become sometimes an object of dread over a large tract of land. There was one great man-eater whom one used to be perpetually hearing about in 1868. Hardly a week passed but there were one or two reports of people carried off by him, and he used to be perfectly well known. He had apparently a charmed life. One day he came on board an Englishman's boat and coolly walked off with one or two of his oarsmen. The Englishman levelled a blunderbus at him, but the instrument burst, and while it much injured the shooter, the tiger got off scoot-free. On another occasion the same tiger passed within a few yards of a gentleman who was accustomed to and prepared for such interviews. He of course fired, but again the beast escaped scatheless. This pest was finally killed by Mr. Morrell of Morrellganj, who laid wait for him, shutting himself up in an iron cage. The tiger was only severely wounded by the shot, and he charged and knocked over the cage, but the cessation of his ravages shewed that the wound had had a mortal effect.

7. It was either this tiger or some other which adopted a habit of attacking boats passing through a certain khal near Morrellganj, and made the passage so dangerous that the route was for a time practically given up as impassable.

8. Suppose, however, that the Sundarban cultivator has got over these difficulties, and the equally formidable though less prominent difficulties entailed by a residence far from the haunts of men, his dangers have not yet passed. Unless the greatest care is taken of the land so cleared, it will spring back into jungle and become as bad as ever. So great is the evil fertility of the soil, that reclaimed land neglected for a single year will present to the next year's cultivator a forest of reed (nal). He may cut it and burn it down, but it will spring up again as thick as ever; and it takes about three eradications to expel this reed when once it has grown. The soil, too, must be cultivated for ten or twelve years before it loses this tendency to at once cover itself with reed jungle.

Fighting with jungle.

9. The first and heaviest part of the clearing of any plot of land is usually done at the expense of the proprietor, the person who has settled with Government for the land; and when the clearing has proceeded to a certain point, he settles ryots upon the lands thus partially cleared and they bring it into cultivation. These ryots call themselves "abad-kari" or reclaiming ryots, and esteem themselves to have a sort of right of occupancy in their lands. When these ryots thus begin, they occasionally themselves extend their lands by additional clearings; but it may, I believe, be stated as a general rule that the greater part of the actual clearing work is done at the expense of the capitalist, and not of the ryots.

System of reclamation.

10. When a sufficient number of people are gathered together, they tend of course to form a settlement, and to remain permanently where they are. But the farthest advanced parts of the cultivation, and some also of those which are not new or remote from old lands, are carried on upon a different principle. A large number of ryots, who live and cultivate lands north of the Sundarbans—that is, near the line of rivers which crosses the district from Kochua, through Baghahat and Khulna, to the Kabadak—have also lands in the Sundarbans, held under different landholders.

Migratory cultivators.

11. The cultivating seasons in the Sundarbans are later than those farther north, and the plan which is followed by these double cultivators is this. The months of Cheit, Bysack, and Jeth, are spent in cultivation

at home. The ryot then, having prepared his home cultivation, embarks his ploughs, and his oxen, and his food, in a boat and takes them away bodily to his "âbâd" or Sundarban cultivation. Assar, Shraban, and Bhadro, are spent in ploughing and sowing and preparing the crops there, the ryot building for himself, with materials he has partly brought with him, a little shed, under which he lives. The water gets high in Shraban and Bhadro, but that is little impediment to cultivation. Many of the lands under rice cultivation are below high-water mark, but the planting is easy, for rice sown on higher lands is transplanted into these low lands when it is strong enough to bear the water.

12. The ryot now again comes home, and these outposts of cultivation are absolutely abandoned—large extents of cultivated rice-fields and not a symptom of human habitation. By the end of Agrayan the ryot has cut and stored his home-cultivated rice, and he then goes to the Sundarbans, re-erects his hut, which has probably been destroyed during his absence (or lives in the open), and reaps his Sundarban rice. At that season of the year (Poos and Magh) reapers, or "dawals," crowd to the district, and they are extensively employed all over the rice-fields of the Sundarbans. When the rice is cut and prepared for sale, the byapáris are sure to come round and buy it up, and the zemindar will also send his agents round to collect the rents from the ryots. The ryot has sold his grain and paid his rent, and the rest of the money he can bring back with him to his home.

13. While a great deal of cultivation in the more remote parts of the Sundarbans follows this method, there are in the nearer parts large settlements of ryots who dwell permanently near the land they have under cultivation. But it must be remembered that these tracts are after all sparsely inhabited, and that many of the ryots who dwell in them, besides having a holding near their own houses, have another eight or ten miles away, which they visit only occasionally when they have work to do. The great fertility of the land renders it easy for ryots to hold large areas under cultivation, and thus, what with resident large-cultivating ryots and non-resident ryots, we do not find in the Sundarban tracts a population at all equal to what the amount of cultivation would lead us to expect.

Sundarban settlements.

14. There is another thing to be noticed with reference to the dwellers in these regions, namely, that they do not tend, as in other places, to group themselves into villages. Probably this is one result of their having holdings so large that it is most convenient to live near them.

But, whatever the cause, many of the village-names on the maps represent no sites of villages as we usually understand a village, but represent great seas of waving paddy with homesteads dotted over them, where families live apparently in perfect seclusion. This description, however, hardly applies to older settled tracts, such as pergunnah Hogla.

15. I have neglected to note another feature in the reclamation and cultivation of these Sundarban lands, namely the embanking of water-inlets. It is a charac-teristic of deltaic formation that the banks of the rivers are higher than the lands further removed from them; and the whole of the Sundarbans may be looked on as an aggregation of basins, where the higher level of the sides prevents the water coming in to overflow the interior. Many of these basins are so formed, that left to themselves they would remain under flood, as they communicate with the surrounding channels by khals which penetrate the bank; and a great part of reclamation work consists in keeping out the water, and thus bringing under cultivation the marsh land inside.

16. This method of reclamation of low lands applies both to the Sundarbans proper (whose northern limit I take to be the line of rivers above noted), and also to that remarkable line of depression which runs across the district immediately north of Khulna. Part of these low lands has been, part still remains to be, drained and reclaimed by the method referred to.

17. In employing this method, all the inlets from the channels surrounding are embanked, and smaller channels, called poyáns, are opened round their ends. The inlets themselves are too big to be kept in control, but these "poyáns" easily can be. This embanking is usually done in Agrayan (November), after the rivers have gone down. Now, when the tide is low, the channels are opened and the water from the inside drains off; when it is high, and would otherwise burst in, the channels are closed. It is evident that by this means the water can be reduced to a level much lower than the half-tide level, and much land can be rendered culturable which otherwise would be marsh.

18. But here also there is the same thing to note, viz. that a year's neglect may at one stroke take away all that has been gained by many years' labour. The effect of the rains and the freshes of each year is to partially destroy all the embankments that were used the previous year and to flood the land. The rice that has been sown has however attained sufficient

Embankments.

Risk of embanking.

hardihood to remain uninjured, and when the waters again go down, harvest may be reaped. But unless the embankments are again renewed in November, the flood will not have ceased to cover the low lands by sowing time, the land will remain unsown, and jungle and marshy reed will take the place of the paddy.

19. These embanking and draining operations are required more or less all over the Sundarbans, where there is always some land that can be by them brought above water-level, but they have been used in their most extensive shape in some parts of the range of marshes which I have mentioned as lying north of Khulna. In the Pabla bhíl, for example, when it was drained after this style, ten large embankments and thirty-two smaller ones were required. The bhíl has since been suffered to go to ruin.

20. One curious testimony to the extent of these embanking operations is shewn in their effect on the tide.

Effect on the tide.

They will plainly have the effect of confining the rising tide within its river channels and preventing it expending itself in lateral overflow. Now, it is a fact that twenty years ago the tide was never observed at Naral, or even for some distance further down stream. At the present day, when the rivers are low, the tide turns the current not only at Naral, but for a few miles above it. The change is plainly the result of twenty years' extension of cultivation in the Sundarbans.

21. With all these drawbacks and risks attached to the cultivation, the soil is nevertheless so very fertile, that it can easily produce a rent of one rupee per bigga. Those who cultivate it without having any right arising from previous occupancy, pay about Re. 1 or 1-4 rent for their lands.

22. It is a question of some interest how long these reclamations in the Sundarbans have been going on, and whether there were any before the occupation of the country by the English. That the Sundarbans were at any time a generally populated region, I have never seen any evidence to shew. But it seems to me beyond doubt that settlers have occasionally appeared in various parts of the Sundarbans and have again disappeared. The history which I have given of Khanja Ali is the history of an ancient and extensive reclamation of land in the neighbourhood of Baghahat—land a great part of which subsequently fell back into jungle and had again to be reclaimed. The mosque at Masjidkur was no doubt in the midst of cultivated lands four hundred

Were the Sundarbans anciently populated?

years ago, yet it is only within the last half century that the new reclamations have reached and spread over that part of the country. The houses and mounds at Kopilmuni are evidences that there was cultivated land when they were built and dwelt in, but the present reclamations in the immediate neighbourhood date only a hundred years back, and the land two or three miles off was jungle till about sixty years back.

23. I think that these are all evidences that cultivation once existed in spots which subsequently relapsed into jungle, and had to be reclaimed in comparatively recent times. Looking at the map, we find that the line which divides the reclaimed lands from those that are still forest, descends further south near Ishwaripur (Pratapaditya's city) than it does either on the west or on the east of that place. In the same manner there seems to be an advanced outpost, Amadi, on the bank of the Kabadak, close to Masjidkur, where the lands have a pergunnah name (Jamira), while there are no pergunnah lands farther north till one comes to Mallai. Chandkhali and its vicinity, as we have seen, is not pergunnah land, for these lands were never reclaimed till 1785 at least. Again, the line of reclamation descends to the south, when we come to the Baghahat side of the river Passar. There is certainly some reason for thinking that the southward march of cultivation has been more rapid at these points, and they are precisely the points where, three or four hundred years ago, Khanja Ali and Pratapaditya established their chieftainships in the Sundarbans.

24. It is also a fact that many persons, in making clearings in the forest, have found in isolated parts the remains of brick gháts and traces of tanks. Few men can give better or more reliable information on this point than the dewan of Morrellganj, and he assured me that not only the Morrellganj reclaimers, but other forest clearers also, found such remains as I have described, and that in one or two instances kilns of bricks have thus been found. It would appear that no houses have been found within his knowledge.

Ancient buildings.

25. There is nothing wonderful in people building masonry gháts to their tanks who themselves dwelt in non-permanent houses; and therefore I do not hesitate to draw from the existence of these tanks the conclusion that not one, but many persons once dwelt in these places and intended to make them their permanent residence. The kilns of bricks testify to unfulfilled intentions, and render it not improbable that the dwellers in these places had sometimes to leave them in a hurry.

The tradition of the place, or rather the account given by the present dwellers, is that the places where these remains are found are really ancient seats of cultivation, but that Mahratta marauders compelled the settlers to abandon such remote places and seek safety in places more thickly inhabited. The Mahratta invaders belong only to last century, and I doubt if they came quite so far east or south as these places. But it is certain that Mughs once dwelt in these regions; and indeed I have heard the fact of the Backerganj cultivation having proceeded so far southward accounted for on the theory that the Mugh settlers had done so much in the way of reclamation. However, I must leave it undecided whether these petty colonies of settlers that used to come down to the Sundarban regions left the place willingly, or because they were driven away, or because they died off.

26. I may mention that there are very many places in the Sundarbans where the present settlers tell one that the lands they now cultivate were cultivated also in ancient times, but permitted to relapse into jungle. It is a sort of general belief, though what its authority is I cannot say. I have found only one place where tradition gives a definite form to the story of these ancient settlers.

Traditions of Ram Pal.

27.. The lands about Rampal and Parikhali have been reclaimed now for sixty or seventy years, but once, long ago, they were reclaimed by two brothers of the potter caste, Ram Pal and Shyam Pal. A tank is shewn as having been made by Ram Pal. It is only of ordinary size, and it is now overgrown with grass thick enough to support animals grazing in it, though as a mass it floats upon the water beneath. Ram Pal was at one time sent for (probably to satisfy revenue demands) by the nawab (or, as others say, by Sitaram Ray, but this is not likely), and when he went he took with him two pigeons, saying that he would bring the pigeons back with him, and if they appeared without him, his family would know that some dire misfortune had befallen him. After a time the pigeons returned alone, and so Ram Pal's family, household, cattle, and all, jumped into this tank and were drowned in it. In attestation of this story, it is declared that up till only five or seven years ago cow-dung used to rise occasionally to the surface of the tank, but in these unbelieving times the miracle has ceased.

28. This tank had another element of sanctity, for when Ram Pal was alive, he used to keep in it the pât, or board, used in the poojah of Shib, in the month of Cheit. On the morning of the poojah the board

used to rise and present itself to Ram Pal, who faithfully returned it
when the poojah was over, to remain for another year in the tank.

29. I give the story in this place as another traditionary evidence
of the existence of ancient settlers in these regions, but the date of
Ram Pal I would not place farther back than two hundred years at most.
I quit now this part of the subject and return to the cultivation.

30. It is difficult to give an idea of the wealth of rice-fields that
one sees in passing during harvest time along the
Sundarban recovery.   rivers which intersect the Sundarban reclamations.
In other parts of the country one's view is always restricted by trees
or by villages, but in these Sundarbans it is different. You look
over one vast plain, stretching for miles upon each side, laden with
golden grain; a homestead is dotted about here and there, and the
course of the rivers is traced by the fringes of low brushwood that
grow upon their banks: but with these exceptions one sees in many
places one unbroken sea of waving dhan, up to the point where the
distant forest bounds the horizon. Of course this is not always the
view: one cannot reclaim a whole estate in one day. In places where
reclamation has only more recently begun, a fringe of half a mile broad
on either side of the river contains all that has as yet been done by the
extending colony.

31. These colonies sometimes suffer most severely from cyclones.
Liability to physical   Their houses and their fields are only a foot or two
calamity.   above high-water mark, and when the cyclone
wave pours up the great streams of the Passar and the Haringhatta,
and from them spreads all over the country, the inundation works cruel
havoc among these low-lying isolated villages. The grain in their fields
is spoiled; their houses are torn away, and all their stores are lost; their
bullocks are carried away, and many of them drowned; and they themselves reduced to the extremest shifts to save their own lives. The
cyclone of 16th May 1869 destroyed 250 lives near Morrellganj alone,
and the loss it caused to property was something immense. One
almost wonders how, in some of those storms, the whole country is not
at once swept bare, for there is no shelter from the storm and little
obstruction to the swelling waters. Liability to cyclones must put a
practical limit to the extension of cultivation: for the nearer one gets
to the sea, the greater the danger; and the more the forest is cleared
away, the smaller the barrier placed between the cultivator and the
devouring wave

32. In the Sundarbans the rice crop is reaped about the first fortnight of January, the soil easily retaining up till
that time all the moisture necessary for the growth
of the grain. The method of reaping, too, is different from that which
prevails over the rest of the district; for as the straw is of absolutely no
value in the Sundarbans, the crop is reaped by only cutting off the heads,
and the straw is subsequently burnt down.

Method of reaping.

33. I have now to shew how the grain finds its way to market,
and here I have first to observe that ryots cultivate
in two ways—either under advances from the
merchant, or without such advances. Many ryots in the Sundarbans
are well enough off to cultivate with their own capital, but several also
receive advances from merchants, who for this purpose send their men
all over the country about Bhadro (August-September), and then again
send their people after harvest to collect in ships the grain which has
been thus pledged to them. Zemindars also make advances in some
cases, but the zemindars of these lands, that is, the large zemindars, are
mostly absentees, and receive back their advances in money, so that the
matter does not influence the distribution of trade. The small taluqdars
are different, and usually take a close interest in their ryots.

Advance system of cultivation.

34. A great quantity of rice, however, is cultivated without any
sort of advances, and the ryots dispose of it themselves, either taking it to the hâts themselves, or
delivering it on the spot to a trader, or byapári, who comes to purchase
it. The latter method is probably the more frequent one in the case of
very remote clearings, but in those which are situated within reach of a
hât, the ryot takes his grain to sell it there. There is a line of hâts situated
in the north of the Sundarbans to which grain in this way is brought—
Chandkhali, Paikgachha, Surkhali, Gauramba, Rampal (or Parikhali),
and Morrellganj; and from long distances the grain is brought up by
ryots in their boats to these hâts.

Sale of grain by the ryots.

35. Of these hâts the chief is Chandkhali, and Monday is the hât
day; convenience of trade causing that only one
day in each week, instead of two, should be set
aside as hât day. If one were to see Chandkhali on an ordinary day, one
would see a few sleepy huts on the river bank and pass it by as some
insignificant village. The huts are many of them shops, and they are
situated round a square; but there are no purchasers to be seen, and the
square is deserted. On Sunday, however, ships come up from all directions,

The Chandkhali hât.

but chiefly from Calcutta, and anchor along the banks of the river and of the khal, waiting for the hât. On Monday boats pour in from all directions laden with grain, and others come with more purchasers. People who trade in eatables bring their tobacco and turmeric, to meet the demands of the thousand ryots who have brought their grain to market and will take away with them a week's stores. The river—a large enough one— and the khal, become alive with native crafts and boats, pushing in among each other and literally covering the face of the water. Sales are going on rapidly amid all the hubbub, and the byapáris and mahajans (traders and merchants) are filling their ships with the grain which the ryots have brought alongside and sold to them.

36. The greater part of the traffic thus goes on the water, but on land, too, it is a busy sight. On water or on land, there is probably a representative from nearly every house for miles around; they have come to sell their grain and to buy their stores; numberless hawkers have come to offer these stores for sale : oil, turmeric, tobacco, vegetables, and all the other luxuries of a ryot's life.

37. By the evening the business is all done; the ryots turn their boats homewards; the hawkers go off to the next hât, or go to procure more supplies; and with the first favorable tide, the ships weigh anchor and take their cargoes away to Calcutta, and to a smaller extent up the river. By Tuesday morning the place is deserted for another week.

38. At this Chandkhali hât alone 3,000 or 4,000 rupees worth of rice on an average change hands every hât day, Extent of its trade. and during the busiest season the amount probably reaches twice that quantity; and about 1,500 boats are brought up by people attending the hât, boats being almost the only means of travelling here. And the rice alone does not measure the amount of trade at this hât; for, as we shall afterwards see, the traffic in firewood equals the rice trade in value, and much surpasses it in bulk.

39. Chandkhali is after all only one out of many hâts, and Migratory and stationary traders. besides the trade that is done in the hâts, there is an immense traffic carried on, less conspicuously, by traders stationed all over the Sundarbans. Some of these have large ships, and with them visit the clearings and fill their ships close to where the grain grows. Others, stationed at some village, buy up grain when they can get it, and ship it off themselves or sell it to larger traders. And everywhere there will be found a class of traders called " farias," who insert themselves between the more petty sellers and the regular

trader or byapári, buying up in very small quantities, and when a certain bulk has been accumulated, waiting for the byapári to come to buy, or taking the grain to him to sell it.

40. In these ways, then, the rice passes from the hand of the cultivator into that of the trader (byapári) or the merchant (mahajan). The trader is a man who has a capital, perhaps, of Rs. 300 or 400; he sometimes exports his purchased rice himself, taking it to the merchant in Calcutta or elsewhere, who will buy it, and so give him money to use for a second similar transaction; or he will sell it on the spot to the larger exporting merchants, men who have large firms in Calcutta, and have agencies in the producing districts.

41. The principal export from the Sundarbans is to Calcutta, and there is a general westward motion of the grain through them, the produce of the Backerganj Sundarbans passing through the Jessore rivers. The routes adopted for this traffic are nearly the same that they were a hundred years ago.

The Sundarban routes.

42. There is the inland route, which goes across the district by Kochua, Baghahat, Khulna, Baitaghatta, Diluti, Paikgachha, and so into the Kabadak. From the notices that appear in the old correspondence, the western half of this route appears to have been much changed since their date, for the boats, after passing Khulna, appear at that time to have gone down the Passar river, and through by the Chunkhuri khal towards Chandkhali. I conclude this from the fact that the route is described as the route by Kochua, Khulna, and Chandkhali, in the magistrate's letter of 31st May 1789. I find also that a boatful of sepoys was plundered by dacoits in 1788, at the mouth of the Chunkhuri khal (M. 23-10-88), shewing that their boat passed by that way.

43. In fact, the rivers near Diluti and Paikgachha do not appear to have been at that time open into the Kabadak; but apparently about forty years ago (though I have not accurate information), the zemindar of pergunnah Mallai cut a khal between them and Sitaganj, on the Kabadak. This allowed easy communication between the north and the Sundarban rivers, and though the route became, and was long used as, the generally adopted one between Khulna and the west, it still involved a long circuit by this artificial khal and the Kabadak.

Artificial canals.

44. Finally, about five years ago, a new excavation was made which communicated directly between the Sipsá Aga which passes Paikgachha and the Kabadak. It is a straight canal of three miles in length, and

it saves a very long detour.   The name of the assistant engineer who cut it is perpetuated in the local appellation of the khal, for people call the little village which has sprung up at the west end of it Millettganj, and call the canal itself the Millettganj khal.

45.   This therefore forms the more inland of the routes, and large numbers of ships pass by it in each direction each day ; of salt-laden ships alone, I have counted more than twenty brought up to Khulna by this route during a single tide.

46.   In the cold season this line of rivers in some places does not afford sufficient water for ships of 1,500 or 2,000

The southern route.

maunds, and these therefore pass by the southern route.   This route enters at Morrellganj and passes by the Ghoskhali and the Chilla Chandpai khal into the Passar.   Thence the ships pass by the Bajua khal and the Dhaki river into the Sipsá, whence the Manus river takes them to Chandkhali.   This route passes through a tract in some parts uninhabited, and is therefore avoided by ships which can take the northern route.

47.   These are the two routes by which the rice passes from east to west in the Sundarbans ; but another route should be mentioned in this place, namely, the one which is used by the ships which are to pass up the Madhumati, or have come down it.   These use the Atharabanka (eighteen bends) between Khulna and the Madhumati, and on the western side of Khulna they use either the northern route just described, or, if they are too big, they use the southern one between Chandkhali and the Chunkhuri khal, coming into the Passar by it, and so passing up to Khulna.

48.   The navigation in all these streams is by tides, for in all these

Navigation by tides.

Sundarban rivers the current flows one way during the ebb and the opposite way during the flood-tide. Part of every journey has to be made with the flood and part with the ebb, and the speed of the voyage depends exactly upon how far the voyager succeeds in catching the ebb and the flood at the proper points.

49.   There are, naturally, some regular anchoring places, places

Solitary traders.

where the voyager has to change from the flood to the ebb, or *vice versá*, and must therefore wait for the turn of the tide, unless he happens to arrive at the exact nick of time. At these points, far as some of them are from the abodes of men, there will be found people present to sell to the passing boatmen some vegetables or some fish.   A fisherman will have stationed himself there and offers his wares to the passing ships, or some solitary boatman will have brought down vegetables in his little craft, hoping by their sale to make a profit sufficient to reimburse him for his long journey. Large ships may take about five days to cross from Morrellganj to Chandkhali, and between these two places they can get no supplies except what they may in this way pick up. The water even is not drinkable, and boats coming from Morrellganj bring water with them from there.

50. The steamer routes through the Sundarbans differ of course from the routes above described. Within the 24-Per-
Steamer routes.
gunnahs district they keep much further south, and they come northwards by the Sipsá river, or by the Passar river, to Khulna, and thence by the Atharabanka to the Madhumati. Steamers that intend to pass through Backerganj district cross Jessore by a route very far south, never coming near human habitations till they appear at Morrellganj.

XLIII.—*The Rice Trade.—(Continued.)*

IN what I have said I have sketched the production of rice only so far as regards the Sundarbans, and it remains to make some remarks about the rice trade as it affects other parts of the district. The general flow of the Sundarban rice is, as has been shewn, a westward flow, as
Local demand for rice.
the great demand in Calcutta draws nearly the whole trade towards itself. But there is another, though of course a smaller, demand all over the western part of Jessore, for in the Sudder and in the Jhenida sub-divisions sufficient rice is not grown to satisfy the local consumption.

2. This tract is mostly supplied from Nalchitti and Jalukati, the Backerganj rice marts; and it is natural that this
Whence supplied.
should be so. The commercial relations between these places in respect of the sugar trade naturally determine, or rather favour, their existence also in respect of the rice trade. Keshabpur, Jinga-gachha, and Chaugachha, have, as we have seen, less direct communication with Nalchitti than the other places, and we find that they accordingly derive their rice rather from places immediately south of them than from the Backerganj Sundarbans.

3. Part of the rice sold at Chandkhali finds its way up the Kabadak, and is landed at Trimohini, Jingagachha, Chaugachha, and Kotchandpur; and rice from the south also pours up the Bhadra river to Keshabpur;

and from all these places it is distributed over the country which I have designated the sugar tract.

4. Nalchitti, however, supplies by far the greatest part of the requirements of the riceless regions. A little goes up by the Madhumati to the north-eastern part of Magurah sub-division, which is somewhat deficient in rice; liability to inundation interfering much with its productiveness. Great quantities are sent up by the Bhairab river, and are landed at Phultalla, Naupara, Basantia, Khajura, Kaliganj; and in a different direction are carried up to Binadpur, Magurah, and Jhenida. Of all these, Basantia is perhaps the greatest mart, the quantity of rice distributed from there being very great: the town of Jessore derives its supplies almost entirely from Basantia. The Nalchitti rice also, to a certain extent, competes with Jessore rice in supplying Keshabpur and the towns on the Kabadak.

5. The sub-division of Naral and the low country near it is almost the only part of the district which neither imports nor exports rice in any quantity. It grows sufficient for itself. In the bhíls about this part of the country is grown the long-stemmed rice. Sown on the edges of the bhíls when the water is low, it rises as the water rises, and is ripe before the water has disappeared. This cultivation is sometimes a very easy cultivation; for after the grass and straw on the dried-up lands is burnt down, there is little to do in the way of ploughing, the seed being sown broadcast upon the soil, which, after a shower or two of rain, is quite ready to receive it.

Naral is self-sufficient.

6. The ordinary system of rice cultivation it is unnecessary to sketch in the same manner as I have done that of the Sundarbans, for it is sufficiently well known. I have noted the matters in which Jessore differs from other districts.

XLIV.—*Other Sundarban Industries.*

BESIDES the cultivation of rice there are some other industries connected with the Sundarbans which deserve specification; and the first of these is the wood trade.

Wood trade.

2. The regular wood-cutters may be first described. These live for the most part just north of the Sundarbans, and when the rains have ceased their season begins. A body of them start in a native ship for the Sundarbans—some far

Wood-cutters.

south portion of them, not very far from the sea. Their ship is provisioned for four months or so, and during that time it remains anchored at the place which they choose as their head-quarters. They themselves leave the ships to go to their work, and come back there at night as they would come back to their home, which the ship really is.

3. A party, of whom some are sure to be of the Bhawali or wood-cutter caste, may consist of ten or fifteen, and *Their system.* they are usually chartered by some regular wood merchant, who has a contract with them, by which they receive advances from him and sell him their wood. During the four months they are absent they cut their wood, shape it to a certain extent, and bind it up into rafts so placed that the high tide will raise them. They are some four days' voyage from home, but some of them occasionally come back to bring news of how the party are progressing, or perhaps to say that one of them has been caught by a tiger or by an alligator. When their rafts are ready, some of the party float them up with the flood tides to the places where they are to deliver them, the rest still remaining engaged in their wood-cutting.

4. These regular expeditions are undertaken chiefly for the purpose of procuring the larger forms of wood—those *Occasional wood-cutters.* which are to be used for posts, or for making boats and other articles; but both these regular wood-cutters and the occasional wood-cutters also bring up large quantities of smaller forms of wood intended to be cut up into firewood. The occasional wood-cutters embrace a very large number of the ryots living within the Sundarban limits, or just without them. If they have an idle season (as they frequently have, for rice cultivation does not employ them all the year round), they take a boat and go down to the Sundarbans, cut a cargo of wood, and bring it up with them to sell it. There are very many ryots who go down to the Sundarbans when they want a post for their house, or some wood for their cooking, preferring a few days' absence from home to spending money in purchasing. The demand for wood, and especially for firewood, is so great, that it offers ample inducement to ryots, who otherwise even are very well off, to engage in it and reap from it a little profit.

5. A great part of the wood thus brought up is sundri wood, and it has this unfortunate characteristic, that it does not *Sundri wood.* in its green state float in water. It is brought up in two shapes—beams, and short pieces of four or five feet long, intended

2 H

for firewood. The former are sometimes brought up by being tied outside boats, or by being made into rafts, floated by being firmly tied up with a mass of lighter wood. The latter are mostly laden in boats.

6. Chandkhali is a great centre towards which the wood trade tends. The ryots who cut the wood meet there (as in the case of the rice-trade) the traders who are ready to carry it off to Calcutta, where by far the most of it goes, or up the Kabadak to the villages and sugar factories on its banks. I was told that Rs. 3,000 worth of wood comes to this hât on one hât day in the busy season, and this represents about 50,000 maunds. Such are the figures that were given me, but I would put down the truth at about half these quantities.

The Wood Trade.—
Chandkhali.

7. The boats used by ryots who only occasionally enter into the trade carry 100 to 150 maunds of wood, but the boats employed in the regular trade are of 1,000 or 1,500 maunds. These last, however, do not come to Chandkhali; they are either employed on the part of mahajans, as above described, or they are managed by parties acting on their own behalf, and in this case they are taken straight to Calcutta and the wood is sold there.

8. Next to Chandkhali, Dhamalia, in Dumuria, is the great place for wood trade. There lived here a wood merchant, Bhikan Sirdar, a man who raised himself from the cooly class to great wealth, and he had an immense trade in wood, both with Calcutta and with other places. From Dhamalia and Dumuria large quantities of wood are sent up the Bhadra river to Keshabpur, where they are used in the sugar manufacture.

Dhamalia.

9. Khulna is also a great place for wood, and a good deal is used in Khulna itself, both in boat-making and in sugar-refining. Much also is sent up the river for the local consumption there.

Khulna.

10. When the Port Canning Company had a lease of the Bankar rights over a large part of the Sundarbans, they used to collect two rupees upon each hundred maunds of wood. At Chandkhali one of their superintendents was stationed, and he had some twenty darogas under him who were always voyaging about and collecting the rates the Company levied. The tract under this superintendent was not so large as the Jessore Sundarbans, but the Chandkhali people say that Rs. 20,000 was sometimes collected within one month. This was made up almost entirely of collections on the

Extent of the trade.

firewood as above described, and it represents a million maunds of wood as the amount cut within the month.

11. Another Sundarban industry is that which has to do with reeds, which are extensively used both for making mats and for making baskets. The mat-makers, Naluas by caste, do not usually dwell within the Sundarbans; their chief places being Phultalla, Satrajitpur, Binadpur, and Magurah. During the cold weather the men, in several trips, bring up a large quantity of reeds from the Sundarbans, and these, when dry, are woven into mats. They are woven sometimes of very large size, and these Naluas are frequently employed by Europeans to make mats for their rooms, as their mats are much better woven than native-made reed mats usually are. During the absence of the men the women alone work at home, but at other times the men work also.

Reeds and mat-making.

12. The reeds are used for baskets also, and there seem to be little colonies of basket-weavers, just as there are of mat-weavers. For instance, there is one colony at Keshabpur, and their habit is this. During the cold weather they migrate to some town in the Sundarbans—Rampal, for example—and remain there weaving baskets, which meet with a ready sale, as they are required for the rice harvest there. When the cold weather is over, they come up to Keshabpur with a stock of reeds, and there again they set about their manufacture and sell their wares to the people of that place who want them. The baskets they make are called "dhama;" they are very thick and substantial, and can be made of almost any size.

Basket-weaving.

13. The remaining products of the Sundarbans may be shortly enumerated. A peculiar long leaf is brought in large quantities, and is used for thatching native huts. Almost every hut in the south of the district is thatched with this leaf, which the natives call "patta." Honey and wax are collected in the forest, and form I believe a rather remunerative trade, though it is naturally a very hazardous one. Shells are collected both on the banks of rivers and marshes, and away down by the sea-shore. These are burnt so as to form lime, and they make an exceedingly good lime. Khulna is the principal place where lime-burning goes on, and the trade seems to be a very ancient one. The old buildings of Khanja Ali appear to have been built with this lime; and I find that at the end of last century large quantities of it were

Thatching leaf.

Honey.

Shell-lime.

sent down to Calcutta, for use in building or repairing Government-house. It is for chunam or plaster that this lime is chiefly useful, and it was for that it was used in this last case. The shells brought are chiefly of two sorts; a long sort called "jongra," and a round sort called "jhinak." The ashes of the shell-lime, mixed with water, form the lime-ash or "chay" which natives chew along with pân leaf.

14. It is unnecessary to say that fishing is a trade plied in all the nearer rivers of the Sundarbans, and also in some of the more remote ones, and it may be convenient to describe it here for the whole district as well as for the Sundarbans. The favorite method of fishing, both here and in other parts of the district, is by having a large bag-net suspended on two long bamboos stuck out at one side of the boat. Sometimes the boat with the net thus expanded under water is driven slowly against the current, and sometimes otters are used, which, tied by a rope to the boat, are made to plunge about on the sides of the net so as to frighten fish into the net. The fisherman, when he thinks proper, raises the net quickly by standing on the inside ends of the bamboos, and thus gets all the fish that may be inside.

Fishing.—Various methods.

15. Another frequent method, applicable however rather to bhíls than to rivers, is this. On the surface of the bhíls form large patches of weed, called "dhap," which on the falling of the waters sometimes get out of the bhíls and float down the streams. These patches the fisherman fixes in their place by staking all round, and then he leaves them for a day or two. The fish then congregate beneath them, and by drawing a net round the place and removing the weeds, they are imprisoned and can easily be caught in very large quantities. On the borders of the shallow rivers branches of trees are placed in the water for the same purpose, the attraction of fish to one place; but this plan I have not seen employed in the Sundarban rivers. On the muddy banks of tidal rivers little branching twigs are placed to attract prawns. The prawns cluster about these twigs in great numbers, and are easily caught. Many of the fishermen in the bhíls carry about with them in their boats an instrument like a long besom, with a little spear-head at the end of each little prong. When they pass near a big fish, which they are very sharp in detecting, they dart this collection of spears at it and usually bring up the fish impaled on some of the points. This is not a regular, but only a supplementary way of fishing, that is to say, men do not go out to fish solely armed with this weapon.

16. On shallow shelving banks a round net is sometimes used. The fisherman goes along the bank watching till he sees a place where some fish are; he then throws his net, which he does so artfully, that before touching the water it has spread out into a large circle. The edges are weighted with lead, and falling on all sides of the fish, imprison them till the fisherman picks them out.

17. Cage-fishing is also frequent all over the district; every little streamlet, even the surface drainage of the fields and the ditches on the roadsides, shew arrays of these cages placed so as to capture fish. The same method is used, on a larger scale, in shallow and sluggish rivers, where in many places lines of the cages may be seen all across them. Cage-fishing is of course inapplicable to the deep rivers of the Sundarbans.

18. There are some other plans used in capturing fish; one, for example, by attracting them at night by a bright light and so capturing them. The methods I have described are those which may be, and are, used by single men, or by a few men together. The fish, however, have sometimes to stand more formidable battles, when a party of men go out with nets or with cages, and laying a large trap drive into it at one time some hundreds of fishes.

19. In most parts of the district the right to fish is a regular tenure, and is paid for like the right to cultivate land. *The right to fish.* In the tidal rivers of Khulna and Baghahat, and especially in the Sundarbans, it is different. There the fishermen are less of a stationary, and more of a migratory class. In the remote parts they pay no rent, and in the nearer parts they only pay when the man who claims the fishery happens to come across them in their migration, and gets a little rent from them as they pass.

20. From the fishing grounds of Backerganj, ships laden with fish are continually passing through the Jessore Sun-*Trade in fish.* darbans to Calcutta. The ships are filled with water and fish in perhaps equal bulk, and the water is continually cast out and new water cast in. The fish die in great numbers, and are cast out as they die, but sufficient reach Calcutta alive to pay for the trip. The stench which comes from these boats is something fearful, and may be perceived a very long distance off.

21. Large quantities of fish are also salted, that is, tumbled into large earthenware jars with a considerable proportion of salt, and so sent off to Calcutta.

22. Another trade of the Sundarbans—if trade it may be called—
is that of wrecking. Boats occasionally make
Wrecking. expeditions to the sea-shore of the Sundarbans, and
are pretty sure there to come across teak beams, the spoil of some ship
that has been destroyed. Thread and other things are also occasionally
found, and sometimes chains or other parts of the furniture of ships.
All this used to be done in secret until some five or six years ago, when
some case occurred in which the authorities refused to interfere. Since
then. the trade is openly carried on, and large teak beams may be seen
at Khulna and at some other places, the product of these expeditions.
Most of these things are however taken straight up to Calcutta, where
they are more likely to find ready sale.

XLV.—Trade in Betelnuts, Cocoanuts, and Pepper.

THE sub-divisions of Khulna and Baghahat are particularly rich in
cocoanut and betelnut palms; and the betel-nut
Exports of nuts. is cultivated also much farther north. From
these regions therefore there is a very great export of betelnuts and
of cocoanut oil.

2. Faqirhat is a great place for the export of these, but almost all
the hâts and bazars in the southern sub-divisions have a share in the
trade. The export of cocoanuts and cocoanut oil is mostly to Calcutta.
Of betelnuts part goes to Calcutta, part is sent north into other parts of the
Jessore district, for local consumption, but the chief export is to Surajganj.

3. The mode of gathering betelnuts is peculiar. They grow, as is
well known, on the top of long, slim trees. The
Gathering betelnuts. collector mounts one of these trees, and after he
has thrown down what he plucks from it, he swings the tree backwards
and forwards, till, receiving sufficient impulse, he throws himself like a
monkey on to the next tree. A great number of accidents and occasional
deaths occur from the falls which the collectors get in this operation,
when they fail to catch hold of the tree towards which they are swung.

4. A few notes may be recorded on the subject
Pepper. · of the pepper trade.

5. The sub-division of Chooadanga, in Nuddea, is a pepper-
producing region, and a little is also grown in those parts of Jessore
which are immediately adjacent to it. Most of the pepper goes down to

Calcutta by train, but no inconsiderable quantity of it is brought across by road to Jhenida and to Kaliganj. From Jhenida it is shipped in small boats to Magurah, where larger ships receive it and take it away to Nalchitti and Jalukati. From Kaliganj it goes to the same places, but a great part, if not most of it, passes through the hât at Kumarganj, opposite Naldi. This seems to be an established place for the pepper traders of Jessore to sell their stock to those who have come, or have been deputed by Nalchitti people, to make purchases for export.

6. The only part of Jessore (except the above) where pepper is a regular article of cultivation is the tract lying between Jingagachha and Trimohini. From there it is sent, chiefly through Keshabpur, to Nalchitti and Jalukati.

7. The manner of preparing pepper for sale is very simple. The pods when first picked are of a yellow or light-red color; they are put out in the sun to dry; and in January and February, the picking season, one may see in the villages large surfaces covered with the bright-colored pepper. After some few days' exposure they are dry, and have attained a deeper hue of red, and they then may be packed in sacks.

*   *   *   *   *   *

PART VI.—GAZETTEER.

XLVI.—*Jessore Sub-division.*

IN arranging according to subjects such remarks as I have to make
Subject and arrange-
ment.
regarding the various matters of interest connected with the Jessore district, I have necessarily omitted many things because they did not refer to any of those particular subjects into which my remarks have been grouped. All that remains to be noticed I shall take up now, going over the district town by town, and noting in connection with each town what seems worthy of mention. It will be convenient also to refer, in passing, to matters stated in other places, so that this part may serve to a certain extent as an index, according to places, of that which has gone before.

2. The towns are arranged in a sort of natural order, namely by sub-divisions and thannahs, so that each part of the district will be dealt with before passing on to another.

Jessore, on the Bhairab river, 75 miles north-east of Calcutta.—A great deal has been written of it in the chapter on the district and its head-quarters in other chapters. Its connection with the story of Khan Jahan Ali has been stated in chapter III.

2. I have stated in chapter IV the manner in which the name Jessore came to be applied to the place. In the earliest records of the district it is called "Kasba," or "Sahibganj" (chapter XXXV). Of these two names the latter one is now entirely forgotten, and arose probably only from temporary circumstances. The first name "Kasba," an Arabic word signifying "chief city," is still the name by which the place is known in its vicinity; and people at a distance in talking of the place call it "Kasba Jessore." Mirzanagar was once the chief city of the district (chapter XV), and we find it in the old correspondence still bearing the name "Kasba Mirzanagar;" and the name is to this day applied in this signification to various places in Bengal. I cannot say how it came to be applied to the town which is now the head-quarters of the district, for it was certainly so applied before the place became the head-quarters; and a remarkable fact is, that the village appears to have had no name to which the title "Kasba" was prefixed, as in the case of other places, but it was called purely "Kasba," and a village close beside it was simply denominated "Purana Kasba," or "the old Kasba." I would conjecture the name to have been used with reference to the place being, as it probably was, the chief market-place, or rather the market-place near the head-quarters, of the zemindari of Isafpur (chapter IX).

Its names.

3. The road to Jessore from Calcutta has been talked of in chapter XXXVI, whence it will be seen that it was an ancient line of road, being the communication between Calcutta and Dacca. Up to ten or fifteen miles beyond Jessore the road is, and has long been, kept up; but between that point and the eastern boundary of the district it was never a well-maintained road. For that part of it which connects Bongong and the vicinity of Jessore, a great deal was done by the liberality of one Kaliprasad Ray, better known as Kali Potdar, a son of the Kábal Ram who is named in chapter XXXIX, paragraph 30. This man lived close to Jessore, and having amassed money, resolved

Road from Calcutta.

Kali Potdar's liberality.

in his old age to spend it in pious uses. His great idea was to make the passage from Jessore to the Ganges, then interrupted by unbridged streams, an easy and unbroken road. He built the bridges over the Bhairab river at Dhaitalla and at Nilganj (five miles and two miles east of Jessore, upon the Dacca road), and both of these bridges are in use up to the present day. He also bridged the two or three streams which lie between the Kabadak and the Ichamati rivers ; that is, between Jingagachha and Bongong. These bridges have now gone to ruin, and have been replaced by more substantial ones built by Government ; the ruins, however, of Kali Potdar's bridge at Jayantipur are to be seen a hundred yards or so south of the present bridge.

4. For the maintenance of all these bridges, and also of the roads from Jessore to Churamankati, and from Jessore to Bongong, Kali Potdar made over to the collector in 1848 a landed estate worth Rs. 301 a year. The papers state that the roads in question as well as the bridges had been made and continually kept up by him; but by making the roads I presume is meant only restoring them.

5. Six or seven miles north of Krishnanagar (in Nuddea) there is a road known as Kali Potdar's Road. It was also made by this Kali Potdar, and I was informed by a zemindar through whose land it passes that it was part of a road which Kali Potdar made all the way from Jessore to Agradwip, on the Bhagirati. The eastern part of this road I do not know, but it may have been that passing through Chaugachha and Maheshur ; and probably by " making" is again meant only " restoring."

6. Besides these works Kali Potdar gave to Government Rs. 9,000 wherewith to bridge the Kabadak at Jingagachha, and Rs. 18,000 wherewith to bridge the Ichamati at Bongong.

Jingagachha suspension-bridge.

7. With the first Rs. 9,000 and another nearly equal sum, the Government, in 1846, erected the chain-bridge at Jingagachha. The Military Board—a department subsequently abolished, in consequence of their numerous failures—had then the management of such works, and about April 1846 they came up to test the new bridge ; they spent more than Rs. 2,500 in this testing, and they pronounced the bridge sufficient.

8. On September 30th of that same year the great festival of the Dúrgapúja was held. People crowded to Jingagachha to see the spectacle, and with great ceremony and show the idol was, as usual, taken out into the stream to be cast into the water. The river was alive with boats, and the bridge was crowded with people, who chose it as a good point

2 I

from which to view the spectacle. All of a sudden the chains gave way, the bridge fell down bodily, and very many people were drowned, both of those upon the bridge and of those who were in the boats beneath it.

9. It cost Rs. 9,000 or Rs. 10,000 more to raise the bridge and fasten it in its place. It has not fallen again as yet.

10. Many years passed before anything was done with the remaining Rs. 18,000 given for the bridge at Bongong; but finally, about 1864-65, with this sum, and about
Bongong bridge-of-boats.
as much given by Government, a bridge-of-boats was erected; and the only breach in the road between Jessore and the Ganges is now filled up.

11. ' Ray Kaliprasad died not long after he had made these great gifts to the public. His present representatives (his grand-children or his great grand-children) are minors, and they live at Bagchar, near Jessore. There should be some remembrance of the old man near the Bongong bridge, his chief work.

12. Communication between Jessore and Calcutta has long forsaken the direct route by Gaighatta and Baraset. The regular route now is to Bongong by the old road, and to Chagdaha, on the Eastern Bengal Railway, by the Bongong feeder road. The metalling of the road between Bongong and Jessore was accomplished in 1866 to 1868.

13. Of course, there is communication by river; but, except during the rains, no boat can come up the Bhairab farther than Dhaitalla.

14. Jessore itself is not a large place, or a great trading place.
The town of Jessore.
There is little in it but the cutcherries and the town which the cutcherries have attracted about them; that is, there are the houses occupied by amla and mukhtars, and the principal zemindars have each a house in the place. Then a bazar must start to supply their wants and those of their attendants, and to meet the necessities of the many people who have to visit on business the head-quarters of their district. It is thus that the place has risen; that is to say, it is not an already great town which has been chosen as the head-quarters of the district, and which would be a great town even if it had not been so chosen, but it is a town which depends for its character almost entirely upon the cutcherries and their surroundings, and which would be little more than a second or third class bazar if they were not there.

15. The place, together with its suburbs, many of which are really in the nature of agricultural villages, was erected into a municipality about 1864. The population in 1869 amounted to 8,776, suburbs included.

16. The trade of Jessore is almost entirely local. There is a good

Trade. deal of sugar manufacture in its vicinity, and it imports a good deal of rice for local consumption. (Chapters XLI and XLIII.) But so far as mere trading and commerce are concerned, Jingagachha, Chaugachha, Khajura, and Basantia, all within a circuit of twelve or fifteen miles from it, are busier places than Jessore is.

17. Of buildings in Jessore, the history of the collectorate cutcherry and of the jail, has been already told. (Chapter XXVII.) The school-house is a good building of its sort, and it was erected, I believe, by private subscriptions collected in the district. A small building, the public library, was erected in 1854 also by subscription, under the auspices of Mr. Raikes, the collector, and it is still the property of the subscribers.

18. The church in Jessore has a history which must be separately

The church. told. It was founded in July 1842 and opened at the end of May 1843. The cost of erection was Rs. 3,467 (Government giving the labour of the prisoners in the jail). Except Rs. 400, which came from the church building fund, Calcutta, the rest was raised by subscription among the residents and indigo planters in the district. Mr. Benthall, the then judge, was the moving spirit in the matter, and along with others subscribed largely to the building, which when erected received the name " Christ Church."

19. In 1846 a new subscription was commenced for the erection of a clock in the tower of the church. To this natives also contributed a little, and the clock was finally put up in February or March 1848 at a cost of Rs. 1,543.

20. About 1846 also a " parsonage" was built, also by subscription among the residents and planters, at a cost of about Rs. 7,064 (prison labour also apparently being used); and Mr. J. Foy, the first clergyman (Additional Clergy Society), occupied this house from his arrival in December 1846 till he left in December 1856.

21. The church was apparently a bare place when he first came— little but walls and seats; but in 1853 and 1854, mainly through his exertions and by subscriptions and donations from the residents in the district, a chancel was built, an altar was set up and decorated, stained windows were put in, the reading desk and pulpit ornamented, and creed and commandment tables were put up. These and other decorations made the church a pretty building, so far as its interior is concerned.

22. Since Mr. Foy left there have been clergymen only in 1859-60 (Mr. Bell) and in 1865-67 (Mr. Glascott). The church building and establishment is maintained partly by a monthly allowance of Rs. 30 from Government and partly by a 1,000-rupee Government paper, which comes down from Mr. Benthall's times. The church has never been consecrated.

23. There are two cemeteries, a new one and an older one close to it. Besides these there are three ancient monuments in the middle of the station under the charge of a man who received from some private grant a little rent-free land on condition of looking after them.

Cemeteries.

24. There is a charity hospital in Jessore, not a good building of its sort, maintained by subscription, a Government grant, and a fund of Rs. 2,500 in the collector's hands.

Charity hospital.

25. Another endowment yet has to be mentioned, that of the idol Raghunath, near Moorly. The endowment was founded in 1813 by Krishna Das Brijabasi, who devoted an estate of five villages to the service of the idol and appointed two sebaits of his own caste for the management of the idol's affairs. He himself did not die till 1827, and then the two sebaits set up a forged will to prove that the estate had been conveyed to them for their own use, and not in trust. The collector heard of it and turned out the sebaits, who failed to regain possession through the civil courts. For a long time the trust was managed by the collector, but under the recent act he made it over to a committee, who are appointed by the caste to whom the idol appertains. The income is about Rs. 2,000 from the land, and Rs. 2,100 from the investment in Government paper of Rs. 42,000, the price paid by the putnidars when the land was settled in putni. It is spent in the maintenance of the temple and its worship, and in the feeding of travellers and religious mendicants.

Raghunath Thakur.

26. The history of this trust remarkably resembles that of the Saydpur Trust Estate (chapter XXXVI) in respect of the attempted fraud and its consequences.

27. The residence of the raja of Jessore is a mile or so south of the town, in a village called Chanchra. The raj-bari once had an ample ramp and fosse surrounding it, but these defences have been utterly neglected for a hundred years. They are, however, distinctly traceable.

The raj-bari.

28. Not very far from them, and on the side of the road between
Chanchra and the outcherries, is a large tank, which
was dug by some ancestor of the raja's family,
and which bears the name of the "Chormâra," or "thief-beating" tank.
It is said that adjacent to it was once the jail in which the raja confined
malefactors, and that from this comes the name.

Jingagachha, nine miles west of Jessore, on the Calcutta road, a
place having considerable sugar trade. (Chapter XLI.) The story of
the suspension-bridge, which here crosses the Kabadak river, is told
under "Jessore."

2. There is, or rather was, an indigo factory here, erected by
Mr. Jenkins about 1800. (Chapter XXXV.) Either this same factory, or,
more likely, another which subsequently took its place, came into the hands
of a Mr. Mackenzie, who died about 1865. He did a great deal for Jingagachha, the bazar and trade being greatly extended by him. A hât was
established by him, and is held on Sunday and Thursday, a minor one being
held on Tuesday. From him the ganj has the name of Mackenzieganj.

3. The factory is now, and has for many years been unoccupied.

4. Through Jingagachha a road runs connecting Chaugachha and
Kotchandpur on the north with Trimohini in the south.

Magurah, or Amrita Bazar, about four miles north of Jingagachha, on
the road just mentioned.—It is only a considerable village, but a family
of Ghoses, small zemindars, resident in the place, established a few years
ago a bazar which they named after their mother, Amrita. They got a
printing press sometime since, and in 1868 established a Bengali news-
paper called the *Amrita Bazar Patrika.* It appears once a week, and
is conspicuous only for its scurrilous tone and its disregard of truth. Its
declared circulation is 500.

Chaugachha, sixteen miles north-west of Jessore, on the Kabadak
river, is mentioned frequently in connection with its sugar manufacture,
as it is one of the great centres of the sugar trade. (Chapter XLI.)

2. The place is marked as a prominent one in Rennel's map,
now 100 years old, and its prominence among its
neighbours is also attested by the fact that a road
to Chaugachha was one of the two or three roads which the collector
proposed in August 1800. The present road, however, was made by
Mr. Beaufort, magistrate, about 1850. He also made a bridge across
the Kabadak here, but not sufficient waterway was left, and it came
down about three years after it was built.

3. There is a large indigo factory here, built by a Mr. Bucksworth (?) when indigo cultivation was first introduced into these districts. It changed hands repeatedly, and came at last to the Bengal Indigo Company, who recently sold it. It is now in ruins, the vats alone being in decent order.

4. There is a small indigo factory which has a little history con-

History.

nected with the history of Chaugachha as a place of commerce, for Chaugachha seems to have made a great start about seventy or eighty years since, when one Majum Paré, who had come from the north-west and had set up a mahajani business in Chaugachha, became a very prominent man. He gathered about himself a very large business, and after he died Sibnarayn, his son, carried it on with equal success. They were the greatest merchants for miles around until Sibnarayn died and Nilkant, his son, who had no talent for business, succeeded. This Nilkant built the small indigo factory which is here, and got on very fairly till one day, when he was bringing back from Calcutta Rs. 14,000, the produce of his indigo sales, he was attacked by dacoits, who robbed him of all. The robbery took place on the river flowing between Hooghly and Nuddea districts, and the two magistrates of the districts had a fight as to who should bear the odium of it. This spoiled any chance there was of successful investigation, and Nilkant recovered none of his money, though a lot of money was found with some suspicious characters near Krishnaganj, in Nuddea.

5. Nilkant never recovered from this loss; and then his debtors failed to repay him, and matters generally went wrong, and he finally died poor a few years ago. Recently a gowala found a number of gold mohurs buried in the foundations of the Paré's house.

6. Nilkant sold the factory to Tarini Charn Ghos, who is the resident landholder of the village, formerly Government pleader at Krishnanagar.

7. A large quantity of indigo seed is grown here by Mr. McLeod,

Indigo seed.

who resides in the house attached to Chaugachha sugar factory.

8. The hât here is an important one, as people flock to it from all

Hât.

sides from distances of ten miles even. It is held on Tuesday and Friday.

Sajiali, a village half way between Jessore and Chaugachha.— Hardly known or heard of now, but noteworthy as having been one of the old thannahs. It was established before 1814, and was in existence till the time of the new police, 1863. (M. 1-3-93. C. 3-5-14.)

Bára Bazar, ten miles north of Jessore, is referred to in chapter III, and again in the history of the Naupara family. (Chapter XXXIX.)

Khajura, eight miles north of Jessore, on the Chitra.—A road leads to it from Jessore.

2. It has a considerable trade in sugar, and also in importing rice. (Chapters XLI and XLIII.)

3. Khajura and its vicinity are a great place for fish, and fish are taken thence even as far as Chaugachha and Maheshpur, in Nuddea.

Basantia, twelve miles east of Jessore, on the Bhairab.—A road leads to it from Jessore.

2. Like Khajura, it has a large sugar trade, and imports rice largely. (Chapters XLI and XLIII.)

3. Being the point nearest to Jessore up to which boats of large size can always come, it acts as a port to Jessore, and the traffic along the road between Basantia

The Piræus of Jessore.

and Jessore, which is metalled almost the whole way, is very great.

4. Pineapples are grown in the lands lying east of Basantia, and they are brought in inconsiderable numbers to Jessore. Many are taken also to Calcutta.

Rajahat, three miles east of Jessore, on the Basantia road.—Acquires considerable trade from its position. Small boats can come up the river to this point, and a good deal of produce from Jessore, and still more from Manirampur and from the vicinity Trimohini and Manikganj, on the Kabadak, is brought across here and passes through Rajahat; of the pepper especially, which grows beside the Jingagachha and Trimohini road, a large quantity is brought to Rajahat and sent off thence. (Chapter XLV.)

2. Of course there is sugar manufacture at Rajahat as there is in every place of any pretensions in this part of the district.

3. The road to Manirampur and Keshabpur goes southward from this point. A cross road, one and a half miles long, made by Azim Biswas of Kazipur, now dead, passes through Kazipur, and cuts off the corner.

Rupdia, which is three miles farther down the Basantia road, may be noted as the site of the first indigo factory in the district, now in ruins and broken up. (Chapter XXXV.)

Singhia, ten miles down the same road from Jessore, is a small place having no bazar or hát. I mention it only because it was one of the old thannahs. It was established at the time of the permanent settlement, and it was abolished only in 1863, on the introduction of the new police. (M. 1-3-93. C. 3-5-14.)

2. The Khulna road strikes south here.

Manirampur, a small town and a very small bazar thirteen miles south of Jessore, on the Harihar, now a dried up river. (Chapter II.) A considerable hât is held upon Monday and Friday, there being no other hâts for a few miles round, not even at Khanpur, which is a much larger village than Manirampur.

2. There is a fine large tank here, one of a set of tanks dug by a lady of the raja of Chanchra's family about seventy years ago or more.

3. A road six miles long was made by the present raja connecting Manirampur with Rajganj, on the Trimohini road.

4. Manirampur has a small sugar factory. (Chapter XLI.) It is referred to also in chapter XVI in a way that leads one to think it was a place of mark about 1785.

Khanpur, a large village, three miles from Manirampur.—It is full of Mussulmans, and they are an exceedingly litigious lot. They date their events by mukaddamas, and talk of the various hours of the day as "the time for filing complaints," and so forth.

Naupara, six miles down the Khulna road from Singhia, and on the bank of the Bhairab.—A considerable bazar, with a large amount of river trade, chiefly in connection with rice and sugar. (Chapters XLI, XLIII.) There are always a large number of boats present here, and its prominence in this respect probably gave it this name of Naupara. It was a prominent market-place even at the permanent settlement time, for it is frequently mentioned in the correspondence of that time. It was then, however, always called Alinagar.

Keshabpur, eighteen miles south of Jessore, on the river Harihar. The Bhaddra also is close to it, but it is a dry bed, while the Harihar, at high tide, has sufficient water to float 500 maund vessels at least. At low tide, however, in the cold season at least, the river is far too shallow; but the merchants have got over the difficulty by digging holes or tanks opening into the river, in which their vessels may remain while detained at Keshabpur.

2. Keshabpur is the second trading place in the district, and a great deal has been said of it in connection with its sugar-refining in chapter XLI. The sugar-refineries are spread all over the town; one pâra, the north-western part of the commercial quarter, which we may call Keshabpur proper, is

Sugar.

called Karkhana-pâra, from the abundance of karkhanas or refineries, there. The Calcutta-poti, which is the principal street, and runs east and west, has several refineries on and near it, and itself obtains its name from the number of Calcutta merchants who have agencies for the purchase of sugar, mostly situated in it. Sriganj, a suburb on the other side the river, contains hardly anything else than sugar-refineries, and in other parts of the town and suburbs also are many refineries.

3. The large import of rice into Keshabpur, its trade in pepper, and its importations of wood from the Sundarbans, have been noticed in chapters XLII, XLIII, XLIV, XLV.

4. It was probably about sixty or seventy years ago that Keshabpur began to become prominent among its neighbours. Rennel's map of 1764-72 does not mark it at all, shewing the whole region about it as a morass, and calling it Barwanny. This name shews that he has been led into a mistake by the name Bara-ani ("twelve annas") given to one of the shares of the Isafpur estate within which the land lay; and as for the region being a morass, it is simply impossible, for only ten or fifteen years afterwards we find a European salt establishment under the Company, at Chupnagar, eight miles south-east of Keshabpur, in the heart of Rennel's morass. Chupnagar is now an insignificant place, and it is likely that Keshabpur would have been chosen in place of it had it then had anything approaching to the prominence it now has.

History.

5. The first we hear of Keshabpur is when the collector, in January 1802, proposes a road to Keshabpur, and thence on to Talla, which he describes as "a great mart." Talla is still a prominent place, but the comparison, if made now, would be made in favour of Keshabpur, and not of Talla. The road then proposed was likely not made, for the present road is of far more recent construction, and, in fact, was not fully bridged until 1868. One of the bridges on the road, that which crosses a khal within the limits of Keshabpur itself, was built a few years ago by a merchant of Keshabpur, named Jitram Shaha.

6. There are two bazars in Keshabpur, both of them very busy places. They are very near to each other, both being on the eastern half of the town. The northern one is the older one; and as the history of the establishment of the southern one affords an example of those frequent rivalries in respect of hâts, of which we shall see some other instances, I shall give it at length.

Rivalries of the two bazars.

2 K

7. The Calcutta-poti is the boundary between Keshabpur proper and Altapol, and the lands on the two sides of it are held by two different zemindars. Of the northern, or Keshabpur part, Sukhamay Mukharjya is the proprietor. It was a lakhiraj estate resumed and settled with a man whose daughter he married. The southern, or Altapol part, is within the trust estate, but is given in patni to Sukhasindu and Sudasindu Banurjya of Altapol. Some share in their patni has been sold, but they still hold full interest in some part of the land within it, which is a subordinate tenure within the patni.

8. Now, up till about twelve years ago, the bazar and hât of Keshabpur were entirely held within Sukhamay Mukharjya's land, and naturally he made great profit from it. So the Banurjyas of Altapol thought they might with advantage set up another hât in their land, just south of the older bazar, and thus there came about a very great rivalry between these two bazars and hâts.

9. The southern or newer bazar had the advantage, however, and that for several reasons. First, it was immediately on the bank of the river, and thus all bulky produce, and all ship traffic, would find it more convenient. Second, fish boats mostly came up the river from the south to both bazars, and all so coming up had not only to pass the Banurjya's house in Altapol, but if they were going to the northern bazar, they had to pass the southern one. So the Banurjyas had men on the look-out, who, by very violent persuasion, induced all the boats so passing to stop at the southern bazar.

10. The Banurjyas could of course exercise the same means of persuasion upon other men going up in boats to the bazars, but the great struggle was for the fish. Almost every body who comes to a hât buys fish before he goes away, and therefore if the fish were confined to the hât held in the southern bazar, every body would have to visit the southern bazar, and this would give it pre-eminence.

11. By these means the Banurjyas did great injury to the old bazar, for they, as the practice in such cases is, fixed upon the same days for holding their hât as had prevailed in the older one,—Sunday, Tuesday, and Friday. A good deal of bad feeling, and a few criminal cases supervened, and at last, as a measure of defence, Sukhamay, the proprietor of the old bazar, gave a four-anna share in it in maurusi tenure to the Naral Baboos, expecting that they, being powerful zemindars, would be able to resist the oppressions of the Banurjyas and guard the interests of the old bazar. The new hât is still the most flourishing, however.

12. The old bazar and hât are called the Bara-ani (or " twelve annas
one") and the new one is called the Char-ani (or
"four annas one"), in allusion to the two shares of
the old Isafpur estate within whose respective limits they are. The
bazars are each of them divided into patis or quarters, named according to
the trade practised by those who are stationed in them. One going up
the river past the southern bazar sees successively the ship-loads and piles
of fire-wood sold in the Kâtia-pati; the heaps of dhan, imported in the
Dhana-pati; vegetables and eatables sold in the Taha-pati; the fish-sellers
who sit in the Machua-pati ; and finally the rice market or Châla-pati.

Business in the bazars.

13. The import of fire-wood is very great, as large quantities
of it are consumed in sugar boiling ; it passes up by Dumuria from the
Sundarbans. (Chapter XLIV.)

14. The manufacture of pottery is a trade which naturally attaches
itself to a sugar-manufacturing place, since in
collecting the juice, in bringing in the goor, in
boiling the sugar, and in keeping and exporting the molasses, there is so
large a consumption of earthenware vessels. The potters or kumars are
mostly collected in one part of the town, called after them the Kumârpâra.
It lies within Altapol, south of the strictly commercial part of the town
and north of the agricultural part of Altapol.

Pottery.

15. A pâru in the west of the bazars, called the Kaora-pâra, is one
of those settlements of non-Aryan laborers which
one meets with here and there in these districts.
They came probably at the time when there was a European factory in
Keshabpur, introduced, as they have been in most cases, as laborers by
European manufacturers and traders. The European factory was here for
a very short time indeed, and has now disappeared (chapter XLI), and
the Kaoras are now employed as laborers by the native sugar refiners.

Coolies.

16. Another great local trade, one which I have not yet mentioned,
is that of the braziers. Mulgram, a village two
miles north-west of Keshabpur, and Jagannathpur,
which is close to it, contain between them some eighty families of kaséries
or braziers. Their manner of trade is this: at the beginning of the cold
season they go out with their wares—all sorts of brass-vessels. Many of
them wander over the eastern parts of the district, and over Backerganj,
travelling in their boats, which are filled with their goods; a few go
landwards, taking their wares in carts. They sell them as occasion offers,
partly for money, partly for old brass, and after they have for four

Braziers.

months or so gone about hawking their goods, they come back to their homes. The old brass which they have obtained, supplemented, if necessary, with brass brought from Calcutta, they hand over to the golândârs or brass-founders, of whom some ten or fifteen coming from Nuddea, the great brass-working place, have settled in Mulgram. These men work up the old brass and the new at the rate of about Rs. 10 per maund, and thus prepare for the kaséries a stock which they go out to sell again in the next cold weather.

17. The brass-working fits in very well with the sugar-refining, as the charcoal left in the latter process may be used in the former.

18. Keshabpur is a police station, and the town with its suburbs was, about 1864, formed into a chaukidary union.

19. Two local zemindar families have been mentioned. The Banur-jyas of Altapol, who have lands about Altapol, and also property in Sahos pergunnah, much of what they hold being in patni under the trust estate; and the Mukharjyas of Chalitabaria, who have lands along the Trimohini road.

20. Madhyakul, a suburb of Keshabpur, about a mile or two long,
Madhyakul.
has at its northern extremity a bazar, whose chief business is the landing of rice from the vessels which bring it up from the Sundarbans, and then sending it northward. The amount of trade done in this single bazar may be judged of from the fact that the bazar is worth to its proprietor more than Rs. 1,000 a year.

Panjhia, a village five miles east of Keshabpur.—Several people of the Kayasth class live in it, especially a family of Bosus. They claim an ancient descent, and have some small zemindari.

Trimohini, five miles west of Keshabpur, and connected with it by a road, whose construction dates within the last few years.—It is situated at the point where the Bhadra river used to leave the Kabadak, and it is perhaps from that circumstance it derives its name; Trimohini being the name applied to any tri-junction of rivers.

2. Trimohini is properly only the name of the bazar, which is a considerable one; Chandra being the name of the village.

3. Trimohini used to be one of the great places of the sugar trade,
Sugar.
but it has of recent years lost almost all its importance in this view. (See chapter XLI.) There are now few or no refiners here, and its business is confined to the exportation to Calcutta of sugar bought up in the neighbourhood and in Keshabpur.

4. Trimohini has two different bazars: a southern one which belongs
Bazars. to a Mahomedan family, and in which a hât is
held on Tuesday and Friday; and a northern one,
the property of the raja, in which a hât is held on other days. A méla or
fair is also held here in March of each year, the Bârani time, as it is called.

5. The ruins near Trimohini have been discussed in chapter VI.
The name Trimohini was apparently not applied at the time they existed,
but Mirzanagar, now a small village, was then a large place and gave
its name to the locality.

6. When the district was first occupied, in 1781, Mirzanagar was
one of the five thannahs then existing; Bhusna and Mirzanagar being, in
fact, the two principal thannahs. It ceased to be kept up when, in 1782, the
Government transferred to zemindars the burden of the police establishments. At the time of the permanent settlement a thannah was established
at Trimohini, and this thannah was kept up until 1863, when the new
police arrangements were made. (M. 18-6-81; 1-3-93; C. 3-5-14.)

7. Mirzanagar was, even in 1815, one of the four largest places in
the district. (Chapter XXXV.)

Gadkhali.—This is the name of a large village, with a bazar, 14 miles
along the Calcutta road from Jessore. When in 1863 part of the land
on the other side the Kabadak was brought within the limits of Jessore
district, it was intended that for these lands a police station should be
established at Gadkhali. Difficulty in respect of water-supply caused a
site two miles nearer Jessore to be preferred; and the police station, though
actually in a village called Beniali, is called by the name of Gadkhali.

2. The large tank close by the thannah, which brought the thannah
Tank. here from Gadkhali, is one of about a dozen tanks
dug by Rani Kasheshwary, a lady of the Chanchra
family. One of the other ones we have seen at Manirampur, and one is
in Jessore. They are all now falling into decay.

3. The very spot where the thannah now stands was a place cele-
Thannah. brated in olden days for outrages. Some traditions
hang about it of robberies that used to be per-
petrated there, and in one of the collector's letters (21st August 1800)
he mentions a patch of jungle at Beniali as a regular lurking place of
bandits upon the Jessore and Calcutta road.

4. One of the features peculiar to the jurisdiction of this police
Bedya tribe. station, and that of Sarsha, the adjacent one in
the Nuddea district, is the existence of a predatory

caste of men. They are usually called bedyas, (from "byâdha," a hunter,) but they call themselves the "shikari" caste (" shikari" having the same meaning in Hindustani). Nominally they are cultivators, and they keep up the semblance of that profession by holding a biggah or two of land, but really they make their living by burglary. During the light half of the moon they are all at home, but in the dark half they leave their houses and wander over Nuddea, 24-Pergunnahs, Hooghly, and other districts, cutting their way into houses at night (an art in which they are adepts) and taking the plunder they can get. They confine themselves chiefly to ornaments in silver and gold, and to cash, because these are things easily carried, and after their fortnight of plunder is over, they return home with the fruit of their thieving. They hardly ever conceal the property in their houses, but place it in distant points of concealment, until they find an opportunity to dispose of it.

5.   These bedyas formerly resided in considerable numbers on the east side of the Kabadak river; but Mr. Beaufort's energetic measures against them in 1852-54 drove them across the river into Nuddea.   The boundary of Jessore has unfortunately travelled westward so as again to include some of their habitations; but they are apparently so mindful of the Jessore magistrate of 1852-54, that Jessore is far less subject to their predatory raids than more distant places, such as the 24-Pergunnahs, Hooghly, and the north of Nuddea, where the railway helps them to speedily retreat from the scene of their operations.

Bodhkhana, four miles north of Gadkhali thannah, is the only place in the jurisdiction that need be named. A méla or fair is held here annually at Bârani time—the same time as the Trimohini fair. In fact, the hawkers who come to it pass on the Trimohini fair, and then still farther on to that at Kopilmuni.

Bodhkhana is mentioned in the history of the Naupara family. (Chapter XXXIX.)

Kaliganj, a place of some trade, eighteen miles north of Jessore, at the point where the Jhenida road crosses the Chitra river, by a bridge built by Mr. Beaufort, magistrate, about 1853.

2.   It was one of the chaukis attached to the Bhusna thannah under

History.

Warren Hastings' police arrangements, but does not appear to have been used as a police station after 1782, until one of the stations of the new police was set up there in 1863.   (M. 18-6-81; 1-12-82; 16-9-91.)

3. Kaliganj dates back, I should think, about 150 years, and it appears to have been rather prominent as a place of trade, for it more than once attracted the cupidity of some of the old robber gangs. One Bishnanath Baboo, who once plundered it, was a great robber. He lived at Asannagar, near Krishnanagar, and used to go about with a body of horsemen, plundering in open daylight. He was finally caught in a boat by Mr. Blacken (?), magistrate of Nuddea, and was hanged.

4. The trade of Kaliganj in sugar and in rice is mentioned in chapters XLI and XLIII.

5. The river Chitra, which passes under Kaliganj, can in December float boats of 200 or 250 maunds, but about February it becomes closed.

6. One of the Eastern Bengal Railway feeders runs from Krishnaganj upon that line to Kaliganj, passing in its way through Kotchandpur; it was completed only two or three years ago, except that it still wants a bridge where it crosses the Kabadak river.

Naldanga, two miles north of Kaliganj, and connected with it by a road, made by the raja of Naldanga. It is the residence of the oldest family in the district, the rajas of Naldanga, to whose history chapter VIII is devoted. It is not otherwise noteworthy, being itself only a small village.

Bagarpara, twelve miles north-east of Jessore, one of the police stations erected in 1863.

Narikelbaria, six miles from Bagarpara, on the Chitra, a place of trade, mentioned for its sugar trade in chapter XLI.

XLVII.—*Jhenida Sub-division.*

Jhenida, or Jhanaidaha, as its name would be if fully spelt, is twenty-eight miles north of Jessore, on the bank of the Nabaganga. It has a large bazar and is a place of some trade.

2. It appears to have been anciently the head-quarters of the Naldanga raja's zemindari of Muhammadshahi, and it was, under Warren Hastings' police arrangements, a chauki under the thannah of Bhusna. It was still kept up, while the police duties were thrown upon the zemindars, and it became a police thannah about 1793, since when it has continually been one. (M. 18-6-81; 16-9-91; 1-3-93. C. 3-5-14.)

History.

3. In 1786 Jhenida was the head-quarters of the collectorate of Muhammadshahi, which was apparently established only about that year, and was absorbed in 1787 into the adjoining district of Jessore. (Chapter XXVI.)

4. In 1861 the indigo disturbances caused a sub-division to be established at Jhenida, which has ever since been kept up. Before 1861 the land was for the most part within the sub-division of Magurah.

5. The road from Jessore through Jhenida to Kamarkhali (Comer-
Road.   colly), in Pubna, is as old as the district, and is
                    mentioned as a regular route in the old correspon-
dence. Rennel's map of 1764-72 shews it, but makes it pass through Khajura, whereas it now goes far west of that line; but north of Naldanga the old and the new lines apparently nearly coincide.

6. In saying that the old road thus existed, I must not be under-stood to mean it was kept up as a road. These very old roads seem to have been then little more than tracks left to take care of themselves, for in fact there were hardly any carts in the district to go upon them. (Chapter XXXVI.) The Jessore and Jhenida road, as it now is, was put into proper order as a road only about twenty years ago.

7. Of the trade carried on in Jhenida I have mentioned something
Trade.   under the sugar trade (XLI), rice trade (XLIII),
                    and pepper trade (XLV), these being the chief
branches. Indigo is cultivated all over the sub-division; the principal European factories being Sinduria, Nagapatam, Jarada, Bijuli, and Porahati. The Naral Baboos have indigo also. Mulberry leaf is cultivated in various parts of the sub-division also, and silk produced from it. (See end of chapter XVII.)

8. Byaparipâra is a village close to Jhenida, which has a consi-derable trade in cotton, or rather a large number of cotton spinners and weavers live in it. They used to obtain their cotton from the Shikdars of Gangutia (fifteen miles north-east of Jhenida), a large mercantile family who have branches for cotton and other trade in Mirzapore, Calcutta, and other places, and are the largest merchants in the Jhenida sub-division. But since the railway opened the cotton weavers get their cotton from Calcutta.

9. These Shikdars, cotton merchants, country produce merchants,
The Shikdars.   and having other trades besides, are a family who
                    have started into prominence only within the last
twenty years. Starting from small beginnings they have now a very

large connection. From the proceeds of their trade they, a few years since, dug a large tank on the side of the Jhenida road, at the village Karikhalli, six miles south of Jhenida, where many brahmans having rent-free lands in the Naldanga estates reside. They were also about to dig a large tank at Jhenida, but from some misunderstanding with the zemindars left it half done.

10. A prominent part of the trade at Jhenida, not yet mentioned, is the export of cold-weather produce.

11. The principal channel of communication between Jhenida and the outside world is the river; but it is gradually shutting up, and after February does not afford more than twelve or eighteen inches of water at its meeting with the Muchikhali at Magurah.

Communications.

12. The railway feeder road leading from Jhenida to Chuhadanga, on the Eastern Bengal line, was completed about five years ago, but has not as yet succeeded in diverting any very large proportion of the local carrying trade.

13. Before the feeder a road of much more simple construction used to connect the places, and in the vicinity of Jhenida this road used thirty or forty years since to be a great place for dacoity. The muchi caste in the sub-division are still in many places notorious for criminality, and to them were chargeable the robberies and murders which so occurred. A big tank, a mile or two from Jhenida, used to be the favorite spot for the perpetration of these outrages, and the tank still bears the suggestive names of Chakshukora (eye-gouging) and Maridhapa (jaw-squashing).

Dacoity.

14. Jhenida has, as I have said, a considerable bazar, and a little distance west of the bazar is the Hâtkhola, or the place where the hât is held every Sunday and every Thursday. It is under the protection of an idol, Kali, who was set up here about thirty or forty years since. The revenue of the idol is a share— say a handful—of everything that is brought into the hât, and it is gathered, so far as I understand, by the kohildars, or scalemen, at the time of weighing out. The persons who profit by it are brahmans and the baishnabs (beggars) who are attached to the idol. The idol herself gets only a new sari (petticoat) and a goat every new moon.

The idol at the hât.

15. These commercial idols must, I am afraid, give way before the spirit of commerce, for I once found a string of pepper carts going back to Chuhadanga because the idol's dues were sufficient to turn the scale of

the market against Jhenida. But there is another divinity near Jhenida
who seems likely to flourish a long time. This is
Child-bearing vows.
Panchu-panchui, who resides in a small village
called Chuhadanga (not the same as that just mentioned), near Jhenida.
She has the reputation of giving children to barren women, and upon
Tuesday, which is her levée day, thirty or forty women may be seen
visiting her. She lives in a small thatched hut, and her guardian is an
old woman. The applicants address this old woman, and she retires
behind a screen, whence some inarticulate sounds are then heard. The
old woman then comes out and states the terms which Panchu-panchui
has dictated as those on which she will accomplish the applicant's desire.
The latter goes away, and when a child is born to her, she returns with
the offering—a two-anna piece, or a cloth, or a bowl of milk, &c., which
Panchu-panchui has demanded. If a child is not born, of course it is
not Panchu-panchui's fault!

16. Another favorite place for child-bearing vows is a temple at
Haibatpur, six miles north of Jessore.

17. Before the Naral Baboos bought this part of the country
(chapter XXXIX), the zemindari cutcherry of
Chakla cutcherry.
their predecessors was at Jhenida, in the same place,
I believe, where the sub-divisional cutcherry now is; but the Naral
Baboos left that site and established their cutcherry two miles farther
west. Of the old cutcherry a reminiscence still remains in Piyâdapâra,
the name of a pâra lying close to the sub-divisional grounds.

Kotchandpur, twenty-five miles north-west of Jessore, on the bank
of the Kabadak, is from a commercial point of view the principal place
in the district.

2. Chandpur is the proper name of the place, and the prefix "kot"
is attached only for the sake of distinction. In
Origin of name.
inquiring as to its origin and meaning, I was told
that in the times of the Mussulman Government, when the revenue used
to be sent from the eastern districts to Moorshedabad, there were along
the route certain stations where there were strong-houses guarded by
sepoys, in which the treasure might stay over-night. One of these was
at Chandpur, and its kot, or strong-house, was upon the spot where the
zemindari cutcherry now is.

3. This explanation, I think, is only part of the truth. We will
find, when we come to it, that Ichakada, in Magurah, was one of the
ancient police stations in the district, and these police stations were in the

nature of little military strongholds. Now, this place is, in the collector's letter of 8th November 1804, mentioned by the name " kot Ichakada," or (as the collector then interprets it in brackets) " Pass Ichakada."

4. The word "kot," then, probably means that Chandpur was in the middle of last century one of these semi-military semi-police stations, of which there were a few here and there; and the guarding of treasure mentioned above was of course one of the many functions that as a kot it performed.

5. The great prominence of Kotchandpur is a creation of the last

History.

thirty or forty years, for it has been made entirely by the sugar trade. (Chapter XLI.) Before that it was only a leading village. In Rennel's map (1764-72) it is marked, but not as a prominent place; moreover, he has placed it at least six miles out of its proper position. It is not mentioned among the thannahs or chaukis occupied at the time the first magistrate came to the district (1781); but I rather think that is to be accounted for by the fact of its then being beyond the boundary of the district. However in 1793, when it was within the district, it was not one of the thannahs, while Kalupol, beyond it, was. In 1814 it does appear among the list of thannahs, and in 1815 the collector writes in a letter of "a place called Kotchandpur, at which a thannah is established, in appearance a town of some importance and magnitude." He had apparently just discovered it, but his knowledge of the interior may be inferred from the fact of his saying it is " ten cos distant from Naldanga," when it is not so much as five.

6. Since 1814, at least, Kotchandpur has remained a thannah, and in 1861 the indigo disturbances caused it to be for a time erected into a sub-division, partly in Jessore and partly in Nuddea. The sub-divisional site was first of all a piece of ground between Kotchandpur and Soliman-pur, but a site was afterwards chosen on the high bank of the Kabadak, west of the town, and a masonry cutcherry was erected. The sub-division was withdrawn in the re-arrangement made in 1863, and the building is now a school building.

7. During the continuance of the sub-division, Kotchandpur and its suburbs were formed into a chaukidary union.

8. Most of what has to be said about Kotchandpur has been said

Sugar.

in chapter XLI, as it is purely a sugar manufacturing place.

9. The roads in the town profit to a great extent from an indirect result of the sugar manufacture. The earthenware pots, of which so

many are broken in the course of manufacture (they use a much smaller size here than they do at Keshabpur) form very fair metalling for the roads, and as they are of no use for anything else, are easily obtained for this purpose. A large and dirty ditch that once ran up into the town has been almost filled up with these broken pots.

10. The Krishnaganj feeder road passes through Kotchandpur to Kaliganj. It was made about five or six years ago, and Kotchandpur is the place that feeds it most; much of the sugar traffic from Kotchandpur goes, however, by another road, namely to Ramnagar on the Eastern Bengal line. Probably, were the feeder road completely bridged, this would cease to be the case.

Feeder road.

11. A very large and important hât is held every Sunday and every Thursday in the bazar at Kotchandpur, and people from every side, and for miles around, attend it. It is most active during the sugar season. Large quantities of cloth are brought chiefly from Bara Bamanda, a suburb where most of the dwellers are weavers, and from Maheshpur; trinkets of all sorts—bracelets, bangles, bead necklaces, and mirrors; a large display of hookahs, and near them a range of tobacco sellers; vegetables in profusion; oil from the neighbouring village of Balahar, and other places; pan-leaf and lime and betelnut brought up from the south of the district; earthenware of all sorts, for which there is a great demand, since almost every one in this part of the country has something to do with the sugar manufacture; and the fish-sellers have also a separate quarter themselves. All these are out in the square and in the roads round it; and at the same time, in the shops which flank them, a busy trade is going on among the sellers of grain and the buyers of goor; and add to the whole an indefinite number of spectators, and everybody—buyer, or seller, or spectator—speaking and clamouring all together,—a hubbub and turmoil which one can hear a mile or two away.

The hât.

12. The European sugar factory at Kotchandpur is noticed in chapter XLI. There are two European houses, each having large compounds, and both situated on the bank of the river.

Solkopa is a large village, with a bazar ten miles north of Jhenida, prettily situated along the north bank of the Kumar river.

2. A thannah was established here in 1863. That part of the thannah jurisdiction which lies north of the Kumar river belonged to the Pubna district before 1863.

3. A good deal of trade goes on at Solkopa, and I find that so early as 1790 it was one of the places from which price lists were sent to the collector of Jessore. (Chapter XXXV.)

Harinakunda is a little place, with a bazar ten miles west of Solkopa. It was one of the thannahs of 1863, but has since been degraded into an outpost.

2. It is marked as a prominent place in Rennel's map (1764-72), but I have not been able to find any old notices of it.

XLVIII.—*Magurah Sub-division.*

Magurah is seventeen miles east of Jhenida, on the bank of the Naba-ganga, at the point where the Muchikhalli brings down the Gorai and Kumar waters into it.

2. It does not seem to have been at all a prominent place before the sub-division was established at it. It is marked

History.

in large letters in Rennel's map, but I find it nowhere alluded to in the old records. It was not on account of its prominence that it was selected as a site for a sub-division, but simply because there was a considerable amount of dacoity going on near the place, and that the confluence of the rivers at Magurah was the most convenient starting point from which to deal with it. Magurah was not then, as I believe, even a thannah, but it was then erected into a phari and afterwards made a thannah.

3. The sub-division of Magurah was established about 1845, and

The sub-division.

Mr. Cockburn, deputy magistrate, was sent to establish it. The place was then low and easily liable to inundation, but there was one pretty high part where the hât was held, and where part of the village was. This place Mr. Cockburn occupied, turning out the villagers and making them hold their hât where the bazar now is. He then dug a few tanks, and with the excavated earth levelled the surface and thus formed the sub-divisional ground.

4. His next step was to build a dwelling-house, and he succeeded marvellously, for with only Rs. 6,000 or 7,000 he erected a house which even now is one of the best sub-divisional residences in Bengal. People on the spot say he had a rather high-handed manner of conducting matters, and that he possessed himself of much of his building material by the simple expedient of fixing his own price upon it. They say that

complaints in respect of this, and in respect of his arbitrary occupation of the sub-divisional grounds, were made to the magistrate of the district, who came down to Magurah, talked a few platitudes, and went away again.

5. Mr. Cockburn then commenced the construction of the road between Magurah and Jhenida. Near Magurah it
The road.
runs through low country, and across the drainage which is by overflow from the Nabaganga; and a considerable amount of work was required. It is a road which has always given much trouble, and even now it requires two considerable bridges, one near Jhenida and one near Magurah, to complete it.

6. It seems, however, to be upon the line of a very ancient road connecting Krishnanagar and Dacca. The large pippul trees found singly or doubly at short intervals near it, and near the Jhenida and Chuha-danga feeder road, are the trees that served as landmarks to travellers when the road was a mere track across the fields.

7. After the sub-divisional residence, the next building erected at Magurah was the jail. It was built, I believe,
The jail.
by the Public Works Department, and, though a very small building, it took seven years (1849-1856) to build.

8. The charity hospital was erected about 1853-54, chiefly by subscription among the indigo planters of the vicinity. It is a very good building of its sort.

9. These and the recently erected cutcherries complete the list of public buildings.

10. The old embankments of the Nabaganga (chapter XXIX) are still traceable along the south side of it, and in two
Old embankments.
places, one on each side of Magurah, where they make a loop to the south, have apparently been repaired in recent times. The one on the east, round the "Madman's Khal," was I am told erected, or at least put into order, by Mr. Cockburn.

11. Another part of the embankment, that near Kasinathpur, has recently been at considerable cost strengthened by the Public Works Department. It was found that the water pouring down to Magurah was flowing up the Nabaganga to this point, and, breaking through at this point, was forming a new river southward. The Public Works Depart-ment stopped this action by a large embankment, simply because the direction of the diverted current at Magurah shewed the Magurah house to be in danger of being swept away. The result is that a natural

action of the rivers (chapter II) has been stopped; and the economy of
it is questionable, for more money has been or will be spent upon the
works than would be required to establish new buildings on some better
protected spot.

12. Of Magurah there are two parts: Magurah proper, where the

The hât.

bazar is, on the east of the sub-divisional ground;
and Dari Magurah, on the west. The latter has
a smaller bazar, and the hât is held on it every Sunday and every
Thursday. The raja of Naldanga (the zemindar) transferred it here
from the bazar about ten years ago. Dari Magurah is very low land.
The roads and the house sites are raised two or three feet so as to be
beyond inundation, and the raja has recently spent money upon raising
the site of the hât.

13. Of trades carried on at Magurah, I have already noted the

Trade.

export of sugar and the importation of rice. (Chapters XLI and XLIII.) For sugar, however, there
are only small refineries about this part of the district. The mat-makers,
who live some of them in Dari Magurah and some in Nanduli, on
the other side of the river, have also been noticed. (Chapter XLIV.)
A considerable amount of mustard seed is brought from the adjacent
parts of the Furreedpore district to be made into oil by the oil-pressers
(kuluas), many of whom live in Magurah and Nanduli. Much of the ·
oil thus made is sent back for sale to the same places whence the mustard
seed came—an arrangement founded rather upon custom than upon
political economy.

14. There are several indigo factories still working within the
Magurah sub-division—the Hazrapur concern, the Burai factory, the
Nohatta concern, and the Amtol-Nohatta factory. The Babukhali
concern has been long shut up, but the house still standing on the bank of
the Madhumati is the most magnificent house in the district.

Sripur is a place of some trade, and a police outpost eight miles
north of Magurah, on the Kumar river.

Ichakada, four miles west of Magurah, is now a small roadside bazar,
where, however, a considerable hât is held.

2. Ichakada was one of the places where, in the time of the

History.

nawab's government, there was a small military
station, subordinate apparently to the faujdar of
Bhusna. When the collector, in 1804, was directed to report if there
were any police lands in the district, he found (C. 8-11-04) that there

were some attached to kot Ichakada, to thannah Dharmpur, and to Bhusna itself. In the first two cases the land was intended for the support of sixteen and eighteen men respectively, the force stationed at the two places; in the last case the lands were apparently for the maintenance of the state boat of the faujdar of Bhusna.

3. When the magistrate came to the district in 1781, Ichakada was a chauki under thannah Bhusna, and it remained so until the thannahs were re-arranged at the time of the permanent settlement, since which time it has never been occupied for police purposes.

4. The hât, which is held here on Tuesdays and Fridays, is very well attended. Much of the goor produced along the Jhenida and Magurah road (chapter XLI) is brought to Ichakada for sale to the refiners, who have small karkhanas in various parts of the sub-division. A considerable quantity of potatoes and of pine-apples is grown in the vicinity, and mostly finds its way ultimately to Calcutta.

Hât.

5. The village Mirzapur, on the other side of the river, is celebrated for the fineness of the rice it grows.

Muhammadpur is on the bank of the Madhumati, fourteen miles south-east of Magurah.

2. A road of recent construction leads to it from Magurah, but the larger half, which lies between Binadpur and Muhammadpur, is so much interrupted by unbridged khals that it can be used only in some places.

3. The story of the foundation, and much of the subsequent history of Muhammadpur, is narrated in chapter V, where an account is given of its antiquities, and all in it connected with Raja Sitaram Ray.

History.

4. At the time of the occupation of the district it was a very large town, and the remains of the forsaken houses still shew how widely it once extended. A space measuring about three-fourths of a mile each way is covered with the foundations of houses that once existed. In Rennel's map its name is marked in the largest letters, and its size and importance is further attested by the fact that it served for a long time as the head-quarters of the Bhusna circle of pergunnahs, and that there was in 1795 a serious proposal to remove to it the head-quarters of the district. (C. 30-3-95.)

5. The story of its devastation is as follows: I am not very sure of the date, but I believe it was about 1836 (1243).

First outbreak of Gangetic fever.

6. In the cold weather of that year five hundred or seven hundred prisoners were employed in making the road which joins Jessore and Dacca, or which was intended to join them, and which passes through Muhammadpur. The work on the side of the river opposite Muhammadpur had been finished, and in January the prisoners crossed the river and began working on the Muhammadpur side. They were making that part of the road which lies between the Ram Sagar and the village Harkrishnapur when, in March, a great sickness broke out. The sirkars who were in charge of the prisoners fled, and of the prisoners one hundred and fifty died.

7. In the town, too, the sickness broke out. It was a fever beginning with a headache, causing great internal heat and carrying off its victims in about ten days. It remained about the town for seven years; and what with the enormous number of deaths by the fever itself, and what with the many people who fled the place to escape the plague, it resulted in desolating Muhammadpur. Where before houses had been crowded together, there remained only deserted "bhitas" and thick jungle.

8. This was the first outbreak of that fever which subsequently spread over Jessore and Nuddea, laying waste, in the latter district, another large village (Oolla, or Bhirnagar), and which a year or two since attracted much attention in Burdwan and Hooghly.

9. Muhammadpur is now composed only of a small bazar situated on part of the elevated rampart just north of the
Bazar.
Ram Sagar where Sitaram Ray established his bazar, and a few houses scattered about in the space once occupied by the town.

10. Two or three years since, Thakur Dass Gosain, who had purchased the land near Muhammadpur, set up
Gosainganj.
a new bazar on the river bank, a mile or less from Muhammadpur bazar. He has given it the name Gosainganj, and has established a Monday and Friday hât. The experiment began badly, for the cyclone of 1867 destroyed the huts, and an outbreak of cholera supervened. The site is so much better, and so much more convenient than the old one, that I have little doubt Gosainganj will ultimately succeed and replace the older bazar.

11. Muhammadpur has little else than a local trade; but during the rains the fishermen here catch a number of
Trade.
hilsa fish, put them into huge earthenware jars with salt to preserve them, and send them down to Calcutta for sale.

2 M

12. Muhammadpur was erected into a thannah somewhere between
1793 and 1814.   Bhusna, on the other side of the
river, was the old thannah, and until the Madhumati
river opened out, probably there was no necessity for one so near it as
Muhammadpur.   The thannah remained at Muhammadpur till a year
or two since, when it was removed to Gosainganj.

Thannah.

13. The jurisdiction of this thannah is during the rains covered with
a number of overflow-channels of the Madhumati,
which in a great measure prevent communication
by the roads leading to it.   The Jessore and Dacca road, which passes
through the thannah jurisdiction, has long been abandoned, and does not
appear to have ever been in a completed state; for with all this body
of water moving southward, it is almost like a road carried across the
bed of a river.   The water finds its way into the large bhîls lying
between the Nabaganga and the Madhumati, and from them into these
two rivers.   I have already mentioned in chapter II that there is a work
of formation going on here, and these overflow-streams are gradually
raising the surface of the country.   Unfortunately the silting up begins
from the outside, and its first operation is therefore the retention of water
over the low country.

The river.

14. Near Muhammadpur a curious feature in the river channel
occurs.   The two streams, the Madhumati proper and the Barasia,
bend towards each other, and their loops meet and form a sort of X.
There will be some great change in the channel within the next ten
years.   The Madhumati at present tends to pour into the Barasia, but it
will not unlikely ultimately break across the neck of its own loop and
leave the X altogether.

Binadpur is a large village half way between Magurah and Muhammadpur—the largest village, in fact, in the sub-division.   It has a bazar
and a hât which is held on Sundays and Thursdays, the same days as
the Magurah hât.

2.   As to its trade, the remarks as to the sugar trade and rice trade,
as to the oil-makers and the mat-makers, which apply to Magurah, apply
also to Binadpur.

3.   There used to be a " sudder distillery" here, which had existed
from before the erection of the sub-division.   It was transferred to Magurah
about ten or twelve years ago.

Salikha, or *Salkhia*, is half way between Magurah and Jessore, and is
situated on the Jessore and Dacca road, which is hardly kept up in this part.

2. It is one of the old thannahs of the district. "Sulka," which is
History. evidently intended to mean this place, is mentioned
in 1781 as a chauki of Bhusna thannah; but it
apparently ceased to be kept up when the police was in the hands of the
zemindars, and it was not one of the ten thannahs established at the time
of the permanent settlement. When, in 1795, the number of thannahs
had increased to seventeen, Salikha was evidently one of them, for it is
mentioned in a letter of 1798, and it is mentioned again in 1814. It
was abolished at the revision of 1863, when a new thannah was set up
at Sitakhali. But this was not a good site, and the thannah was
removed first to Simakhali, and in 1867 back to its old site at Salikha.
(M. 18-6-81; 16-9-91; 1-3-93; 2-6-95. J. 12-2-98. C. 3-5-14.)

XLIX.—Naral Sub-division.

Naral is twenty-two miles east of Jessore, upon the Chitra river, which
at this place is very deep, and is throughout the year a regular route for
large boats passing northward or southward through the district.

2. Most of what was to be narrated of the history of Naral has been
said in chapter XL.

3. Naral extends for a mile or more along the river bank, the sub-
The bazar and hât. divisional buildings being the northern extremity,
and the principal bazar and ganj the southern.
Just south of the bazar is a masonry ghât known as Rattan Baboo's Ghât.

4. The bazar, which is now a considerable one, was established by
Rupram, one of the ancestors of the Naral family, and the ganj is named
after him Rupganj. It has hardly anything but local trade. The
country produces enough rice for its own consumption, and as for its sugar
trade, it imports a little for its own use from Basantia. Date trees indeed
grow in the vicinity, but their juice does not produce good sugar.

5. A hât is held on Sunday and Thursday at the place where the
bazar is, and there is a smaller hât, on Monday and Friday, on a site
farther north, namely, in that smaller bazar where the thannah is.

6. Naral has been the seat of a sub-division since 1861. The
The sub-division. sub-division was one of those which were started
during the indigo disturbances, and its first site
was Gopalganj, which is on the Furreedpore bank of the Madhumati,
just above the separation of the Atharabanka. Thence it was brought

to Bhatiapara, opposite Lohagara, thence to Lohagara (which was then
a munsiffi), thence to Kumarganj, opposite Naldi, and then a permanent
site was chosen at Naral. All these wanderings occurred within a very
short space—a year at most, and the final site was chosen upon the
principle that it was well to exercise moral restraint over the powerful
zemindars who resided at Naral.

7. Mr. Bainbridge, c.s., was the first magistrate, and he accompanied
the sub-division in the wanderings noted above.

8. When Naral was first occupied, the sub-divisional site was little
better than a bleak spot surrounded by marsh, and so it remained for a
long time. Now the level of the grounds has been raised, and they
have been laid out and planted with shrubs and trees, and a garden
intervenes between the house and the river, most of the land of which
has been gained from the river. These changes have been wrought by
Mr. Deare, the present sub-divisional magistrate.

9. Naral sub-division is part of what I have in the first chapter
described as the low bhíl tract of the district, and
Communications.   it is therefore almost devoid of communication by
road. A road at the sub-divisional head-quarters to Ghorakhali is almost
the only one in the sub-division. The Naral Baboos, or rather one of
them, Ray Harnath Ray Bahadur, commenced the construction of a road
joining Jessore and Naral, and upon this road a good deal of money has
been spent, both in making it, by the Baboos, and in occupying the land
for it, by Government. It is a road difficult of construction, passing as it
does through bhíl lands, and directly athwart the drainage of the country.
The work on it has almost stopped since Ray Harnath's death.

10. Communication, therefore, throughout the sub-divisions is
chiefly by water, and the rivers and cross-khals enable one to go by boat
over a great part of the sub-division. The Madhumati, unfortunately,
is nearly cut off from its connection with the rivers flowing within the
district. Its connection with the Nabaganga has recently ceased to exist,
for the channel of the latter stream, where it passes Lohagara, is dry,
except during the rains. Rani Rasmani (chapter XXXIX) cut a half-
mile khal to join the Bankána with the Madhumati at Tona; but this,
too, is now so far silted up, that in February it is dry at low tide, and at
high tide has only some eighteen inches of water. The dissensions of the
zemindars will prevent anything being done to re-open it.

11. The communication between the Naral rivers and the Madhumati is thus almost shut off, and it is a drawback to the internal traffic of

the district that this noble river has no connection with the district rivers between Ramnagar, north of Magurah, and the Atharabanka river, which runs down to Khulna.

12. The usual line of communication between Jessore and Naral is by water, through the Gobra khal; but this khal becomes difficult of passage after the middle of March, and one must then either use a circuitous route, or go straight across country by land, which in the dry months is not difficult.

13. Of Naral the staple produce is rice, and in many of its
Rice.
bhíls the long-stemmed variety is grown. Sown broadcast when the bhíls are dry, the stem rises with the water, and twelve or fourteen feet is not an unusual depth for the water in which this long rice grows.

14. Naral was not occupied as a thannah before it was a sub-division.

Naldi, five miles north of Naral, is a large village, with a bazar, a ganj, and a hât; the latter held on Sundays and Thursdays.

2. Naldi is probably an extremely ancient place, for the large and important pergunnah of Naldi no doubt derives from it its name.

3. The inhabitants are almost all of two classes: firstly, an agricultural class, living by agriculture in the vicinity; secondly, a great number of petty traders of all sorts—telis (grocers), kuris, sekras (gold and silver workers), shahas (general traders), whose petty trading operations extend all over the country, as far even as Jessore and Calcutta; that is to say, their home is in Naldi, but they set up and carry on shops all over the country.

4. There are some small sugar-refineries in Naldi, and the raw material comes mostly from Khajura. The sugar is exported to Nalchitti.

5. An ancient idol, Kalachand, has a temple and service in Naldi.

6. Naldi was a police chauki in the latter days of the old police.

Kumarganj is the name of the ganj in the village Chandibarpur, opposite Naldi.

2. It was, I am told, a very prominent place a hundred years ago, being the only ganj within a considerable tract of country, Rupganj at Naral not being then established; and in a letter of 1794 (C. 18-10-94) Kumarganj is mentioned as a great mart for the purchase of grain. I doubt, however, whether these remarks apply to this Kumarganj, or to another Kumarganj, marked in Rennel's map on the opposite side of the Barasia from Muhammadpur; but the fact that the place was a salt

chauki up till about twenty years ago, is some evidence that it was not altogether an unknown place.

3. Now there is not even a bazar in the place. There seems to have been about twenty or thirty years ago some squabbling among zemindars as to who should have the bazar in this part of the country. Guru Dass Ray strove to have it in Naldi, because he had land there; Ram Rattan Ray, for a similar reason, strove to attract it to Kumarganj; and one Shaha, who had taken in patni some lands of Naldi village, desired to have it within his limits. The latter had no chance against the first two, who were powerful zemindars; and of these two Guru Dass Ray prevailed, because his lands contained the majority of the population to be served. The bazar of Naldi, therefore, has out out that at Kumarganj, and now all that is at Kumarganj is an open space where a hât is held every Monday and Friday.

4. One peculiar feature in this hât is, that it is here that the purchasers of pepper from the east mostly meet the sellers of it from the west. The latter bring their goods from Jhenida and Kaliganj by the Nabaganga and Chitra rivers and transfer it to the former, who carry it off by the Tona khal into Backerganj.

Lakshmipassa is ten miles east of Naral, on the Nabaganga, at the point where it flows into the Bankána. The main stream used to flow eastward, under Lohagara, into the Madhumati; but for a few years that bed has been closed, except during the rains, and the Bankána, flowing southward, is now the continuation of the Nabaganga.

2. Lakshmipassa is the site of a thannah whose history is this.

Thannah.

Bhatiaparra, on the other side of the Madhumati, was in 1781 one of the chaukis of Bhusna thannah, but it ceased to be kept up when the zemindars had charge. In 1793 no new thannah was proposed to take its place, but it seems to have been revived shortly afterwards; either the thannah at Bhatiaparra was revived and shortly afterwards transferred to Lohagara, or a thannah at Lohagara was made to take the place of the previous one. The Lohagara thannah was certainly in existence in 1814 (C. 3-5-14), and it remained till about 1867 or 1868, when the drying up of the river channel beneath it caused its transference to Lakshmipassa.

3. Between these two places, Lohagara and Lakshmipassa, there has long been a rivalry for the possession of the local trade. Both places have bazars, and both hâts. In Lohagara the hât days are Monday and Thursday, and in

Trade.

Lakshmipassa they are Sunday and Wednesday; whence we may safely conclude that the latter is the more modern, and was established to cut out the former. Lohagara possessed the greater part of the trade, until the closing of its river turned the advantage in favour of the other place.

4. Besides the ordinary local trade there is a trade in sugar. Goor is brought from Khajura, manufactured into pucka sugar, and exported to Nalchitti and to Calcutta. A little rice is sent westward, and some cold-weather produce—kallai, sarshya, and rai—sent to Calcutta. (Chapters XLI to XLIII.)

5. All the coarse cloth used in this part of the district comes

Cloth.

from Boalmari hât, about sixteen miles north, in the Furreedpore district. A large number of Mohamedans of the Ferazi sect, many of whom are weavers (Jalâhas), live in that part of Furreedpore, and bring their cloths for sale to this large hât, which is held only one day in the week, Sunday. The cloth trade of that place must be very great, for in Lakshmipassa, which gets its cloth thence, 5,000 rupees worth are sometimes sold in a single hât day at the time of the Dúrgapúja.

6. Lakshmipassa is remarkable as the habitation of a number

Kulin brahmans.

of the pure Kulin brahmans. This place and its immediate vicinity, and Kamalpur, five miles south of Jessore, are the only places in the district where they reside.

7. The peculiar features of Kulinism are less known than are the abuses of it, and I shall therefore state them very shortly here.

8. The Kulins are a caste of brahmans who are esteemed very

Their caste, history, and customs.

sacred, and are held in the highest honour. Their separation into a special caste, endowed with these distinctions, they date from Ballal Sen, the ancient king of Bengal, the remains of whose palace are still to be seen near Nuddea, and from Lakhan Sen, his son (about 1100 A.D.) The preservation of their Kulinism depends upon their strict abstinence from inter-marriage with other stocks and their strict adherence to the limitation as to inter-marriage among themselves prescribed by the rules of their caste. One of these rules is that the two persons marrying must be descended from the original stock by exactly the same number of generations. But there are many other rules, and the system of rules (which is called parjyá) is, I believe, attributed to Lakhan Sen. So great is the practical restriction which they impose upon marriage, that to each person born there are only, in the whole world, a few persons with whom he may marry.

9. The genealogical records are kept by the Ghataks, and when any marriage takes place it is entered in their books, and they define the persons with whom the offspring of the marriage may intermarry, and to these they are absolutely confined, if they would keep their caste. Of the persons so defined, some may not be born and some may die, but the restriction remains. A father with half-a-dozen daughters may find he has only one bridegroom for all his daughters, so they are all married off to him. Perhaps another father has only the same man as a possible bridegroom for his daughters too, so the man gets another batch of wives. Little boys sometimes marry aged women, and little girls are married to aged men. There is no help for it; they must be married, and these are the only bridegrooms the rules allow. Many women find themselves without any possible bridegrooms, and these are held in immense reverence, and are called "daughters of houses of Taika."

10. Fathers compel a rigid adherence to all these rules, for it is their honour that suffers by an infringement; but there are many fathers who are not Kulins, and who would pay large sums to Kulin bridegrooms to obtain from them the honour involved in having their daughters married to Kulins. There are several Kulins, therefore, who go abroad seeking for such fathers and obtaining from them considerable sums of money to marry their daughters. The father only cares to have his daughter so married, and does not in the least insist upon his Kulin son-in-law keeping or staying with his new wife, and so the Kulin leaves this place, and goes on to find another father with a sum of money and a daughter to spare.

Abuse.

11. There are some Kulins at Lakshmipassa who have gone on these marrying tours and have returned to set up a trade with the money they have obtained as the price of their marriages to all these wives.

12. When Kulins do this, their Kulinism is of course gone for ever, and it is looked upon by Kulins as a scandalous sort of proceeding thus to prostitute one's Kulinism for money.

13. It will be seen from the above that both the legitimate exercise of Kulinism and its abuse operate in restraint of marriage. Women are married to Kulins and never see them again. Some cannot be married at all. Hardly any wife can possess a husband to herself, or even a considerable share in one. The evils that follow from this state of things—the unchastity and child-murder that are prevalent—are acknowledged even by those who live according to the rules of Kulinism.

14. The story of the immigration of Kulins into this place is as
Their immigration. follows. A number of Kulin families lived at Sar-
mangal, near Khalia, in Backerganj, and the Mughs
who resided in that part of the country used to annoy these families
excessively by forcibly marrying their daughters to Kulin boys. One
old man, Ramanand Chackravarti, determined to save himself from this
desecration and left the place, intending to find a new residence on the
banks of the Ganges. When he passed this place, the Mazumdars of
Dhopadaha, a village three miles west of Lakshmipassa, induced him to
stay there and marry one of their daughters, paying him for the honour
by giving him their jumma rights in the village. He and his nine sons
therefore remained in that village, and though their caste was slightly
blemished by this marriage, still, as the Mazumdars were of high caste,
the Chackravarti family did not lose their Kulinism.

15. From that time to this is five generations, and all the Kulins
here derive their descent from this Ramanand.

16. There remains one note to be made on this place, namely, respect-
Temple of Kali. ing the temple of Kali which stands close to the bazar.

17. A hundred years ago, and more, there lived here a pious black-
smith who used frequently to make images of Kali, and after worshipping
them to cast them into the river, according to the ceremony of " bissarjan."
But one night Kali appeared to him and told him that she had determined permanently to take up her abode with him; so he gave her a
house, and her fame went abroad.

18. Not very long since a masonry temple was built for her by
one of the ranis of the Naldi family, I think, and to this temple people
crowd every day to worship her and make their offerings. Tuesdays and
Saturdays are the principal days. A large number of goats are sacrificed
here, and now and then a bullock is sacrificed; and there are some twenty-
five or thirty brahmans engaged in the service of the goddess.

19. In 1866 the body of a Mussulman boy, who had been murdered,
was found lying in the place of sacrifice, and it was at first supposed it
was a case of human sacrifice. But though no definite information was
arrived at, enough was found to shew that the murder had nothing to do
with the temple, and most likely the body of a boy otherwise murdered
had been, to divert inquiry, cast at the door of the temple.

20. Lakshmipassa is the head-quarters of the Naldi zemindari.
Naldi cutcherry. They were removed from Muhammadpur after
the outbreak of the great fever there.

2 N

21. There is a criminal population down the banks of the Madhumati, within Lakshmipassa thannah. They used to
Criminals.
commit dacoities on the river, until the improve-
ment of the police in recent years restrained their operations. They are
still ready for anything of the sort, but they are held in check by the
police. Alphadanga outpost was established a few years since especially
for their benefit.

Digalia, four or five miles south of Lakshmipassa, contains some
ruins connected with Sitaram Ray. (Chapter V.)

Khalia, ten or twelve miles south of Lakshmipassa, is a considerable
town, with a bazar and hât, situate at the junction of two small rivers.

2. Khalia is one of those places, of which there are only two or
three in the district, which are filled with resi-
Residents.
dents of the Kayasth class. The residents are in
professional employment, such as moonsiffs, deputy collectors, vakeels,
serishtadars, mukhtars, &c., and they are absent from their homes except
at Dúrgapúja time, when they bring home their money and spend
it in " tamasha."

3. A favorite holiday spectacle here is boat-racing. The racing
boats, which are kept solely for this purpose, are
Spectacles.
about a hundred feet long and rather heavily built.
The villagers who are going to form the crew come each with his own
paddle (for in these watery parts each villager has a paddle, and many
have boats). They seat themselves on the cross-bars of the boat, and
when full there are about fifty paddles upon each side, with which very
rapid progress indeed is made.

4. I have obtained the following account of the origin of the place,
and the reason why so many "bhadra-lok" are collected in it. The
southern tracts used to be liable to the attacks of the Mughs, and the
western and north-western were subject to the ravages of the "Bargies"
or Mahrattas. A number of people who were sufficiently well off, desirous
to live in peace, sought a residence in the more inaccessible parts, where
neither Mugh nor Bargi would approach, and established themselves
at Khalia, which then was, as shewn in Rennel's map, in the midst of a
marshy tract.

5. Khalia is not inconveniently situated. The Bânkâna from the
north is open all the year round to large boats, and
Communications.
a cross khal, except during the dry months, enables
one to come also by a direct route from Naral. The continuation of the

Bânkâna, open all the year round, leads south to the Bhairab, near Khulna. A strong tide runs in this river.

6. Khalia has only local trade. It has a flourishing school, and
Trade. a dispensary kept up by the residents, chiefly by the leading family, the Sens.

7. Khalia was formerly part of Lohagara thannah, but about 1867
Thannah. the necessity of watching Gurudas Ray, who has a cutcherry here, caused the erection of a separate thannah at Khalia.

L.—*Khulna Sub-division.*

Khulna.—The geographical situation of Khulna, at the point where
Important position. the Bhairab meets the chief Sundarban route, has rendered it, for a hundred years at least, a very prominent place. It is, as it were, the capital of the Sundarbans. It was the head-quarters of the salt department when the Company's salt manufacture was still carried on in the Sundarbans, and now it is a grand mart for all Sundarban trades, whether rice, or firewood, or lime, or anything else. (Chapters XLII, XLIII, and XLIV.)

2. All the ship traffic from the east and north-east, and during the dry months that from up-country also, passes it on its way to Calcutta. Rice from Dacca and Backerganj; lime, lemons, and oranges from Sylhet; mustard-seed, linseed, and kallai from Pubna, Rajshahye, and Furreedpore; ghee from Patna,—such are the cargoes which are perpetually passing Khulna on their way to Calcutta. From Calcutta the principal cargoes brought are salt, and I have seen twenty salt boats arrive by one tide and pull up opposite the thannah to deliver up their rawanas before passing northward.

3. Khulna is in its commercial position a forwarding mart; rice,
Trade. sugar, betelnut, and coocanut, the produce of its vicinity, is collected for exportation to Calcutta, and partly also northward; and the trade in salt is also very great, for Khulna as it were taps the line of salt traffic and supplies salt to all the country roundabout.

4. At Khulna there are a few sugar refineries, supplied with goor, partly the produce of the vicinity, partly from Naupara and Basantia. The cheapness of firewood encourages the sugar manufacture here.

5. At Khulna there are three bazars, and of these Sen's Bazar, as
Bazars.
it is called, on the opposite side of the Bhairab from
Khulna proper, is the chief one. The particular
circumstances whence the name is derived, I do not know; but the records
quoted in chapter XXXV shew that in 1790 and 1793 Sen's Bazar was,
as it is now, the chief bazar of Khulna. There is no hât held at this bazar.

6. On the west side of the river there are two bazars; one a small
one, at the confluence of the rivers, and one a large one, a mile north of
the first. In this northern one a hât is held on Tuesdays and Saturdays.
The ganj is called "Charliganj," deriving its name from a Mr. Charles,
who about thirty years since had an indigo factory close by.

7. The official history of Khulna, apart from its connection with the
Company's salt manufacture, is as follows. It was
History.
the site of thannah Nauabad which is mentioned
in 1781, 1791, 1793, and 1814, and has continued in existence, with a
change of name, up to the present time. It is therefore the only place
in the district where a *thannah* existing from before the permanent
settlement has lasted up to the present time.

8. A sub-division, the first established in Bengal, was set up here
in 1842. Its chief object was to hold in check Mr. Rainey, who had
purchased a zemindari in the vicinity and resided at Nihalpur, and who
did not seem inclined to acknowledge the restraints of law. The first
sub-divisional officer was Mr. Shore, then Mr. E. Lushington, then
Mr. Montresor; and the jurisdiction extended over not only the present
Khulna sub-division, but also over almost the whole of the present
Baghahat sub-division.

9. From Singhia, twelve miles east of Jessore, a road leads south-
wards, following the river bank, to Khulna. The
Roads.
road is mentioned in 1794 (chapter XXXVI),
but it was then no more than a track. Even now, though in fair order,
it is little used, as the river affords easier means of communication
between the various towns and villages which the road connects.

10. There are no other roads in the sub-division except a mere
track that goes down the southern bank of the Bhairab. Communication everywhere is by water, and the net-work of rivers and khals
that covers the sub-division renders water communication available to
almost every village.

11. The principal product of the sub-division (excluding the Sundarban forest) is rice, and the soil is very fertile. Cocoanut trees and

betelnut trees are abundant all over the northern parts, but in some of the lower parts there is not a tree or a bush of any sort to be seen for miles.

12. In chapters XLII and XLIII enough has been said about the Sundarbans.

Phultalla is a police outpost under Khulna thannah, eight miles north of it, and on the bank of the Bhairab. It has a considerable bazar, and has some sugar manufacture. (Chapter XLI.)

Senhati is four miles north of Khulna, on the banks of the Bhairab.

2. With its suburbs it forms the largest collection of houses in the district, and I think it may claim also to be the

Jungle.

most jungly place in the whole district. Old tanks filled with weed and mud, and their sides covered with rank jungle, are everywhere scattered over it, and the many unoccupied spaces within its limits, which anywhere else would be cultivated, are a mass of underwood. The roads and paths of the village, except one very fair one that runs north and south, and is kept in order, wind through masses of brushwood.

3. Many of the chief inhabitants of the village are of the class described with regard to Khalia, and are at home only at Dúrgapúja time.

4. Upon a road, part of Khanja Ali's great road (chapter III), which runs east and west along the river bank,

Nimai Ray's Bazar.

is the bazar of Senhati, called Nimai Ray's Bazar. It is a bazar of some importance, and it is a very old one. It has a local trade supplying all the country around, and there are in it one or two large sugar refineries. Their raw material comes from farther up the river, and their export is chiefly to Calcutta.

5. Nimai Ray, who established the bazar, was, in the time of the Musulman Government, a mukhtar in the service of Rani Bhawani, of Nattore, and he had a taluq or ganti here. The widow of one of his descendants is now alive, but poor enough, as all the property has long since been sold up. The ruins of Nimai Ray's house are still to be seen in Senhati, about half a mile north of the bazar. The walls of one house, and the pucka verandah of another, are still standing. It appears to have once been a fine house although it is only of small dimensions.

6. In Nimai Ray's Bazar there is a temple to Kali built by Raja Srikant Ray (of Jessore), who was proprietor of these lands till about 1797. It is beginning to be dilapidated.

7. I found two other shrines on the bank of the river, set up in thatched huts, one to Shital (god of small-pox) and one to Jalnarayn

(god of fever). Púja is done to these two gods to ward off small-pox
and fever. The inhabitants might take the more practical means of
clearing their superabundant jungle.

Tálla, on the river Kabadak, is now, and has long been, a great
place of trade. It is mentioned as such by the collector in a letter of
9th January 1802. Its produce is chiefly sugar, in respect of which
it is, as it were, a companion mart to Keshabpur. Not having visited
the place, I am unable to give further particulars.

2. Tálla was one of the old thannahs established in 1793, but since
1863 it has been only an outpost under Dumuria thannah.

Kopilmuni, on the Kabadak, is five or six miles below Tálla.

Antiquities.

2. The antiquities connected with this place
I have described in chapter VII.

3. The tomb of Jafr Ali I did not there mention. This Jafr Ali is
much more recent in date than Kopil, and is perhaps not a hundred years
dead. He was a man of extreme piety, and like Kopil, had superhuman
power. When he died a small tomb was erected, a little to the east of
Kopil's ancient hermitage. The tomb is covered by a thatched roof, and
it is kept by some faqirs who have lands for its support. The tomb is a
place of pilgrimage for devout Mahomedans.

4. At Kopilmuni there is a bazar, and a hát is held on Sundays
and Thursdays.

Chandkhali, on the Kabadak, is about ten miles north of where the
river enters the forest.

2. I have already said so much of Chandkhali, that I have little to
do here but to refer to what has been said.

3. The story of its establishment is given in chapter XXV, and that
of the sub-division once held here in chapter XXVI. Its position as a
leading Sundarban mart is fully described in chapters XLII and XLIV.

4. On the opposite side of the river from Chandkhali there is a

The hát.

place called Bardal, where there is held a hát called
"The Sahibs' Hát." It was formerly a greater hát
than it now is, as Chandkhali has completely eclipsed it. But looking
to the name of it, and to the fact that there is so frequently between
adjacent zemindars great rivalry for the possession of a hát, it seems not
improbable that the hát and ganj first established by Mr. Henckell at
Chandkhali got transferred at some time to Bardal, on the opposite side
of the river, and carried its name with it. The present zemindar, Uma
Nath Ray, is said to have encouraged the Chandkhali hát so as to give

it the predominance over the Bardal hât, which belongs to a zemindar of less power. There is now, in fact, no comparison between the two, for the trade of the ever-increasing Sundarban reclamations always gravitates towards Chandkhali.

5. Chandkhali is a police outpost under Diluti, or as it should rather now be called, "Paikgachha" thannah.

6. Khanja Ali's ruins at Masjidkur, six miles south of Chandkhali, have been described in chapter III.

Kâtipara, which, together with Râruli, occupies a peninsula on the Kabadak, about ten miles north of Chandkhali, deserves separate notice.

2. It appears to have been one of the early outposts of advancing reclamation. The leading family in it is a Kayasth
History.
family of Ghoses who migrated hither from Khali-shakhali, somewhat to the north-west, about a hundred years ago, or at least at a time when the land hereabout was mostly jungle. They were then poor enough, but now have zemindari in Bhaluka, the pergunnah on the opposite side of the river. Their wealth is founded upon the acquisitions made by one of them, who was serishtadar of the salt chauki of Baripur; and these salt serishtadarships, it is everywhere notorious, were sources of very great wealth to all who occupied them. One man who officiated in one for only a month or two (and that in their later days) told me himself what grand mines of wealth they were.

3. This family have since that time brought to the village other Kayasth families, with which they have intermarried, and there is now in the village a Kayasth society like that I have described at Khalia, in Naral.

4. The rest of the inhabitants are engaged in cultivation, either in the vicinity or in the Sundarban reclamations.

5. The village is a good specimen of a village. The Baboos' houses are for the most part well kept, and the village roads are wide and are maintained in fair order by the Baboos.

LI.—*Baghahat Sub-division.*

Baghahat is twenty miles south-east of Khulna, on the Bhairab river.

2. The ruins in the vicinity connected with Khanja Ali have received full description in chapter III, but there are in Baghahat itself some ruins which deserve to be recorded.

3. Immediately adjacent to the sub-divisional compound there is a rectangular space of ground, a biggah or two in area, raised about five or six feet above the level of the surrounding land, and at the southern end of this raised area one finds the foundation of what was once a small pucka house.

The Básábárí.

4. Two brick walls at different distances enclosed this raised area, and it is very easy still to follow their lines, as that part of the walls which was below the surface of the ground is still existing. I am not sure, but, in case of the inner line at least, these brick-built lines mark the position of a built path rather than that of a wall. This line in two places is connected with the outer line, and these connections may have been pathways leading to the gates on the outer wall. Moreover, the line leads directly upon the ghât of an old tank, which is within the enclosure, a position which would be that of a road, and not of a wall.

5. This tank, called the Mitha Pokar, or sweet tank, is still the chief tank in Baghahat—the only one that gives good water. When it was being re-excavated two years ago, there was found upon the western side of it, about two feet below the surface, an ancient ghât. The steps of it were somewhat worn away and dilapidated, but the floor above the steps was still in good order,—a floor of circular shape, with its border composed of ornamental brick-work.

The sweet tank.

6. On the other side of the same tank a lady of the family of Mahima Chandra Ray of Karapara, a year or two since, built a ghât.

7. At the southern end of the enclosure there are two other tanks, the largest of which is known as the Natkhana, or ball-room tank.

8. These ruins do not date further back than the middle of last century, and they mark the site of the cutcherry of a certain begum of the family of the nawab of Moorshedabad. In those days it was necessary, especially so near the Sundarbans, to make places where money was kept sufficiently strong to resist the attacks of robbers.

The Baho Begum.

9. About the middle of last century the nawab conferred upon a begum, known as the Baho Begum, a jaghir which consisted of certain allowances in this part of the country. It included six annas of pergunnah Khalifat-abad, within which Baghahat is, and it included also certain allowances, both of money and of guards, leviable from some of the other lands, the begum of course having to collect them herself.

10. When the permanent settlement was made, it was considered that the system by which both the revenue authorities and the begum

made collections of their respective dues from the same zemindars was open to objection; and the begum's jaghir was then commuted into a money allowance payable by Government, and the zemindar's contributions to her were incorporated with their revenue. The allowances which composed the jaghir were then stated to be Rs. 6,300 undisputed and Rs. 2,900 disputed. The begum enjoyed the commuted allowance for only a year or two, for she died in 1794, and it lapsed to Government. (C. 15-12-86; 31-7-91; 5-3-92; 30-8-94.)

11. This old cutcherry at Baghahat was therefore the cutcherry of collection of this jaghir. It is known in the vicinity as the Básábárí (residence), and has given its name to an adjacent village. Another village in the immediate vicinity is called Das-áni (ten annas), a name evidently founded upon the old division of the pergunnah into ten annas revenue-paying and six annas jaghir.

12. It may be mentioned that the bricks found about these ruins have been to a large extent used in metalling the roads about the sub-divisional station, so abundant is the supply of them.

13. Baghahat is in itself only a small bazar, where a hât is held
Recent improvements. every Sunday and Wednesday. The ganj is called
Madhabganj, named, I believe, after a certain member of the Karapara family. Baghahat was erected into a subdivision in 1863, and since then has naturally increased in size. It was then only a piece of low jungle on the bank of the river; but since its occupation the jungle has been cleared away, a house built for the subdivisional office, grounds acquired and partly laid out, and a few roads made about the place. A good deal has been done by the residents themselves, the chief private work of the sort being a ghât in the river, opposite the sub-divisional house, built by Baboo Mahima Chandra Ray of Bangaon (Selimabad).

14. Before the sub-division was erected the lands were partly in
Character of the inhabit- Khulna sub-division and partly in Backerganj dis-
ants. trict. The people dwelling in it are still much
more of the Backerganj sort than of the Jessore sort, mostly Mahomedans, turbulent and lawless, and excessively fond of litigation. Both the police and the courts in Baghahat find more to do than in other sub-divisions.

15. The sub-division partakes for the most part of the character of
the Sundarbans, and this character has been fully
Cultivation. described in chapter XLII. Rice is its staple
produce, and it grows very luxuriantly over the whole sub-division; that

2 o

is, wherever the lands have been reclaimed. The system of land tenure is peculiar, and I have described it in chapter XXXIX, where I have stated that I ascribe its peculiarities to the relations arising from the reclamation of land through ryots and others, who thus acquire certain recognized rights in the land they bring under cultivation.

16. Baghahat has been a thannah ever since 1863, and it has at present two outposts, Kochua and Faqirhat.

17. Communication in Baghahat sub-division, it need hardly be remarked, is entirely by water.

Kochua is eight miles east of Baghahat, upon the Bhairab, which here carries little water, as most of the water of the Bhairab now goes southward from Baghahat.

2. Kochua is now a police outpost of Baghahat thannah, but before 1863 it was itself a thannah, and there was then also a munsiffi and a salt chauki in the place.

3. Kochua possesses a considerable bazar and a hât. The village is in two parts separated by a khal, and across this khal is built a masonry bridge, which bears a somewhat rudely carved inscription declaring it to have been built by Bangshi Kundu. He was, I am told, a merchant of Kochua, and he built the bridge about forty or fifty years since. He built also a small temple close by.

4. The hât and bazar were previously close to the bridge, but the

Trade.

oppressions and exactions of the zemindars caused its removal to a site half a mile farther west, where another zemindar offered it a place and promised less severe terms.

5. Kochua exports rice, as do all the places in this part of the country. Large quantities of the vegetable kochu are grown in the vicinity, and it is not unlikely that the place derives its name from that fact.

6. The story of the first establishment of Kochua by Mr. Henckell has been told in chapter XXV.

7. As a place of trade, Kochua has now a rival in Taleshwar, a mile or two farther west.

Fakirhat is midway between Khulna and Baghahat. It is still a place of considerable importance, with a large bazar; but it appears to have been previously a still more important place, for in 1815 the collector notes it as one of the three most considerable towns in the district. (C. 28-4-15.)

2. Its situation, or at least the situation of its bazar, has been

The hât.

slightly changed. First of all, Radha Mohun Ghose Chaudhry, the zemindar, changed its situation from a place which is now desert (where he had only a share of the proprietorship) to a place two hundred yards farther south, which belonged entirely to him. This last place is still occupied by a bazar, but some ten or fifteen years since, another of the zemindars, Shamaprasad Ray, caused the removal of the principal part of the bazar to a site half a mile farther south still, which belonged to him. This is the largest bazar, and the ganj is also here, and is called Kaliganj, from Kaliprasad Ray, Shamaprasad's brother and partner. A hât is held in the ganj every Sunday and Wednesday.

3. The land about Faqirhat is exceptionally high, and grows date

Trade. trees to a certain extent. From the produce of these date trees, and from goor imported from other parts of the district, sugar is manufactured in Faqirhat. (Chapter XLI.)

4. The rest of the trade is chiefly in rice, betelnuts, and cocoanuts, all of which are exported.

5. There is a police outpost at Faqirhat.

Jatrapur is half way between Baghahat and Faqirhat, upon the Bhairab river, which makes a detour of about four miles, and then returns to a point quite close to where it began. There have been proposals for cutting through the narrow neck of land here, but this has not been done as yet. It would be of great benefit to the navigation, not only because it would shorten the course of the stream, but also because it would, by increasing the strength of the tidal current, tend to keep it open and of greater depth.

2. Jatrapur is a considerable village, with a bazar, but it is note-

Baishnab temple. worthy chiefly for its possession of a great temple of the Baishnab sect. The god Gopal who dwells in the temple is an ancient resident of Jatrapur, but his temple was erected only two generations back by a Baishnab named Ballab Dass, known as "Babaji." The wealth which he employed to raise and endow the temple was acquired, as the livelihood of all proper Baishnabs is, by begging. But his followers attribute to him miraculous powers, because he, after coming to the country a penniless beggar, managed to build a fine temple to his god.

3. To this temple of Gopal therefore a new temple has been added, dedicated to this "Babaji." It was built by his followers upon the spot where he is buried, for Baishnabs bury their dead.

4. These temples are frequently visited by pilgrims, who make to it journeys from even three or four days' distance.

5.   Jatrapur is the site of the head cutcherry of the zemindari of the late Sarada Prasanna Mukharjya.

Múlnahàt is the northern thannah of Baghahat sub-division, which was about 1867 removed to a more convenient site, Udaypur, on the Madhumati.

2.   The jurisdiction of this thannah contains only two places which need be mentioned: *Chitalmari,* a bazar on the Madhumati, having a little local trade, and exporting rice; and *Alaypur,* at the point where the Atharabanka meets the Bhairab, which has a considerable local trade, and whose pottery is known all over the south of the district.

Rampal is a police station about twelve miles south-west of Baghahat, but having no direct communication with it; there is, however, a circuitous route by water.

2.   Rampal is of itself a small place, but on the opposite side of the river Mangla, on which it is situated, is the village Parikhali, where a hât is held.   Like most Sundarban hâts, the place presents on ordinary days the appearance of a few deserted huts, and on hât days only does it appear to have any life about it.

3.   There is an old story connected with Rampal which I have narrated in chapter XLII.

Morrellganj is on the Panguchi river, two miles above its confluence with the Baleshwar.   Morrellganj is a new name given to the ganj and bazar, Sarulia being the name of the village.

2.   Where thirty years ago there were miles of impenetrable jungle
Its recent origin.   coming down to the water's edge and forbidding all access to the land, the country is now covered with rice fields and dotted with prosperous villages, with Morrellganj in the middle of all, a busy place of trade, and becoming more and more important every day.

3.   The whole work is due to the Messrs. Morrell, who, beginning with small beginnings, have now extended, and are still continuing to extend, their cultivation over a wide area.   Their residence, which, in such unsure, foundationless ground, it took some years of patient labour to erect, stands on the bank of the river at Morrellganj, which of course is named after them; and half a mile north of it, at the confluence of three rivers and a khal besides, is the village and bazar of Morrellganj.

4.   Morrellganj has thus a great advantage in its position; for not
Importance of the site.   only is it the natural centre of all the country round it—the place to which all who reside in this

part of the district send their produce for export, and to which they look for their own supplies—but it also lies directly upon the route by which most of the produce of the eastern districts finds its way to Calcutta.

5. The deep channel of the Panguchi river affords a harbour for sea-going vessels, which now can reach it by the *Its future.* Baleshwar river. The Messrs. Morrell have had the place declared a port, and more than one vessel has already taken cargo from it. So great are the natural advantages of the situations, that I feel sure there is a great future in store for the place, and that it will in a few years attract to itself no mean share of the export trade of the Sundarbans of Backerganj and Jessore. The place has not yet established itself as a great centre of local trade, like Nalchitti and Jalukati, in Backerganj; but when it does so, (and with the encouragement afforded by the visit of a few ships it shortly will do so,) it is sure to become the commercial capital of the Sundarbans.

6. There is a daily bazar in the place, and on Fridays and Mondays a hât is held. The river and khal is then crowded *Trade.* with boats and with native ships, and a great quantity of rice and of other articles changes hands; the rice being carried off at present to Calcutta.

7. There is a considerable trade in boat-building, and pottery is prominent also among the articles sold. The reason of this is that, for the many boats passing westward, Morrellganj is the last place where they obtain fresh water, and they therefore carry a supply with them in large earthenware vessels into the Sundarbans.

8. The land upon which the bazar is, and also that on which the Morrells' residence is, has been artificially raised in level. Its natural level is that of an extreme spring tide.

9. Morrellganj was within the Rampal thannah from 1863 till about 1866, when it was erected into a separate thannah. Before 1863 it was within the Backerganj district.

APPENDIX.

A.

Population Statement.—District Jessore.—Autumn 1869.

Sub-division	Police jurisdiction	No. of "bargee" or houses	Men	Women	Boys	Girls	Total	Hindoos	Mahomedans	Europeans and Christians
Sunder.	Jessore	16,363	32,765	33,171	15,274	10,396	91,606	34,640	56,823	134
	O. Chaugachha	3,904	8,017	8,439	4,783	3,133	24,372	6,975	17,397	...
	Bagarpara	8,238	17,113	18,451	8,358	5,593	49,515	23,193	26,322	...
	Gadkhali	7,158	15,250	15,564	7,117	5,111	43,042	15,782	27,191	69
	Manirampur	17,465	43,798	45,205	23,251	15,260	127,514	48,754	78,760	...
	Kaliganj	11,488	26,357	27,456	14,146	9,519	77,280	28,982	48,298	...
	Keshabpur	11,855	25,439	26,872	12,623	8,602	73,536	26,419	47,080	37
	Total	76,449	168,739	175,158	85,554	57,414	486,865	184,754	301,871	240
Jhenidah.	Jhenidah	10,790	22,429	23,638	10,452	6,702	63,221	24,968	38,353	...
	Kotchandpur	4,814	8,098	8,184	4,170	3,200	23,652	9,044	14,608	...
	Solcopa	12,607	29,106	30,332	14,662	10,776	84,876	33,651	51,225	...
	O. Harinakundu	3,409	7,453	7,677	4,104	2,710	21,944	6,995	14,949	...
	Total	31,610	67,086	69,831	33,388	23,388	193,693	74,558	119,135	...
Magurah.	Magurah	10,412	28,523	30,115	14,045	10,141	82,824	40,748	42,076	5
	O. Sripur	3,878	6,938	7,178	3,280	2,470	19,866	9,961	9,965	...
	Salikha	5,958	12,275	14,024	6,302	4,510	37,111	17,000	20,111	...
	Muhammadpur	8,540	17,573	17,090	8,115	6,503	49,281	20,535	28,746	...
	Total	28,788	65,309	68,407	31,742	23,624	189,082	88,179	100,898	5
Naral.	Naral	14,981	34,919	36,705	18,373	12,780	102,777	56,865	45,903	9
	Khalia	6,190	19,878	8,945	5,548	4,148	29,519	21,306	8,213	...
	Lohagara	6,776	18,283	18,911	9,346	6,460	53,000	29,846	23,154	...
	O. Alfadanga	2,463	5,615	5,770	3,196	2,333	16,914	7,103	9,811	...
	Total	30,410	69,695	70,331	36,463	25,721	202,210	115,120	87,081	9
Khulna.	Khulna	9,607	22,143	22,220	12,636	8,392	65,391	36,133	29,173	85
	O. Phultalla	1,947	6,234	6,522	2,885	1,855	17,496	6,231	11,265	...
	Baitaghatta	2,168	5,181	5,610	3,341	2,516	16,648	8,952	7,696	...
	O. Barcari	456	1,002	960	629	421	3,002	1,425	1,577	...
	Diluti	4,777	9,831	9,868	5,369	3,761	28,669	16,501	12,168	...
	O. Chandkhali	1,021	2,465	2,156	1,211	870	6,702	2,244	4,458	...
	Dumuria	5,778	16,068	16,066	8,307	5,839	46,180	20,015	26,165	...
	O. Tullah	4,099	9,984	10,681	5,078	3,240	28,963	10,618	18,365	...
	Total	29,853	72,908	74,073	39,256	26,834	213,071	102,119	110,867	85
Baghahat.	Baghahat	8,077	19,481	19,811	11,146	8,071	58,509	33,170	25,339	...
	O. Faqirhat	5,771	11,733	12,505	6,497	4,485	35,190	21,045	14,145	...
	O. Kochua	4,102	9,474	10,557	6,360	4,663	31,054	18,360	12,694	...
	Mulnahat	4,290	11,541	12,250	7,421	5,804	37,016	21,116	15,870	...
	Morrellganj	6,400	14,026	14,567	8,950	7,146	44,591	16,752	27,939	...
	Rampal	3,936	10,937	10,839	6,870	4,780	33,426	15,705	17,663	58
	Total	32,636	77,192	80,529	47,214	34,951	239,886	126,178	113,650	58
	District total	229,746	520,929	538,329	273,617	191,932	1,524,907	690,908	833,502	397

The above is the result of a census taken in the autumn of 1869. The figures were filled into a printed form by the chief inhabitants of each chaukidar's ward, and the printed forms thus filled up were collected through the police. There is reason to believe the return to be accurate, or nearly so, except that the Native Christians appear to have been in some places classed according to race instead of according to religion. The reason why boys so far outnumber girls is that males are classed as boys up to a later age than that up to which females are classed as girls.

APPENDIX.

B.

Statistics of Agriculture.—

AREA CULTIVATED IN ACRES.	RICE CROPS.			Date Sugar.	Cocoa-nut.	Areca-nut.	DALL.			Barley.	Til.
	Aman.	Aus.	Boro.				Mustard.	Musuri.	Kallai.		
				See col. of remarks.*							
Sub-divn. Jessore...	50,000	70,000	500	10,000	500	1,000	20,000	20,000	5,000	5,000	500
„ Jhenida..	50,000	25,000	......	4,000	300	100	5,000	5,000	3,000	1,000	500
„ Magurah	40,000	20,000	7,000	1,000	300	100	......	1,500	1,500	500	1,500
„ Naral ...	50,000	25,000	3,000	500	2,000	1,500	......	1,000	2,000	1,000	1,000
„ Khulna..	180,000	16,000	30,000	1,500	4,000	4,000	2,000	There is a little only of			
„ Baghahat	120,000	8,000	3,000	500	2,000	2,000	A little only.	1,000		A little	
District total...	490,000	158,000	43,500	17,500	9,100	8,700	27,000	27,500	12,500	7,500	3,500
Preparation of land begins about	Feb. & March Sund June 15.	Jan. 7	Nov. 15	......	......	......	Oct. 15	Oct. 15	Oct. 15	Oct. 15 Na. Nov. 20.	July South Jan. 1.
Sowing time ...	April & May Sund. July 1.	March April.	Nov. 25	......	......	......	Nov. 5	Nov. 15	Nov. 5	Nov. 5 Na. Nov. 25.	Aug. South Jan. 25.
Reaping time ...	Nov. & Dec. Sund. Jan.	Aug. 15 to Sept. 15.	Mar. 15 to Apl. 15.	Nov. till Feb.	During the rains.	......	Feb. 15 to Mar. 15.	Feb. 15 to Mar. 15.	Feb. 15 to Mar. 1.	Feb. 15 to Mar. 1. Rather later in Ma. Na.	Nov. South July.
Produce of one acre	30-35 mds. paddy. 15-18 mds. rice.	25 mds. paddy. 12 mds. rice.	25-30 mds. paddy. 12-15 mds. rice.	250 mds. goor.† 80 to 100 mds. sugar.	......	100 nuts each tree.	6 mds.	10 mds.	7 mds.	10 mds.	6 mds.
Value of produce of one acre.	22-26 Rs.	18 Rs.	18-23 Rs.	500-600 Rs.	......	......	12 Rs.	8 Rs.	9 Rs.	10 Rs.	12 Rs.
Rent of one biggah equal to ½ acre... {	Je. Jh. Ma. 14 annas ... Na. Kh. Ba. Re. 1-4 or 1-8 }			3 Rs. to 5 Rs.	3 Rs. to 5 Rs.	3 Rs. to 5 Rs.	Re. 1-2 or 1-4.	1 Re. or 1-4.	Re. 1	14 as. or Re. 1.	14 as. or Re. 1.

NOTES REGARDING CULTIVATION.

Land ploughed four times. Except in bheel lands the paddy is transplanted about July. In the Sunderbunds the high extrancy variety, called boro aman, is sown; the stubble being first burnt down and ploughed into the soil.

Land ploughed five or six times.

Land hardly ploughed. The seed is scattered broadcast in the bheels as they dry up. The plants are transplanted when about a month old, and sometimes again a month later.

The trees do not bear till six or seven years old. After that they continue bearing for some thirty years. The trees are tapped and the juice collected at night, and then boiled into goor. (See column of remarks.‡)

The trees are scattered about rather than grown in groves.

Areca trees are mostly scattered amid other cultivation, and may be found in every village in some parts of the district. Of course, there are also occasional groves of them, especially in the south.

The land is ploughed three or four times. Cow-dung and ashes are occasionally used as manure.

Land ploughed three or four times.

Land is ploughed three or four times. But kallai is also sown, without ploughing, in the bheels, as they dry up.

Land ploughed three or four times.

Land ploughed about three times.

District Jessore.

Red pepper.	Fruit trees.	Indigo.	Sugar-cane.	Turmeric.	Jute.	Other crops.	REMARKS.
3,000	3,000	Very little.	......	A little	......	Begun tobacco, potato	There exists no means of obtaining statistics even approximately accurate; and these are merely rough estimates, based on information gathered by local inquiry.
2,000	2,000	30,000	6,000	A little	A little	Begun potato, mulberry.	
1,500	1,500	12,000	A little	A little	......	Begun tobacco	
300	1,000	12,000	......	A little	1,000	Begun tobacco, pineapple	
these.	2,000	......	A little	......	......	Tobacco. Begun ginger	
only.	1,500	......	......	......	......	....	
6,800	11,000	54,000	6,000	......	1,000		
July 1	......	Sept. and Feb.	Dec.	March	April 1		* The area given under the heads "date sugar," "cocoanut," and "areca-nut," does not represent any specific land. It is rather the area which would be occupied if the trees which are everywhere scattered about were all collected into groves.
July 10	....	Oct. and Mar.	Jan.	May	April 15		
Nov. and Dec.	....	June, July, and Aug.	Next Dec.	Feb.	Aug.		† This is the full measure of a well-stocked date grove in full bearing. Only a quarter of the land cultivated comes up to this. Most of it will produce only half as much to the acre. Each tree will produce, when in good bearing, seven or eight maunds of juice, from which a maund of goor, or about fifteen or sixteen seers of sugar, may be made.
12 mds.	......	32 bundles 8 or 10 seers indigo.	30 mds. goor.	12 mds.	9 mds. fibre.		
30 Rs.	......	5 to 8 Rs. (plant) 50 or 60 Rs. indigo.	75 Rs.	60 Rs.	12 Rs.		
Rs 2.	5 Rs.	Re. 1 or 1-8.	Rs. 3 or 4.	Re. 1-8	Re. 1-4		
Cow-dung is used as manure. The land is very frequently ploughed. Plants are transplanted in August, and the pods picked in the cold weather and put out in the sun to dry. The plants require careful tending and weeding.		Land is ploughed four or six times; but October sowings on alluvial lands require almost no ploughing.	Land ploughed about eight times. Plant transplanted about February. It is planted chiefly along river banks, so as to get rich soil. Requires careful weeding.		Land is very frequently ploughed. The plant when cut is steeped in water till it decomposes, and the fibre is then easily separated.		‡ The trees, besides being planted in groves, are scattered about singly and in groups over fields, especially along their margins, and among villages. They are everywhere a leading feature in the scenery of the first two sub-divisions. Sund. stands for Sundarbans; the sub-divisions are indicated by their first letters.

C.

Revenue and Expenditure of the District of Jessore.

(FIGURES OF 1868-69.)

HEADING.	Revenue.	Expenditure.	Nett revenue.	Nett expenditure.	REMARKS.
Land Revenue Administration.	Rs.	Rs.	Rs.	Rs.	
By land revenue, net ...	9,86,305	......			
„ lapsed deposits, net ...	34,842	......			
„ ward fund, excess ...	1,113	......			
„ improvement, Government estates ...	478	......			
„ establishment ...	...,...	33,046	9,54,692		Being ⅓rd of magistrate and collector's establishment.
Criminal Administration.					
By establishment ...	......	33,046			Being ⅓rd of magistrate and collector's establishment.
„ sessions court ...	......	9,600			Estimated share.
„ police ...	......	1,58,578			
„ jail ...	......	41,468			
„ fines ...	9,845	......			
„ cattle pounds ...	5,404	......			
„ jail manufactures ...	9,221	......			
„ unclaimed property ...	1,301	......			
„ law expenses ...	......	1,218			Government pleader.
„ miscellaneous ...	......	330		2,03,519	Mukhtar examination.
Civil Courts.					
By civil courts' establishment...	......	91,149			Exclusive of sessions court.
„ excess on process fund ...	4,293	......			
„ small cause court's establishment ...	......	40,954			
„ excess on small cause court process fund ...	17,364	......			
„ stamp revenue ...	1,12,473	......	2,127		Estimated share.
Act X. (Rent Law) Administration.					
By establishment ...	......	33,046			Being ⅓rd of magistrate and collector's establishment.
„ revenue process fund	5,929	......			
„ stamp revenue ...	64,000	......			
„ fees and fines ...	1,851	......			
„ miscellaneous ...	330	......	33,614		Revenue agents' examination.
Excise Administration.					
By excise revenue ...	35,573	......			
„ establishment ...	......	6,693	28,880		
Opium.					
By sales ...	22,220	......	22,220		
Assessed Taxes.					
By certificate tax ...	32,461	......			
„ establishment ...	......	9,696	22,765		
Stamp Revenue (Schedule A).					
By stamps on documents ...	60,000	......	60,000		Estimated.
Registration.					
By establishment ...	......	9,968			
„ fees ...	22,068	......	12,200		

Heading.	Revenue.	Expenditure.	Net revenue.	Net expenditure.	Remarks.
Post Office.					
	Rs.	Rs.	Rs.	Rs.	
By establishment	......	15,313			
„ stamps, &c.	15,926	......	613		
Telegraph.					
By establishment	......	3,346			Maintained chiefly for Dacca.
„ collections	377	......		2,969	
Medical.					
By establishment	......	14,347		14,347	
Education.					
By establishment (less subscriptions and fees)	......	57,628		57,628	
Roads.					
By district roads	......	44,136			
„ ferries, net	5,965	......			
„ tolls, net	3,452	......			
„ 1 per cent. road fund	517	......		34,202	
Public Works Imperial.					

(Expenditure not known, as it is mixed up with that of the Nuddea district, and drawn chiefly from the Nuddea treasury. Rs. 22,083 was drawn in Jessore.)

Heading.	Revenue.	Expenditure.	Net revenue.	Net expenditure.	Remarks.
Miscellaneous.					
Dâk bungalow	331				
Church	......	420			
Civil suits	......	3,137			
Pensions and gratuities	......	5,307			
Land acquired	......	669			
Circuit-house	......	189			
Miscellaneous	4,409	5,515	4,749	15,187	

Revenue as above	...	11,71,851		
Expenditure as above	...		3,49,935	
Net revenue	...	8,21,916		

After deducting from this Rs. 7,000 as the cost price of the opium, whose sale price is above put down as revenue, and Rs. 60,000 as the amount drawn from the Nuddea treasury by the Public Works Department and spent on Jessore, there remains to the credit of the *district* a net revenue of 7½ lakhs, besides about 7 lakhs of salt revenue which are contributed by it.

No account has been taken of charges incurred on account of offices of supervision or inspection in any department, as such charges are not met within the district ; nor, on the other hand, of customs revenue. It is, of course, impossible to say what, everything included, is the revenue derived from, and the charges incurred on account of, any particular district ; and the figures I give are those merely of the direct revenue and expenditure of the district.

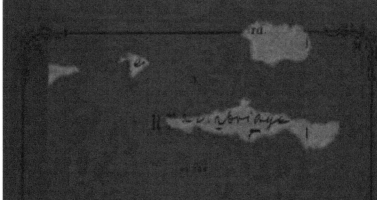

DISTRICT OF JESSORE:

ITS ANTIQUITIES,

ITS HISTORY, AND ITS COMMERCE.

J. WESTLAND, Bengal

Civil Service.

Calcutta.

1871.

www.ingramcontent.com/pod-product-compliance
Lightning Source LLC
LaVergne TN
LVHW012205040326
832903LV00003B/131